The "Family Jewels"

Declassified Documents Released by the CIA under the Freedom of Information Act, June 2007

Central Intelligence Agency

REPUBLISHED BY NIMBLE BOOKS LLC

Nimble Books LLC
1521 Martha Avenue
Ann Arbor, MI, USA 48103
http://www.NimbleBooks.com
wfz@nimblebooks.com
+1.734-330-2593

Version 1.0; last saved 2010-11-09.

Printed in the United States of America
ISBN-13: 978-1-60888-097-3

∞ The paper used in this publication meets the minimum requirements of the American National Standard for Information Sciences—Permanence of Paper for Printed Library Materials, ANSI Z39.48-1992. The paper is acid-free and lignin-free.

CONTENTS

The reports describe numerous activities conducted by the CIA during the 1950s to 1970s that violated its charter. According to a briefing provided by CIA Director William Colby to the Justice Department on December 31, 1974, these included 18 issues which were of legal concern:

Confinement of a KGB defector, Yuri Ivanovich Nosenko, that "might be regarded as a violation of the kidnapping laws."

Wiretapping of two syndicated columnists, Robert Allen and Paul Scott, approved by US Attorney General Robert Kennedy and Secretary of Defense Robert McNamara (see also Project Mockingbird).

Physical surveillance of investigative journalist and muckraker Jack Anderson and his associates, including Les Whitten of the Washington Post and future Fox News Channel anchor and managing editor Brit Hume. Jack Anderson had written two articles on CIA-backed assassination attempts on Cuban leader Fidel Castro.

Physical surveillance of then-Washington Post reporter Michael Getler, who later was an ombudsman for the Washington Post and PBS.

Break-in at the home of a former CIA employee.

Break-in at the office of a former defector.

Warrantless entry into the apartment of a former CIA employee.

Opening of mail to and from the Soviet Union from 1953 to 1973 (including letters associated with actress Jane Fonda) (project SRPOINTER/HTLINGUAL at JFK airport).

Opening of mail to and from the People's Republic of China from 1969 to 1972 (project SRPOINTER/HTLINGUAL at JFK airport - see also Project SHAMROCK by the NSA).

Funding of behavior modification research on unwitting US citizens, including unscientific, non-consensual human experiments. (see also Project MKULTRA concerning LSD experiments).

Assassination plots against Cuban President Fidel Castro (authorized by Robert Kennedy)[8]; Congolese leader Patrice Lumumba; President Rafael Trujillo of the Dominican Republic; and René Schneider, Commander-in-chief of the Chilean Army. All of these plots were said to be unsuccessful ones.

Surveillance of dissident groups between 1967 and 1971 (see Project RESISTANCE, Project MERRIMAC and Operation CHAOS).

Surveillance of a particular Latin American female, and of US citizens in Detroit.

Surveillance of former CIA officer and Agency critic, Victor Marchetti, author of the book, The CIA and the Cult of Intelligence, published in 1974.

Amassing of files on 9,900-plus US citizens related to the antiwar movement (see Project RESISTANCE, Project MERRIMAC and Operation CHAOS).

Polygraph experiments with the sheriff of San Mateo County, California.

Fake CIA identification documents that might violate state laws.

Testing of electronic equipment on US telephone circuits.

UNCLASSIFIED [ ] INTERNAL USE ONLY [ ] CONFIDENTIAL [X] SECRET

ROUTING AND RECORD SHEET

SUBJECT: (Optional)

FROM:	EXTENSION	NO.
Howard J. Osborn Director of Security		DATE 16 May 1973

TO: (Officer designation, room number, and building)	DATE RECEIVED	DATE FORWARDED	OFFICER'S INITIALS	COMMENTS (Number each comment to show from whom to whom. Draw a line across column after each comment.)
1. Executive Secretary, CIA Management Committee				~~EYES ONLY~~
2.				
3.				
4.				(b)(1) (b)(3) (b)(5) (b)(6)
5.				
6.				
7.				APPROVED FOR RELEASE DATE: JUN 2007
8.				
9.				
10.				
11.				00001
12.				
13.				
14.				
15.				~~EYES ONLY~~

610 USE PREVIOUS EDITIONS [X] SECRET [ ] CONFIDENTIAL [ ] INTERNAL USE ONLY [ ] UNCLASSIFIED

16 May 1973

MEMORANDUM FOR: Executive Secretary,
CIA Management Committee

SUBJECT : "Family Jewels"

1. The purpose of this memorandum is to forward for your personal review summaries of activities conducted either by or under the sponsorship of the Office of Security in the past which in my opinion conflict with the provisions of the National Security Act of 1947.

2. These activities cover the period from March 1959 to date and represent as accurate a record as is available in our files. Those activities which took place prior to the date of my appointment as Director of Security on 1 July 1964 have been developed to a certain extent through the recollection of the senior people in this Office who were involved or who had knowledge of the activities at the time they occurred.

3. I have gone back to March 1959 because I believe that the activities occurring since that time still have a viable "flap potential" in that many of the people involved, both Agency and non-Agency are still alive and through their knowledge of the activity represent a possible potential threat or embarrassment to the Agency. I would be glad to provide clarification or an explanation of any of these activities if desired. You have my assurance that unless otherwise stated each of these activities was approved by higher authority--the

00002

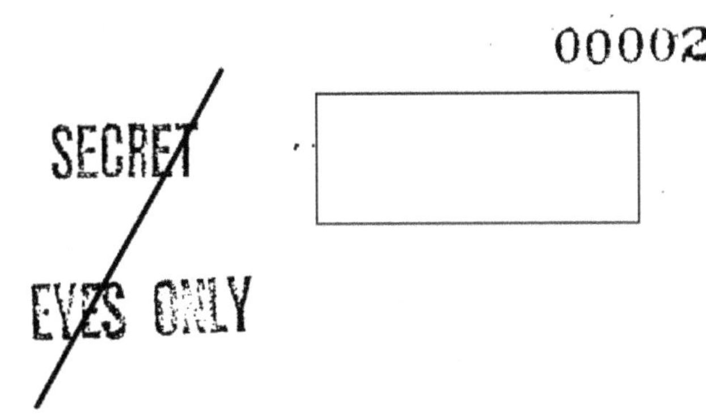

Director of Central Intelligence, the Deputy Director of Central Intelligence, the Executive Director-Comptroller, or the Deputy Director for Support.

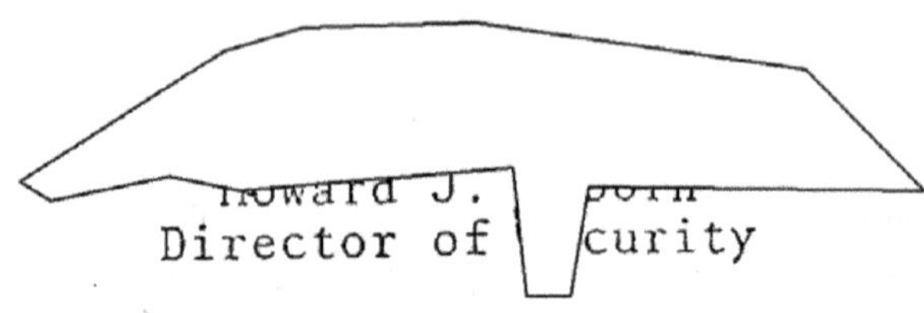

Director of [redacted]curity

Attachments

00003

00004

Attachment A

"FAMILY JEWELS"

1.

2. Johnny Roselli -- The use of a member of the Mafia in an attempt to assassinate Fidel Castro.

3. Project MOCKINGBIRD -- During the period from 12 March 1963 to 15 June 1963, this Office installed telephone taps on two Washington-based newsmen who were suspected of disclosing classified information obtained from a variety of governmental and congressional sources.

4. Yuriy Ivanovich Nosenko -- A KGB defector who from the period 13 August 1965 to 27 October 1967 was confined in a specially constructed "jail" at He was literally confined in a cell behind bars with nothing but a cot in it for this period.

5. Various Surveillance and Support Activities -- These are briefly summarized and range from the surveillance of newsmen to the provision of specialized support of local police officials in the Metropolitan area. I believe that each one is self-explanatory and, therefore, no further comment is needed here.

6. Equipment Support to Local Police -- Attached is a list provided me by the Director of Logistics (he will simply report these items in his report) which we have provided local police in the Metropolitan D. C. area over the past four or five years on indefinite loan. During the period when the Agency's installations in this area appeared to be a target of dissident elements

a conscious decision was made by the Agency to utilize the services of local police to repel invaders in case of riot or dissension as opposed to utilization of our GSA guards, who are not trained in this type of activity. This equipment has been issued over the years to local police, principally Fairfax and Arlington County Police Departments. I do not believe that this is totally illegal under the provisions of the National Security Act of 1947, but I am including it since I am sure that it would be considered as such in light of the recent congressional fuss over our police training activities.

7. Audio Countermeasures Support to the United States Secret Service

8. Test of Specialized Equipment in Miami Immediately Prior to the Political Convention There

00006

00007

SECRET

EYES ONLY

00008

SECRET

EYES ONLY

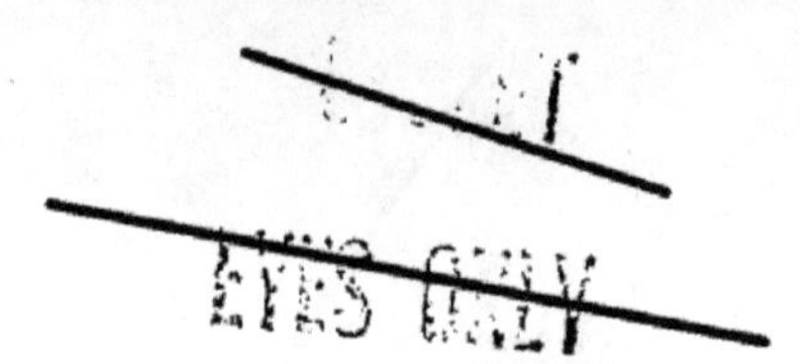

2

00009

SECRET
EYES ONLY

00010

3

SECRET
EYES ONLY

00011

SUBJECT: Johnny Roselli

1. In August 1960, Mr. Richard M. Bissell approached Colonel Sheffield Edwards to determine if the Office of Security had assets that may assist in a sensitive mission requiring gangster-type action. The mission target was Fidel Castro.

2. Because of its extreme sensitivity, only a small group was made privy to the project. The DCI was briefed and gave his approval. Colonel J. C. King, Chief, WH Division, was briefed, but all details were deliberately concealed from any of the JMWAVE officials. Certain TSD and Communications personnel participated in the initial planning stages, but were not witting of the purpose of the mission.

3. Robert A. Maheu, a cleared source of the Office of Security, was contacted, briefed generally on the project, and requested to ascertain if he could develop an entree into the gangster elements as the first step toward accomplishing the desired goal.

4. Mr. Maheu advised that he had met one Johnny Roselli on several occasions while visiting Las Vegas. He only knew him casually through clients, but was given to understand that he was a high-ranking member of the "syndicate" and controlled all of the ice-making machines on the Strip. Maheu reasoned that, if Roselli was in fact a member of the clan, he undoubtedly had connections leading into the Cuban gambling interests.

5. Maheu was asked to approach Roselli, who knew Maheu as a personal relations executive handling domestic and foreign accounts, and tell him that he had recently been retained by a client who represented several international business firms which were suffering heavy financial losses in Cuba as a result of Castro's action. They were convinced that Castro's removal was the answer to their

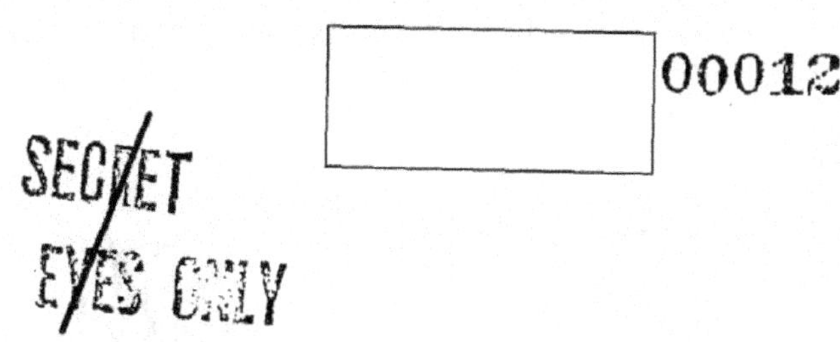

00012

problem and were willing to pay a price of $150,000 for its successful accomplishment. It was to be made clear to Roselli that the United States Government was not, and should not, become aware of this operation.

6. The pitch was made to Roselli on 14 September 1960 at the Hilton Plaza Hotel, New York City. Mr. James O'Connell, Office of Security, was present during this meeting and was identified to Roselli as an employee of Maheu. O'Connell actively served as Roselli's contact until May 1962 at which time he phased out due to an overseas assignment. His initial reaction was to avoid getting involved, but through Maheu's persuasion, he agreed to introduce him to a friend, Sam Gold, who knew the "Cuban crowd." Roselli made it clear he did not want any money for his part and believed Sam would feel the same way. Neither of these individuals were ever paid out of Agency funds.

7. During the week of 25 September, Maheu was introduced to Sam who was staying at the Fontainebleau Hotel, Miami Beach. It was several weeks after his meeting with Sam and Joe, who was identified to him as a courier operating between Havana and Miami, that he saw photographs of both of these individuals in the Sunday supplemental "Parade." They were identified as Momo Salvatore Giancana and Santos Trafficant, respectively. Both were on the list of the Attorney General's ten most-wanted men. The former was described as the Chicago chieftain of the Cosa Nostra and successor to Al Capone, and the latter, the Cosa Nostra boss of Cuban operations. Maheu called this office immediately upon ascertaining this information.

8. In discussing the possible methods of accomplishing this mission, Sam suggested that they not resort to firearms but, if he could be furnished some type of potent pill, that could be placed in Castro's food or drink, it would be a much more effective operation. Sam indicated that he had a prospective nominee in the person of Juan Orta, a Cuban official who had been receiving kick-back payments from the gambling interests, who still had access to Castro, and was in a financial bind.

00013

9. TSD was requested to produce six pills of high lethal content.

10. Joe delivered the pills to Orta. After several weeks of reported attempts, Orta apparently got cold feet and asked out of the assignment. He suggested another candidate who made several attempts without success.

11. Joe then indicated that Dr. Anthony Verona, one of the principal officers in the Cuban Exile Junta, had become disaffected with the apparent ineffectual progress of the Junta and was willing to handle the mission through his own resources.

12. He asked, as a prerequisite to the deal, that he be given $10,000 for organizational expenses and requested $1,000 worth of communications equipment.

13. Dr. Verona's potential was never fully exploited, as the project was canceled shortly after the Bay of Pigs episode. Verona was advised that the offer was withdrawn, and the pills were retrieved.

14. Of significant interest was an incident which involved a request levied by Sam upon Maheu.

> At the height of the project negotiations, Sam expressed concern about his girlfriend, Phyllis McGuire, who he learned was getting much attention from Dan Rowan while both were booked at a Las Vegas night club. Sam asked Maheu to put a bug in Rowan's room to determine the extent of his intimacy with Miss McGuire. The technician involved in the assignment was discovered in the process, arrested, and taken to the Sheriff's office for questioning. He called Maheu and informed him that he had been detained by the police. This call was made in the presence of the Sheriff's personnel.
>
> Subsequently, the Department of Justice announced its intention to prosecute Maheu along

00014

with the technician. On 7 February 1962, the Director of Security briefed the Attorney General, Robert Kennedy, on the circumstances leading up to Maheu's involvement in the wiretap. At our request, prosecution was dropped.

15. In May 1962, Mr. William Harvey took over as Case Officer, and it is not known by this office whether Roselli was used operationally from that point on.

16. It was subsequently learned from the FBI that Roselli had been convicted on six counts involving illegal entry into the United States. Our records do not reflect the date of conviction, but it is believed to have been sometime during November 1967.

17. On 2 December 1968, Roselli, along with four other individuals, was convicted of conspiracy to cheat members of the Friars Club of $400,000 in a rigged gin rummy game.

18. Mr. Harvey reported to the Office of Security of his contacts with Roselli during November and December 1967 and January 1968. It was his belief that Johnny would not seek out the Agency for assistance in the deportation proceedings unless he actually faced deportation. Roselli expressed confidence that he would win an appeal.

19. On 17 November 1970, Maheu called James O'Connell, Roselli's first Case Officer, to advise that Maheu's attorney, Ed Morgan, had received a call from a Thomas Waddin, Roselli's lawyer, who stated that all avenues of appeal had been exhausted, and his client now faces deportation. Waddin indicated that, if someone did not intercede on Roselli's behalf, he would make a complete expose of his activities with the Agency.

20. On 18 November 1970, Mr. Helms was briefed on the latest development in this case, and it was decided that the Agency would not in any way assist Roselli. Maheu was so advised of the Agency's position, and he was in

complete agreement with our stand. He further advised that he was not concerned about any publicity as it affected him personally should Roselli decide to tell all.

21. Subsequently, Roselli or someone on his behalf furnished Jack Anderson details of the operation. Attached are two Anderson columns dealing with this matter.

22. The last known residence of Roselli was the Federal Penitentiary in Seattle, Washington.

Attachments

00016

00017

The Washington Merry-Go-Round THE WASHINGTON POST Monday, Jan. 18, 1971 B7

6 Attempts to Kill Castro Laid to CIA

By Jack Anderson

Locked in the darkest recesses of the Central Intelligence Agency is the story of six assassination attempts against Cuba's Fidel Castro.

For 10 years, only a few key people have known the terrible secret. They have sworn never to talk. Yet we have learned the details from sources whose credentials are beyond question.

We spoke to John McCone, who headed the CIA at the time of the assassination attempts. He acknowledged the idea had been discussed inside the CIA but insisted it had been "rejected immediately." He vigorously denied that the CIA had ever participated in any plot on Castro's life. Asked whether the attempts could have been made with his knowledge, he replied: "It could not have happened."

We have complete confidence, however, in our sources.

The plot to knock off Castro began as part of the Bay of Pigs operation. The intent was to eliminate the Cuban dictator before the motley invaders landed on the island. Their arrival was expected to touch off a general uprising, which the Communist militia would have had more trouble putting down without the charismatic Castro to lead them.

After the first attempt failed, five more assassination teams were sent to Cuba. The last team reportedly made it to a rooftop within shooting distance of Castro before they were apprehended. This happened around the last of February or first of March, 1963.

Nine months later, President Kennedy was gunned down in Dallas by Lee Harvey Oswald, a fanatic who previously had agitated for Castro in New Orleans and had made a mysterious trip to the Cuban Embassy in Mexico City.

Among those privy to the CIA conspiracy, there is still a nagging suspicion—unsupported by the Warren Commission's findings—that Castro became aware of the U.S. plot upon his life and somehow recruited Oswald to retaliate against President Kennedy.

To set up the Castro assassination, the CIA enlisted Robert Maheu, a former FBI agent with shadowy contacts, who had handled other undercover assignments for the CIA out of his Washington public relations office. He later moved to Las Vegas to head up billionaire Howard Hughes' Nevada operations.

Maheu recruited John Roselli, a ruggedly handsome gambler with contacts in both the American and Cuban underworlds, to arrange the assassination. The dapper, hawk-faced Roselli, formerly married to movie actress June Lang, was a power in the movie industry until his conviction with racketeer Willie Bioff in a million-dollar Hollywood labor shakedown. The CIA assigned two of its most trusted operatives, William Harvey and James (Big Jim) O'Connell, to the hush-hush murder mission. Using phony names, they accompanied Roselli on trips to Miami to line up the assassination teams.

The full story reads like the script of a James Bond movie, complete with secret trysts at glittering Miami Beach hotels and midnight powerboat dashes to secret landing spots on the Cuban coast. Once, Roselli's boat was shot out from under him.

For the first try, the CIA furnished Roselli with special poison capsules to slip into Castro's food. The poison was supposed to take three days to act. By the time Castro died, his system would throw off all traces of the poison, so he would appear to be the victim of a natural if mysterious ailment.

Roselli arranged with a Cuban related to one of Castro's chefs, to plant the deadly pellets in the dictator's food. On March 13, 1961, Roselli delivered the capsules to his contact at Miami Beach's glamorous Fontainebleau Hotel.

A couple of weeks later, just about the right time for the plot to have been carried out, a report out of Havana said Castro was ill. But he recovered before the Bay of Pigs invasion on April 17, 1961.

Four more attempts were made on Castro's life.

00018

The Washington Merry-Go-Round THE WASHINGTON POST Tuesday, Feb. 23, 1971 B11

Castro Stalker Worked for the CIA

By Jack Anderson

The mystery man whom the Central Intelligence Agency recruited to assassinate Cuba's Fidel Castro has been laid up in the sick ward of the Los Angeles County jail.

He is handsome, hawk-faced John Roselli, once a dashing figure around Hollywood and Las Vegas, now a gray, 66-year-old inmate with a respiratory ailment.

Confidential FBI files identify him as "a top Mafia figure" who watched over "the concealed interests in Las Vegas casinos of the Chicago underworld."

Roselli has admitted to friends that he was a rum runner during the Roaring Twenties. Operating along the East Coast, he learned how to evade Coast Guard cutters and police patrols.

His name later became linked with the biggest names in the Chicago and Los Angeles underworlds. He also developed contacts in the Cuban underworld before Castro took over the Havana gambling casinos.

He had the right background for a hush-hush mission that the CIA was planning in 1961. As part of the Bay of Pigs invasion, the CIA hoped to knock off Castro and leave Cuba leaderless.

Risks Neck

Roselli was recruited for the job by Robert Maheu, a former FBI agent, who admitted to us that he had handled undercover assignments for the CIA. He refused, however, to discuss the details. This is the same Maheu, incidentally, who is now involved in a legal battle over phantom billionaire Howard Hughes' Nevada operations.

Roselli was so flattered over being asked to perform a secret mission for the U.S. government that he paid all his expenses out of his own pocket and risked his neck to land the assassination teams on the Cuban coast.

In James Bond fashion, he held whispered meetings in Miami Beach hotels with Cubans willing to make an attempt on Castro's life. Once, he called on Chicago racket boss Sam Giancana to line up a contact. The confidential files report that Giancana had "gambling interest and an interest in the shrimp business in Cuba." However, the Chicago gangster took no direct part in the assassination plot.

Roselli made midnight dashes to Cuba with his hired assassins in twin powerboats. Once a Cuban patrol ship turned its guns on his darkened boat, tore a hole in the bottom and sank the boat. Roselli was fished out of the water by the other boat, which escaped into the shadows.

In earlier columns, we reported how the CIA furnished Roselli with deadly poison capsules which he tried through a relative of Castro's chef to plant in the dictator's food. Later, marksmen armed with high-powered Belgian rifles attempted to infiltrate close enough to gun Castro down.

All told, six assassination attempts were made, the last in the spring of 1963. Throughout this period, Roselli worked under the direct supervision of two secret CIA agents, William Harvey and James (Big Jim) O'Connell.

Roselli's Reward

The FBI which got wind of the assassination plot, has tried to pump Roselli for information. But he was sworn to silence by the CIA, and up to this moment, he hasn't broken it.

Meanwhile, the Justice Department, as part of its crackdown on organized crime, tried to nail Roselli. The FBI discovered that his Chicago birth records had been forged, that his name was really Filippo Sacco and that he had come to this country from Italy as a child. He was convicted for failing to register as an alien.

He was also convicted for conspiracy to rig card games at Los Angeles' exclusive Friar's Club.

Of Roselli's two CIA associates, Harvey has now retired to Indianapolis and O'Connell is still on the CIA payroll. Both admitted to us a friendship with Roselli but refused to discuss their CIA activities. Harvey said he had a "high regard" for Roselli and called the Friar's Club case a "bum rap." Said Harvey: "The Friar's Club indictment is phony. Roselli had no more to do with that than I had."

Roselli's lawyers are now trying to get clemency for their client, citing our stories about his secret CIA service.

Firearms Fiasco

Under pressure from the firearms lobby, the Treasury Department has failed to enforce a vital section of the 1968 federal firearms act.

The law was passed after the murders of Sen. Robert Kennedy and Dr. Martin Luther King. It authorizes the Treasury Secretary to require full reports of all firearms and ammunition sales.

For the two years that the law has been in force, the Treasury Department has ignored this key provision. The gun industry has complained it would be a bookkeeping nightmare.

The federal government, which would have to compile all the sales data, has also been reluctant to spend the $100 million it would cost the computers and staff to maintain the firearms files.

00019

00020

PROJECT MOCKINGBIRD

Project Mockingbird, a telephone intercept activity, was conducted between 12 March 1963 and 15 June 1963, and targeted two Washington-based newsmen who, at the time, had been publishing news articles based on, and frequently quoting, classified materials of this Agency and others, including Top Secret and Special Intelligence.

Telephone intercept connections were installed at the newmen's office and at each of their homes, for a total of 3. The connections were established with the assistance of a telephone company official who responded to a personal request by the Director of Security, Col. Sheffield Edwards. Col. Edwards' authority for the activity was Mr. John A. McCone, Director of Central Intelligence. The latter conducted the activity in coordination with the Attorney General (Mr. Robert Kennedy), the Secretary of Defense (Mr. Robert McNamara), and the Director of the Defense Intelligence Agency (Gen. Joseph Carroll). In addition to Office of Security personnel directly involved in the intercepts and research of materials acquired therefrom, only 3 other Agency officials are on record as witting of the activity: the Deputy Director of Central Intelligence (General Marshall S. Carter), the Inspector General (Lyman Kirkpatrick) and the General Counsel. (Mr. Lawrence Houston).

The intercept activity was particularly productive in identifying contacts of the newsmen, their method of operation and many of their sources of information. For example, it was determined that during the period they received data from 13 newsmen, 12 of whom were identified; 12 senators and 6 members of Congress, all identified; 21 Congressional staff members, of whom 11 were identified; 16 government employees, including a staff member of the White House, members of the Vice President's office, an Assistant Attorney General, and other well-placed individuals. A number of other sources were partially or tentatively identified, but the short span of the activity precluded positive identification. It was observed that through these contacts the newsmen actually received more classified and official data than they could use, and passed some of the stories to other newsmen for release, establishing that many "leaks" appearing under other by-lines were actually from the sources of the target newsmen.

Since the termination of Project Mockingbird, those materials related to it which were retained, have been maintained under strict security access of two Office of Security professionals.

00021

SECRET ~~EYES~~ ONLY

00022

SUBJECT: Yuriy Ivanovich Nosenko

Yuriy Ivanovich Nosenko, an officer of the KGB, defected to a representative of this Agency in Geneva, Switzerland, on 4 February 1964. The responsibility for his exploitation was assigned to the then SR Division of the Clandestine Service and he was brought to this country on 12 February 1964. After initial interrogation by representatives of the SR Division, he was moved to a safehouse in Clinton, Maryland, from 4 April 1964 where he was confined and interrogated until 13 August 1965 when he was moved to a specially constructed "jail" in a remote wooded area at [ ] The SR Division was convinced that he was a dispatched agent but even after a long period of hostile interrogation was unable to prove their contention and he was confined at [ ] in an effort to convince him to "confess."

This Office together with the Office of General Counsel became increasingly concerned with the illegality of the Agency's position in handling a defector under these conditions for such a long period of time. Strong representations were made to the Director (Mr. Helms) by this Office, the Office of General Counsel, and the Legislative Liaison Counsel, and on 27 October 1967, the responsibility for Nosenko's further handling was transferred to the Office of Security under the direction of the Deputy Director of Central Intelligence, then Admiral Rufus Taylor.

Nosenko was moved to a comfortable safehouse in the Washington area and was interviewed under friendly, sympathetic conditions by his Security Case Officer, Mr. Bruce Solie, for more than a year. It soon became apparent that Nosenko was bona fide and he was moved to more comfortable surroundings with considerable freedom of independent movement and has continued to cooperate fully with the Federal Bureau of Investigation and this Office since that time. He has proven to be the most

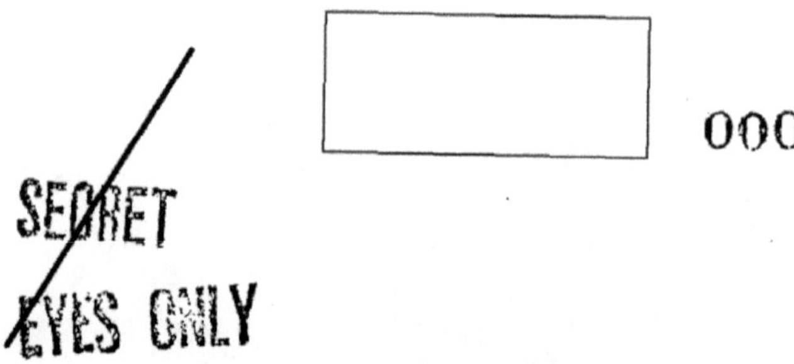

00023

valuable and economical defector this Agency has ever had and leads which were ignored by the SR Division were explored and have resulted in the arrest and prosecution [redacted] He currently is living under an alias; secured a divorce from his Russian wife and remarried an American citizen. He is happy, relaxed, and appreciative of the treatment accorded him and states "while I regret my three years of incarceration, I have no bitterness and now understand how it could happen."

2

00024

SECRET
EYES ONLY

00025

I. SURVEILLANCES

A.

During the periods 1-20 February, 12 April-7 May, and 9-20 August 1971, a surveillance was conducted of a former staff employee, and a Cuban national with whom become professionally and emotionally involved. Surveillance was predicated upon information that had been seeking from employees information in Information Processing Division files, and that employees were visiting a photographic studio operated by in Fairfax City, Virginia. In addition to physical surveillance, one surreptitious entry of the photographic studio was made, and an attempt to enter the apartment of was aborted because of a door lock problem.

B.

Pursuant to a request from the CI Staff, approved by the DCI, surveillances were conducted of and her associates at various times from May to September 1971. had long been a source of the WH Division and had given information regarding a plot to assassinate or kidnap Vice President Agnew and the DCI. Surveillances included coverage of the activities of Miss King during two visits to the United States, technical coverage of debriefings of her by WH Division representatives in New York City, and surveillance, including mail coverage, of several American citizens alleged to be part of the plot. Although most of the surveillance occurred in New York City, surveillance of one of the individuals included extensive coverage of a commune in Detroit.

C. CELOTEX I

At the direction of the DCI, a surveillance was conducted of Michael Getler of the Washington Post during

SECRET
EYES ONLY

00026

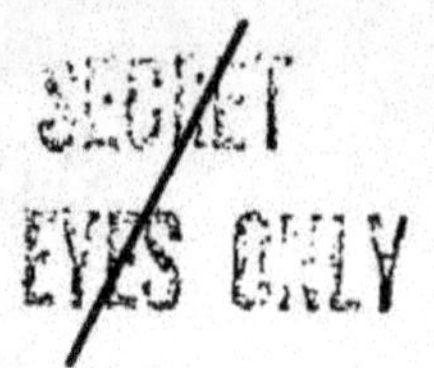

the periods 6-9 October, 27 October-10 December 1971 and on 3 January 1972. In addition to physical surveillance, an observation post was maintained in the Statler Hilton Hotel where observation could be maintained of the building housing his office. The surveillance was designed to determine Getler's sources of classified information of interest to the Agency which had appeared in a number of his columns.

D. CELOTEX II

At the direction of the DCI, surveillance was conducted of Jack Anderson and at various times his "leg men," Britt Hume, Leslie Whitten, and Joseph Spear, from 15 February to 12 April 1972. In addition to the physical surveillance, an observation post was maintained in the Statler Hilton Hotel directly opposite Anderson's office. The purpose of this surveillance was to attempt to determine Anderson's sources for highly classified Agency information appearing in his syndicated columns.

E. BUTANE

At the direction of the DCI, a surveillance was conducted on Victor L. Marchetti from 23 March to 20 April 1972. The purpose of this surveillance was to determine his activities and contacts both with Agency employees and other individuals in regard to his proposed book and published magazine articles exposing Agency operations.

II. POLICE SUPPORT

A. During 1969, 1970, and 1971, on several occasions, the Intelligence Division of the Metropolitan Police Department was provided a communications system to monitor major anti-Vietnam war demonstrations in the Washington area. This system consisted of a radio receiver and an Agent at the Intelligence Division Headquarters and several automobiles from the Washington Field Office equipped with radio receivers and transmitters and manned by two WFO Agents, as well as a representative of the Intelligence Division, Metropolitan Police Department. The benefit to the Agency was that the communications over this system were monitored at the Headquarters Building to provide instant notice of possible actions by the dissidents against Agency installations.

00027

SECRET EYES ONLY

B. During the period from 1968 to 1973, several items of positive audio equipment consisting primarily of clandestine transmitters and touch-tone dial recorders were loaned to the Metropolitan Police Department, Fairfax County, Virginia, Police Department, Montgomery County, Maryland, Police Department, New York City Police Department, and the San Francisco, California, Police Department.

III. GENERAL SUPPORT

A. SRPOINTER

Since 1953, this office has operated a mail intercept program of incoming and outgoing Russian mail and, at various times, other selective mail at Kennedy Airport in New York City. This operation included not only the photographing of envelopes but also surreptitious opening and photographing of selected items of mail. The bulk of the take involved matters of internal security interest which was disseminated to the Federal Bureau of Investigation. This program is now in a dormant state pending a decision as to whether the operation will be continued or abolished.

B. AELADLE

For several years the Office of Security has provided support to Anatole Golitsyn, a Russian defector of interest to the CI Staff.

C. REDFACE I

In July 1970, this office made a surreptitious entry of an office in Silver Spring, Maryland, occupied by a former defector working under contract for the Agency. This involved by-passing a contact and

3

00028

sonic alarm system, entering a vault, and entering a safe within the vault. The purpose of the operation was to determine whether the individual had any unauthorized classified information in his possession.

D. BUREAU OF NARCOTICS AND DANGEROUS DRUGS

In January 1971, the Director approved a request from the Director, Bureau of Narcotics and Dangerous Drugs, to provide covert recruitment and security clearance support to BNDD. This has been accomplished through the medium of a proprietary of the Office of Security known as [ ] and operating as [ ] [ ]. Support includes covert recruitment, investigation, polygraph, medical clearance, and training. It has been divided into three phases: (1) A CI operation to place individuals in BNDD field offices to monitor any illegal activities of other BNDD employees; (2) [ ] [ ] and (3) Recruitment of an individual used as an Agent by BNDD but actually employed by BNDD, although this fact is known only to the Director and Chief Inspector, BNDD. In this case, arrangements were made for all pay and other employee benefits to come from CIA on a reimbursable basis.

E. [ ]

[ ]

F. MERRIMAC

From February 1967 to November 1971, [ ] an Office of Security proprietary, recruited and handled several Agents for the purpose of covertly monitoring

SECRET
EYES ONLY

00029

dissident groups in the Washington area considered to be potential threats to Agency personnel and installations. One of these Agents so successfully penetrated one dissident group that she was turned over to the FBI for handling. In addition, during this period, the Office of Security field offices were tasked with collecting available intelligence on dissident groups. All such information was included in a periodic report distributed to appropriate parts of the Agency and to certain outside Government agencies.

G.? F.

5

SECRET EYES ONLY

00030

00031

MATERIAL REQUISITIONED FROM LOGISTICS
BY SECURITY FOR ISSUANCE TO
LOCAL POLICE

ITEM	QUANITY
Gas Mask M-9	200
Gas Mask M-17	196
Steel Helmet and Liners	231
Vest and Groin Protector	96
Vest, Flak M-52	34
Vest, Protective	46
Vest, Grenade	105
Execuvest	6
Emergency Flashing Red Light	22
*Searchlight, Tear Gas	36
*Chemical Baton 6 1/2"	36
*Chemical Baton 12"	24
*Chemical Baton 26"	24
*Mustang 35 Pistol	6
*Searchlight with Shoulder Strap	36
*Stun Gun	3

*NOTE: Various quantities and types of replacement chemical cartridges, loading kits, and batteries were also ordered for asterisk items.

032

00033

SUBJECT: Audio Countermeasures Support to the United States Secret Service

On 25 July 1968, and at the specific request of the United States Secret Service, this Office provided two audio countermeasures technicians to the United States Secret Service in connection with the Democratic National Convention held in Chicago, Illinois. This was not an official detail although both men were provided with temporary credentials identifying them as being affiliated with the United States Secret Service.

On 15 August 1968, we detailed the same two men to the United States Secret Service to cover the Republican National Convention in Miami, Florida. On both occasions, the team members were debriefed upon their return and it is clear that their activities were confined exclusively to sweeping the candidates and potential candidates quarters.

00034

SECRET

EYES ONLY

00035

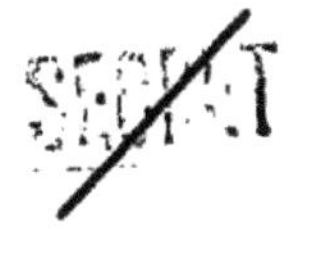

15 May 1973

MEMORANDUM FOR: Mr. Howard Osborn
Director of Security

SUBJECT : Identification of Activities with Embarrassment Potential for the Agency

1. In responding on 7 May by memorandum to the DDO's request for the identification of any incident which might conceivably have an embarrassment potential for the Agency, I cited the equipment test which is mentioned in the attached memo. The test in question was related to the development of [redacted] and in the course of running these tests, our technicians were in and out of some four hotels in Miami, with radio equipment. This was shortly before the political conventions, and at least one of the hotels was within a block of the convention hall.

2. Although this completely innocent--although subject to misconstrual--activity may already have been drawn to your attention by your own staff, it has occurred to us that we should ensure you are aware of it, given the involvement of a Security officer, [redacted]

[redacted]

Chief, Division D

Att:
M/R dated 7 May 73 by [redacted]
subj: [redacted] Equipment Test, Miami, Fla., Aug 71

00036

cc: [redacted]

SECRET

7 May 1973

MEMORANDUM FOR THE RECORD

SUBJECT : Equipment Test, Miami, Florida, August 1971

The following details concerning the arrangements for Subject tests were provided by during a telephone conversation with the undersigned, 7 May 1973.

now retired, formerly assigned to was the for the August 1971 Field Test of the Security arrangements for the test were handled on behalf of and the visitors by in conjunction with the Security Officer, who was at the time. was in daily contact with Miami Police in the course of his official liaison duties.

was reluctant to call at home over an open telephone line to inquire about the specifics of the arrangements at this point, and suggested that the Security Officer by this time might have been transferred back to Headquarters and be available for a direct query.

The writer called , DIV/D Security Officer, who verified the fact that indeed is stationed at Headquarters, with a current assignment to a located in is available via the following telephone connections:

The above details were provided by telephone to Chief, Division D at 1650 hours this date.

(signed)

Distribution:
Orig - File

00037

SECRET

UNCLASSIFIED ☐ INTERNAL ONLY ☐ CONFIDENTIAL ☒ ~~SECRET~~

ROUTING AND RECORD SHEET

SUBJECT: (Optional)

FROM:			EXTENSION	NO.
Director of Security				DATE

TO: (Officer designation, room number, and building)	DATE RECEIVED	DATE FORWARDED	OFFICER'S INITIALS	COMMENTS (Number each comment to show from whom to whom. Draw a line across column after each comment.)
1. Ex. Dir. -Compt.				
2.				
3.				
4.				
5.				
6.				
7.				
8.				
9.				
10.				
11.				
12.				00038
13.				
14.				
15.				

~~EYES ONLY~~

FORM 3-62 610 USE PREVIOUS EDITIONS ☒ ~~SECRET~~ ☐ CONFIDENTIAL ☐ INTERNAL USE ONLY ☐ UNCLASSIFIED

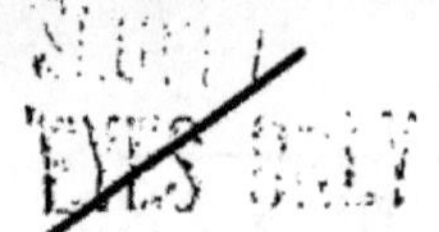

15 FEB 1972

MEMORANDUM FOR: Executive Director-Comptroller

SUBJECT : ROSELLI, John

1. This memorandum is for your information only.

2. Reference is made to our recent conversation regarding the Agency's participation in political assassinations. Attached hereto is a memorandum dated 19 November 1970 which was furnished to Mr. Helms setting forth the circumstances of the Subject's activities on behalf of the Agency. Initially Roselli was unwitting of Government interest, but as time went on, he suspected that the U. S. Government was involved and specifically the CIA.

3. Roselli is presently serving a prison sentence for conspiracy in a Federal penitentiary in Seattle, Washington and awaits deportation upon completion of his current sentence.

4. This Agency was aware that Roselli intended to expose his participation in the plot should we not intervene on his behalf. The DCI decided to ignore his threats and take a calculated risk as to the consequences that may occur with the disclosure of his story. This was subsequently done by Roselli or someone on his behalf furnishing Jack Anderson details of the incident. Attached hereto are two of Anderson's articles dealing with Roselli. Anderson is also Editor of the Washington Bureau of the Washington Post, Sunday supplemental "Parade."

5. Individuals who were aware of this project were: Messrs. Dulles, Bissell, Colonel J. C. King, Colonel Sheffield Edwards,

00039

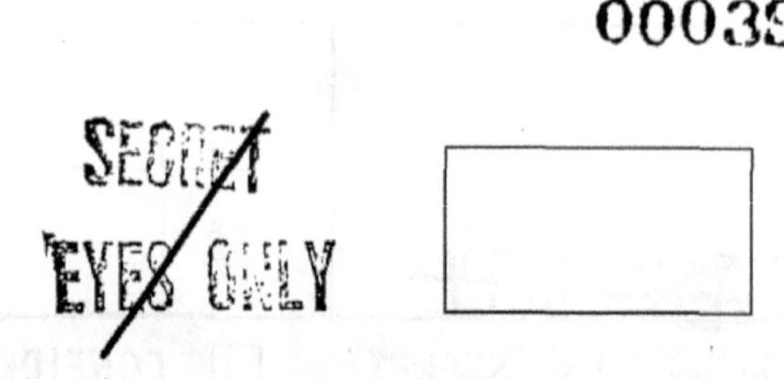

William Harvey, and James P. O'Connell. Also included were Robert A. Maheu and his attorneys Edward P. Morgan and Edward Bennett Williams.

6. On 26 February 1971 arrangements were made with Immigration and Naturalization Service Commissioner Raymond Farrell to flag any action that may be taken by his organization regarding deportation proceedings against Roselli. On 26 January 1972 James F. Green, Associate Commissioner for I&NS, advised that they were deferring any deportation action for another year and would again call it to our attention upon expiration of the deferral.

[illegible]ward J. [illegible]
Director of [illegible]urity

Atts

SECRET
EYES ONLY

00040

15 FEB 1972

MEMORANDUM FOR: Executive Director-Comptroller

SUBJECT : ROSELLI, John

1. This memorandum is for your information only.

2. Reference is made to our recent conversation regarding the Agency's participation in political assassinations. Attached hereto is a memorandum dated 19 November 1970 which was furnished to Mr. Helms setting forth the circumstances of the Subject's activities on behalf of the Agency. Initially Roselli was unwitting of Government interest, but as time went on, he suspected that the U. S. Government was involved and specifically the CIA.

3. Roselli is presently serving a prison sentence for conspiracy in a Federal penitentiary in Seattle, Washington and awaits deportation upon completion of his current sentence.

4. This Agency was aware that Roselli intended to expose his participation in the plot should we not intervene on his behalf. The DCI decided to ignore his threats and take a calculated risk as to the consequences that may occur with the disclosure of his story. This was subsequently done by Roselli or someone on his behalf furnishing Jack Anderson details of the incident. Attached hereto are two of Anderson's articles dealing with Roselli. Anderson is also Editor of the Washington Bureau of the Washington Post, Sunday supplemental "Parade."

5. Individuals who were aware of this project were: Messrs. Dulles, Bissell, Colonel J. C. King, Colonel Sheffield Edwards,

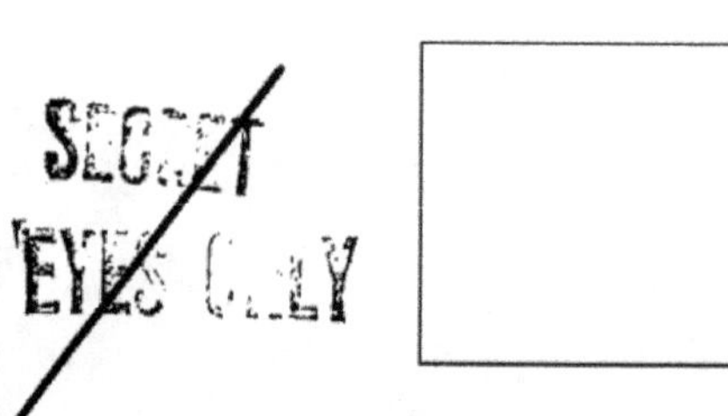

00041

William Harvey, and James P. O'Connell. Also included were Robert A. Maheu and his attorneys Edward P. Morgan and Edward Bennett Williams.

6. On 26 February 1971 arrangements were made with Immigration and Naturalization Service Commissioner Raymond Farrell to flag any action that may be taken by his organization regarding deportation proceedings against Roselli. On 26 January 1972 James F. Green, Associate Commissioner for I&NS, advised that they were deferring any deportation action for another year and would again call it to our attention upon expiration of the deferral.

Howard J. Osborn
Director of Security

Atts

00042

Atts

00043

19 NOV 1970

MEMORANDUM FOR: Director of Central Intelligence

SUBJECT : ROSELLI, Johnny

1. This memorandum is for information only.

2. In August 1960, Mr. Richard M. Bissell approached Colonel Sheffield Edwards to determine if the Office of Security had assets that may assist in a sensitive mission requiring gangster-type action. The mission target was Fidel Castro.

3. Because of its extreme sensitivity, only a small group was made privy to the project. The DCI was briefed and gave his approval. Colonel J. C. King, Chief, WH Division, was briefed, but all details were deliberately concealed from any of the JMWAVE officials. Certain TSD and Commo personnel participated in the initial planning stages, but were not witting of the purpose of the mission.

4. Robert A. Maheu was contacted, briefed generally on the project, and requested to ascertain if he could develop an entree into the gangster elements as the first step toward accomplishing the desired goal.

5. Mr. Maheu advised that he had met one Johnny Roselli on several occasions while visiting Las Vegas. He only knew him casually through clients, but was given to understand that he was a high-ranking member of the "syndicate" and controlled all of the ice-making machines on the Strip. Maheu reasoned that, if Roselli was in fact a member of the clan, he undoubtedly had connections leading into the Cuban gambling interests.

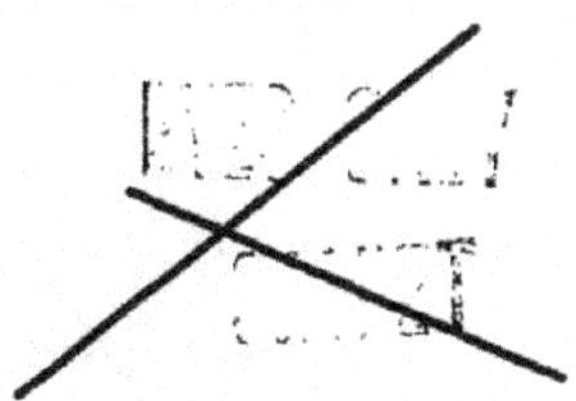

00044

6. Maheu was asked to approach Roselli, who knew Maheu as a personal relations executive handling domestic and foreign accounts, and tell him that he had recently been retained by a client who represented several international business firms which were suffering heavy financial losses in Cuba as a result of Castro's action. They were convinced that Castro's removal was the answer to their problem and were willing to pay a price of $150,000 for its successful accomplishment. It was to be made clear to Roselli that the U. S. Government was not, and should not, become aware of this operation.

7. The pitch was made to Roselli on 14 September 1960 at the Hilton Plaza Hotel, New York City. His initial reaction was to avoid getting involved but, through Maheu's persuasion, he agreed to introduce him to a friend, Sam Gold, who knew the "Cuban crowd." Roselli made it clear he did not want any money for his part and believed Sam would feel the same way. Neither of these individuals was ever paid out of Agency funds.

8. During the week of 25 September, Maheu was introduced to Sam who was staying at the Fontainebleau Hotel, Miami Beach. It was several weeks after his meeting with Sam and Joe, who was identified to him as a courier operating between Havana and Miami, that he saw photographs of both of these individuals in the Sunday supplemental "Parade." They were identified as Momo Salvatore Giancana and Santos Trafficant, respectively. Both were on the list of the Attorney General's ten most-wanted men. The former was described as the Chicago chieftain of the Cosa Nostra and successor to Al Capone, and the latter, the Cosa Nostra boss of Cuban operations. Maheu called this office immediately upon ascertaining this information.

9. In discussing the possible methods of accomplishing this mission, Sam suggested that they not resort to firearms but, if he could be furnished some type of potent pill, that could be placed in Castro's food or drink, it would be a much more effective operation. Sam indicated that he had a prospective nominee in the person of Juan Orta, a Cuban official who had been receiving kick-back payments from the gambling interests, who still had access to Castro, and was in a financial bind.

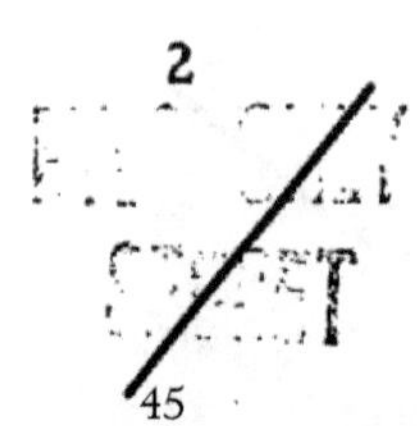

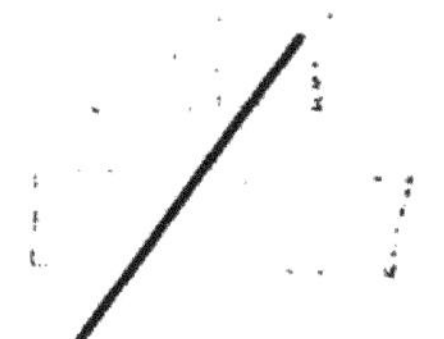

10. TSD was requested to produce six pills of high lethal content.

11. Joe delivered the pills to Orta. After several weeks of reported attempts, Orta apparently got cold feet and asked out of the assignment. He suggested another candidate who made several attempts without success.

12. Joe then indicated that Dr. Anthony Verona, one of the principal officers in the Cuban Exile Junta, had become disaffected with the apparent ineffectual progress of the Junta and was willing to handle the mission through his own resources.

13. He asked, as a prerequisite to the deal, that he be given $10,000 for organizational expenses and requested $1,000 worth of communications equipment.

14. Dr. Verona's potential was never fully exploited, as the project was canceled shortly after the Bay of Pigs episode. Verona was advised that the offer was withdrawn, and the pills were retrieved.

15. Of significant interest was an incident which involved a request levied by Sam upon Maheu.

> At the height of the project negotiations, Sam expressed concern about his girlfriend, Phyllis McGuire, who he learned was getting much attention from Dan Rowan while both were booked at a Las Vegas night club. Sam asked Maheu to put a bug in Rowan's room to determine the extent of his intimacy with Miss McGuire. The technician involved in the assignment was discovered in the process, arrested, and taken to the Sheriff's office for questioning. He called Maheu and informed him that he had been detained by the police. This call was made in the presence of the Sheriff's personnel.
>
> Subsequently, the Department of Justice announced its intention to prosecute Maheu along with the technician. On 7 February 1962, the Director of

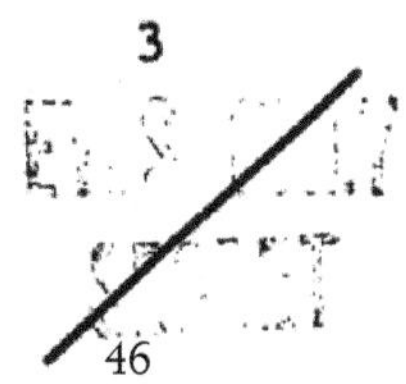

00046

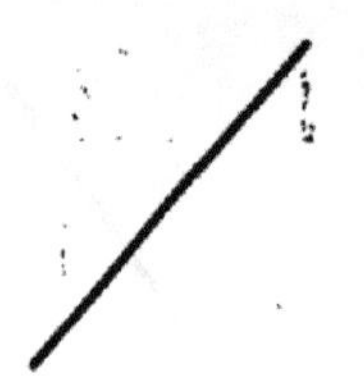

Security briefed the Attorney General, Robert Kennedy, on the circumstances leading up to Maheu's involvement in the wiretap. At our request, prosecution was dropped.

16. In May 1962, Mr. William Harvey took over as Case Officer, and it is not known by this Office whether Roselli was used operationally from that point on.

17. It was subsequently learned from the FBI that Roselli had been convicted on six counts involving illegal entry into the United States. Our records do not reflect the date of conviction, but it is believed to have been sometime during November 1967.

18. On 2 December 1968, Roselli, along with four other individuals, was convicted of conspiracy to cheat members of the Friars Club of $400,000 in a rigged gin gummy game.

19. Mr. Harvey reported to the Office of Security of his contacts with Roselli during November and December 1967 and January 1968. It was his belief that Johnny would not seek out the Agency for assistance in the deportation proceedings unless he actually faced deportation. Roselli expressed confidence that he would win an appeal.

20. On 17 November 1970, Maheu called James O'Connell, Roselli's first Case Officer, to advise that Maheu's attorney, Ed Morgan, had received a call from a Thomas Waddin, Roselli's lawyer, who stated that all avenues of appeal had been exhausted, and his client now faces deportation. Waddin indicated that, if someone did not intercede on Roselli's behalf, he would make a complete expose of his activities with the Agency.

21. On 18 November 1970, you were briefed on the latest development in this case, and it was decided that the Agency would not in any way assist Roselli. Maheu was so advised of the Agency's position, and he was in complete agreement with our stand. He further advised that he was not concerned about

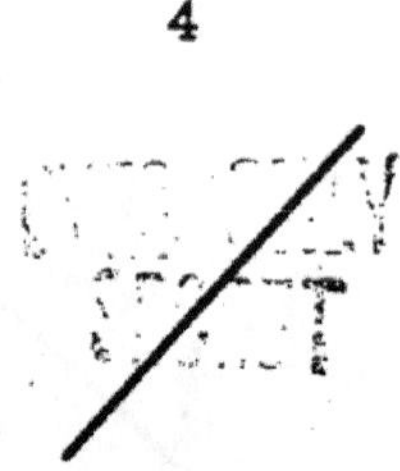

any publicity as it affected him personally should Roselli decide to tell all. He stated he would advise us promptly of any developments that he may become aware of in this matter.

Howard J. Osborn
Director of Security

5

00048

The Washington Merry-Go-Round THE WASHINGTON POST Monday, Jan. 18, 1971 B7

6 Attempts to Kill Castro Laid to CIA

By Jack Anderson

Locked in the darkest recesses of the Central Intelligence Agency is the story of six assassination attempts against Cuba's Fidel Castro.

For 10 years, only a few key people have known the terrible secret. They have sworn never to talk. Yet we have learned the details from sources whose credentials are beyond question.

We spoke to John McCone, who headed the CIA at the time of the assassination attempts. He acknowledged the idea had been discussed inside the CIA but insisted it had been "rejected immediately." He vigorously denied that the CIA had ever participated in any plot on Castro's life. Asked whether the attempts could have been made with his knowledge, he replied: "It could not have happened."

We have complete confidence, however, in our sources.

The plot to knock off Castro began as part of the Bay of Pigs operation. The intent was to eliminate the Cuban dictator before the motley invaders landed on the island. Their arrival was expected to touch off a general uprising, which the Communist militia would have had more trouble putting down without the charismatic Castro to lead them.

After the first attempt failed, five more assassination teams were sent to Cuba. The last team reportedly made it to a rooftop within shooting distance of Castro before they were apprehended. This happened around the last of February or first of March, 1963.

Nine months later, President Kennedy was gunned down in Dallas by Lee Harvey Oswald, a fanatic who previously had agitated for Castro in New Orleans and had made a mysterious trip to the Cuban Embassy in Mexico City.

Among those privy to the CIA conspiracy, there is still a nagging suspicion—unsupported by the Warren Commission's findings—that Castro became aware of the U.S. plot upon his life and somehow recruited Oswald to retaliate against President Kennedy.

To set up the Castro assassination, the CIA enlisted Robert Maheu, a former FBI agent with shadowy contacts, who had handled other undercover assignments for the CIA out of his Washington public relations office. He later moved to Las Vegas to head up billionaire Howard Hughes' Nevada operations.

Maheu recruited John Roselli, a ruggedly handsome gambler with contacts in both the American and Cuban underworlds, to arrange the assassination. The dapper, hawk-faced Roselli, formerly married to movie actress June Lang, was a power in the movie industry until his conviction with racketeer Willie Bioff in a million-dollar Hollywood labor shakedown. The CIA assigned two of its most trusted operatives, William Harvey and James (Big Jim) O'Connell, to the hush-hush murder mission. Using phony names, they accompanied Roselli on trips to Miami to line up the assassination teams.

The full story reads like the script of a James Bond movie, complete with secret trysts at glittering Miami Beach hotels and midnight powerboat dashes to secret landing spots on the Cuban coast. Once, Roselli's boat was shot out from under him.

For the first try, the CIA furnished Roselli with special poison capsules to slip into Castro's food. The poison was supposed to take three days to act. By the time Castro died, his system would throw off all traces of the poison, so he would appear to be the victim of a natural if mysterious ailment.

Roselli arranged with a Cuban, related to one of Castro's chefs, to plant the deadly pellets in the dictator's food. On March 13, 1961, Roselli delivered the capsules to his contact at Miami Beach's glamorous Fontainebleau Hotel.

A couple of weeks later, just about the right time for the plot to have been carried out a report out of Havana said Castro was ill. But he recovered before the Bay of Pigs invasion on April 17, 1961.

Four more attempts were made on Castro's life.

00049

The Washington Merry-Go-Round THE WASHINGTON POST *Tuesday, Feb. 23, 1971* B11

Castro Stalker Worked for the CIA

By Jack Anderson

The mystery man whom the Central Intelligence Agency recruited to assassinate Cuba's Fidel Castro has been laid up in the sick ward of the Los Angeles County jail.

He is handsome, hawk-faced John Roselli, once a dashing figure around Hollywood and Las Vegas, now a gray, 66-year-old inmate with a respiratory ailment.

Confidential FBI files identify him as "a top Mafia figure" who watched over "the concealed interests in Las Vegas casinos of the Chicago underworld."

Roselli has admitted to friends that he was a rum runner during the Roaring Twenties. Operating along the East Coast, he learned how to evade Coast Guard cutters and police patrols.

His name later became linked with the biggest names in the Chicago and Los Angeles underworlds. He also developed contacts in the Cuban underworld before Castro took over the Havana gambling casinos.

He had the right background for a hush-hush mission that the CIA was planning in 1961. As part of the Bay of Pigs invasion, the CIA hoped to knock off Castro and leave Cuba leaderless.

Risks Neck

Roselli was recruited for the job by Robert Maheu, a former FBI agent, who admitted to us that he had handled undercover assignments for the CIA. He refused, however, to discuss the details. This is the same Maheu, incidentally, who is now involved in a legal battle over phantom billionaire Howard Hughes' Nevada operations.

Roselli was so flattered over being asked to perform a secret mission for the U.S. government that he paid all his expenses out of his own pocket and risked his neck to land the assassination teams on the Cuban coast.

In James Bond fashion, he held whispered meetings in Miami Beach hotels with Cubans willing to make an attempt on Castro's life. Once, he called on Chicago racket boss Sam Giancana to line up a contact. The confidential files report that Giancana had "gambling interest and an interest in the shrimp business in Cuba." However, the Chicago gangster took no direct part in the assassination plot.

Roselli made midnight dashes to Cuba with his hired assassins in twin powerboats. Once a Cuban patrol ship turned its guns on his darkened boat, tore a hole in the bottom and sank the boat. Roselli was fished out of the water by the other boat, which escaped into the shadows.

In earlier columns, we reported how the CIA furnished Roselli with deadly poison capsules which he tried through a relative of Castro's chef to plant in the dictator's food. Later, marksmen armed with high-powered Belgian rifles attempted to infiltrate close enough to gun Castro down.

All told, six assassination attempts were made, the last in the spring of 1963. Throughout this period, Roselli worked under the direct supervision of two secret CIA agents, William Harvey and James (Big Jim) O'Connell.

Roselli's Reward

The FBI which got wind of the assassination plot, has tried to pump Roselli for information. But he was sworn to silence by the CIA, and up to this moment, he hasn't broken it.

Meanwhile, the Justice Department, as part of its crackdown on organized crime, tried to nail Roselli. The FBI discovered that his Chicago birth records had been forged, that his name was really Filippo Sacco and that he had come to this country from Italy as a child. He was convicted for failing to register as an alien.

He was also convicted for conspiracy to rig card games at Los Angeles' exclusive Friar's Club.

Of Roselli's two CIA associates, Harvey has now retired to Indianapolis and O'Connell is still on the CIA payroll. Both admitted to us a friendship with Roselli but refused to discuss their CIA activities. Harvey said he had a "high regard" for Roselli and called the Friar's Club case a "bum rap." Said Harvey: "The Friar's Club indictment is phony. Roselli had no more to do with that than I had."

Roselli's lawyers are now trying to get clemency for their client, citing our stories about his secret CIA service.

Firearms Fiasco

Under pressure from the firearms lobby, the Treasury Department has failed to enforce a vital section of the 1968 federal firearms act.

The law was passed after the murders of Sen. Robert Kennedy and Dr. Martin Luther King. It authorizes the Treasury Secretary to require full reports of all firearms and ammunition sales.

For the two years that the law has been in force, the Treasury Department has ignored this key provision. The gun industry has complained it would be a bookkeeping nightmare.

The federal government, which would have to compile all the sales data, has [illegible] been reluctant to spend the $100 million it would cost for computers and staff to maintain the firearms files.

UNCLASSIFIED | INTERNAL USE ONLY | CONFIDENTIAL | ~~SECRET~~

ROUTING AND RECORD SHEET

SUBJECT: (Optional)

FROM: Howard J. Osborn HJO
Director of Security
[redacted] Hqs.

EXTENSION: [redacted]

NO.

DATE: 17 December 1973

TO: (Officer designation, room number, and building)	DATE RECEIVED	DATE FORWARDED	OFFICER'S INITIALS	COMMENTS (Number each comment to show from whom to whom. Draw a line across column after each comment.)
1. IG Staff Attn: [redacted] ~~2E-24 Hqs.~~			S [redacted]	John — I believe you are aware of the "other activities" referred to in #4. If not I will be happy to brief you. Oz
2. [illegible]				
3. DFC				
4. SDB	16 Jan '74			
5.				
6.				
7.				
8.				
9.				
10.				
11.				
12.				
13.				
14.				
15.				

00051

FORM 3-62 610 USE PREVIOUS EDITIONS ~~SECRET~~ CONFIDENTIAL INTERNAL USE ONLY UNCLASSIFIED

17 December 1973

MEMORANDUM FOR THE RECORD

SUBJECT: Recent Activities of the Watergate Special Prosecution Staff

1. Early in the evening of 10 December 1973, I received a telephone call from [redacted] [redacted] who informed me that he, in turn, had received a call from [redacted] Intelligence Division, Washington Metropolitan Police Department.

2. It seems that [redacted] had just spent an hour in conversation at his home with a [redacted] in the Washington Metropolitan Police Department who had reported to him on his interview that afternoon with a Mr. Martin and a Mr. Horowitz, prosecutors of the Watergate Special Prosecution Staff. [redacted] had been subpoenaed for his appearance and he indicated to [redacted] that the two prosecutors were principally concerned with two matters:

a. What type of training had the Agency given members of the Washington Metropolitan Police Department? how long were the courses? and how often were they given?

b. What support did the Agency provide to the Washington Metropolitan Police Department during demonstrations occurring in the Washington area in late 1969 and early 1970?

3. [redacted] said that he had been shown a long list of names and asked if any of them had been involved either with the training given the Washington Metropolitan Police Department or the support to the Washington Metropolitan Police Department during the demonstrations. [redacted] could remember only three names on the list. They were: [redacted]

SECRET/~~SENSITIVE~~

4. The three individuals named by [redacted] did in fact participate in both the training and support during the demonstrations. They are only three among others of my [redacted] special support group who were involved in these activities. Of extreme sensitivity is the fact that these same individuals were engaged in other highly sensitive activities which could cause the Agency severe embarrassment if they were surfaced today in the current 'Watergate climate."

5. I briefed the Director personally on this development and he indicated that if the training and demonstrations surfaced that he would simply acknowledge that this had occurred but as he had assured members of Congress, we would not engage in this type of activity in the future. He agreed with my suggestion that we have the Legislative Counsel brief Congressman Nedzi and Senator Stennis on this since they have already been briefed on all activities of this nature undertaken by the Agency in the past. I briefed Mr. John Warner, Acting General Counsel, and agreed with him that we would make no effort to brief members of my [redacted] until and if they are subpoenaed. Mr. Warner or members of his Staff will then caution them to only answer questions asked and not volunteer additional information. I am making a copy of this memorandum available to [redacted] of the Inspector General's Staff at the suggestion of the Inspector General, who I also briefed on this development.

Howard J. Osborn
Director of Security

cc: IG Staff Attn: [redacted]

00053

[ ] UNCLASSIFIED [ ] INTERNAL USE ONLY [ ] CONFIDENTIAL [X] ~~SECRET~~

ROUTING AND RECORD SHEET

SUBJECT: (Optional)

FROM: Howard J. Osborn, Director of Security #10

EXTENSION:

NO.:

DATE: 25 MAY 1973

TO: (Officer designation, room number, and building)	DATE RECEIVED	DATE FORWARDED	OFFICER'S INITIALS	COMMENTS (Number each comment to show from whom to whom. Draw a line across column after each comment.)
1. Executive Secretary, CIA Management Com.	5/25	5/25	[illegible]	Recommend we terminate para 2 & continue para 3 only as the activity pertains to foreign assignments to collect narcotics intellig.
2. DCI				
3. D/Security [redacted] - Hdqs.				
4.				
5.				
6.				
7.				
8.				
9.				
10.				
11.				
12.				
13.				
14.				
15.				

MEMORANDUM FOR: D/M&S
D/Sec

Pls comply -

WEC
5/29/73

(DATE)

00054

FORM NO. 101 REPLACES FORM 10-101 WHICH MAY BE USED.
1 AUG 54

FORM 3-62 610 USE PREVIOUS EDITIONS [X] ~~SECRET~~

(47)

UNCLASSIFIED ☐ INTERNAL USE ONLY ☐ CONFIDENTIAL ☒ ~~SECRET~~ The "Family Jewels"

ROUTING AND RECORD SHEET

SUBJECT: (Optional)

FROM:	EXTENSION	NO.
Howard J. Osborn, Director of Security HJO		DATE 25 MAY 1973

TO: (Officer designation, room number, and building)	DATE RECEIVED	DATE FORWARDED	OFFICER'S INITIALS	COMMENTS (Number each comment to show from whom to whom. Draw a line across column after each comment.)
1. Executive Secretary, CIA Management Com.	5/25	5/25		
2. DCI				Recommend we terminate para 2 & continue para 3 only as the activity pertains to foreign assignments to collect narcotics intelligence abroad — WEC
3. D/Security [redacted] - Hdqs.				
4.				
5.				
6.				
7.				
8.				
9.				
10.				
11.				
12.				
13.				
14.				
15.				

00055

FORM 610 USE PREVIOUS EDITIONS ☒ ~~SECRET~~ ☐ CONFIDENTIAL ☐ INTERNAL USE ONLY ☐ UNCLASSIFIED

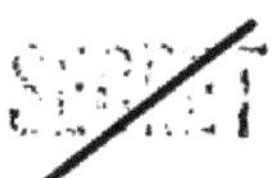

Executive Registry
73-3426

25 MAY 1973

MEMORANDUM FOR: Executive Secretary,
CIA Management Committee

SUBJECT : Project TWO-FOLD

1. This memorandum sets forth a recommendation for your approval in paragraph 5.

2. For the past several years, this office has been supporting the Bureau of Narcotics and Dangerous Drugs (BNDD) by spotting, assessing, and recruiting personnel to form an internal security unit whose primary mission is the detection of corruption within the BNDD. Subsequent to the recruitment and training stage, the individuals selected are turned over to the Chief Inspector of BNDD for operational guidance and handling in their various domestic assignments.

3. Recently, this Agency has extended this activity by supporting BNDD in the covert acquisition of individuals who are hired as Staff Agents utilized under nonofficial cover and directed against the principal international drug traffickers. These individuals are true employees of the BNDD and, although all administrative details relative to their employment are handled within the Agency, they are unaware of any Agency involvement.

4. It is felt at this time that a reaffirmation of our support to BNDD in Project TWO-FOLD is necessary and desirable.

5. Therefore, it is recommended that approval be granted for the continuation of Project TWO-FOLD as originally approved by the Director of Central Intelligence on 12 February 1971.

Howard J. Osborn
Director of Security

00056

SECRET

SECRET

SUBJECT: Project TWO-FOLD

APPROVED: ______________________ *

DISAPPROVED: ______________________

Distribution:
Orig. - Return to OS
1 - ER
1 - IG

* Per Mr. Colby's recommendation and DCI concurrence, terminate paragraph 2 activity and continue paragraph 3 only as the activity pertains to foreign assignments to collect narcotics intelligence abroad. Copy furnished IG.

Ben C. Evans, Jr.
O/ES/

29 MAY 1973

00057

ROUTING AND RECORD SHEET

SUBJECT: (Optional)

FROM:	EXTENSION	NO.
		DATE 11 May 1973

TO: (Officer designation, room number, and building)	DATE RECEIVED	DATE FORWARDED	OFFICER'S INITIALS	COMMENTS (Number each comment to show from whom to whom. Draw a line across column after each comment.)
1. Broe				
2.				
3.				
4.				
5.				
6.				
7.				
8.				
9.				
10.				
11.				
12.				
13.				
14.				
15.				00058

FORM 3-62 610 USE PREVIOUS EDITIONS ☒ SECRET ☐ CONFIDENTIAL ☐ INTERNAL USE ONLY ☐ UNCLASSIFIED

~~SECRET~~

11 May 1973

MEMORANDUM FOR THE RECORD

SUBJECT: General: Office of Security Survey

1. At the Director's instruction, and with the concurrence of the then DD/P, the Office of Security developed informants in RID to report on the activities of RID employees on whom security questions had arisen. This program, which included upwards of a dozen informants at its peak, has declined to its present level of three, only one of whom is reporting regularly on matters of current interest.

2. The principal object of Security's interest through this informant is a female who was employed in RID for a number of years until she resigned in 1969. Her resignation coincided with the initiation of a security review on her by the Office of Security, but Security does not know whether the employee was aware of this security review at the time of her resignation.

3. Security's interest in this employee was occasioned by reports that she had developed an increasingly intimate acquaintance with a Cuban national. Reporting by one informant, who was also being developed by the Cuban, suggested that the Cuban might have an intelligence interest in the female. The same informant also subsequently reported that the Cuban had numerous other contacts among clerical and secretarial employees of the Agency.

4. Subsequent to her departure from the Agency, the ex-RID employee entered into a common-law marital relationship with the Cuban and joined him as partner in a photographic business. In this capacity she solicited business among CIA employees, especially those requiring passport photos. Recently, she and the Cuban sought to employ Security's informant in this business on a part-time basis.

00059 35

~~SECRET~~

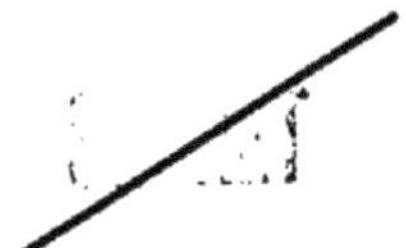

5. Information on the background of the Cuban is fairly extensive, but it is inconclusive. He is known to have been a member of anti-Castro organizations in this country. There are also reports that his mother was imprisoned in Cuba at one time. There are other episodes in his life that suggest intelligence involvement on his part with some hostile service, but this is not yet definitely established.

6. The Office of Security has had at times a second informant in this case. His reporting has tended to confirm reporting by the principal informant.

8. The Office of Security has been running this operation for over two years, in an effort to obtain conclusive proof of its intelligence nature. CI Staff has been kept informed. The FBI, which was informed of the case at an early stage, has declined to take responsibility for it, on grounds that it concerns CIA's internal security. As a result, the Office ofSecurity has been inhi bited in the actions it can take against the Cuban suspect. On the other hand, Security has not taken any action against Agency employees for fear of compromising the operation.

9. It would appear to me that the Office of Security has dallied with this case long enough. Apparently unable through positive measures to resolve doubts about the case, O/S has followed the course of watchful waiting, hoping the Cuban would take precipitate action himself that would give us the evidence we seek. In the meantime, our knowledge of the relationship between the Cuban and the several other current Agency employees with whom he is known to have contact continues

00060

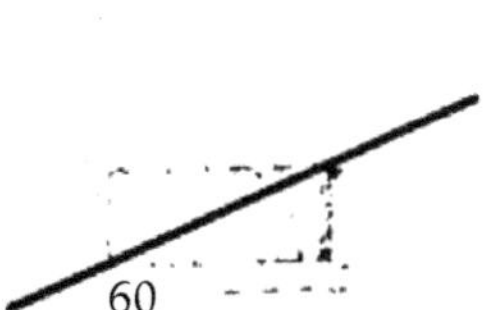

The possibility that the employee in SB Division may be passing information on CIA's Soviet operations is too great to warrant further delay in moving against her.

00061

7 May 1973

Memorandum to: The Inspector General

Subject: Office of Security Survey - Office of Security Support to BNDD

1. In December 1970 Robert Ingersoll, head of the Bureau of Narcotics and Dangerous Drugs, asked Mr. Helms if the Agency could give him some assistance in shoring up the internal integrity of the BNDD. According to Ingersoll, the old Federal Bureau of Narcotics had been heavily infiltrated by dishonest and corrupt elements, who were believed to have ties with the narcotics smuggling industry. Ingersoll wanted us to help him recruit some thoroughly reliable people who could be used, not only as special agents in his various offices around the country, but also to serve as informants on the other BNDD employees in these offices.

)62

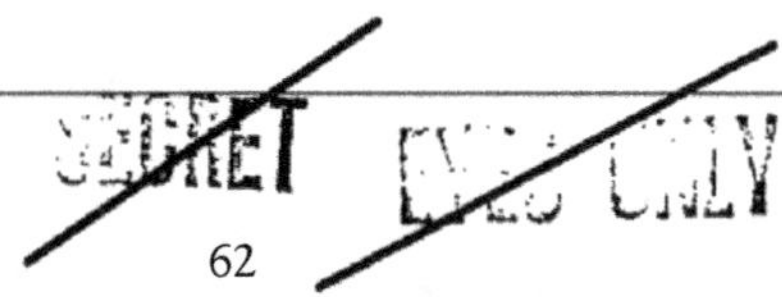

JOLawrence

00063

SECRET ~~EYES ONLY~~

☐ UNCLASSIFIED [X] ADMIN - INTERNAL USE ONLY ☐ CONFIDENTIAL ☐ SECRET

ROUTING AND RECORD SHEET

SUBJECT: (Optional)

FROM:	EXTENSION	NO.
Howard J. Osborn Director of Security		DATE 9 May 1973

TO: (Officer designation, room number, and building)	DATE RECEIVED	DATE FORWARDED	OFFICER'S INITIALS	COMMENTS (Number each comment to show from whom to whom. Draw a line across column after each comment.)
1. Deputy Director for Management & Services				
2.				
3. IG				
4.				
5.				
6.				
7.				
8.				
9.				
10.				
11.				
12.				
13.				
14.				
15.				00064 ADMIN -

FORM 3-62 610 USE PREVIOUS EDITIONS ☐ SECRET ☐ CONFIDENTIAL [X] INTERNAL USE ONLY ☐ UNCLASSIFIED

ADMINISTRATIVE-INTERNAL USE ONLY

9 May 1973

MEMORANDUM FOR: Deputy Director for Management & Services

SUBJECT : Press Allegations re Use of Agency Polygraph

1. This memorandum is for your information only and confirms a report I made to you by telephone earlier today.

2. On 22 July 1971, an article was carried on American proposals relative to the SALT talks in The New York Times over the by-line of William Beecher. It was devastatingly accurate and contained direct quotes from a Presidential advisory memorandum the White House had sent to Mr. Gerard Smith, Director, Arms Control and Disarmament Agency, a few days earlier. The President was alleged to be furious with this unauthorized disclosure of classified information and directed a sweeping investigation within the United States Government to determine the source of the disclosure. Investigation was conducted under the direction of Mr. Egil Krogh and Mr. David Young, Staff Assistants to Mr. John Ehrlichman, Counsel to the President for Domestic Affairs.

3. On the basis of investigations conducted by State Security and Defense officials, four individuals--one individual in the Department of Defense and three individuals in the Arms Control and Disarmament Agency--were tabbed as leading suspects. Mr. Egil Krogh contacted me on 26 July 1971 and requested that we arrange to polygraph the three suspects in the Arms Control and Disarmament Agency and volunteered the information that the Federal Bureau of Investigation would be asked to polygraph the one suspect in the Department of Defense.

00065

4. I informed Mr. Krogh that from time to time in matters involving the national security the Agency had detailed to Mr. G. Marvin Gentile, Director of State Security, a polygraph operator and a polygraph machine for his use in polygraphing State Department employees who were recipients of allegations concerning their loyalty. I emphasized that this procedure had the Director's approval and that State clearly understood that the examination was their total responsibility. I further informed him that this was the only way we could undertake to entertain his request and that even then it would require the specific approval of the Director. Mr. Krogh asked me to obtain such approval and work out such arrangements with Mr. Gentile.

5. Later that same day, Mr. Krogh called Mr. Gentile and inquired as to whether the arrangements had been made. Mr. Gentile indicated they had and suggested that the same polygraph operator be used to examine the Defense suspect. Mr. Krogh informed Mr. Gentile that he considered this an excellent idea and that he would instruct Defense officials to make their man available to Mr. Gentile for a polygraph examination.

6. The four individuals were [redacted] The polygraph examinations resulted in clearing the four men and the results of the examinations were forwarded over my signature to Mr. Gentile on 29 July 1971. A copy of my covering memorandum is attached.

7. Mr. Murrey Marder, a staff writer for The Washington Post, in an article dated 3 September 1971, stated that a State Department spokesman had acknowledged at a news briefing that agents of the Federal Bureau of Investigation had polygraphed State Department employees suspected of leaking information on the SALT talks in July. Mr. John Edgar Hoover, then Director of the Federal

Bureau of Investigation, denied this allegation in a letter to The Washington Post and said that the polygraph examinations had been conducted by another agency. Speculation centered around the Agency, but after a day or so, press speculation in this regard died away.

8. Mr. Marder apparently has never been satisfied and has been pressing Mr. Charles Bray, State Department spokesman, for confirmation of Agency involvement. Mr. Bray learned today that Mr. Marder plans to use a press conference to be held at 2:00 p.m. this afternoon to press this point further. Mr. Bray has been given guidance by Mr. Gentile to avoid confirmation but if this is impossible he will indicate the examinations were conducted by State Department Security officials utilizing an operator and a machine detailed to the Department for this purpose. I do not know whether or not the fact that the government-wide investigation was directed by Mr. Egil Krogh is known to Mr. Marder but I suspect that it is and that this is the reason why the matter has been raised again. Mr. David Young was instrumental in pushing my office to conduct an internal Agency investigation of this disclosure and the White House was satisfied that no Agency employee was the source.

Howard J. Osborn
Director of Security

Attachment

00067

00068

30 JUL 1971

MEMORANDUM FOR: Mr. G. Marvin Gentile
Deputy Assistant Secretary
for Security
Department of State

SUBJECT : Special Technical Interviews

1. Attached are the technical interview reports on

2. As in other cases involving the use of polygraph, it is imperative no reference be made to this Agency's involvement in these actions.

3. As you will note, the reports are not classified and I shall defer to your judgment in regard to the level of classification.

FOR THE DIRECTOR OF CENTRAL INTELLIGENCE:

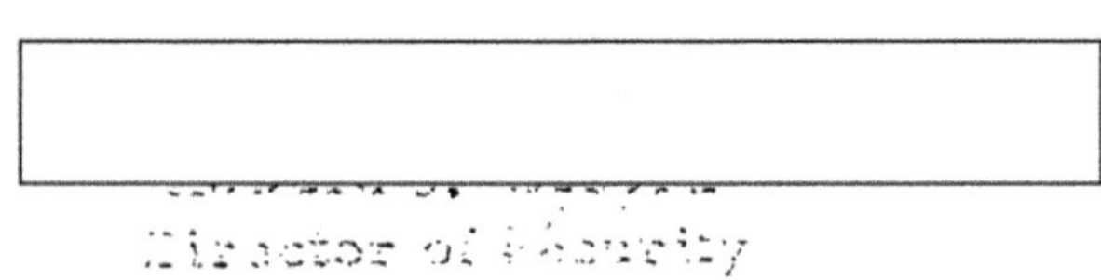

Director of Security

Atts.

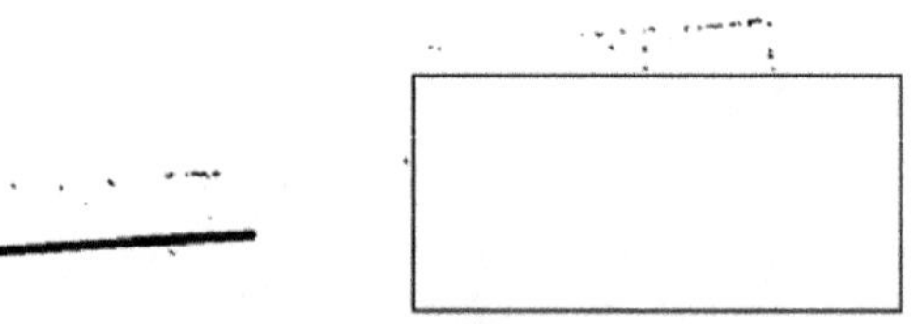

00069

SECRET EYES ONLY

5 June 1973

MEMORANDUM FOR: Inspector General

SUBJECT : Items in John Clarke Memorandum to the Director of Central Intelligence, dated 9 May 1973

1. Two items in the attached memorandum had not previously been reported. The first: "-- Use of CIA funds and facilities to [redacted] for FBI and provision of technical equipments by NSA [redacted] for use against a [redacted]

2. In a follow-up meeting with Mr. Clarke, he advised that involved here was the use of funds appropriated for CIA being given to the FBI in cashiers checks for the purpose of [redacted] There was also Agency help given in [redacted] Further, other CIA monies in cashiers checks were given to NSA who, with some [redacted] assistance, was working on [redacted] Mr. Clarke said he thought the only problem here was in the use of funds, not in the operation. He thought the only source of additional information on this subject was Mr. [redacted] of the DDO/CI Staff.

3. The second item: "-- Use of CIA funds to help State Department defer Presidential representational expenses of President Lyndon B. Johnson's trip to Southeast Asia."

4. Mr. Clarke said the total amount of money requested by State Department was $3,000,000 but that the Director would not agree to this amount. The Director did supply funds in those instances where some operational activity was involved or could be inferred, i.e., [redacted] Mr. Clarke was not sure of the amount of Agency

00070

SECRET EYES ONLY

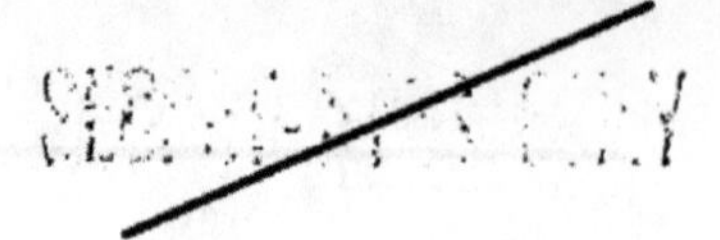

funds used. He felt that only Colonel White could supply additional details. He said Senator Russell and Representative Mahon were advised of this Agency activity but asked not to be briefed in detail.

Inspector

Attachment

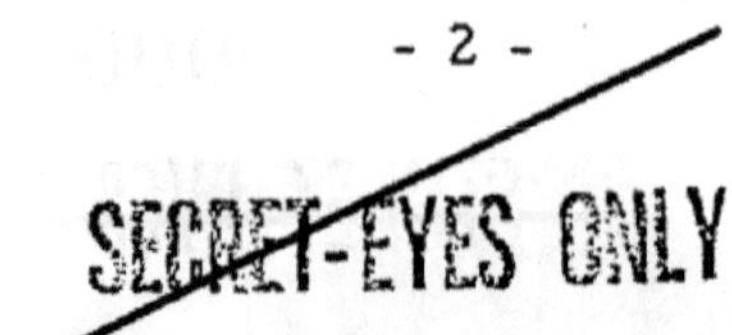

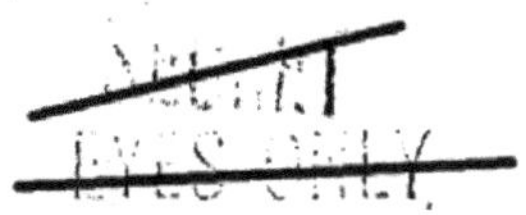

9 May 1973

MEMORANDUM FOR: Director of Central Intelligence

SUBJECT : Per your instructions

1. I have no recollection of specific contacts with the Ellsberg case, Watergate, or Young. Dick Helms' instructions at the time regarding discussion of Hunt's previous employment should be a matter of record.

2. Other activities of the Agency which could at some point raise public questions should they be exposed and on which Bill Colby is fully conversant are:

-- CI activity of Dick Ober, DD/O.

-- [redacted] and [redacted] investments and accumulation of Government capital.

-- Use of CIA funds and facilities to acquire U. S. real estate for FBI and provision of technical equipments by NSA [redacted] for use against [redacted]

-- Use of CIA funds to help State Department defer Presidential representational expenses of L. B. J. trip to SEA.

John M. Clarke

00072

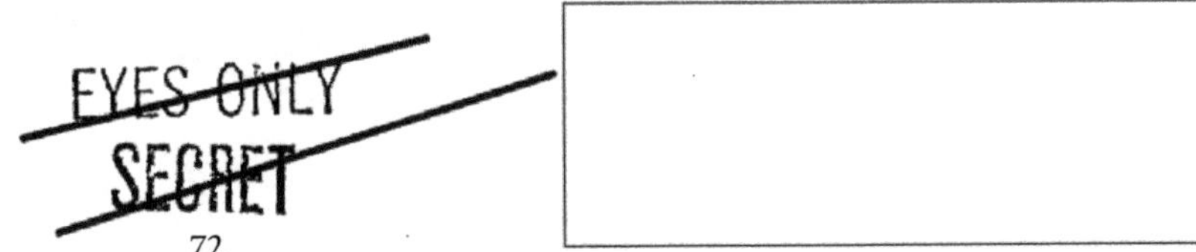

5 June 1973

MEMORANDUM FOR: Inspector General

SUBJECT : Items in John Clarke Memorandum to the Director of Central Intelligence, dated 9 May 1973

1. Two items in the attached memorandum had not previously been reported. The first: "-- Use of CIA funds and facilities to acquire U.S. real estate for FBI and provision of technical equipments by NSA [redacted] for use against a [redacted]

2. In a follow-up meeting with Mr. Clarke, he advised that involved here was the use of funds appropriated for CIA being given to the FBI in cashiers checks for the purpose of [redacted] There was also Agency help given in [redacted] Further, other CIA monies in cashiers checks were given to NSA who, with some [redacted] assistance, was working on [redacted] Mr. Clarke said he thought the only problem here was in the use of funds, not in the operation. He thought the only source of additional information on this subject was Mr. [redacted] of the DDO/CI Staff.

3. The second item: "-- Use of CIA funds to help State Department defer Presidential representational expenses of President Lyndon B. Johnson's trip to Southeast Asia."

4. Mr. Clarke said the total amount of money requested by State Department was $3,000,000 but that the Director would not agree to this amount. The Director did supply funds in those instances where some operational activity was involved or could be inferred, i.e., [redacted] Mr. Clarke was not sure of the amount of Agency

00073

SECRET-EYES ONLY

funds used. He felt that only Colonel White could supply additional details. He said Senator Russell and Representative Mahon were advised of this Agency activity but asked not to be briefed in detail.

Inspector

Attachment

- 2 -

00074

SECRET-EYES ONLY

UNCLASSIFIED | INTERNAL USE ONLY | CONFIDENTIAL | SECRET

ROUTING AND RECORD SHEET

SUBJECT: (Optional)

FROM: Director of Finance
1212 Key Building

EXTENSION

NO.

DATE 7 May 1973

TO: (Officer designation, room number, and building)	DATE RECEIVED	DATE FORWARDED	OFFICER'S INITIALS	COMMENTS (Number each comment to show from whom to whom. Draw a line across column after each comment.)
1. Deputy Director for Management & Services [redacted] Headquarters				
2.				
3.				
4. Director of Central Intelligence [redacted] Headquarters				
5.				
6.				
7.				
8.				
9.				
10.				
11.				
12.				
13.				
14.				
15.				

EYES ONLY

00075

FORM 3-62 610 USE PREVIOUS EDITIONS [X] SECRET [ ] CONFIDENTIAL [ ] INTERNAL USE ONLY [ ] UNCLASSIFIED

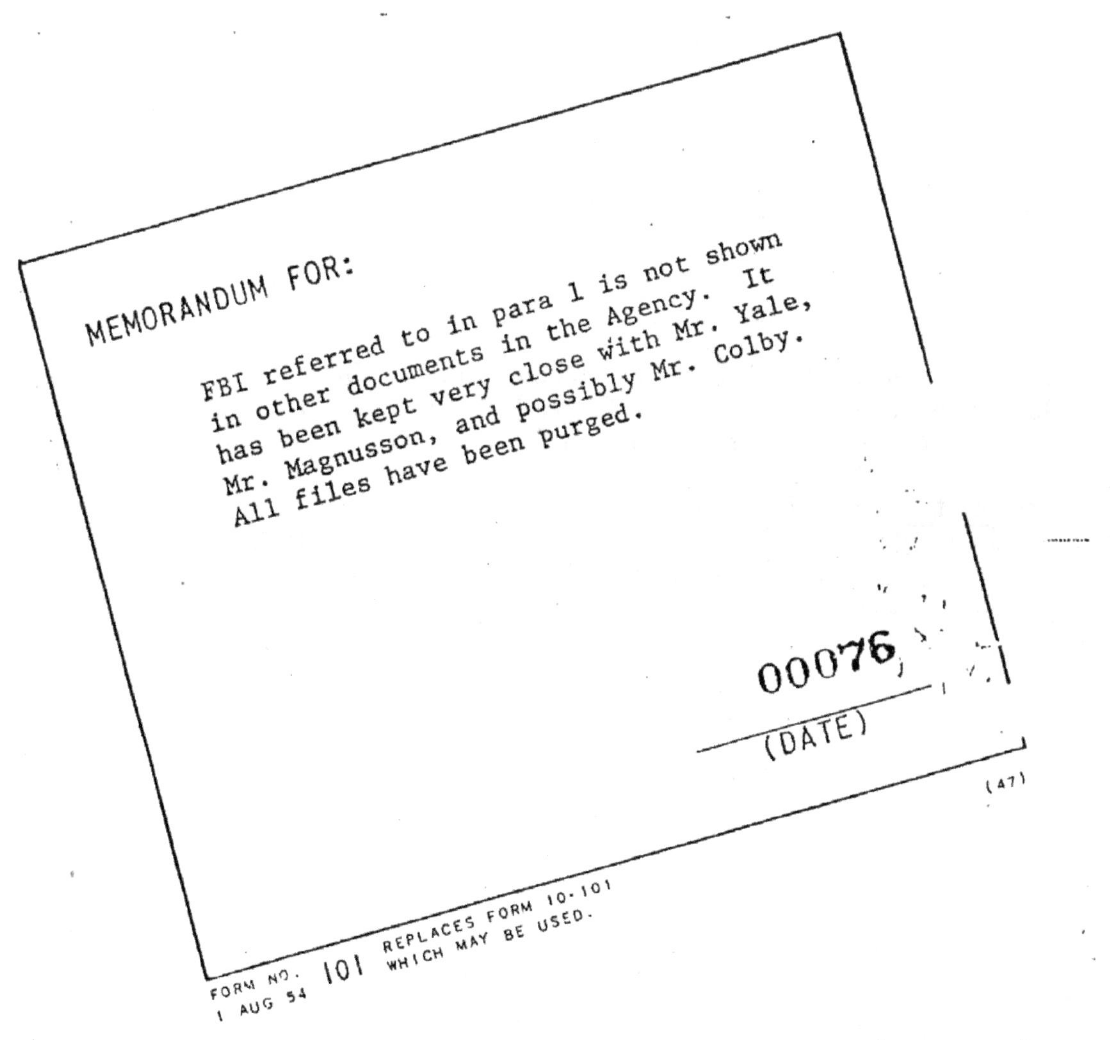

MEMORANDUM FOR:

FBI referred to in para 1 is not shown in other documents in the Agency. It has been kept very close with Mr. Yale, Mr. Magnusson, and possibly Mr. Colby. All files have been purged.

00076

(DATE)

(47)

FORM NO. 101 REPLACES FORM 10-101 WHICH MAY BE USED.
1 AUG 54

07 MAY 1973

MEMORANDUM FOR: Director of Central Intelligence

VIA : Deputy Director for Management and Services

FROM : Director of Finance

SUBJECT : Special Other Government Agency Activities

1. Colonel White, Executive Director-

2.

3. Detailees - The Agency has reimbursable and non-reimbursable agreements with the White House, Department of Justice, Defense Agencies, etc., based on signed memoranda between the Director of Personnel and the various Agencies.

4. Project TWOFOLD - Reimbursement from Bureau of Narcotics and Dangerous Drugs for training of BNDD agents by a domestic Agency Security proprietary.

5.

SECRET EYES ONLY

00077

SUBJECT: Special Other Government Agency Activities

6. Payment to White House - Reimbursement to White House as approved by Executive Director-Comptroller for $33,655.68 representing cost of postage, stationery and addressing of replies to letters and telegrams received by the White House as a result of the President's speech on Cambodia in May 1970.

Thomas [redacted] ale
Director of Finance

00078

07 MAY 1973

MEMORANDUM FOR: Director of Central Intelligence

VIA : Deputy Director for Management and Services

FROM : Director of Finance

SUBJECT : Special Other Government Agency Activities

Colonel White, Executive Director-

2.

3. Detailees - The Agency has reimbursable and non-reimbursable agreements with the White House, Department of Justice, Defense Agencies, etc., based on signed memoranda between the Director of Personnel and the various Agencies.

4. Project ~~TWOFOLD~~ - Reimbursement from Bureau of Narcotics and Dangerous Drugs for training of BNDD agents by a domestic Agency Security proprietary.

5.

~~SECRET EYES ONLY~~

00079

SUBJECT: Special Other Government Agency Activities

6. Payment to White House - Reimbursement to White House as approved by Executive Director-Comptroller for $33,655.68 representing cost of postage, stationery and addressing of replies to letters and telegrams received by the White House as a result of the President's speech on Cambodia in May 1970.

(signed) Thomas B. Yale

Thomas B. Yale
Director of Finance

~~SECRET EYES ONLY~~

07 MAY 1973

MEMORANDUM FOR: Director of Central Intelligence

VIA : Deputy Director for Management and Services

FROM : Director of Finance

SUBJECT : Special Other Government Agency Activities

Colonel White, Executive Director-

2.

3. Detailees - The Agency has reimbursable and non-reimbursable agreements with the White House, Department of Justice, Defense Agencies, etc., based on signed memoranda between the Director of Personnel and the various Agencies.

4. Project TWOFOLD - Reimbursement from Bureau of Narcotics and Dangerous Drugs for training of BNDD agents by a domestic Agency Security proprietary.

5.

~~SECRET EYES ONLY~~

00081

SUBJECT: Special Other Government Agency Activities

6. Payment to White House - Reimbursement to White House as approved by Executive Director-Comptroller for $33,655.68 representing cost of postage, stationery and addressing of replies to letters and telegrams received by the White House as a result of the President's speech on Cambodia in May 1970.

(signed) Thomas B. Yale

Thomas B. Yale
Director of Finance

00082

ROUTING AND RECORD SHEET

SUBJECT: (Optional)

FROM:	EXTENSION	NO.
Deputy Director of Finance 1212 Key Building		DATE 24 May 1973

TO: (Officer designation, room number, and building)	DATE RECEIVED	DATE FORWARDED	OFFICER'S INITIALS	COMMENTS (Number each comment to show from whom to whom. Draw a line across column after each comment.)
1. [redacted] [redacted] Headquarters				Attached are pertinent documents and papers relatin to Para 6 of the Director of Finance's memo to the DCI dated 7 May 1973, Subject: "Special Other Government Agency Activities" [redacted] Warren D. Magnusso Atts
2.				
3.				
4.				
5.				
6.				
7.				
8.				
9.				
10.				
11.				
12.				
13.				
14.				
15.				00083

EYES ONLY

Mr. Magnusson's phone conversation with Mr. John Brown at approximately 10:20 on 26 May 1970:

B: Guess we're back together again!

M: Got more problems?

B: Yes, don't know how much Watts told you.

M: I didn't talk to Watts. Think he called Colonel White.

B: Let me explain background. As a result of the Cambodia speech, we're getting relatively inundated with correspondence and normally all of this is sent to the Department of State for answering. What we're doing -- we're continuing to send all cons correspondence to State. However, the President made determination he'd like to answer support over his signature here and we asked the Department of State to support us on this effort. They're in a position where they can provide only limited support at this time. They're committed for $10,000 which would probably handle in the area of maybe 60,000 responses.

M: How many responses altogether counting pros and cons?

B: The cons are quite a large group that they're handling themselves also.

M: Are they going to be handling pros too?

B: $10,000 is for pros. They're doing cons. On pros they can pick up only $10,000 worth. We estimate it will be around $8,000 per 50,000 and it looks like at present time we've got over 100,000 responses in and it could go upwards of 150,000 or greater. Looks like we'll need a minimum of another $10,000, probably in area of $15,000, additional. This covers cost of printing, postage and addressing.

M: Just printing, postage and addressing? Not any overtime for any salaries or anything like that?

B: No, the posting of the things we'll do ourselves -- by hand. No problem. We're talking about physical costs of job -- cost of stamps, cost of envelopes and cards, and cost of having them addressed by outside firm. We'll handle putting stamp on, inserting, and sealing and mailing. Only talking about cost associated with three aspects of the operation.

M: Postage, addressing and printing.

B: Yes, reason I asked NSC to see if they could arrange -- depending on how volume goes -- probably another $10,000 to $15,000.

M: These are just pros? State is handling all cons themselves?

(continued)

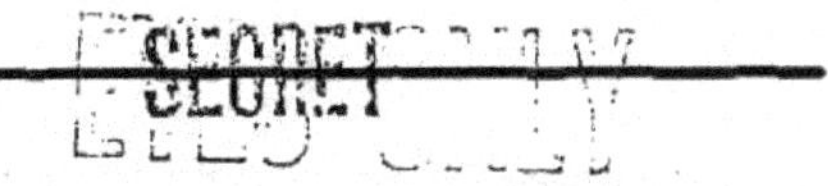

00084

Messrs. Magnusson and Brown (continued - Page 2)

B: Yes, this is just portion of pros we're talking about. My understanding get in touch with you to work out mechanics of how we would handle the billing to make sure it's straight and we do it properly so it fits in with your accounting system.

M: This is only portion of pros. State doing some too?

B: They're contributing $10,000 to the pros as well as doing all the cons. They're picking up quite a load as a result of this. One hell of a lot of response coming in on this.

M: Bound to be. Tell you, John, let me give you a call back later today if I may. Have to take a look about where I would fit this stuff in. Are you going to be in this afternoon?

B: I'll be around. If I'm not in my office I'll get back to you as soon as I come back.

M: I'll give you a call then.

B: Can't be real definite -- not sure how we're going to peak out. Not sure what backlog is. I'll check into that so when we talk this afternoon I can be little more definite. Probably run into that area, I think.

M: Okay, I'll get back in touch with you.

B: Okay, thank you, Warren.

End of Conversation

00085

Mr. Magnusson's phone conversation with Col. White at 15:40 on 26 May 1970:

M: I talked with John Brown today and it seems like -- as you mentioned -- as a result of Cambodia, inquiries going into White House. The State Department is doing all the work on the cons -- there are pros and cons. The State Department is going to answer all the cons and the President has determined that he wants to answer personally all the pros. However, the State has agreed to pick up some of those too in the amount of $10,000. That will cover maybe 60,000 of the answers. They estimate there's going to be from 100,000 to 150,000 answers that will have to be put out by the White House. Estimate it's going to cost about $8,000 per 50,000. Think it might go to 150,000. $10,000 to $15,000 additional which the White House will have to pay for. The charges are only going to be for printing, postage and addressing by an outside firm. No salaries for overtime or anything like that. They're going to lick the stamps in the White House, paste the stamps on and insert the message into the envelopes. John Brown said he had requested NSC to see if they could arrange, presumably with us, I guess, for another $10,000 to $15,000 depending on volume. He was talking as more or less foregone conclusion we would do it. I made no commitment. Told him I'd look into it.

W: How would we do this?

M: We would do it by asking them to pay amount and then send over 1080 to us with bill for the postage, bill for the addressing of the envelopes and bill for the printing accompanying this and we would just send check back. They would send short memorandum with it certifying these are the charges.

W: I think we want to know what we spend our money for but I don't think we want the public records to show that we paid for it.

M: What we can do, Sir -- I can ask them to send over a 1080 with certification that these are the charges for classified services per our conversation, and if you're willing to take that we can certainly do it that way.

W: Will this be an outside firm? Couldn't we just pay the firm? What would be better? I'm not sure.

M: I think a short memo just saying attached 1080 is for charges previously agreed to between this Agency and themselves and that's all and then we send them check for that. Otherwise, there's always chance that an outside firm might realize it was us paying for it.

W: I guess it's the best way to do it. I'd like to have in our records -- nobody else has access to -- exactly what it was for -- all about it; their records, which are audited by the General Accounting Office, as little as possible.

(continued)

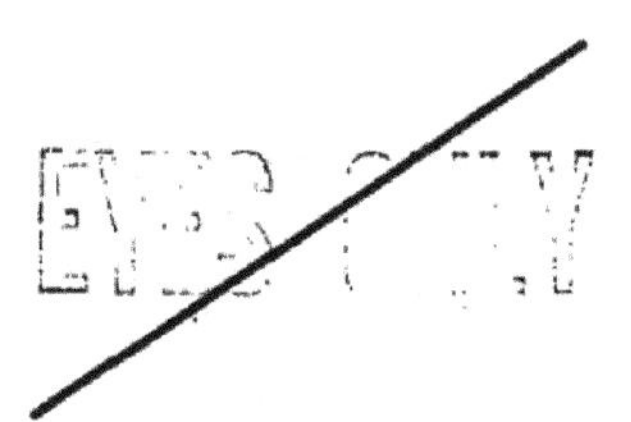

00086

Mr. Magnusson and Col. White (continued - Page 2)

M: Think I can talk to them and arrange that so he just sends unclassified 1080.

W: Go ahead and do it. I'll have to sign off on it, I suppose. You go ahead and arrange it in way that will give us full record. As far as any records of their's are concerned, I would prefer to have minimum.

M: I can write memo and John Brown can refer to this and our phone conversation in a memo accompanying the 1080.

W: Okay, go ahead and do it. Put limit on it. When they talked to me they said $10,000.

M: He said $10,000 to $15,000 because they're just pouring in. Might run above $10,000.

W: Approximately $10,000 but in no case will it exceed $15,000 -- something like that. Okay.

M: All right, Sir.

W: Thank you, Warren.

End of Conversation

145-2167

00087

Mr. Magnusson's phone conversation with Mr. John Brown at approximately 17:00 on 26 May 1970:

M: Think we can go ahead and do this. Have to be careful as to way this is documented -- that's the only thing. Would like to suggest that I write memo for the record -- kind of co-sign it -- agreeing to amount and so forth and the way we do this. Memo would have in it what it's for and then you would send us a 1080 for this, referencing this memo and our conversation.

B: You're thinking in terms of reimbursing us again? Wouldn't it be better for us to have direct charge to you?

M: No, because of public record. In order to have all the things in our hands. It wouldn't look good for us to pay the bills direct for this sort of thing.

B: It would not?

M: No, if you people pay the bills .....

B: (interrupting) Even to pay a large postage fee? Bulk of expense will be postage.

M: But we have to document what it's for -- if you people can just pay it, then we'll give you money for it.

B: What would our memo say?

M: Say attached is 1080 referencing memo dated such and such.

B: What does the memo say -- that we're making reference to?

M: I'll write that up and bring over to you.

B: What, basically, are we going to say it's about?

M: Have $10,000 with limit of $15,000 and would be for printing of these things and so on.

B: Just wondering if you have direct billing it seems to me that serves purpose of memorandum.

M: The direct billing from, let's say, the printer, the addressograph company or something like that, to us might raise questions outside and I think powers that be don't want to have fact that we're paying for this sort of thing anyplace where it can be dug up. Easiest and cleanest way to do this is you people go ahead and pay and we'll reimburse you immediately.

B: Do we have to have this memo?

(continued) 00088

Messrs. Magnusson and Brown (continued - Page 2)

M: I'd keep in my safe here.

B: Wouldn't it be adequate to send 1080?

M: Don't forget, you people keep copies of 1080's -- you have to by law. 1080 would have to cite what billing is for because of that, then that would open up to GAO or somebody else as to who's paying for this sort of thing.

B: We have to cite what it's for?

M: Let's say it's "XYZ Printing Company" and you pay bill. This looks like you're paying it. You send us 1080 which says nothing and we give you money for this. We ourselves have to have on our records what we're paying for for our own auditors which doesn't get outside of our Agency.

B: It's for your internal auditors? It would not get outside? Okay, that sounds all right.

M: I'll draw the memo up and bring it over there and you can see it.

B: That sounds good, Warren.

M: Would next Monday be all right with that memo?

B: Yes, we'll go ahead and order.

M: You can get going and so on.

B: Don't know what final cost is going to be. Hate to restrict ourselves. We figure total cost is going to be around $25,000. Got over 100,000 already that are just pro. 200,000 that haven't been analyzed yet. Of 200,000 they estimate possibly upwards of 50,000 or 60,000 could pertain to Cambodia. Of the backlog of 200,000, 60,000 could be of type that will be answered in this mailing. Our best estimate would be it may run over.

M: I've got instructions, John, to indicate in memo that it's for approximately $10,000 but not to exceed $15,000. If and when it exceeds $15,000, we'll start over again and I'll inquire further as to whether we can cover the other -- okay?

B: Okay.

M: Open to negotiation if it runs higher.

(continued)

00089

Messrs. Magnusson and Brown (continued - Page 3)

B: It may run higher. If 60,000 letters come out being pro, will take us to $26,000 or somewhere in that vicinity.

M: Then I'd have to go back and inquire to see if powers that be will cover the other part. I think it's best to wait 'til that happens.

B: Okay, good enough.

M: What time Monday?

B: Why don't you give us call here Monday? My secretary will line it up.

M: Okay.

B: Thank you, Warren.

End of Conversation

00090

CENTRAL INTELLIGENCE AGENCY
WASHINGTON, D.C. 20505

8 JUN 1970

MEMORANDUM FOR THE RECORD

SUBJECT: Reimbursement to the White House for Certain Printing, Postage and Addressing Expenses

1. Reference is made to the telephone conversation between Mr. John Brown, Staff Secretary, White House, and the undersigned concerning the accounting and the reimbursement procedure for White House expenditures in connection with the printing, postage and addressing of replies to certain mail addressed to the President.

2. It was estimated and agreed that these expenditures would amount to approximately $10,000, but not exceed $15,000, and the request for reimbursement to this Agency would be based upon receipt of a memorandum categorizing the expenses and certifying to their validity. The memorandum will also transmit a Standard Form 1081 and copies of the vendors' invoices where applicable.

3. Upon receipt of the above memorandum, Standard Form 1081 and copies of vendors' invoices, a U. S. Government Treasury check will be drawn and forwarded to the White House.

WARREN D. MAGNUSSON
Deputy Director for Liaison and Planning
Office of Finance

CONCUR:

John Brown

SECRET

00091

24 AUG 1970

MEMORANDUM FOR THE RECORD

SUBJECT: Reimbursement to the White House for Certain Printing, Postage and Addressing Expenses

1. On 18 August 1970, the undersigned received a telephone call from Mr. John Brown (145-2167) advising that the mailing had been heavier than anticipated (increased to 250,000 pieces) and that the dollar requirement for subject purpose had increased from $15,000 to $25,000.

2. I apologetically advised Mr. Brown that since our records showed that prior approval was limited to $15,000 I would have to advise and confirm with my superiors that the increase to $25,000 was acceptable, as I was sure it was.

3. In the absence of Col. White (on leave), Mr. Bush immediately contacted Mr. Clarke, [redacted], who was not in his office. On 19 August, Mr. Clarke telephonically approved the increased level and Mr. Brown was duly informed.

Chief, [redacted]

OF[redacted]

[redacted]

SECRET [redacted] 00092

THE WHITE HOUSE

WASHINGTON

September 10, 1970

Dear Mr. Magnusson:

Pursuant to your telephone call to Mr. John Brown regarding the breakdown of costs in connection with the mailing of the Acknowledgement Cards concerning The President's Speech on The Situation in Southeast Asia, the following costs were incurred:

Computer Marketing Industries, Inc.	$ 12,746.15
Acknowledgement Cards	3,185.07
Envelopes	1,051.20
Total -	$ 16,982.42

Sincerely yours,

Carson M. Howell

Carson M. Howell
Administrative Officer

Mr. Warren D. Magnusson
Deputy Director for Liaison and Planning
Office of Finance
Central Intelligence Agency
Washington, D. C.

00093

~~SECRET~~

15 SEP 1970

MEMORANDUM FOR: Director of Planning, Programming and Budgeting

SUBJECT : Reimbursement to the White House for Certain Printing, Postage and Addressing Expenses

REFERENCE : Memorandum for the Record, dated 24 August 1970, same subject

1. Attached hereto is accounting submitted from the White House for mailing expenses.

2. It is requested that the original voucher be administratively approved and certified as to the availability of funds and returned to this office for payment.

[illegible]
Deputy Director for Liaison and Planning
Office of Finance

Attachments
Memo from Mr. Howell
dtd 10 Sept 1970
SF 1081 (orig and 2)

OF (15 Sept 70)

00094

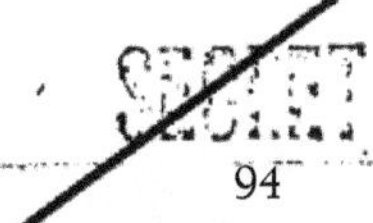

15 SEP 1970

MEMORANDUM FOR: Director of Planning, Programming and Budgeting

SUBJECT : Reimbursement to the White House for Certain Printing, Postage and Addressing Expenses

REFERENCE : Memorandum for the Record, dated 24 August 1970, same subject

1. Attached hereto is accounting submitted from the White House for mailing expenses.

2. It is requested that the original voucher be administratively approved and certified as to the availability of funds and returned to this office for payment.

WARREN D. MAGNUSSON
Deputy Director for Liaison and Planning
Office of Finance

Attachments
Memo from Mr. Howell
dtd 10 Sept 1970
SF 1081 (orig and 2)

OK
[signature]
23 Sept 70

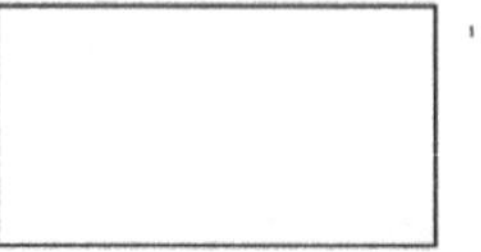

00095

Standard Form No. 1081
7 GAO 4010
1081-101-10

VOUCHER AND SCHEDULE OF WITHDRAWALS AND CREDITS

D. O. No. ______
Bu. No. ______ (Office billed)
Bu. No. 13-71 (Billing office)

To ______ (Disbursing officer—office billed) 300 (D. O. symbol)

You are authorized to effect the withdrawals and credits indicated below.

______ 300 (Disbursing officer—billing office) 300 (D. O. symbol)

Washington, D. C. (Address)

PAID BY

WITHDRAW FROM—	PAY TO—
Department	Department: Executive Office of the Presi
Bureau	Bureau: The White House Office 11-01-0001
Address	Address: Washington, D. C. 20500

Bureau Reference	Summary: Appropriation or Fund Symbol	Amount	Bureau Reference	Summary: Appropriation or Fund Symbol	Amount
				1100110.001	$16,982.
	Total			Total	$16,982.

Details of charges or reference to attached supporting documents

For the printing of Acknowledgment Cards, Envelopes, and to Keypunch names & addr and place on magnetic tape and the preparation of heat transfer labels and affixi to envelopes, in connection with the acknowledging of mail concerning the Preside speech on the Situation in Southeast Asia.

For use of office billed:	For use of billing office:
I certify funds are available. FAN ______ MOR ______ CODE ______	

IFICATE OF OFFICE BILLED

I certify that the items listed herein are correct and proper for payment from the appropriation(s) designated.

______ (Date) ______ (Authorized administrative or certifying officer)

Paid by check No. ______ C/D No. ______, dated 00096

☆ U. S. GOVERNMENT PRINTING OFFICE: 1961—607821

30 SEP 19[illegible]

MEMORANDUM FOR: Chief, [redacted]

SUBJECT : Reimbursement to The White House

1. It is requested that a check in the amount of $16,[illegible].42 be drawn payable to the Treasurer of the United States.

2. This disbursement is chargeable as follows:

FAN [redacted] MOR [redacted] CODE [redacted]

3. All documentation concerning this transaction is being held in this office for security reasons and is available to the Agency auditors.

4. Please forward the check to this office for transmittal to the appropriate official.

[redacted]

WARREN D. MAGNUSON
Deputy Director for Liaison and Planning

OF

[redacted]

00097

Mr. John Brown
Staff Secretary
The White House Office
Washington, D. C. 20500

Dear Mr. Brown:

Enclosed is U. S. Treasury Check No. [redacted] in the amount of $16,982.42 which represents reimbursement of Bureau Schedule No. [redacted] copy enclosed. This schedule was forwarded to this Office by Mr. Carson M. Howell, Administrative Officer, on 10 September 1970.

Yours very truly,

[redacted]

WARREN D. MA[redacted]USSON
Deputy Director for Liaison and Planning
Office of Finance

Enclosures

OF [redacted] 1 Oct. 70)

Note: [redacted] called me to advise that Document Receipt was not sent back with Courier (2 Oct). I called Mr. Brown's secretary who said she'd call me when they received it from the Guard's desk. They hadn't called back as of noon 5 October, so I called again and she said they had received it Friday [illegible] and notified [illegible] accordingly.
J.H.

00098

THE WHITE HOUSE

WASHINGTON

December 7, 1970

CONFIDENTIAL

MEMORANDUM FOR: WARREN MAGNUSON

We have finally received the cost breakdown for acknowledging the mail in connection with the President's speech on the situation in Southeast Asia. By copy of this memorandum I am requesting our administrative office to forward that portion of the bill applicable to you.

If there are any problems in handling this, please let me know.

Thank you.

JRB

JOHN R. BROWN III

cc: Carson Howell

00099

Keypunch names, place on magnetic tape prepare and affix to envelopes heat transfer labels, and furnish printout.	$7,410.35
Print acknowledgment Cards	2,244.27
Print Envelopes	728.00
Postage	6,290.64
	$16,673.26

00100

MEMORANDUM FOR: Director of Planning, Programming and Budgeting

SUBJECT : Reimbursement to the White House for Certain Printing, Postage and Addressing Expenses

REFERENCE : Memorandum for the Record, dated 24 August 1970, same subject

1. Attached hereto is the second accounting, in the amount of $16,673.26, submitted from the White House for mailing expenses. Check for the first accounting in the amount of $16,982.42 was forwarded to the White House on 2 October 1970.

2. It is requested that the original voucher be administratively approved and certified as to the availability of funds and returned to this office for payment.

WARREN D. MAGNUSSON
Deputy Director for Liaison and Planning
Office of Finance

Attachments
SF 1081 (orig & 2 w/att)
Memo from the White House dated 7 Dec 1970
Memo to D/PPB, transmitting 1st accounting, dated 15 Sept 70
Copy of 1st 1081
Memo from the White House dated 10 Sept 70
Memo for the Record dated 24 Aug 70

OK

26 Jan 71

00101

Standard Form No. 1081
GAO 1010
1081-104-16

VOUCHER AND SCHEDULE OF WITHDRAWALS AND CREDITS

D. O. No.

Bu. No. (Office billed)

Bu. No. 3[illegible] (Billing office)

PAID BY

To [redacted] (Disbursing officer—office billed) 300 (D. O. symbol)

You are authorized to effect the withdrawals and credits indicated below.

[redacted] (Disbursing officer—billing office) 300 (D. O. symbol)

Washington, D.C. (Address)

WITHDRAW FROM—		PAY TO—	
DEPARTMENT		DEPARTMENT	Executive Office of the Presic
BUREAU		BUREAU	The White House Office 11-01-0001
ADDRESS		ADDRESS	Washington, D.C. 20500

Bureau Reference	Summary: Appropriation or Fund Symbol	Summary: Amount	Bureau Reference	Summary: Appropriation or Fund Symbol	Summary: Amount
			[redacted]	1110110.001	$16,673.26
	Total			Total	[illegible],673.26

Details of charges or reference to attached supporting documents

For the printing of Acknowledgement Cards, Envelopes and Postage for mailing, and to Keypunch names, place on magnetic tape, prepare and affix to envelopes heat transfer labels, and furnish printout, in connection with the acknowledging of mail concerning the President's Second speech on the Situation in Southeast Asia. See attached list for breakdown of costs.

For use of office billed:

I certify funds are available.

[illegible] [redacted] MGR [redacted] CODE [redacted]

[redacted]

For use of billing office:

CERTIFICATE OF OFFICE BILLED

I certify that the items listed herein are correct and proper for payment from the appropriation(s) designated.

Feb 5, 1971 (Date)

[redacted] (Certifying officer)

Paid by check No. C/D No. , dated

00102

☆ U. S. GOVERNMENT PRINTING OFFICE: 1961-607821

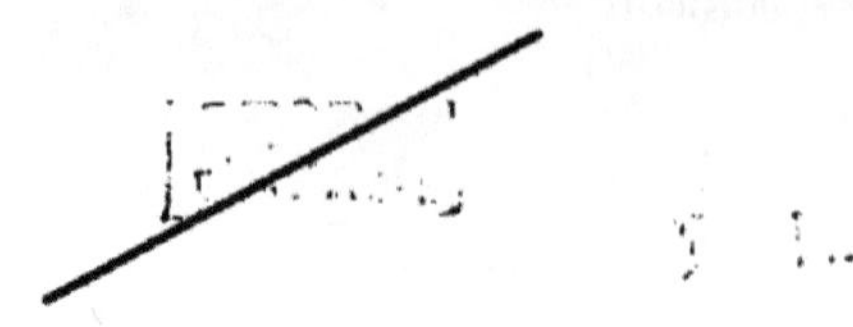

MEMORANDUM FOR: Chief, Certification and Liaison Division

SUBJECT : Reimbursement to The White House

1. It is requested that a check in the amount of $16,673.26 be drawn payable to the Treasurer of the United States.

2. This disbursement is chargeable as follows:

FAN MOR Code

3. All documentation concerning this transaction is being held in this office for security reasons and is available to the Agency auditors.

4. Please forward the check to this office for transmittal to the appropriate official.

WARREN D. MAG
Deputy Director for Liaison and

OF

00103

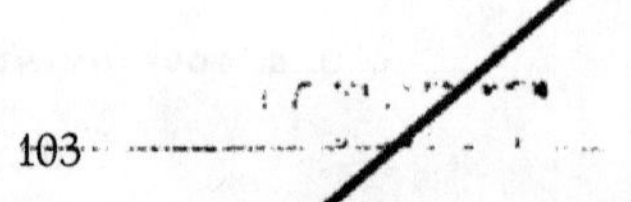

1? FEB 1971

Mr. John R. Brown III
Staff Secretary
The White House Office
Washington, D. C. 20500

Dear Mr. Brown:

Enclosed is U. S Treasury Check No. [redacted] in the amount of $16,673.26 which represents reimbursement of Bureau Schedule No. [redacted] copy enclosed.

Yours very truly,

[redacted]

De[redacted] Director for Liaison and Planning
Office of Finance

Enclosures

OF/[redacted]

[redacted]

00104

[redacted]

CONFIDENTIAL

MEMORANDUM FOR: Deputy Director for Management and Services

SUBJECT : Special Report

1. This memorandum is in response to a request to provide information on situations or associations that might appear to be irregular on the surface.

2. Details to the White House and Government Agencies - Background: For many years the Central Intelligence Agency has detailed employees to the immediate office of the White House per se and to components associated intimately with the immediate office of the President such as the Council on International Economic Policy and the President's Foreign Intelligence Advisory Board. We have furnished secretaries, clerical employees and certain professional employees on a reimbursable and non-reimbursable basis. At the present time, we have no clericals or professionals assigned to the immediate White House office, but we do have one young man detailed to their Communications Section. There are detailees to PFIAB and CIEP. I might point out that we had detailed to the White House as late as the fall of 1970 couriers, telephone operators, a laborer assigned to the grounds and a graphics man who designed invitations for State dinners. By October of 1970, more funds were apparently available to run the White House and most of our detailees were hired as bona fide White House employees. CIA is not the only Agency furnishing the White House with detailees. Levies have been made by this Administration and others on Defense and State and other Government entities whose employees have Top Secret clearances.

Professional officers have been and are at the present time assigned to the National Security Council and we have seven clericals on detail to NSC on a reimbursable basis.

In addition to the above, we have technical specialists detailed to NSA, an instructor at the National War College and security officers detailed to the Department of State to

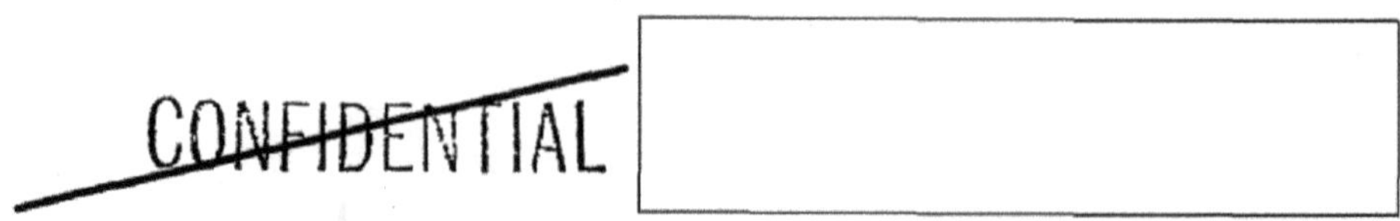

00105

protect foreign visitors. Recently, [redacted] was detailed to the Secretary of the Treasury along with four other Agency employees. We have even, in rare instances, detailed our people to Congressional Staffs for short periods of time.

3. Details to the White House and Government Agencies - Discussion: Details to NSC, the White House, NSA and the National War College are probably quite defensible. On the other hand, there may be those who would question Agency employees currently working at the Bureau of Narcotics and Dangerous Drugs and Mr. Peter Peterson having an Agency employee as his secretary when he was the Secretary of Commerce (she also made a trip with him to Moscow). She is still with him in his present assignment but we expect that she will report to NSC for a new detail sometime this month. [redacted] served for over ten years as Director of the Office of Public Safety for AID. This information has been kept "close to the vest" during that entire period of time. He has been approved for disability retirement and is presently on sick leave and will retire automatically at the expiration of this leave.

Each detail of an Agency employee to the White House or other Government agency has been carefully considered and approval at a higher level obtained when professionals were involved.

4. Project TWOFOLD: I believe the support we are providing to Project TWOFOLD is an activity that should be reported under your guidelines. Since this is an extremely sensitive Project and the Office of Security is reporting on it, I will not repeat the details in my memorandum.

5. Individuals Engaged in Domestic Activities: In a more general sense, Contract Personnel Division prepares and executes contracts with individuals engaged by the Agency to carry out domestic activities. We also process Staff Agents who are domestically assigned. None of these assignments are decided in OP. I really have no way of knowing with any degree of certainty what the specific duties of these individuals will be.

6. [redacted]

7. [redacted]

8. Hunt Requests a Lockpicker: This is a record of External Employment Assistance Branch's action on a request from Howard Hunt for a lockpicker who might be retiring or resigning from the Agency.

Sometime in the spring of 1972, Frank O'Malley of EEAB received a call from Howard Hunt who asked Frank if he had a retiree or resignee who was accomplished at picking locks. Mr. O'Malley sent him a resume on Thomas Amato who retired 31 July 1971. Mr. O'Malley did not document his EEAB record to show the date of this exchange, but [redacted] (who also works in EEAB) opines that it occurred sometime between March and May 1972.

All of the above information was reported to the Office of Security on 4 October 1972 following the FBI's contact with the Agency regarding Howard Hunt.

9. Resume Sent to McCord: [redacted] a contract employee who retired in September 1971, was a client of the External Employment Assistance Branch in his search for a job after retirement. One of the leads given to [redacted] was James McCord's security business. EEAB sent a resume to McCord, but [redacted] was not hired.

In mid-summer 1972, [redacted] telephoned EEAB from Chicago. (He had a job there with the Halifax Security Co., a lead provided by EEAB, but until this telephone call he had

not notified EEAB that he had the job and had moved from the D.C. area.) He said he had been visited by a Special Agent of the FBI who told [redacted] that his resume had been found among McCord's papers. The Agent wanted to know if [redacted] had any connection with McCord. [redacted] explained how the resume got to McCord. After the Agent left him, [redacted] telephoned EEAB. [redacted] of OP and [redacted] of OS were notified immediately.

[redacted]
Harry B. Fisher
Director of Personnel

4

UNCLASSIFIED | INTERNAL USE ONLY | CONFIDENTIAL | SECRET

ROUTING AND RECORD SHEET

SUBJECT: (Optional)

Sensitive Activities Performed by the Office of Logistics

FROM:	EXTENSION	NO.
Director of Logistics	2551	DATE 14 MAY 1973

TO: (Officer designation, room number, and building)	DATE RECEIVED	DATE FORWARDED	OFFICER'S INITIALS	COMMENTS (Number each comment to show from whom to whom. Draw a line across column after each comment.)
1. Deputy Director for Management and Services	5/14	5/14	[illegible]	EYES ONLY
2.				
3. Director of Central Intelligence				
4.				
5.				
6.				
7.				
8.				
9.				
10.				
11.				
12.				
13.				
14.				00109
15.				

FORM 3-62 610 USE PREVIOUS EDITIONS ☐ SECRET ☐ CONFIDENTIAL ☐ INTERNAL USE ONLY ☐ UNCLASSIFIED

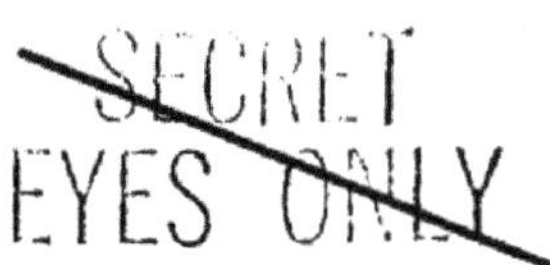

14 MAY 1973

MEMORANDUM FOR: Director of Central Intelligence

THROUGH : Deputy Director for Management and Services

SUBJECT : Sensitive Activities Performed by the Office of Logistics

1. This memorandum contains information for the Director of Central Intelligence.

2. This memorandum is submitted pursuant to advice given by the Deputy Director for Management and Services on 7 May that Office Directors report on activities, either under their cognizance or otherwise known to them, the nature of which could possibly need explanation or justification when viewed within the statutory responsibility and authority of the Director of Central Intelligence. The responsibilities of the Office of Logistics (OL) are such that in all matters herein reported, except two, the actions undertaken were at the request of another Agency component. We have prepared a brief description of each action involved and then have included the name of the sponsoring component. The substantive reason for the requests for action by this Office will have to be determined by inquiry to the designated sponsoring component.

3. Facts pertaining to both actions undertaken at the initiative of this Office are as follows:

00110

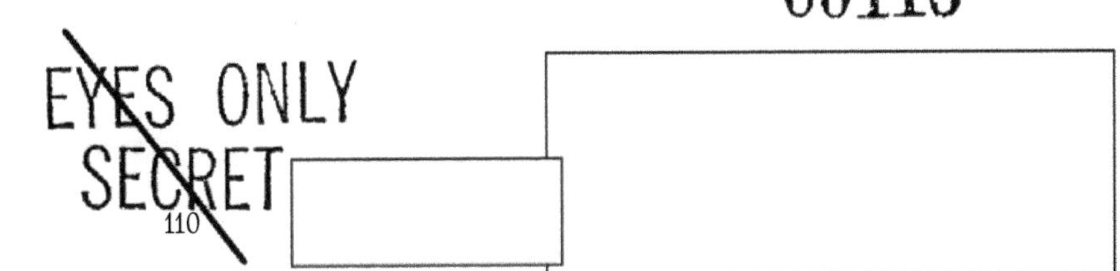

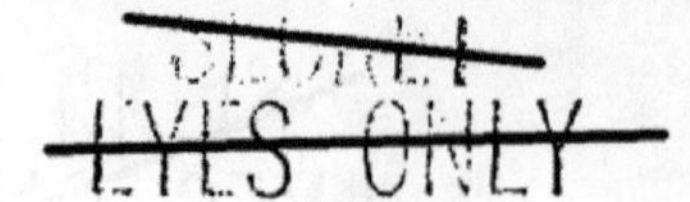

SUBJECT: Sensitive Activities Performed by the Office of Logistics

~~EYES ONLY~~

~~SECRET~~

00111

the DD/O, we will not honor any requisition for surveillance equipment unless it has been approved by the CI Staff of the DD/O.

4. Within the area of contractual responsibilities, the following items are pertinent:

a. In February 1971, Colonel L. K. White, the then Executive Director-Comptroller, called me to attend a meeting in his office, also attended by Mr. William Colby. Colonel White explained that the Technical Services Division (TSD) had been requested to provide assistance to the FBI for a sensitive project designated [redacted] (currently designated [redacted] Colonel White did not disclose the purpose of the assistance being provided by TSD but did instruct me to assist TSD on purely contractual matters. Since the Office of Logistics has no information concerning the mission or purpose of Project [redacted] substantive questions concerning the subject should be addressed to TSD. Other procurement actions accomplished for the FBI are reported below. Specific mention is made, however, of [redacted] because of the dollar magnitude, approximately $1 million, and the complex technical equipment that has been involved in the undertaking.

b. The Procurement Division, OL, currently has two requisitions in hand from TSD which would involve reimbursable sales to the FBI. One such requisition in the amount of $36,900 is for two Westinghouse television cameras. The second requisition in the amount of $11,200 is for two wide-angle surveillance probes manufactured by Bausch and Lomb. No action is being taken on either of these requirements pending further instructions which will be sought from the Deputy Director for Management and Services.

c. Over the years, this Agency has often supported other Government agencies from a contractual or materiel standpoint. Upon the submission of an officially approved request, supported by a transfer of funds, the Agency would either enter into "accommodation procurements" for the requesting agency or support the requesting agency by the issuance of materiel from stock. Such actions are legally accomplished under the Economy Act of 1925. This Act authorizes one agency to support the needs of, or provide a service for, another Government agency when such

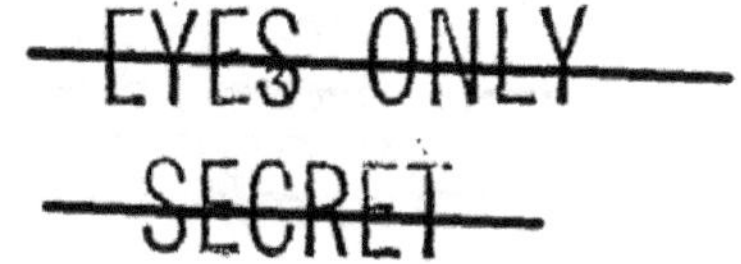

00112

SUBJECT: Sensitive Activities Performed by the Office of Logistics

action would be more economical and eliminate the need for one agency of the Government to duplicate facilities readily available from another. A typical example of this procedure is purchasing photointerpretation gear for the Defense Intelligence Agency element located at NPIC. In connection with the current reporting requirement, however, I have had our records researched for the past 2 years and Attachment 1 reflects those transactions which appear to be relevant to the subject of this memorandum.

d. In connection with the disclosures during the summer of 1971 that the Rand Corporation was not properly safeguarding classified documents, this Office undertook two acts. I directed the Security Officer from our West Coast Procurement Office at the Moffet Naval Air Station in California to visit the Rand Corporation and satisfy himself that classified material furnished them by the Agency was both properly safeguarded and accounted for. His report was affirmative. On 23 August 1971, the senior Security Officer assigned to this Office forwarded a letter to the Rand Corporation stressing and reaffirming the procedures Rand must follow in safeguarding classified information furnished them by the Agency. Of residual interest in this matter, there is summarized the contents of a memorandum of 2 July 1971 to the Executive Director-Comptroller from the DD/I which is in our possession.

> This memorandum reports that FBIS regularly disseminated reports to the Rand Corporation but that instructions had been issued to cease distribution of classified reports. While no other direct dissemination went to Rand, other USIB agencies, primarily USAF, were passing "many" copies of DD/I products to Rand as authorized under USIB regulations. The memorandum also states that Rand personnel had requested searches and document retrieval from the CRS facility.

5. In connection with action taken for the Office of Security, there are three relevant items:

a. The Printing Services Division, OL, was requested by the Office of Security to print a book written by Harry J. Murphy, Office of Security. The book was prepared by Mr. Murphy under a Brookings Institution Federal

00113

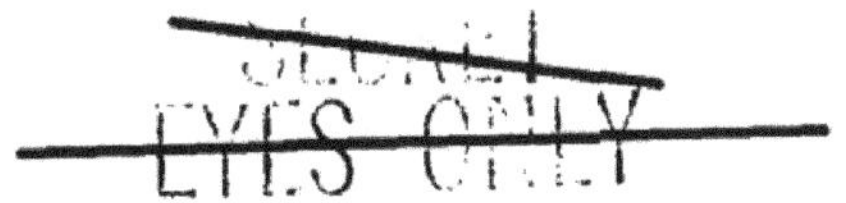

SUBJECT: Sensitive Activities Performed by the Office of Logistics

Executive Fellowship. The book is entitled "Where's What -- Sources of Information for Federal Investigators." It is a full treatise on the existence of sources of information that may be useful to an investigator. The book's first printing of 300 copies was made in June 1967. Due to demand, a second printing of 600 copies was made in September 1968. The title page of the book gives attribution to Mr. Murphy, Office of Security, Central Intelligence Agency, and the Brookings Institution Federal Executive Fellowship. The book is classified Confidential, and it is our understanding that the distribution was made to appropriate agencies of the Federal Government. A copy of Mr. Murphy's book can be made available for review if desired.

Sometime in 1972, a representative of the Law Enforcement Assistance Administration (LEAA) requested that the Agency give consideration to our publishing, at LEAA expense, an unclassified version of this volume. It was the intent of LEAA to make broad-scale distribution to Police Departments throughout the country. The Director of Security and I consulted on this matter and jointly determined that the LEAA request should not be honored because the Agency should not put itself in the position of publishing law enforcement material for general and unclassified purposes, and it would be an abuse of our printing facilities.

b. On 5 January 1971, the Director of Security requested that I approve his leasing up to eleven motor vehicles for use in connection with a special support operation which would last approximately 3 months. The Director of Security informed me, in his requesting memorandum of 5 January 1971, that "This support activity has been undertaken at the specific instruction of the Director and has his personal approval." The request was approved.

c. From 1968 to date, the Office of Security has requisitioned from this Office a considerable amount of materiel which we understand was to be given or loaned by them to local Police Departments. In certain cases some of this materiel was issued from Agency stocks and, in other cases, direct procurement of the materiel was made by funds furnished by the Office of Security. A complete listing of such materiel is found in Attachment 2.

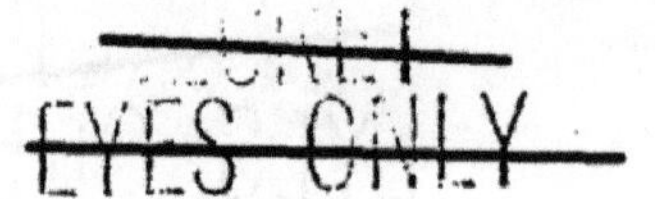

SUBJECT: Sensitive Activities Performed by the Office of Logistics

b. This Office is aware, although it had no cognizance nor responsibility, that an apartment was rented in Miami Beach, Florida, during the period of the Democratic National Convention, 10-14 July 1972, and the Republican National Convention, 21-24 August 1972. The apartment was used as a meeting place [redacted] in liaison with members of the Secret Service and rendering

~~EYES ONLY~~
~~SECRET~~

00115

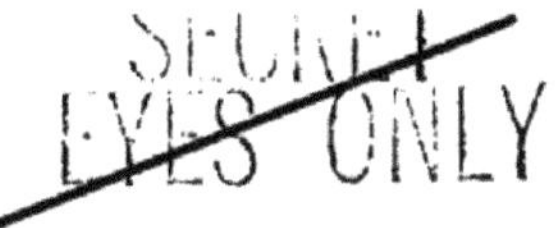

SUBJECT: Sensitive Activities Performed by the Office of Logistics

assistance in connection with the political conventions that were being held. WH Division is the cognizant operating component on this matter.

7. The above recitation of facts represents, to the best of my knowledge and memory, those matters which appear to be relevant to subject tasking given by the Director.

John F. Blake
Director of Logistics

2 Atts

cc: DD/M&S

00116

~~SECRET~~
~~EYES ONLY~~

Requesting Office	Date of Request	Item	Quantity	Unit Cost	Receiving U.S. Department or Agency
OS	3/23/72	Telephone Analyzer	1	1,350	BNDD
TSD	5/16/72	Transmitters, Radio Beacon	8	313	BNDD
OS	3/23/72	Telephone Analyzer	1	1,350	White House Communications Agency
OS	3/23/72	Telephone Analyzers	13	1,400	Air Force
OS	3/23/72	Telephone Analyzers	10	1,350	State
OS	3/23/72	Telephone Analyzers	2	1,375	AEC
TSD	11/16/72	Camera Sets	20	656	FBI
TSD	4/17/72	Camera Sets	10	700	FBI
TSD	11/18/71	Actuators, Recorders	50	488	FBI
TSD	4/19/72	Tessina Cameras	3	700	BNDD
TSD	12/ 7/72	Camera, Video	1	18,045	FBI
TSD	10/13/72	Tube, Image, Burn-Resistance, Equivalent of W L 30691	1	4,639	FBI
TSD	3/26/71	Tubes, Image, W L 30691	2	4,607	FBI
TSD	4/20/73	Cameras, Television	2	18,300	FBI

00118

~~EYES ONLY~~
~~SECRET~~

~~SECRET~~
~~EYES ONLY~~

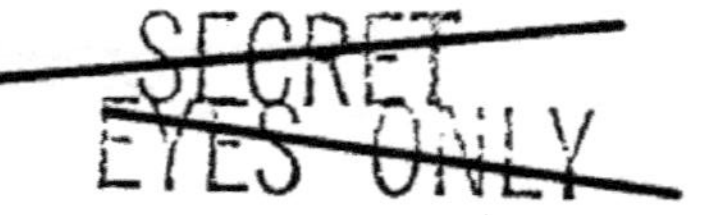

Requesting Office	Date of Request	Item	Quantity	Unit Cost	Receiving U.S. Department or Agency
TSD	12/14/72	Transmitters, Radio	3	313	BNDD
TSD	10/20/72	Actuators, Recorder	25	591	FBI
TSD	10/13/72	Tube, Image, Burn-Resistance, Equivalent of W L 30691	1	4,639	FBI
TSD	5/26/71	Tube, Image, W L 30691	2	4,639	FBI
TSD	4/22/71	Transmitters	3	1,372	FBI
TSD	4/22/71	Module, Plug-In	1	1,247	FBI
TSD	4/22/71	Power Supply - UWP-39A	1	568	FBI
OL	2/25/71	Telephone Analyzers	2	1,350	Treasury
OS	1/30/71	Telephone Analyzers	22	1,350	Treasury
OL	8/12/70	Cable, Special-Purpose Electrical	5,000 ft.	.42	White House Communications Agency
TSD	1/10/73	Ink, Special Formula	1 lot	1,825	Immigration and Naturalization Service
TSD	6/28/72	Ink, Special Formula	1 lot	3,700	Immigration and Naturalization Service
TSD	7/26/71	Transmitter, Radio Beacon	1	728	U.S. Forestry

~~EYES ONLY~~
~~SECRET~~

00119

00120

MATERIAL REQUISITIONED FROM LOGISTICS
BY SECURITY FOR ISSUANCE TO
LOCAL POLICE

ITEM	QUANITY
Gas Mask M-9	200
Gas Mask M-17	196
Steel Helmet and Liners	231
Vest and Groin Protector	96
Vest, Flak M-52	34
Vest, Protective	46
Vest, Grenade	105
Execuvest	6
Emergency Flashing Red Light	22
*Searchlight, Tear Gas	36
*Chemical Baton 6 1/2"	36
*Chemical Baton 12"	24
*Chemical Baton 26"	24
*Mustang 35 Pistol	6
*Searchlight with Shoulder Strap	36
*Stun Gun	3

*NOTE: Various quantities and types of replacement chemical cartridges, loading kits, and batteries were also ordered for asterisk items.

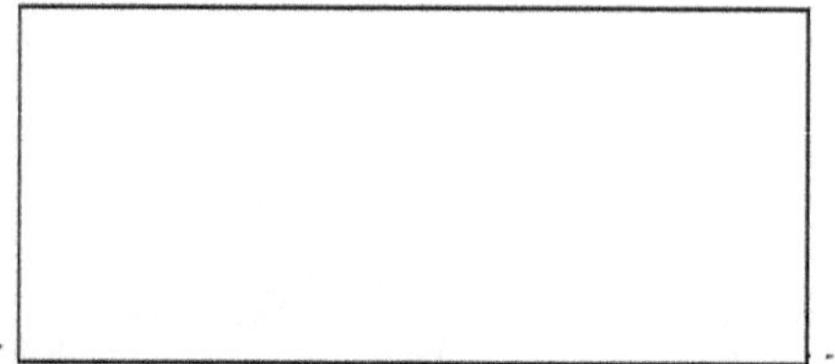

00121

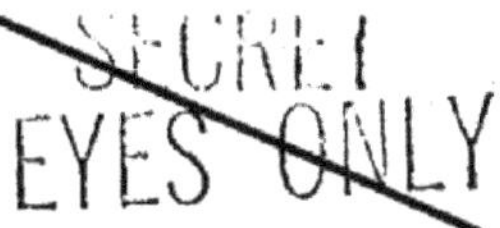

14 MAY 1973

MEMORANDUM FOR: Director of Central Intelligence

THROUGH : Deputy Director for Management and Services

SUBJECT : Sensitive Activities Performed by the Office of Logistics

1. This memorandum contains information for the Director of Central Intelligence.

2. This memorandum is submitted pursuant to advice given by the Deputy Director for Management and Services on 7 May that Office Directors report on activities, either under their cognizance or otherwise known to them, the nature of which could possibly need explanation or justification when viewed within the statutory responsibility and authority of the Director of Central Intelligence. The responsibilities of the Office of Logistics (OL) are such that in all matters herein reported, except two, the actions undertaken were at the request of another Agency component. We have prepared a brief description of each action involved and then have included the name of the sponsoring component. The substantive reason for the requests for action by this Office will have to be determined by inquiry to the designated sponsoring component.

3. Facts pertaining to both actions undertaken at the initiative of this Office are as follows:

00122

EYES ONLY
SECRET

~~SECRET~~
EYES ~~ONLY~~

SUBJECT: Sensitive Activities Performed by the Office of Logistics

2

~~EYES~~ ONLY
~~SECRET~~

00123

SUBJECT: Sensitive Activities Performed by the Office of Logistics

the DD/O, we will not honor any requisition for surveillance equipment unless it has been approved by the CI Staff of the DD/O.

4. Within the area of contractual responsibilities, the following items are pertinent:

a. In February 1971, Colonel L. K. White, the then Executive Director-Comptroller, called me to attend a meeting in his office, also attended by Mr. William Colby. Colonel White explained that the Technical Services Division (TSD) had been requested to provide assistance to the FBI for a sensitive project designated [redacted] (currently designated [redacted] Colonel White did not disclose the purpose of the assistance being provided by TSD but did instruct me to assist TSD on purely contractual matters. Since the Office of Logistics has no information concerning the mission or purpose of Project [redacted] substantive questions concerning the subject should be addressed to TSD. Other procurement actions accomplished for the FBI are reported below. Specific mention is made, however, of [redacted] because of the dollar magnitude, approximately $1 million, and the complex technical equipment that has been involved in the undertaking.

b. The Procurement Division, OL, currently has two requisitions in hand from TSD which would involve reimbursable sales to the FBI. One such requisition in the amount of $36,900 is for two Westinghouse television cameras. The second requisition in the amount of $11,200 is for two wide-angle surveillance probes manufactured by Bausch and Lomb. No action is being taken on either of these requirements pending further instructions which will be sought from the Deputy Director for Management and Services.

c. Over the years, this Agency has often supported other Government agencies from a contractual or materiel standpoint. Upon the submission of an officially approved request, supported by a transfer of funds, the Agency would either enter into "accommodation procurements" for the requesting agency or support the requesting agency by the issuance of materiel from stock. Such actions are legally accomplished under the Economy Act of 1925. This Act authorizes one agency to support the needs of, or provide a service for, another Government agency when such

00124

SUBJECT: Sensitive Activities Performed by the Office of Logistics

action would be more economical and eliminate the need for one agency of the Government to duplicate facilities readily available from another. A typical example of this procedure is purchasing photointerpretation gear for the Defense Intelligence Agency element located at NPIC. In connection with the current reporting requirement, however, I have had our records researched for the past 2 years and Attachment 1 reflects those transactions which appear to be relevant to the subject of this memorandum.

d. In connection with the disclosures during the summer of 1971 that the Rand Corporation was not properly safeguarding classified documents, this Office undertook two acts. I directed the Security Officer from our West Coast Procurement Office at the Moffet Naval Air Station in California to visit the Rand Corporation and satisfy himself that classified material furnished them by the Agency was both properly safeguarded and accounted for. His report was affirmative. On 23 August 1971, the senior Security Officer assigned to this Office forwarded a letter to the Rand Corporation stressing and reaffirming the procedures Rand must follow in safeguarding classified information furnished them by the Agency. Of residual interest in this matter, there is summarized the contents of a memorandum of 2 July 1971 to the Executive Director-Comptroller from the DD/I which is in our possession.

> This memorandum reports that FBIS regularly disseminated reports to the Rand Corporation but that instructions had been issued to cease distribution of classified reports. While no other direct dissemination went to Rand, other USIB agencies, primarily USAF, were passing "many" copies of DD/I products to Rand as authorized under USIB regulations. The memorandum also states that Rand personnel had requested searches and document retrieval from the CRS facility.

5. In connection with action taken for the Office of Security, there are three relevant items:

a. The Printing Services Division, OL, was requested by the Office of Security to print a book written by Harry J. Murphy, Office of Security. The book was prepared by Mr. Murphy under a Brookings Institution Federal

00125

SUBJECT: Sensitive Activities Performed by the Office of Logistics

Executive Fellowship. The book is entitled "Where's What -- Sources of Information for Federal Investigators." It is a full treatise on the existence of sources of information that may be useful to an investigator. The book's first printing of 300 copies was made in June 1967. Due to demand, a second printing of 600 copies was made in September 1968. The title page of the book gives attribution to Mr. Murphy, Office of Security, Central Intelligence Agency, and the Brookings Institution Federal Executive Fellowship. The book is classified Confidential, and it is our understanding that the distribution was made to appropriate agencies of the Federal Government. A copy of Mr. Murphy's book can be made available for review if desired.

Sometime in 1972, a representative of the Law Enforcement Assistance Administration (LEAA) requested that the Agency give consideration to our publishing, at LEAA expense, an unclassified version of this volume. It was the intent of LEAA to make broad-scale distribution to Police Departments throughout the country. The Director of Security and I consulted on this matter and jointly determined that the LEAA request should not be honored because the Agency should not put itself in the position of publishing law enforcement material for general and unclassified purposes, and it would be an abuse of our printing facilities.

b. On 5 January 1971, the Director of Security requested that I approve his leasing up to eleven motor vehicles for use in connection with a special support operation which would last approximately 3 months. The Director of Security informed me, in his requesting memorandum of 5 January 1971, that "This support activity has been undertaken at the specific instruction of the Director and has his personal approval." The request was approved.

c. From 1968 to date, the Office of Security has requisitioned from this Office a considerable amount of materiel which we understand was to be given or loaned by them to local Police Departments. In certain cases some of this materiel was issued from Agency stocks and, in other cases, direct procurement of the materiel was made by funds furnished by the Office of Security. A complete listing of such materiel is found in Attachment 2.

00126

SUBJECT: Sensitive Activities Performed by the Office of Logistics

b. This Office is aware, although it had no cognizance nor responsibility, that an apartment was rented in Miami Beach, Florida, during the period of the Democratic National Convention, 10-14 July 1972, and the Republican National Convention, 21-24 August 1972. The apartment was used as a meeting place [redacted] in liaison with members of the Secret Service and rendering

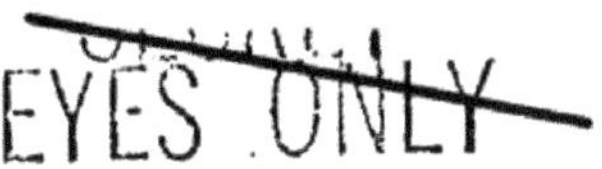

SUBJECT: Sensitive Activities Performed by the Office of Logistics

assistance in connection with the political conventions that were being held. WH Division is the cognizant operating component on this matter.

7. The above recitation of facts represents, to the best of my knowledge and memory, those matters which appear to be relevant to subject tasking given by the Director.

John F. Blake
Director of Logistics

2 Atts

cc: DD/M&S

00128

SECRET
EYES ONLY

Requesting Office	Date of Request	Item	Quantity	Unit Cost	Receiving U.S. Department or Agency
OS	3/23/72	Telephone Analyzer	1	1,350	BNDD
TSD	5/16/72	Transmitters, Radio Beacon	8	313	BNDD
OS	3/23/72	Telephone Analyzer	1	1,350	White House Communications Agency
OS	3/23/72	Telephone Analyzers	13	1,400	Air Force
OS	3/23/72	Telephone Analyzers	10	1,350	State
OS	3/23/72	Telephone Analyzers	2	1,375	AEC
TSD	11/16/72	Camera Sets	20	656	FBI
TSD	4/17/72	Camera Sets	10	700	FBI
TSD	11/18/71	Actuators, Recorders	50	488	FBI
TSD	4/19/72	Tessina Cameras	3	700	BNDD
TSD	12/ 7/72	Camera, Video	1	18,045	FBI
TSD	10/13/72	Tube, Image, Burn-Resistance, Equivalent of W L 30691	1	4,639	FBI
TSD	3/26/71	Tubes, Image, W L 30691	2	4,607	FBI
TSD	4/20/73	Cameras, Television	2	18,300	FBI

00130

EYES ONLY
SECRET

SECRET EYES ONLY

Requesting Office	Date of Request	Item	Quantity	Unit Cost	Receiving U.S. Department or Agency
TSD	12/14/72	Transmitters, Radio	3	313	BNDD
TSD	10/20/72	Actuators, Recorder	25	591	FBI
TSD	10/13/72	Tube, Image, Burn-Resistance, Equivalent of W L 30691	1	4,639	FBI
TSD	5/26/71	Tube, Image, W L 30691	2	4,639	FBI
TSD	4/22/71	Transmitters	3	1,372	FBI
TSD	4/22/71	Module, Plug-In	1	1,247	FBI
TSD	4/22/71	Power Supply - UWP-39A	1	568	FBI
OL	2/25/71	Telephone Analyzers	2	1,350	Treasury
OS	1/30/71	Telephone Analyzers	22	1,350	Treasury
OL	8/12/70	Cable, Special-Purpose Electrical	5,000 ft.	.42	White House Communications Agency
TSD	1/10/73	Ink, Special Formula	1 lot	1,825	Immigration and Naturalization Service
TSD	6/28/72	Ink, Special Formula	1 lot	3,700	Immigration and Naturalization Service
TSD	7/26/71	Transmitter, Radio Beacon	1	728	U.S. Forestry

EYES ONLY SECRET

00131

00132

MATERIAL REQUISITIONED FROM LOGISTICS
BY SECURITY FOR ISSUANCE TO
LOCAL POLICE

ITEM	QUANITY
Gas Mask M-9	200
Gas Mask M-17	196
Steel Helmet and Liners	231
Vest and Groin Protector	96
Vest, Flak M-52	34
Vest, Protective	46
Vest, Grenade	105
Execuvest	6
Emergency Flashing Red Light	22
*Searchlight, Tear Gas	36
*Chemical Baton 6 1/2"	36
*Chemical Baton 12"	24
*Chemical Baton 26"	24
*Mustang 35 Pistol	6
*Searchlight with Shoulder Strap	36
*Stun Gun	3

*NOTE: Various quantities and types of replacement chemical cartridges, loading kits, and batteries were also ordered for asterisk items.

00133

[ ] UNCLASSIFIED [ ] INTERNAL USE ONLY [ ] CONFIDENTIAL [X] SECRET

ROUTING AND RECORD SHEET

SUBJECT: (Optional)

FROM: D/OJCS, [redacted] Hq.	EXTENSION [redacted]	NO. OJCS[redacted] DATE 11 MAY 1973

TO: (Officer designation, room number, and building)	DATE RECEIVED	DATE FORWARDED	OFFICER'S INITIALS	COMMENTS (Number each comment to show from whom to whom. Draw a line across column after each comment.)
1. DD/M&S [redacted] Hq.			[redacted]	
2.				
3. DCI [redacted] Hq.				
4. IG			[redacted]	
5.				
6.				carbon copy removed for use (and destruction) in working up check on OJCS status on these programs.
7.				
8.				
9.				
10.				[redacted] 15 October 1973
11.				
12.				
13.				
14.				
15.				00134

FORM 3-62 610 USE PREVIOUS EDITIONS [ ] SECRET [ ] CONFIDENTIAL [ ] INTERNAL USE ONLY [ ] UNCLASSIFIED

OJCS [redacted]
11 MAY 1973

MEMORANDUM FOR: Director, Central Intelligence Agency

THROUGH : Deputy Director for Management and Services

SUBJECT : Activities which might be considered sensitive issues.

I have listed below computer processing projects which the Office of Joint Computer Support has participated in or is aware of and which might be considered sensitive issues.

Most Sensitive Projects

OJCS Project Identification	Project Officer Organization, & Telephone	Nature of Project	OJCS Reason for Listing
HYDRA	Richard Ober CI Staff [redacted]	A special project initiated by DCI	Type of data being collected.
SANCA	[redacted] OS [redacted]	Machine index to security files	Type of data in index.
[redacted]	[redacted] ORD [redacted]	Information storage & retrieval of drug related data (ORD's project OFTEN)	Type of data in files.

Sensitive Projects

[redacted]	[redacted]	Computer file of drug data.	Type of data in file.

00135

EYES ONLY
SECRET

~~SECRET~~ ~~EYES ONLY~~

DO 72

Sensitive Projects (Continued)

OJCS Project Identification	Project Officer Organization, & Telephone	Nature of Project	OJCS Reason for Listing
[redacted]	[redacted] TSD [redacted]	Statistical analysis of psychological data.	Source of data. Contractors are involved with project.

Sensitivity Unknown, but Possibly a Matter for Concern

OJCS Project Identification	Project Officer Organization, & Telephone	Nature of Project	OJCS Reason for Listing
[redacted]			Nature of data. Techniques of system discussed with FBI.
SPYDER	[redacted] OS [redacted]	Data on radio frequencies used for support of In-Place Monitoring System, a system to identify unauthorized transmitters.	[redacted]
DMVREC	[redacted] OS [redacted]	File of automobile license numbers.	Nature of data.
[redacted]		File of Agency applicants who were not hired.	Nature of data.

2

00136

~~EYES ONLY~~

Sensitivity Unknown, but Possibly a Matter for Concern (Continued)

OJCS Project Identification	Project Officer Organization, & Telephone	Nature of Project	OJCS Reason for Listing
--	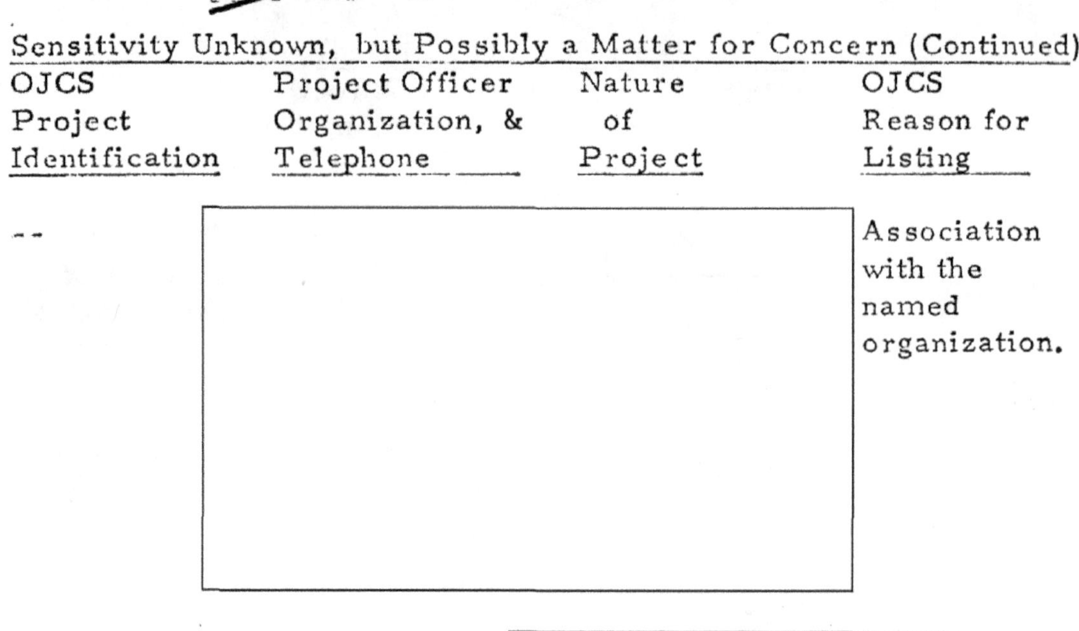		Association with the named organization.

For

JOHN D. IAMS
Director of Joint Computer Support

3

~~EYES ONLY~~
~~SECRET~~

00137

[ ] UNCLASSIFIED [ ] INTERNAL USE ONLY [ ] CONFIDENTIAL [ ] SECRET

ROUTING AND RECORD SHEET

SUBJECT: (Optional)

FROM:	EXTENSION	NO.
Director of Communications [redacted] Hqrs.	[redacted]	DATE 10 May 1973

TO: (Officer designation, room number, and building)	DATE RECEIVED	DATE FORWARDED	OFFICER'S INITIALS	COMMENTS (Number each comment to show from whom to whom. Draw a line across column after each comment.)
1. DDM&S [redacted] Hqrs.				Ref SC [redacted] - The attached is in further response to your request.
2.				
3.				
4.				
5.				
6.				
7.				
8.				
9.				
10.				
11.				
12.				
13.				
14.				00138
15.				

FORM 3-62 610 USE PREVIOUS EDITIONS [ ] SECRET [ ] CONFIDENTIAL [ ] INTERNAL USE ONLY [ ] UNCLASSIFIED

TOP SECRET
SECRET
CONFIDENTIAL

DOCUMENT DESCRIPTION	REGISTRY
SOURCE: OC	CONTROL NUMBER: SC
DATE OF DOCUMENT: 8 May 1973	DATE DOCUMENT RECEIVED:
COPY NUMBER (S):	LOGGED BY:
NUMBER OF PAGES: two DOCUMENT NO:	
NUMBER OF ATTACHMENTS: one	

FROM: Special Programs Division, OC — DATE: 10 May 73

	TO OFFICE	NAME	SIGNATURE	DATE
1	D/CO	Mr. Jack J. Keith		10 May
2	DDM&S			
3				
4				
5				

- [ ] Approval
- [ ] Action
- [ ] Comment
- [ ] Concurrences
- [ ] Information
- [ ] Direct Reply
- [ ] Preparation of Reply
- [ ] Recommendation
- [ ] Signature
- [ ] Return
- [ ] Dispatch
- [ ] File

REMARKS

1-2: Forwarded per your request of 7 May to identify operations that are not clearly within CIA's "charter". All of these operations have been levied on us by the Directorate of Operations — those of para 3 have been accompanied by assurances of approval by the (then) DCI.

CONFIDENTIAL
SECRET
TOP SECRET

00139

~~TOP SECRET~~

SC

8 May 1973

MEMORANDUM FOR THE RECORD

SUBJECT: Summary, Special Programs Division (SPD), Office of Communications, Operational Contacts with Other U.S. Government Agencies

1. Prior to 1969 the OC COMINT intercept unit, which was then in Miami, had relatively frequent contact with the Miami bureaus of the FBI and FCC, Miami Police and the Miami Beach Police. The staff provided support to these activities in monitoring, identification and DF of specific illegal agent transmissions conducted by foreign nationals and American citizens in the greater Miami area. Arrangements for this support were made through the DDO's

2. In late September 1972, NSA, through Division D/DDO, requested that the Special Programs Division initiate a hearability survey of certain HF long-distance commercial telephone circuits between the U.S. and South America. The circuits carried drug related long-distance calls of interest to the BNDD and other U.S. agencies. Because of the availability of personnel and technical capabilities, where the circuits could be satisfactorily intercepted. On 15 January 1973, formal NSA tasking of the intercept was instituted. On 30 January 1973, all coverage was terminated by Division D because of possible legal complications.

3. The Chief and Deputy Chief, SPD and SPD/Special Electronic Operations Branch have been engaged in informal technical liaison with operating components of the FBI for a number of years. Initial contacts and arrangements for support of specific activities have been made by the Division D/DDO. Support has been provided in the form of

~~DOWNGRADED TO SECRET UPON REMOVAL OF ATTACHMENT~~

~~TOP SECRET~~

00140

~~TOP SECRET~~

8 May 1973

exchanges of technical information on techniques, technical assistance and training, and the loan of Agency equipment. In the past several years, support has been rendered to sensitive FBI projects [redacted] and [redacted] Support has been and is presently being given to FBI projects [redacted] These projects are described in the attached sealed envelope.

4. An operational test of an [redacted] HF/DF system was [redacted] conducted [redacted] Division D/DDO and OC-SPD personnel in the early part of the summer of 1972. A location in Miami Beach, Florida was selected for the tests because of similarity to the actual target site and environment in Saigon. Receiving antennas were placed on the roof of the hotel being used as the receiving/DF site. A hotel employee asked why the materiel was placed on the roof. A team member in effect told him that the group was an advance security segment for the Democratic National Convention. No further questions were asked; the tests were completed and the equipment was returned to the Washington area.

[redacted]

Chief, Special Programs Division, OC

Att.

~~TOP SECRET~~

00141

TOP SECRET

SENSITIVE

9 May 1973

9 May 1973

MEMORANDUM FOR THE RECORD

SUBJECT: Organizational Dealings with Activities Inside the United States

1. This MFR records organizational dealings with activities inside the United States known to this office.

2. In September 1972, [redacted] requested secure communications in the Miami Area with local offices of BNDD and Customs. [redacted] The communications link was never installed [redacted] advised in April 1973 that there were plans underway in Miami to combine various Federal agencies anti-drug efforts under a new Justice Department Division, and at this time it was not known where the new anti-drug office would be located. [redacted]

3. During the Democratic and Republican conventions, [redacted] supported requirements levied by the Secret Service concerning name traces and other intelligence information relating to subversive influences which might affect those conventions. [redacted] provided some technical advice and procedural assistance in establishing a useful means of communicating between the two correspondents. WHD should be able to provide a detailed resume of activities supported in this matter.

Thomas E. O'Donnell
Chief, Americas Staff, OC

CONFIDENTIAL

SENDER WILL CHECK CLASSIFICATION TOP AND BOTTOM

UNCLASSIFIED | CONFIDENTIAL | SECRET

OFFICIAL ROUTING SLIP

TO	NAME AND ADDRESS	DATE	INITIALS
1	Mr. William E. Colby	6/1	WEC
2	IG	6/1	WVB
3			
4	C/MPS		
5			
6			

	ACTION		DIRECT REPLY		PREPARE REPLY
	APPROVAL		DISPATCH		RECOMMENDATION
	COMMENT		FILE		RETURN
	CONCURRENCE		INFORMATION		SIGNATURE

Remarks: file — WEC **

Bill:

The attached memorandum identifies the funds referred to in Chuck Briggs' notes of 13 and 20 January 1972.

WVB

FOLD HERE TO RETURN TO SENDER

FROM: NAME, ADDRESS AND PHONE NO.	DATE
Inspector General	30 May 73

UNCLASSIFIED | CONFIDENTIAL | SECRET

FORM NO. 237 1-67 Use previous editions (40)

** "Since these notes are on a totally separate sensitive subject, pls pull them from this file -- WEC " (Note to C/MPS)

00144

29 May 1973

MEMORANDUM FOR: Inspector General

SUBJECT : Mr. Colby's Request to Inspector General to Determine Subject Referred to by Two Notes in a PP/B Memo to DD/M&S

REFERENCE : D/PPB Memo to DD/M&S dated 23 May 1973, Subject: Watergate Principals - Direct or Indirect Involvement

00145

SENDER WILL CHECK CLASSIFICATION TOP AND BOTTOM

	UNCLASSIFIED		CONFIDENTIAL		SECRET

OFFICIAL ROUTING SLIP

TO	NAME AND ADDRESS	DATE	INITIALS
1	IG	5/24/73	
2		5/24	
3			
4			
5			
6			

	ACTION		DIRECT REPLY		PREPARE REPLY
	APPROVAL		DISPATCH		RECOMMENDATION
	COMMENT		FILE		RETURN
	CONCURRENCE		INFORMATION		SIGNATURE

Remarks:

Note action required by IG.

1288

00146

FOLD HERE TO RETURN TO SENDER

FROM: NAME, ADDRESS AND PHONE NO.	DATE
W. E. Colby	23 May 73

	UNCLASSIFIED		CONFIDENTIAL		SECRET

FORM NO. 1-67 237 Use previous editions (40)

MEMORANDUM FOR: IG —

Pls find out what the two notes refer to — Maybe DDO files will show

WEC

2 3 MAY 1973

(DATE)

FORM NO. 1 AUG 54 101 REPLACES FORM 10-101 WHICH MAY BE USED. (47)

00147

SENDER WILL CHECK CLASSIFICATION TOP AND BOTTOM

UNCLASSIFIED		CONFIDENTIAL		SECRET

OFFICIAL ROUTING SLIP

TO	NAME AND ADDRESS	DATE	INITIALS
1	W. E. Colby	5/23	wec
2			
3			
4			
5			
6			

	ACTION		DIRECT REPLY		PREPARE REPLY
	APPROVAL		DISPATCH		RECOMMENDATION
	COMMENT		FILE		RETURN
	CONCURRENCE		INFORMATION		SIGNATURE

Remarks:

See second sheet of notes on your copy only (at paginatio). Do not know if this was related in any way. We have no details in OPPB of this DCI-approved expenditure.

FOLD HERE TO RETURN TO SENDER

FROM: NAME, ADDRESS AND PHONE NO.	DATE
Charles A. Briggs, D/PPB	5/23/73

UNCLASSIFIED		CONFIDENTIAL		SECRET

FORM NO. 1-67 237 Use previous editions (40)

00148

23 May 1973

DD-70

MEMORANDUM FOR: Deputy Director for Management and Services

SUBJECT: Watergate Principals - Direct or Indirect Involvement

1. This memorandum responds to the Director's request for a report of any involvement in any capacity since 1 January 1969 with Messrs. Hunt, McCord, Liddy, Young, or Krogh.

2. I have had none with Hunt, Liddy or Young.

3. My McCord contact was indirect and occurred sometime during the late 1960's when I was Director, Office of Computer Services. I opposed plans for Technical Division, Office of Security (under Mr. McCord) to acquire a separate computer for its In-Place Monitoring System. [redacted] of DD/S&T (then ORD) was the computer individual working with TD and, I think, would have details.

4. The Krogh contact also was indirect and involved his request, first through OMB, that CIA fund foreign travel on behalf of the Cabinet Committee on International Narcotics Control. Individual phone discussions are noted in the attached. The Agency focal points were [redacted] and [redacted] I understand [redacted] has forwarded relevant documentation. Copies of memoranda from Messrs. Krogh, [redacted] and Colby are attached also.

5. I held a staff meeting yesterday to pass the request to all OPPB employees. One officer who was attending a funeral will not be available until tomorrow.

/s/ Charles A. Briggs

Charles A. Briggs
Director of Planning,
Programming, and Budgeting

Distribution:
Orig & 1 - Addressee
1 - W. E. Colby
1 - D/PPB Eyes Only File
O/PPB/CABriggs/mrm:4456(23May73)

Attachment
As stated

00149

SECRET

SECRET

Attachment
23 May 1973

D 0 70

4 Feb 72	Call from Jim Taylor, OMB re "Bud" Krogh and his deputy, Walter Minnick, of the Domestic Council who plan foreign travel in connection with their narcotics interests. Jim was alerting us to their intention to ask us for funds for the travel.
7 Feb 72	Follow-up from Taylor: Plan 3-5 trips for 3 individuals--all in FY 72. Cost probably $10K. Minnick ready to make first trip. [redacted] is plugged in. ExDir said OK re Tehran visit.
7 Feb 72	See attached memo from Egil Krogh, Jr. to Bill Colby and follow-on memos from [redacted] (21 Jul 72) and Colby (2 Aug 72).
12(?) May 72	John Hurley, OMB called, mentioning possible Krogh/Minnick attendance at a Latin American (Station Chief?) conference on narcotics. He also said Jeff Shepherd, White House, was laying on a trip with [redacted] for himself, Shepherd and Mark Alger, OMB to Europe.
23 Jun 72	[redacted] commented on Krogh/Minnick interest in getting CA activities, including large-scale PM, on narcotics front. [redacted] pushing small-scale PP.
6 Jul 72	[redacted] called. Notes say only: "Minnick-Hurley film. We will send."
2 Aug 72	[redacted] called re Colby letter (attached). Said travel orders ready; need money this PM (No record in my notes as to who was traveling when, but have faint recollection of its being to Mexico City). [redacted] and [redacted] contacted by [redacted]
1 Nov 72	Related? [redacted] call. Again notes are cryptic: [redacted] GAO-Grace [redacted] Survey BNDD problems/Mexico."

00150

SECRET

DO 70

On Mr. Colby's copy only:

13 Jan 72 ExDir (Colby) said DCI had approved $30K for sensitive CS project - no details.

20 Jan 72 Reminded ExDir re $32K he said DCI OK'd.

THE WHITE HOUSE

WASHINGTON

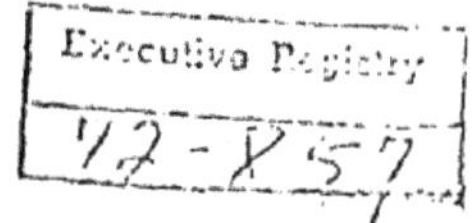
Executive Registry

72-857

February 7, 1972

MEMORANDUM FOR BILL COLBY

SUBJECT: BUDGETARY SUPPORT FOR THE CABINET COMMITTEE ON INTERNATIONAL NARCOTICS CONTROL

The Cabinet Committee on International Narcotics Control was created September 7, 1971, by the President to centralize his attack on the international drug traffic.

The Committee does not have a separate budget.

Salary and administrative support for its small, full-time staff has been provided by the Executive Office of the President. Other expenses are being charged to the constituent agencies and departments.

The Bureau of Customs, BNDD, and AID/Office of Public Safety have provided support to date.

The CIA should be prepared to defray not more than fifteen thousand dollars in overseas travel expenses for Cabinet Committee staff during the remainder of FY-1972.

Walter C. Minnick, the Committee's Staff Coordinator, can be contacted for further details.

Thank you for your assistance.

Egil Krogh Jr.

Egil Krogh, Jr.
Executive Director
Cabinet Committee on
International Narcotics Control

CC: John Ehrlichman
Assistant to the President for Domestic Affairs
Mark Alger
OMB, Chief, General Government Programs Division
[redacted]
CIA Representative, CCINC Working Group

00152

2 AUG 1972

Count 1
DO-1

MEMORANDUM FOR: Deputy Director for Plans

SUBJECT: Fiscal Year 1973 Budgetary Support for the Cabinet Committee on International Narcotics Control (CCINC)

REFERENCE: Memo to ExDir frm C/DDP/NARCOG dtd 21 July 1972; same subject

1. This is in response to the referenced memo regarding use of CIA funds to cover travel expenses for the White House Cabinet Committee Staff for Fiscal Year 1973.

2. You are authorized to obligated up to $15,000 for the use of the White House Cabinet Committee Staff for travel expenses during FY 1973. Obligation should be recorded against the O/DDP allotment and travel orders issued against your own appropriate fan number.

3. To the extent that you are unable to absorb this requirement within your present allotment, we will have to arrange some reprogramming later in the year to cover this unbudgeted item.

/s/

W. E. Colby
Executive Director-Comptroller

O/PPB [redacted] /hg 2 Aug 72

FULL TEXT COPY - DO NOT RELEASE

Distribution:
Orig & 1 - addressee
1 - ExDir
1 - ER
1 - PPB Subj (BMS
1 - O/F
1 - Reading
[redacted] Chrono

00153

SECRET

PPB [illegible]

Executive R
72-46

21 July 1972

MEMORANDUM FOR: Executive Director - Comptroller

VIA : [redacted] Deputy Director for Plans

SUBJECT : Fiscal Year 1973 Budgetary Support for the Cabinet Committee on International Narcotics Control (CCINC)

1. At our invitation, Mr. Walter C. Minnick, Staff Member of the CCINC, is scheduled to attend and participate in the Regional Narcotics Seminar sponsored by WH Division on 27-28 July 1972.

2. In accordance with procedures adopted for travel of White House Cabinet Committee Staff in FY 1972, it is requested that funds to cover the cost of Mr. Minnick's trip be released. Attached herewith is a copy of a formal request from Mr. Egil Krogh dated 7 February 1972 to Mr. William Colby requesting travel funds for the balance of FY 1972. Mr. Krogh is now preparing a formal request for $15,000.00 to cover travel expenses for White House Cabinet Committee staff for FY 1973. I will forward this request to your office as soon as it arrives.

C/DDP/NARCOG

Attachment: A/S

00154

SECRET

RECORD COPY

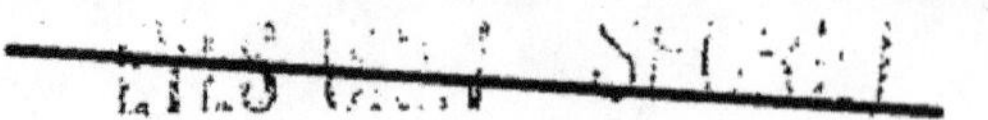

DD/M&S 73-1809

MEMORANDUM FOR: Deputy Director for Management and Services

SUBJECT : Contacts with Individuals Named in the Watergate Matter

1. I am addressing this to you instead of to the Director of Central Intelligence since I doubt that the information contained herein is of such significance to warrant his interest and because it has been on record with the Agency since July 1972. However, if you feel that the information is of such interest that it should be forwarded to the Director I shall put it in the proper format to do so.

2. My only contact with anyone named in connection with the Watergate and related matters was through [redacted] a former Agency employee now retired and living in Winterhaven, Florida. In December 1971 [redacted] called me from Florida and advised that he wanted to get in touch with Howard Hunt. He said that he did not have Hunt's home phone number and that it was probably unlisted but that since Hunt was a former employee, could I contact Hunt and ask him to give [redacted] a call. I had only met Hunt once about 10 years before but I agreed to relay the message. I called Howard Hunt at his home and told him that [redacted] did not have his home phone and requested he call [redacted] Mr. Hunt thanked me for relaying the message and said that he would call [redacted] This seemed of little consequence to me in December 1971 but in July 1972 [redacted] of the Office of Security contacted me in regard to the FBI investigation of the Watergate situation. At that time I informed [redacted] of the telephone call from [redacted] in December 1971. Attached is a copy of a Memorandum for the Record prepared by [redacted] as a result of our conversation.

3. In the summer of 1972 I took my family to Disney World in Florida and took that occasion to drop in to see [redacted] [redacted] told me in a private conversation that he had been interviewed three or four times by the FBI in connection with the Watergate affair and he related to me his contact

00155

~~EYES ONLY~~ SECRET

with Howard Hunt. On 19 July 1972 after my return from Florida I reported this conversation to the Director of Security and made it a Memorandum for the Record. This memorandum was sent to Mr. Colby and a copy of the memorandum is attached.

4. Other than knowing Mr. McCord through his employment with the Agency and meeting Howard Hunt once in about 1959, I do not know nor have I had any contact with any individuals named or knowledge of related matters now receiving attention in the press.

Charles W. Kane
Special Assistant to the
Deputy Director
for Management and Services

Atts

MEMORANDUM FOR: Executive Director-Comptroller

Per our conversation on Monday.

Thanks —
WEC
7/20/72

Ho[redacted] J. Osborn
D[redacted] of Security

20 July 1972
(DATE)

FORM NO. 101 REPLACES FORM 10-101
1 AUG 54 WHICH MAY BE USED. (47)

00157

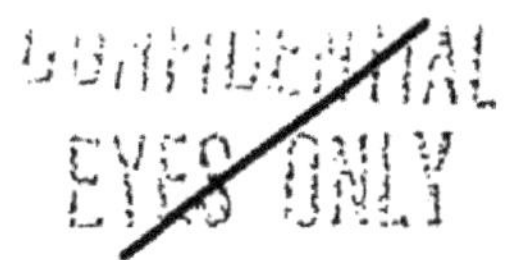

19 July 1972

MEMORANDUM FOR THE RECORD

SUBJECT: Conversation with

1. While on leave visiting Disney World in Florida, I dropped in to see who lives in Winterhaven, Florida. retired from the Agency about five years ago on disability due to a serious heart condition. He was with the Office of Security for about 20 years prior to his retirement.

2. During a private conversation told me that he had been interviewed three or four times by the FBI in connection with the McCord-Hunt affair. I asked him why he had been interviewed, and he told me that in late 1971 he had been contacted by Howard Hunt who suggested that he consider an assignment as Security Officer for the Republican Party. visited Washington in January 1972 to discuss the proposed position with Howard Hunt who apparently was acting on behalf of the Republican Party. furnished a resume to Hunt and discussed the position with him. Ultimately, he decided not to accept the position because he felt that his heart condition would not allow him to become involved in such activity.

3. According to during the meeting with Mr. Hunt they discussed some of the requirements of the job. At that time they discussed a need for both a positive and a counteraudio program and a need for a good security system both before and during the National Convention. indicated that he sincerely believed that the Republican Party did need a security officer and a good security programmer but felt that he could not afford to accept the job even though it was a very lucrative offer. Apparently, money was not a problem.

00158

CONFIDENTIAL
EYES ONLY

4. When [redacted] declined, he indicated that Mr. Hunt asked for any other recommendations he might have. According to [redacted] he told Mr. Hunt that most of the people he knew were still in the Agency, but he did furnish the name of [redacted] who might be possibly ready to retire from the Agency.

5. [redacted] informed me that he assumed that the Bureau obtained his name due to the resume he furnished Mr. Hunt. He said that the Bureau had talked to him on three or four occasions and that he had written up about a 40 page statement concerning his dealings with Mr. Hunt. When asked about Mr. McCord, [redacted] said that he really did not know McCord that well and declined any knowledge of Mr. McCord's technical capability.

6. [redacted] indicated that he had not been in touch with Mr. Hunt since the early part of 1972 and knew nothing of the Watergate operation. He stated that he had gained the impression from the Bureau interview that the technical devices were being removed at the time of the arrest and were not being installed as originally reported.

7. All of the above information was volunteered by [redacted] [redacted] and I really did not get involved in any discussion on the matter other than to comment that I hated to see the Agency's name connected with such an incident in any way. The above conversation took place during a 10 or 15 minute period and no other discussion relating to this incident was held. It is being reported for the record and for information of the Director of Security.

Charles W. Kane

CONFIDENTIAL

EYES ONLY

00159

17 July 1972

MEMORANDUM FOR THE RECORD

SUBJECT: Charles W. Kane
[redacted]

1. Last week Special Agent Arnold Parham of the FBI contacted the Acting DD/OS. He asked whether or not the Subjects worked for the Central Intelligence Agency. Previously, requests of this nature were followed up by the FBI with an interview of the subjects.

2. I briefed Mr. Colby who is the Agency's focal point on the "Watergate" case and the Acting DD/S of the FBI inquiry. Mr. Colby suggested that we determine the extent of involvement and indicated that we advise the Bureau of their employment.

3. When Agent Parham was again contacted and advised of the Subjects' employment with the Agency, he indicated that the Bureau does not wish to interview them.

4. The office of the DD/PS will interview [redacted] in the same fashion as [redacted] was previously interviewed. / Already in the file ? 7/21

5. I called Mr. Kane both at his office and his residence and learned that he is in Florida and will return to duty on 17 July. I called Mr. Kane this morning to advise him of the inquiry.

6. Mr. Kane stated that he has no firm conclusion as to how the Bureau obtained his name. He stated that he has seen Mr. Hunt on only one occasion in 1959. At that time Hunt was the Chief of Station, [redacted] The meeting was occasioned

00160

by the fact that Mr. Kane [redacted] Mr. Kane stated further that around Christmas time of 1971 he received a call from [redacted] who wanted to get in touch with Mr. Hunt. [redacted] asked Mr. Kane how he could get in touch with him. Mr. Kane obtained Mr. Hunt's telephone number through telephone information channels whereupon he passed the number on to [redacted]

7. Mr. Kane stated that he has information that [redacted] has talked to the FBI on several occasions in connection with the current investigation and that he surmises that the Bureau may have obtained his name from him.

[redacted]
Deputy Director of Security

00161

MORI 75-15[illegible]

SENDER WILL CHECK CLASSIFICATION TOP AND BOTTOM

	UNCLASSIFIED		CONFIDENTIAL		SECRET

OFFICIAL ROUTING SLIP

TO	NAME AND ADDRESS	DATE	INITIALS
1	DDM&S, [redacted] Hqs.		
2	DCI, [redacted] Hqs.		
3			
4			
5			
6			

	ACTION		DIRECT REPLY		PREPARE REPLY
	APPROVAL		DISPATCH		RECOMMENDATION
	COMMENT		FILE		RETURN
	CONCURRENCE		INFORMATION		SIGNATURE

Remarks:

00162

FOLD HERE TO RETURN TO SENDER

FROM: NAME, ADDRESS AND PHONE NO.	DATE
[redacted] D/PPB/[redacted]	8 May 73

UNCLASSIFIED		CONFIDENTIAL		SECRET

FORM NO. 237 Use previous editions (40)
1-67

Not a record

8 May 1973

MEMORANDUM FOR: Director of Central Intelligence

THROUGH: Deputy Director for Management and Services

SUBJECT: Involvement in Sensitive Domestic Activities

1. As chief of the DDP Systems Group prior to 1969, I was involved in providing data processing support for the following sensitive projects:

a. CI Staff Mr. Richard Ober's program for processing data of U.S. citizens believed to be militants, subversives, terrorists, etc.

b. FI Staff and Office of Medical Services program [redacted] for recording data on foreign and U.S. physicians [redacted]

c. A Systems Group sponsored program of common concern listing travel of U.S. citizens to and from Communist countries.

2. In the same capacity my staff and I briefed police officers from New York State and Chicago at the DCI's request (Admiral Rayborn) on data processing techniques related to biographic intelligence (unclassified).

3. As a member of O/PPB, I have been aware of five programs with possibly sensitive domestic overtones.

a. DDS&T/ORD's contract with the [redacted] The VIP Health and Behavior Prediction System."

b. DDS&T/ORD's Project OFTEN which involved the collection of data on dangerous drugs from U.S. firms. I believe Mr. Helms terminated this program last Fall.

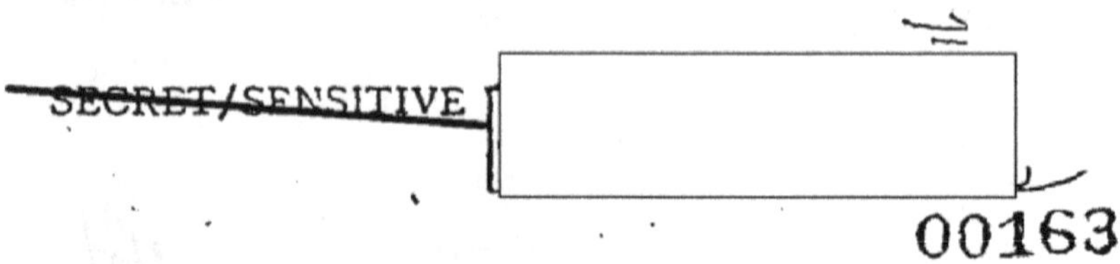

~~SECRET/SENSITIVE~~

00163

c. DDS&T/ORD's project [redacted]

d. DDS&T/ORD's use of ERTS-A data to analyze Soviet wheat yields.

e. DDS&T Special Projects Staff - the [redacted] program.

[redacted]

Science and Technology Group
O/PPB

~~EYES ONLY~~

8 MAY 1973

MEMORANDUM FOR: Director of Central Intelligence

VIA: Deputy Director for Management and Services

SUBJECT: Watergate/Ellsberg and Like Matters

1. No personal involvement, direct or indirect to my knowledge on my part or my staff, with the Watergate or Pentagon papers cases, with Young on security regulations or with classified releases to RAND. I was aware, many years back when in the DDI, that certain classified papers were released to RAND from the production offices. One staff member, [redacted] while a member of the IC Staff, did have a RAND contact which he is elaborating on separately.

2. There are some sensitive activities or projects of which I am aware, which are mighty close to the borderline of legality in terms of Agency mission, including:

a. The CI Staff (Ober) project

b. The [redacted] proprietary, [redacted]

c. An Office of Security narcotics cover project

d. A CI Staff funding-channel project with the FBI [redacted]

~~SECRET/SENSITIVE~~
EYES ONLY

00165

~~EYES ONLY~~

3. One of my staff officers, [redacted] while in OCI was the briefing officer for the former Attorney General, but can recall nothing in his dealing with Mr. Mitchell which would have any relevance to the current issues. A couple other staff officers are reporting separately on some sensitive activities in which they were involved prior to coming to this staff.

Charles A. Briggs
Director of Planning,
Programming, and Budgeting

00166

2

~~SECRET/SENSITIVE~~
~~EYES ONLY~~

UNCLASSIFIED ☐ INTERNAL USE ONLY ☐ CONFIDENTIAL ☐ SECRET ☐

ROUTING AND RECORD SHEET

SUBJECT: (Optional)

FROM:	EXTENSION	NO.
C.V.S. Roosevelt Chairman, TSCC [redacted] Hqs	[redacted]	DATE 8 May 1973

TO: (Officer designation, room number, and building)	DATE RECEIVED	DATE FORWARDED	OFFICER'S INITIALS	COMMENTS (Number each comment to show from whom to whom. Draw a line across column after each comment.)
1. DCI [redacted]				
2.				
3.				
4.				
5.				
6.				
7.				
8.				
9.				
10.				
11.				
12.				
13.				
14.				
15.				00167

FORM 3-62 610 USE PREVIOUS EDITIONS ☐ ~~SECRET~~ ☐ ~~CONFIDENTIAL~~ ☐ INTERNAL USE ONLY ☐ UNCLASSIFIED

UNITED STATES INTELLIGENCE BOARD

TECHNICAL SURVEILLANCE COUNTERMEASURES COMMITTEE

OFFICE OF THE CHAIRMAN

TSCC-D-386
8 May 1973

MEMORANDUM FOR: Director of Central Intelligence

SUBJECT : Support Furnished to Elements of the Government Outside of the Intelligence Community

The Interagency Audio Surveillance Countermeasures Training Center (ITC) was established at the instigation of this Committee and opened in late 1968 under the executive management of CIA. The need for such a school had been recognized by the National Security Council's Technical Subcommittee as far back as 1962 and was re-emphasized by the Security Committee of the USIB in their October 1964 report titled "Damage Assessment of the Technical Surveillance Penetration of the US Embassy, Moscow."

Membership on the TSCC has been confined to agencies and departments who are represented on the USIB. From time to time other elements of the Government have indicated their concern over the audio surveillance threat and asked for membership on the Committee. In all cases they have been turned down with the suggestion that they take advantage of the TSCC's product either through liaison with the security organizations of the Committee's members or by nominating students to attend the ITC. During CY-72 the following students were trained at the ITC:

Central Intelligence Agency	10
Defense Intelligence Agency	5
Department of the Air Force	25
Department of the Army	50
Department of Justice (BNDD)	4
Department of the Navy	5
Department of State	3

00168

Department of Transportation	3
Internal Revenue Service	3
National Security Agency	1
United States Secret Service	6
White House Communications Agency	2
	117

The ITC has furnished training only to employees of the agencies and departments of the Federal Government. State and local police departments have not been detailed to the ITC.

CVS Roosevelt

Cornelius V. S. Roosevelt
Chairman

00169

CONFIDENTIAL

Retirement Information - E. Howard Hunt

1. Date of retirement: 30 April 1970

2. System: CIA Retirement and Disability System

3. Grade and salary at time of retirement: GS-15, Step 8 - $28,226

4. Creditable civilian service used in computing annuity:

   17 May 1948 to 8 June 1948 - Economic Cooperation Administration

   9 June 1948 to 19 February 1949 - State (ECA)

   8 November 1949 to 30 April 1970 - CIA

5. Annuity:

   At retirement - $1,020 per month

   At present - $1,181 per month (which includes cost-of-living increases since date of retirement)

6. At the time of retirement Mr. Hunt did not elect survivorship benefits. This meant that upon his death, his wife would not draw a survivorship annuity. By letter of 5 April 1971 he raised the question of changing his election but was informed by the General Counsel on 6 May 1971 that this could not be done. By letter dated 5 May 1972 Mr. Hunt asked Mr. Houston to raise with the Director the possibility of being recalled to duty for a short period of time, after which he could retire again and elect survivorship benefits. By letter of 16 May 1972 Mr. Houston advised Mr. Hunt that to call him back to duty solely for the purpose of permitting him to change survivorship benefits would be in violation of the spirit of the CIA Retirement Act.

00170

SECRET/SENSITIVE

22 May 1973

MEMORANDUM FOR: Inspector General

Bill--

Attached are the reports Bill Colby asked to see:

1. Restless Youth (September 1968), No. 0613/68, Secret/Sensitive/No Foreign Dissem (Copy 78).

This document was produced in two versions--one with the chapter on radical students in America (pages 25-39) which was sent only to the President, Walt Rostow, and Cy Vance (former Deputy Secretary of Defense); the other version without the references to the American scene was disseminated to twenty people outside the Agency. This document without the material on the US was updated in February 1969 and copies were sent to the Vice President and Dr. Kissinger. A still more abbreviated edition was sent to the Attorney General in March 1969.

2. Black Radicalism in the Caribbean (6 August 1969), No. 1839/69, Secret/No Foreign Dissem (Copy 142).

3. Black Radicalism in the Caribbean--Another Look (12 June 1970), No. 0517/70, Secret/No Foreign Dissem (Copy 98).

Please note that these are our record copies and should be returned.

Edward W. Proctor
Deputy Director for Intelligence

Attachments

00171

2 013329

SENDER WILL CHECK CLASSIFICATION TOP AND BOTTOM

	UNCLASSIFIED		CONFIDENTIAL		SECRET

OFFICIAL ROUTING SLIP

TO	NAME AND ADDRESS	DATE	INITIALS
1	Mr. Breckinridge		
2			
3			
4			
5			
6			

	ACTION		DIRECT REPLY		PREPARE REPLY
	APPROVAL		DISPATCH		RECOMMENDATION
	COMMENT		FILE		RETURN
	CONCURRENCE		INFORMATION		SIGNATURE

Remarks:

00172

FOLD HERE TO RETURN TO SENDER

FROM: NAME, ADDRESS AND PHONE NO.	DATE
O/DCI	12/24/74

	UNCLASSIFIED		CONFIDENTIAL		SECRET

FORM NO. 1-67 237 Use previous editions (40)

17 September 1968

MEMORANDUM

SUBJECT: Dissemination of OCI Paper on Student Dissidents

1. Dissemination to the Cabinet and within the Intelligence Community--The paper Restless Youth is sensitive because of its subject matter, because of the likelihood that public exposure of the Agency's interest in the problem of student dissidence would result in considerable notoriety, particularly in the university world, and because pursuant to Mr. Rostow's instructions, the author included in his text a study of student radicals in the United States, thereby exceeding the Agency's charter. We have sanitized the paper for dissemination to the members of the President's Cabinet and within the Intelligence Community by eliminating altogether the chapter which discusses Students for a Democratic Society (SDS) and by striking from the Prospects section all mention of SDS.

2. Outside the Community but within the Government--We believe that the basic text should be further edited for the purpose of eliminating even the most casual reference to the domestic scene--lest someone infer from such a chance reference that the original paper had contained a section on American students. The nineteen country chapters which form Part II of Restless Youth can be disseminated within the Government, provided that the controls appropriate to their classification are observed. To do the editing and reprinting required would take several days at least.

3. Release to the academic world or to the public--For the reasons set forth above, we believe that release of the basic text would harm the Agency. The country chapters could not be released without first being rewritten to eliminate all classified information. Once this was done,

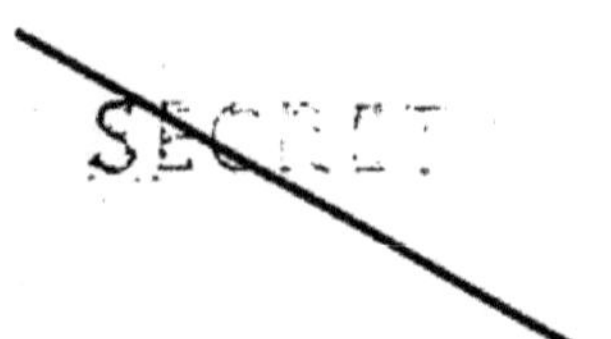

00173

SECRET

they would duplicate information already available in the open press. There is no lack of overt literature on the subject of student dissent; virtually every publisher includes at least one title on his current listing. Moreover, other agencies of government, such as Health, Education and Welfare, have sponsored research on the subject and are prepared to publish their findings. Consequently, we recommend against public release.

SECRET

00174

ADDI's Personal Copy

No further dissemination or reading without ADDI's permission.

per ADDI
16 September 1968

limited
distribution
includes
VS.

00175

SECRET
No Foreign Dissem
Sensitive

Restless Youth

SEPTEMBER 1968
No. 0613/68

00176

78

Sensitive
No Foreign Dissem
SECRET

3 Jan 75

Black Radicalism in Caribbean

II 142

6 Aug '69

No 1837/69

Black Radicalism in Caribbean –

An Air Look

II 96

12 June 1970

No 0517/70

00177

14 May 1973

MEMORANDUM FOR THE RECORD

SUBJECT: Research Project on Robert Vesco

1. On 16 October 1972 Messrs. Breckinridge and [redacted] in the course of a Survey, were briefed on activities of the Atlantic/Pacific Division of the Office of Economic Reports. One project cited was a query from the Director, apparently at the request of Secretary Shultz, to the effect, "What do we know about Vesco," the man then running IOS. Two of OER's analysts were assigned to the project and, working through the Domestic Contact Service, spent a day going over the files of the Securities and Exchange Commission. There apparently was some contact also with EUR Division of the Deputy Directorate for Plans and with the Office of Current Intelligence.

"Research"

2. The information above is based on rough notes and obviously is sketchy. It is cited now not to suggest any wrongdoing but because of the current publicity about Vesco and the probability of continuing probes into the subject by the press and the courts.

Scott D. Breckinridge

[redacted]

00178

Director of Central Intelligence

Please handle in this channel due to classification of attachment.

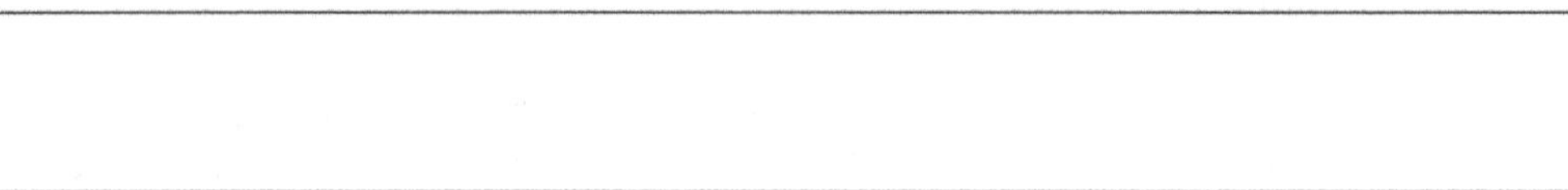

WARNING

This document contains classified information affecting the national security of the United States within the meaning of the espionage laws, US Code, Title 18, Sections 793, 794, and 798. The law prohibits its transmission or the revelation of its contents in any manner to an unauthorized person, as well as its use in any manner prejudicial to the safety or interest of the United States or for the benefit of any foreign government to the detriment of the United States.

THIS DOCUMENT MUST BE KEPT IN COMMUNICATIONS INTELLIGENCE CHANNELS AT ALL TIMES

It is to be seen only by US personnel especially indoctrinated and authorized to receive COMMUNICATIONS INTELLIGENCE information; its security must be maintained in accordance with COMMUNICATIONS INTELLIGENCE REGULATIONS.

No action is to be taken on any COMMUNICATIONS INTELLIGENCE which may be contained herein, regardless of the advantages to be gained, unless such action is first approved by the Director of Central Intelligence.

~~TOP SECRET~~

00179

8 May 1973

MEMORANDUM FOR: Director of Central Intelligence

FROM : Deputy Director for Intelligence

SUBJECT : Activities Possibly Outside CIA's Legislative Charter

1. This memorandum responds to your instruction to report any activities which might be considered outside CIA's legislative charter.

2. All Office and Staff chiefs in the Intelligence Directorate have reviewed the past and present activities of their components. I have received responses from all of them, and none reported any activities related to either the Watergate affair or the break into the offices of Ellsberg's psychiatrist. Although contacts with three of the people allegedly implicated in these incidents were reported, these contacts were on matters other than the two improper activities:

Hunt: Col. White, Richard Lehman, and I talked to Hunt in late 1970 regarding his preparation of a recommendation in support of the Agency's nomination of R. Jack Smith for the National Civil Service League Award.

Mitchell: While Mr. Mitchell was Attorney General, an OCI officer was assigned the task of providing him with daily briefings on foreign developments.

00180

~~SECRET~~
CIA INTERNAL USE ONLY

Young: Harry Eisenbeiss and [redacted] of CRS had frequent contacts with Young during the summer of 1972 in connection with Executive Order 11652 and the implementing NSC directive. This involved visits by Young to CIA to discuss information storage and retrieval and several meetings of an inter-agency group dealing with the implementation of the Executive Order and directive.

3. In accordance with my instructions, several Offices reported domestic activities which might appear questionable to outsiders. Their responses are attached. Most of these activities are clearly within the Agency's charter, but there are a few which could be viewed as borderline.

- [redacted]
- [redacted]
- DCS accepts information on possible foreign involvement in US dissident groups and on the narcotics trade when sources refuse to deal with the FBI and BNDD directly.
- [redacted]
- DCS, for six months in late 1972 and early 1973, was acquiring telephone routing slips on overseas calls.
- [redacted]
- NPIC and COMIREX review satellite imagery from NASA programs to identify photography too "sensitive" for public release.

-2-

SECRET
CIA INTERNAL USE ONLY

00181

- NPIC has examined domestic coverage for special purposes such as natural catastrophes and civil disturbances.

- OCI, in 1967 and 1968, prepared intelligence memoranda on possible foreign connections with the US anti-war movement and world-wide student dissidence (including the SDS) at the request of the White House.

-

- FBIS has on occasion supplied linguists to work directly for another agency, e.g., to the FBI to translate Arabic in Washington.

- FBIS monitors radio press dispatches and reports covered by copyright. These are circulated within the Government and stamped "Official Use Only". This has gone on for three decades without problems.

- FBIS has monitored and reported on foreign radio broadcasts of statements and speeches of US citizens such as those by US POWs in Hanoi, Jane Fonda, and Ramsey Clarke.

-

EDWARD W. PROCTOR
Deputy Director for Intelligence

Attachments

-3-

SECRET
CIA INTERNAL USE ONLY

00182

00183

7 May 1973 DD 54

MEMORANDUM FOR: Deputy Director for Intelligence

SUBJECT: DCS Domestic Activity

To the best of my knowledge, DCS has not engaged in any activity outside the CIA charter or that could be construed as illegal. Some of the functions that we perform under HR 1-13f (i) of providing operational support within the US to all elements of CIA and to the USIB-member agencies, however, are perhaps borderline or could be construed as illegal if misinterpreted. For example:

5. Collect information on possible foreign involvement or penetration of US dissident groups, but only in a passive manner and only when the source has refused to pass the information directly to the FBI.

6. Collect information on the narcotics trade, but again only in a passive manner when the source has refused to pass the information directly to BNDD or the FBI.

00184

SECRET/SENSITIVE

SUBJECT: DCS Domestic Activity

10. Acquire routing slips recording the fact of overseas telephone calls between persons in the US and persons overseas and telephone calls between two foreign points routed through US switchboards. This activity lasted for approximately six months but has ceased.

JAMES R. MURPHY
Director, Domestic Contact Service

-2-

~~SECRET/SENSITIVE~~

00185

00186

7 May 1973

MEMORANDUM FOR: Director of Central Intelligence

VIA : Deputy Director for Intelligence

FROM : Director of Current Intelligence

SUBJECT : Activity Related to Domestic Events

1. OCI provided current intelligence briefings to John Mitchell as Attorney General. With the approval of the DCI, this practice began in the pre-inaugural period in New York and continued until Mr. Mitchell's resignation as Attorney General. The OCI officer assigned to this duty had a daily appointment with Mr. Mitchell in his office at Justice.

2. The briefings provided were strictly on foreign intelligence, and were a legitimate service for CIA to provide to an official advisor to the President who sat on, among other bodies, the 40 Committee. It must be presumed, however, that our man's daily visits were known and speculated on elsewhere in Justice. The problem comes in the potential press treatment: "CIA Officer in Continuous Contact with Mitchell."

Richard Lehman
Director of Current Intelligence

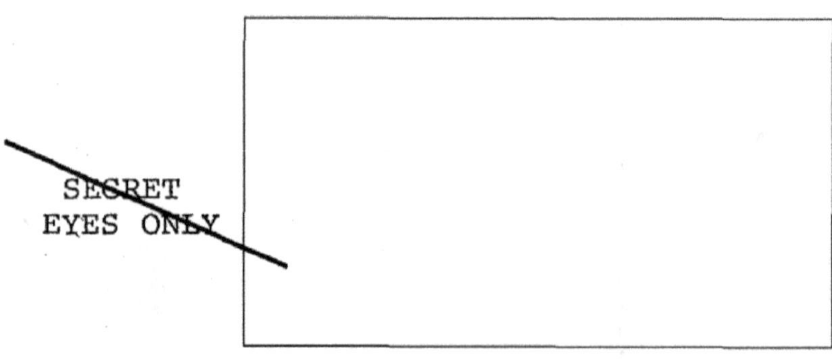

00187

7 May 1973

MEMORANDUM FOR: Director of Central Intelligence

VIA : Deputy Director for Intelligence

FROM : Director of Current Intelligence

SUBJECT : Activity Related to Domestic Events

1. OCI began following Caribbean black radicalism in earnest in 1968. The emphasis of our analysis was on black nationalism as a political force in the Caribbean and as a threat to the security of the Caribbean states. Two DDI memoranda were produced on the subject: "Black Radicalism in the Caribbean" (6 August 1969), and "Black Radicalism in the Caribbean--Another Look" (12 June 1970). In each a single paragraph was devoted to ties with the US black power movement; the discussion primarily concerned visits of Stokely Carmichael and other US black power activists to the Caribbean and other overt contacts.

2. In June 1970, Archer Bush of OCI was asked to write a memorandum with special attention to links between black radicalism in the Caribbean and advocates of black power in the US. The record is not clear where this request originated, but it came through channels from the DCI. The paper was to be treated as especially sensitive and was to include material provided by the Special Operations group of the CI Staff. The CI Staff material was voluminous but did not provide meaningful evidence of important links between militant blacks in the US and the Caribbean. This, in fact, was one of the conclusions of the paper. The memorandum was produced in typescript form and given to the DCI.

3. For several months in the first half of 1968 the Caribbean Branch wrote periodic typescript memoranda on Stokely Carmichael's travels abroad during a period when he had dropped out of public view. Our recollection is that the memoranda were for internal CIA use only, although a copy of one was inadvertently sent to the FBI.

Richard Lehman
Director of Current Intelligence

SECRET
EYES ONLY

7 May 1973

MEMORANDUM FOR: Director of Central Intelligence

VIA : Deputy Director for Intelligence

FROM : Director of Current Intelligence

SUBJECT : Activity Related to Domestic Events

1. In late spring of 1968 Walt Rostow, then Special Assistant to the President for National Security Affairs, tasked the DCI with undertaking a survey of worldwide student dissidence. Confronted by tumult at campuses like Columbia and mindful of the violence accompanying student outbursts at Berlin's Free University and elsewhere, Rostow sought to learn whether youthful dissidence was interconnected: spawned by the same causes; financed and hence manipulated by forces or influences hostile to the interests of the US and its allies; or likely to come under inimical sway to the detriment of US interests.

2. The paper was prepared by [redacted] of OCI with the assistance of the CA and CI Staffs. The DDI, D/OCI, and [redacted] met with Rostow to elicit the reasons for his or the President's concerns and to agree on the sources to be examined, the research methods to be followed, etc.

3. Written during the summer of 1968, the most sensitive version of Restless Youth comprised two sections. The first was a philosophical treatment of student unrest, its motivation, history, and tactics. This section drew heavily on overt literature and FBI reporting on Students for a Democratic Society and affiliated groups. In a sense, the survey of dissent emerged from a shorter (30 page) typescript study of SDS and its foreign ties the same author had done for Mr. Rostow at the DCI's request in December 1967. (We no longer have a copy.)

00190

SECRET
EYES ONLY

4. Because of the paucity of information on foreign student movements, it was necessary to focus on SDS which then monopolized the field of student action here and abroad. A second section comprised 19 country chapters--ranging from Argentina to Yugoslavia--and stood by itself as a review of foreign student dissidence.

5. Because SDS was a domestic organization, the full paper Restless Youth, including the essay on world-wide dissent went only to nine readers. A copy may be in the Johnson Library.

6. Following the paper's favorable reception by the President and Mr. Rostow, the DCI briefed the NSC on student dissent. The sensitive version subsequently was updated and sent to the White House in February 1969.

7. The less sensitive text was disseminated in September 1968 and then updated and issued again in March 1969 and August 1970.

Richard Lehman
Director of Current Intelligence

WARNING

This document contains classified information affecting the national security of the United States within the meaning of the espionage laws, US Code, Title 18, Sections 793, 794, and 798. The law prohibits its transmission or the revelation of its contents in any manner to an unauthorized person, as well as its use in any manner prejudicial to the safety or interest of the United States or for the benefit of any foreign government to the detriment of the United States.

THIS DOCUMENT MUST BE KEPT IN COMMUNICATIONS INTELLIGENCE CHANNELS AT ALL TIMES

It is to be seen only by US personnel especially indoctrinated and authorized to receive COMMUNICATIONS INTELLIGENCE information; its security must be maintained in accordance with COMMUNICATIONS INTELLIGENCE REGULATIONS.

No action is to be taken on any COMMUNICATIONS INTELLIGENCE which may be contained herein, regardless of the advantages to be gained, unless such action is first approved by the Director of Central Intelligence.

00192

~~TOP SECRET~~

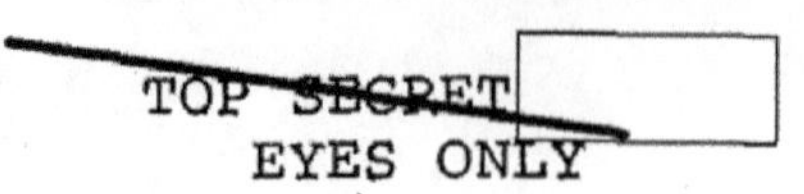
TOP SECRET
EYES ONLY

7 May 1973

MEMORANDUM FOR: Director of Central Intelligence

VIA : Deputy Director for Intelligence

FROM : Director of Current Intelligence

SUBJECT : Activity Related to Domestic Events

1. In late 1967 OCI participated in the preparation of several short intelligence memoranda dealing with the foreign connections of US organizations and activists involved in the anti-war movement. The main purpose of these reports, prepared at the request of the White House, was to determine whether any links existed between international Communist elements or foreign governments and the American peace movement. The conclusion reached was that there was some evidence of ad hoc contacts between anti-war activists at home and abroad but no evidence of direction or formal coordination.

2. In October 1967 President Johnson expressed interest in this subject and ordered a high level interdepartmental survey. In response to his personal request to the DCI, Mr. Helms asked the CI Staff to collect whatever information was available through our own sources and through liaison with the FBI and to pass it to OCI, which was directed to prepare a memorandum from the DCI to the President.

3. A book message requirement was sent to all stations to report whatever information was on hand relevant to this subject. Although agent reports on Communist front operations overseas were of some value, the primary source of information on the activities of US activists--and that was quite limited--was sensitive intercepts produced by NSA, which had been similarly tasked by the White House.

TOP SECRET
EYES ONLY

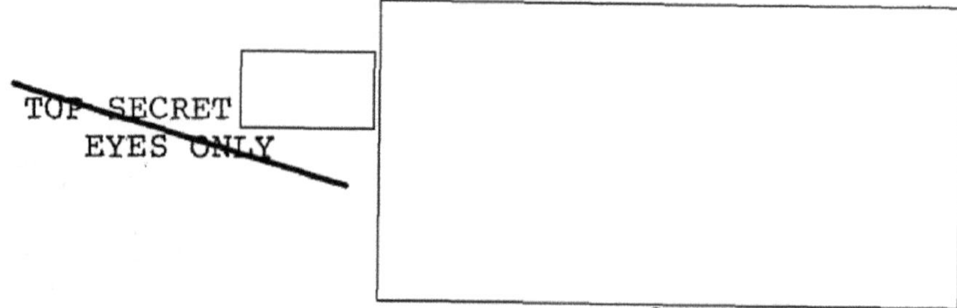

00193

4. A draft memorandum was jointly prepared by OCI and CI Staff and forwarded to the DCI. He passed this typescript memo, dated 15 November 1967, to the President personally. The White House copy is now in the files of President Johnson's papers at the library in Austin.

5. Brief follow-up memoranda were prepared and forwarded to the White House on 21 December and 17 January 1968. According to our best recollection, no further finished intelligence reports on international connections of the peace movement were produced.

Director of Current Intelligence

TOP SECRET
EYES ONLY

00194

00195

7 May 1973

MEMORANDUM FOR: Deputy Director for Intelligence

SUBJECT: Contacts with David Young

1. In the summer of 1972, I had frequent contacts with David Young. He was in this building under my control once. These contacts related solely to Executive Order 11652 and the NSC directive concerned therewith. Young was apparently at the time in the process of drafting the NSC directive. The visit to the building under my control was for a briefing on CRS processes for storage and retrieval of documents and is apparently reflected in the paragraph of the directive concerned with the Data Index. I visited him in his White House office at least twice in the company of an inter-Agency group concerned with the Data Index.

2. In August of 1972, [redacted] also visited Mr. Young's office in the company of an inter-Agency group to discuss CIA compliance with the data index instructions. To the best of my knowledge no one in CRS had any contact with Mr. Young in his role as a "plumber."

[redacted]

H. C. EISENBEISS
Director, Central Reference Service

00196

7 May 1973

MEMORANDUM FOR: O/DDI

SUBJECT: Involvement In Domestic Affairs

1. This memorandum responds to the DDI's request for a listing of any questionable involvements in domestic affairs. I do not believe that CRS is doing anything that a reasonable man could construe as improper.

2. CRS does, of course, have several programs to acquire still pictures, movies, videotapes

3. CRS files do not generally bear on U.S. citizens or organizations. The biographic file-building criteria specifically excludes U.S. nationals unless the person has become of such major importance in the political life of a foreign country that the file is essential. (To my knowledge, only 2 persons so qualify.

Our Cuban files probably include some persons who are now U.S. citizens but we have no way to separate them; we have files on U.S. defectors to Cuba.)

~~SECRET~~

00197

SUBJECT: Involvement In Domestic Affairs

4. The CIA Library has several informal snag files intended to aid the librarians in answering the kinds of questions that they know they will get on a continuing basis. An appointments file is a collection of clippings on appointed federal officials: who holds what job when and what is his background? The extremist files are a collection of folders on a variety of organizations and a few people with intricate organizational links. Any sort of extremism is grist for these particular files. And a few persons, e.g., Rap Brown and Eldridge Cleaver, have dossiers consisting almost exclusively of clippings from public media. These files are unclassified and consist mostly of clippings from the public press: U.S., foreign, underground, scholarly.

5. I am not aware of any other kind of involvement in domestic activities that is not related to development of techniques or logistics or legitimate training of CRS personnel.

H. C. EISENBEISS
Director, Central Reference Service

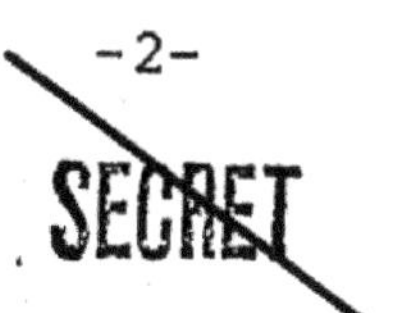

00198

8 May 1973

Questionable NPIC Projects

1. Leaks of Jack Anderson

In January 1972, NPIC performed image enhancement techniques on TV tapes of a Jack Anderson show. The purpose was to try to identify serial numbers of CIA documents in Anderson's possession. The request was levied on NPIC through the Office of Security.

2. The Poppy Project

NPIC has provided the services of one PI to assist an interagency effort to detect poppy cultivation. In addition the Center has provided the contractual mechanism in support of the Bureau of Narcotics and Dangerous Drugs for a multispectral crop study by a private company.

3. Reviews of NASA Collected Imagery

NPIC has and continues to conduct reviews of satellite imagery from NASA programs to identify "sensitive" frames of photography not releasable to the public and to ascertain the intelligence potential of the imagery. This service has been provided for GEMINI and ERTS photography and preparations are underway for review of SKY LAB imagery.

4. Peaceful Uses of Satellite Imagery

NPIC has been requested to provide a number of looks at domestic coverage for special purposes. Examples include:

- Santa Barbara Oil Spill
- Los Angeles Earthquake
- Sierra Snow (flood threat)
- Current Mississippi Floods
- Hurricane Cammile Damage on the Coast of the Gulf of Mexico
- Civil Disturbance in Detroit
- OEP U.S. Data Base

00200

8 May 1973

MEMORANDUM FOR: DDI

SUBJECT : Sensitive Activities

1. FBIS has been engaged in no activities related to the Ellsberg and Watergate cases.

2. FBIS operations occasionally extend to the domestic arena. From time to time, FBIS linguists are made available to DDO or Office of Communications components for special operations (usually abroad) involving close-support SIGINT work or translation of audio take. On one occasion recently DDO, on behalf of the FBI, requested the services of several FBIS linguists skilled in Arabic to work directly for the FBI on a short-term project here in Washington. The arrangements were made by Mr. Oberg of the DDO CI Staff. He said the project was very highly classified and that FBIS participation was approved by Mr. Colby and the Director. FBIS participation was approved by the Director of FBIS after a check with the ADDI. Other examples of sensitive linguistic support work are help in the handling and resettlement of defectors, the recent assignment of an employee to the Bureau of Narcotics and Dangerous Drugs to transcribe recordings in a rare Chinese dialect, and the detailing of another Chinese linguist on two occasions to assist in the U.S. military training of Chinese Nationalist cadets.

3. Within its responsibility for monitoring press agency transmissions for intelligence information, FBIS publishes and distributes some material which falls in a "gray" area of copyright protection, libel, and privacy of international communications. Press services controlled by national governments and transmitted by radioteletype without specific addressees, e.g. the Soviet TASS service and the PRC's NCNA, are monitored by FBIS and the material is disseminated without restriction. The legality of this has been affirmed by decisions of the Office of General Counsel.

00202

~~SECRET~~

SENSITIVE

4. The routine FBIS monitoring of foreign radio broadcasts often involves statements or speeches made by U.S. citizens using those radio facilities. Examples are statements made or allegedly made by American POW's in Hanoi, by Jane Fonda in Hanoi and by Ramsey Clark in Vietnam. At the request of FBI and the Department of Justice, and with the approval of the CIA Office of General Counsel, we have on occasion submitted transcripts of such broadcasts to the Department of Justice as part of that Department's consideration of a possible trial. In such cases, we have been required to submit names of FBIS monitors involved, presumably because of the possibility they might be required as witnesses. (In one case in 1971, an FBIS staff employee was directed to appear as an expert witness in the court-martial of a Marine enlisted man charged with aiding the enemy in a broadcast from Hanoi.) FBIS views all this with misgivings. Monitoring of such broadcasts is incidental and we rue attribution of their news to FBIS, and we should not be considered policemen maintaining surveillance of traveling Americans.

E. H. KNOCHE
Director
Foreign Broadcast Information Service

-2-

SECRET
SENSITIVE

00203

ROUTING AND RECORD SHEET

SUBJECT: (Optional)

FROM:
Director
Office of Technical Service

EXTENSION	NO.
	DATE 29 [illegible]

TO: (Officer designation, room number, and building)	DATE RECEIVED	DATE FORWARDED	OFFICER'S INITIALS	COMMENTS (Number each comment to show from whom to whom. Draw a line across column after each comment.)
1. ADDO 31 [illegible]			[illegible]	[illegible]
2.				
3. IG	6/1	6/1		
4.				
5.				
6.				
7.				
8.				
9.				
10.				
11.				
12.				
13.				
14.				00204
15.				

FORM 3-62 610 USE PREVIOUS EDITIONS ☐ SECRET ☐ CONFIDENTIAL ☐ INTERNAL USE ONLY ☐ UNCLASSIFIED

29 MAY 1973

MEMORANDUM FOR: Deputy Director for Operations

SUBJECT: Documentation Support for Use in the United States

1. As you are aware this office provides document support for a variety of covert activities. Specific use is not always available to this office and should properly come from the requesting office who can provide the details. U.S. alias documentation use in the United States is approved by the Office of Security and normally has the concurrence of Central Cover Staff or FI and CI Staffs. Requests received by this office from outside the Clandestine Service are approved by an appropriate office of the DDO.

2. A review of this office's document support files for the period 1 January 1972 to date indicates that the following number of U.S. alias document requests were fulfilled for probable use in the United States. The statistics below are broken down by requester:

SECRET

00205

2

SECRET

00206

3

00207

SECRET

4

00208

John N. McMahon
Director
Office of Technical Service

cc:DD/S&T

5

00209

SECRET

UNCLASSIFIED [ ] CONFIDENTIAL [ ] INTERNAL USE ONLY [X] SECRET [ ]

ROUTING AND RECORD SHEET

SUBJECT: (Optional)

FROM:	EXTENSION	NO.
OTS/ [redacted]	[redacted]	DATE 29 May 1973

TO: (Officer designation, room number, and building)	DATE RECEIVED	DATE FORWARDED	OFFICER'S INITIALS	COMMENTS (Number each comment to show from whom to whom. Draw a line across column after each comment.)
1. OTS/TRAINING [redacted]		30 MAY 1973	[redacted]	1: Please comment or concur.
2.				
3.				
4. OTS/ [redacted] Attn: [redacted]		31 MAY 1973	[redacted]	
5. OTS/EXO	5/31/73		[redacted]	7-5 [redacted] Innocent enough but very right wish to know about —
6. DD/OTS		4 JUN 1973	[redacted]	
7. D/OTS		4 JUN 1973	[redacted]	[redacted]
8. DDS&T			[redacted]	
9. IG 2E24	6/6/73		[redacted]	8-9 [redacted]
10. TSD/MPS:File [redacted]	6 June		[redacted]	Sounds OK but should be in your file
11. [redacted] "Jewels"				
12.				[redacted]
13.				
14.				
15.				00210

FORM 3-62 610 USE PREVIOUS EDITIONS [ ] ~~SECRET~~ [ ] ~~CONFIDENTIAL~~ [ ] INTERNAL USE ONLY [ ] UNCLASSIFIED

25 May 1973

MEMORANDUM FOR THE RECORD

SUBJECT: Loan of Tape Recorder to Passport Office

1. Late in 1971 (December, I believe) the Deputy Director for the Passport Office, Department of State, (Mr. Robert Johnson) informally queried me on whether that office might borrow a small tape recorder for use by the Director of the Passport Office (Miss Frances Knight) to record a meeting she had scheduled with representatives of a foreign government.

2. I conveyed this request to the then Chief, [redacted] and subsequently held several discussions with representatives of our [redacted] office. It was decided to loan the Passport Office a small commercial recorder (Norelco Cassette Recorder, Model 150), which we had in stock.

3. A representative of our Training Branch [redacted] and I delivered the recorder to Miss Knight's office and [redacted] demonstrated the recorder's capabilities and instructed her in its use. She did not seem too pleased at the recording quality; however, the recorder was left with her.

4. On this date (21 May 1973) I asked Mr. Johnson to check on the status of the recorder. He said it was never used in any way. I therefore retrieved it from the Passport Office and delivered it to Training Branch [redacted]

[redacted]

OTS/[redacted]

00211

CONFIDENTIAL

FORM NO. 1 MAY 56	238	REPLACES FORM 35-1 WHICH IS OBSOLETE	DOCUMENT CONTROL	(13-40) MFG 7-71

	SEC. CL.	ORIGIN		CONTROL NO.
DATE OF DOC	DATE REC'D	DATE OUT	SUSPENSE DATE	CROSS REFERENCE OR POINT OF FILING

TO
FROM
SUBJ.

ROUTING	DATE SENT

00212

COURIER NO.	ANSWERED	NO REPLY		3

MEMORANDUM FOR: Mr. Colby

Carl Duckett brought this up and said he is very uncomfortable with what Sid Gottlieb is reporting and thinks the Director would be ill-advised to say he is acquainted with this program. Duckett plans to scrub it down with Gottlieb but obviously cannot do it this afternoon.

Ben Evans
8 May 1973
(DATE)

00213

FORM NO. 101 REPLACES FORM 10-101
1 AUG 54 WHICH MAY BE USED. (47)

☐ UNCLASSIFIED ☐ USE ONLY ☐ CONFIDENTIAL ☐ SECRET

ROUTING AND RECORD SHEET

SUBJECT: (Optional)

FROM:	EXTENSION	NO.
Sidney Gottlieb Chief, TSD		DATE 8 May 1973

TO: (Officer designation, room number, and building)	DATE RECEIVED	DATE FORWARDED	OFFICER'S INITIALS	COMMENTS (Number each comment to show from whom to whom. Draw a line across column after each comment.)
1. Carl E. Duckett DDS&T				~~SECRET~~
2.				
3.				
4.				
5.				
6.				
7.				
8.				
9.				
10.				
11.				
12.				
13.				
14.				
15.				~~SECRET~~ 00214

FORM 3-62 610 USE PREVIOUS EDITIONS ☐ SECRET ☐ CONFIDENTIAL ☐ INTERNAL USE ONLY ☐ UNCLASSIFIED

8 May 1973

MEMORANDUM FOR: Deputy Director for Science & Technology

SUBJECT : TSD Support to Other Agencies

1. Technical Services Division's charter (CSI 1-8) requires that it provide technical assistance to both CIA operations and other activities as may be directed by the Deputy Director for Operations.

2. Over the years the chief non-CIA recipients of this support have been the Department of Defense, the Federal Bureau of Investigation, Bureau of Narcotics and Dangerous Drugs, Immigration and Naturalization Service, Department of State, United States Postal Service, Secret Service, Agency for International Development, and the White House.

3. While varying widely among the different recipients, these services have included training and materials, and in a few instances participation in the fields of audio and visual surveillance, secret writing and related communications, personal protection, alias documentation and questioned document examination, disguise, concealment devices, electronic beaconry, illicit narcotics detection, and counter-sabotage/terrorism.

4. In most instances requirements for this support are received by TSD through higher echelons (Office of the Director or Deputy Director for Operations). Unless the service involved is a trivial or continuing one, the request is referred to the Foreign Intelligence Staff Departmental Coordination Group for coordination and approval at the appropriate Agency levels. Approval within TSD by the Chief of Operations or Development and Engineering and the Chief of TSD or his Deputy also is required.

5. The attachment lists the primary services provided to the organizations named in Paragraph two.

E2 IMPDET
CL BY 059098

00215

6. Issuance of forged personal identity documentation by TSD is controlled according to two broad criteria: type of requester; and type of documentation requested. A request for denied area documentation from a DDO Area Division is honored after proper validation. Free world documentation may require some extra coordination however.

7. Unless ordered otherwise by higher Agency authority, no U.S. documentation is issued by TSD Headquarters without prior coordination with the Office of Security and the Central Cover Staff. TSD Regional Bases require at least the validation of U.S. documentation requests by the COS, or his designated representative, of the requesting Station. Because it could be used no U.S. Birth Certificate is issued without approval of the DDO via Central Cover Staff. Backstopped major credit cards are issued by Office of Security, not TSD.

8. Provision of forged documentation to non-DDO requesters, whether they be CIA or other Agency requesters, always requires approval of non-TSD offices. Support to the military for instance would be validated by FI Staff/Departmental Coordination Group at Headquarters or by the COS overseas having responsibility for coordination of the operation. BNDD requests are coordinated with DDO/NARCOG. Requests for documentation of Immigration and Naturalization Service is coordinated via the Alien Affairs Staff.

9. Authentication items are issued on a loan basis and must be returned to TSD or accounted for. After any documentation has been issued, TSD retains photographs and records of such support until the documentation has been returned to TSD. If the material is not returned after a reasonable time, the requester is reminded of the outstanding documentation.

Sidney Gottlieb
Chief
Technical Services Division

Attachment

Distribution:
O & 1 - Addressee, w/att

00216

ATTACHMENT

Department of Defense

Documents, disguise, concealment devices, secret writing, flaps and seals; counterinsurgency and counter sabotage courses have been furnished to all intelligence elements of the Department of Defense and certain elements of the Special Forces. All requests are coordinated with the FI Departmental Coordination Group at Headquarters and with the Chief of Stations overseas. In turn these elements furnished TSD with exemplars of foreign identities documents, foreign cachets, foreign intelligence secret writing systems, foreign intelligence concealment devices. Selected audio requirements have been furnished overseas for CI -type cases.

Federal Bureau of Investigation

At the request of the FBI we cooperate with the Bureau in a few audio surveillance operations against sensitive foreign targets in the United States.

Bureau of Narcotics and Dangerous Drugs

Beacons, cameras, audio and telephone devices for overseas operations, identity documents, car-trailing devices, SRAC, flaps and seals and training of selected personnel responsible for use thereof has been furnished this Bureau. All requirements are sent to DDO/NARCOG for coordination with area divisions and for action by TSD if appropriate. Requests overseas are coordinated with the COS or his designee before action by TSD is taken.

Immigration and Naturalization

CI analyses of foreign passports and visas, guidance in developing tamperproof alien registration cards, [redacted] [redacted] have been furnished the Service. Requests are forwarded directly to TSD for coordination within TSD if technical, with the FI Departmental Coordination Group if operational.

00217

Department of State

Technical graphics guidance on developing a new United States Passport, analyses of foreign passports, car-armoring and personnel locators (beacons) for Ambassadors have been supplied the State Department. In addition analyses and exposure of black letter operations against the United States abroad are made. All graphics requirements are forwarded to TSD for further coordination within the Division. The Department of State furnishes exemplars of foreign passports, foreign visas and in the past passports on a priority basis.

Postal Service

The Office of Chief Postal Inspector has had selected personnel attend basic surveillance photographic courses, has been furnished foreign postal information and has been the recipient of letter bomb analyses, furnished [redacted] typewriter analyses. Requirements are coordinated with the DDO and DDO/EA. The Post Office has furnished TSD with exemplars of letter bombs and [redacted] We also have an arrangement with the Post Office to examine and reinsert a low volume of certain foreign mail arriving in the United States.

Secret Service

Gate passes, security passes, passes for Presidential campaign, emblems for Presidential vehicles; a secure ID photo system have been furnished this Service. Blanket approval for graphics support has been granted to the Deputy Director for Operations. In each case TSD requests approval from the DDO.

U. S. Agency for International Development

We furnish instructors to a USAID-sponsored Technical Investigation Course (Counter Terror) at [redacted]

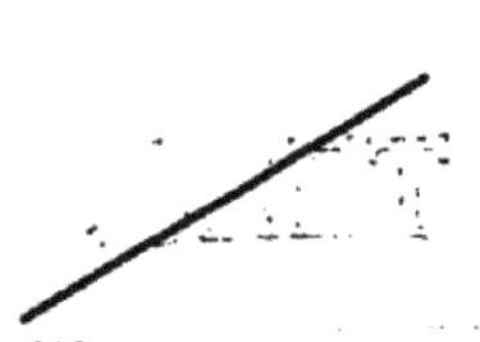

White House

Stationery, special memoranda, molds of the Great Seal have been furnished the Social Secretary. The Deputy Director for Operations is apprised of these requirements.

Police Respresenting Washington, Arlington, Fairfax and Alexandria

During the period 1968 - 1969 a series of classes reflecting basic and surveillance photography, basic audio, locks and picks, countersabotage and surreptitious entry were given to selected members from the above mentioned cities. Overall training was approved by the Director of Centeral Intelligence and in turn validation was required for each course from the Director of Security.

00219

SUBJECT: (Optional)

FROM:			EXTENSION	NO.
Sidney Gottlieb Chief, TSD				DATE 8 May 1973
TO: (Officer designation, room number, and building)	DATE RECEIVED	DATE FORWARDED	OFFICER'S INITIALS	COMMENTS (Number each comment to show from whom to whom. Draw a line across column after each comment.)
1. DDS&T				Attached herewith are additional explanations of TSD support to other U.S. Government agencies.
2.				
3.				
4.				
5.				
6.				
7.				
8.				SECRET EYES ONLY
9.				
10.				
11.				
12.				
13.				
14.				00220
15.				SECRET EYES ONLY

FORM 3-62 610 USE PREVIOUS EDITIONS ☐ SECRET ☐ CONFIDENTIAL ☐ INTERNAL USE ONLY ☐ UNCLASSIFIED

ATTACHMENT

FEDERAL BUREAU OF INVESTIGATION

TSD has had a close working relationship with the FBI over the past few years. The FBI is the only organization that has been fully briefed on TSD audio techniques and equipment. The following are situations where TSD equipment and guidance were involved in operations:

SECRET

00221

- 2 -

SECRET

00222

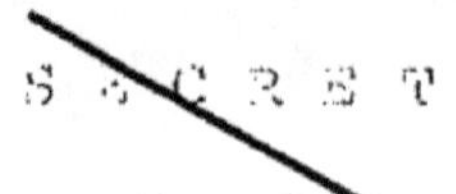

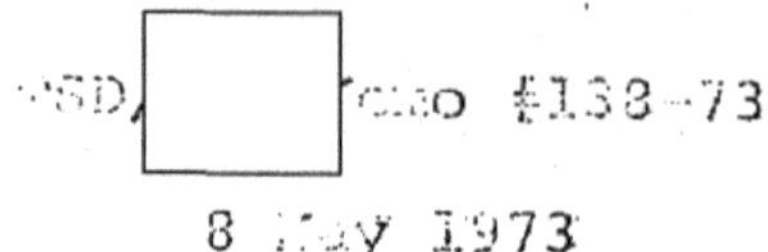

TSD/ Memo #138-73

8 May 1973

MEMORANDUM FOR: Chief, TSD

ATTENTION: Executive Officer

SUBJECT: Contacts with Domestic Police Organizations

1. In December 1968, July 1969 and December 1970, SDB provided basic countersabotage familiarization training for selected members of the Washington metropolitan area police departments. The training was given at the Fairfax County police pistol and rifle range. Authorization for the training came from DDP and Chief, Office of Security.

2. On occasion during the past few years, under the auspices of the Law Enforcement Assistance Administration of the Department of Justice and with the approval of CI Staff and Office of Security, SDB provided training and familiarization to police officers of several domestic police departments in the uses of the Explosives Residue Detection Technique and Trace Metals Detection Technique. These techniques had been declassified and are currently available to the law enforcement community. The National Bomb Data Center publishes periodic guidance in their uses.

3. In order to augment the SDB mission responsibilities in the field of countersabotage and counterterror, SDB officers have in the past two years visited, under appropriate covers, the explosives disposal units of the New York City police department, Dade County (Miami) Florida Dept. and the Los Angeles Police Dept. Also, in March 1973, two SDB officers attended the Explosives and Ordnance Disposal Conference in Sacramento, California, sponsored by LEAA. When the recent letter bomb menace began in September 1972, our liaison with the NYCPD bomb squad paid off in that we had complete information on letter bomb construction in hours, enabling the Agency to make worldwide dissemination within a day.

C/TSD/OPS/SDB

00223

SECRET

SECRET SERVICE

In addition to printing of various passes and identification emblems, TSD has also supplied the Secret Service with some U.S. alias documentation:

00224

Technical Training for Local Police Department

I. The first segment of technical training by Training Branch was conducted during the period 7 October - 26 November 1968. The following schedule and subjects were used in the training of six members of the Metropolitan Police Department.

A. 7-18 October - Surreptitious Entry
Content of Subject taught:

1. Familiarization and identity of American locks.

2. Method of manipulation of locks.

3. Methods and techniques of conducting Surreptitious Entry Survey.

B. 21-29 October - Photo Surveillance
Content of Subject taught:

1. Familiarization with cameras: Pentax Spotmatic, Leica, Nikon F, Robot and Polaroid.

2. Lens, telephoto and wide angle.

3. Exposure Meter, Tripods, Bowum, etc.

4. Film, film processing and print processing.

5. Document copy exercises.

6. Night Photography and night exercises.

7. TV Surveillance.

C. 18-23 November - Audio Surveillance
Content of Subject taught:

1. Microphones, wire impedances and line amplifiers. (Shure MC-30, Sennheiser MM-22, RCA - BK - 6B and RCA BK-12a all commercially available)

2. RF commercial transmitter. (Research Products, Tracer Inc., Scientific Research Corp.)

00225

3. [illegible]. (Military and [illegible] - [illegible]R-4 and [illegible] respectfully.)

4. Telephone Taps. (Obsolete model DR-2 equipment which [illegible] available to government and law enforcement agencies).

5. Recorders ([illegible]pex-601-2 Stereo, Revere T-204 Mona, Uher 4000L, all commercially obtainable).

6. Plastering and Wall Restoration.

D. 24-26 November - Operational Problem and Exercise

1. This problem entailed an operational exercise against three of our Safesties. The students had to survey, case and peetrate these locations using surreptitious entry, photography and audio surveillance.

2. All these safesites, two apartments in and one on have been turned back to Agency Real Estate and have since then been terminated. Formal class instruction was conducted at

II. After this first MPD group other police departments personnel trained using the identical safe sites and employing the same subject matter and commercial equipment as indicated above were taught on the following dates. The Fairfax Police Department and Arlington Police Department. Date - 21 October - 10 December 1968. Six officers, 4 from APD and 2 from FPD.

III. In 1969 additional officers from the Metropolitan Police Department, Fairfax Police Department and Arlington Police Department received identifical training as that stated above. In total 24 police officers were trained in our facilities.

00226

ROUTING AND RECORD SHEET

SUBJECT: (Optional) Repeated Survey of ORD for Non-Foreign Intelligence Activities

FROM: D/ORD

NO. ORD-2328-73

DATE 9 May 1973

TO: (Officer designation, room number, and building)	DATE RECEIVED	DATE FORWARDED	OFFICER'S INITIALS	COMMENTS (Number each comment to show from whom to whom. Draw a line across column after each comment.)
1. DDS&T			CEP	To 2 This is a revision which Carl Duckett accepted to me with the request you & DCI know
2. Mr Colby		5/14		
3. [illegible]	5/14			2-3: [illegible]
4. DCI				
5.				
6.				
7.				
8.				
9.				
10.				
11.				
12.				
13.				
14.				00227
15.				

FORM 3-62 610 USE PREVIOUS EDITIONS [X] SECRET [ ] CONFIDENTIAL [ ] INTERNAL USE ONLY [ ] UNCLASSIFIED

ORD-2528-73
9 MAY 1973

MEMORANDUM FOR: Deputy Director for Science and Technology

SUBJECT : Repeated Survey of ORD for Non-Foreign Intelligence Activities

The 7 May survey has been repeated and refined with respect to all ORD services or dealings with other agencies on domestic, non-foreign matters. In addition, this report covers all our activities dealing with the research and development of intelligence equipment for foreign use which has been tested in the United States and might have collected domestic information. Again, each member of ORD available today was asked either directly or through his supervisor to provide the above requested information, whether he was directly involved or not. We have used all diligence to search our records available to us during this time period to ensure this is a complete and factual list.

for Sayre Stevens
Director of Research & Development

Attachments:
1 - Contacts with Other Government Agencies
2 - Domestic Tests

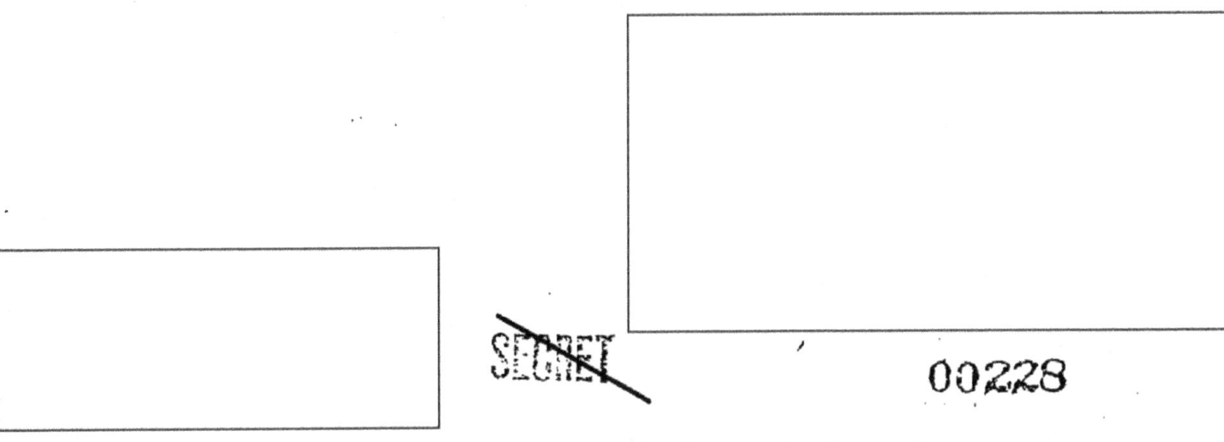

SECRET

00228

CONTACTS WITH OTHER U.S. GOVERNMENT AGENCIES WHICH COULD OR HAVE RESULTED IN USE OF CIA-DEVELOPED TECHNOLOGY IN ADDRESSING DOMESTIC PROBLEMS

Executive Office of the President

ORD represents DD/S&T on the R&D Sub-Committee of the Cabinet Committee for International Narcotics Control that is concerned with research support of the narcotics control problem.

(Dr. Leonard Laster, OST)

Office of Telecommunications Policy

Technical surveillance countermeasures and physical security information was exchanged with them.

Bureau of Narcotics and Dangerous Drugs (BNDD)

Techniques and equipment for navigation and tracking was discussed with BNDD.

BNDD)

BNDD)

Audio tapes were processed to improve their intelligibility. The source of the tapes was unknown.

BNDD)

00229

SUBJECT: Contacts With Other U.S. Government Agencies Which Could or Have Resulted In Use of CIA-Developed Technology in Addressing Domestic Problems

BNDD (cont'd)

BNDD was given permission in the fall of 1972 to receive proposals from Aerospace, Inc., concerning a Radar People Detector developed for OSD.

BNDD)

BNDD)

USIB Technical Surveillance Countermeasures Committee

Continuing contacts were maintained with the intelligence community regarding technical surveillance countermeasurs and physical security. This exchange of information, reports, and equipment has been conducted under the auspices of USIB TSCC and involves State, FBI, Secret Service, NSA, DIA, Army, AF, and Navy.

State Department

Two contracts for development of countermeasures techniques were funded jointly with the State Department.

00230

SECRET

SUBJECT: Contacts With Other U.S. Government Agencies Which Could or Have Resulted In Use of CIA-Developed Technology In Addressing Domestic Problems

Atomic Energy Commission (AEC)

Some of the AEC Laboratories, e.g., Savannah River Laboratory, are supported by CIA to develop radio nuclide sampling and detection techniques and devices. These Laboratories have used sampling techniques developed for CIA to measure CONUS nuclear plant releases.

(Mr. B. Benson, AEC)

At the request of AEC Security Officer, Mr. Richard Cowan, the walls of the office of the Chairman of the AEC (then Mr. Schlesinger) were X-rayed. The operation occurred one evening and was an attempt to resolve some anomalies created by the use of the

(Mr. Richard Cowan, AEC)

Law Enforcement Assistance Agency (LEAA)

Reports and information about the ORD-developed Adhesive Restraint, Non-Lethal Incapacitation System were made available to Department of Justice, LEAA in August 1972. If they developed the system, it would be used for civilian crowd and riot control.

(Mr. Les Schubin, LEAA)

Technical surveillance countermeasures and physical security information were exchanged with LEAA.

00231

SECRET

SUBJECT: Contacts With Other U.S. Government Agencies Which Could or Have Resulted In Use of CIA-Developed Technology in Addressing Domestic Problems

Treasury

[redacted] is being detailed to Treasury Department to assist in formulating their R&D program and organization in anticipation of the establishment of the new drug enforcement administration. The request for his services was made by [redacted] the Agency's Narcotics Coordinator. Mr. [redacted] discussed the request and cleared the detailing through Mr. Colby.

Customs/Treasury Department

Technical discussions were held with Customs relating to detecting illicit nighttime aircraft intrusions over the U.S.-Mexico border.

(Mr. Martin Pera, Customs)

Alcohol & Tobacco Tax Div/IRS

About five years ago, assistance was requested in domestic search of "moonshine" stills using CIA infrared scanners. This was turned down.

Secret Service

We have had numerous discussions with the Secret Service regarding navigation and tracking techniques and equipment.

4

00232

SUBJECT: Contacts With Other U.S. Government Agencies Which Could or Have Resulted In Use of CIA-Developed Technology in Addressing Domestic Problems

Federal Aviation Agency (FAA)

The results of our research work in the detection of metals [redacted] were reported to FAA for possible use in the detection of hijacker weapons.

National Institute of Health (NIH)

At the request of ORD, OCS assigned a staff technician to undertake to write a computer program for the Wisswesser Line Notation (WLN) chemical notation method. This work was done in cooperation with NIH.

(Ms. Conivcr, NIH)

Arms Control and Disarmament Agency (ACDA)

[redacted] ORD met frequently with ACDA personnel in order to structure ORD's BW/CW research programs to support ACDA needs.

Environmental Protection Agency (EPA)

Technical information relating to detection of radio nuclides in the environment was exchanged with them.

(Mr. Charles Weaver, EPA)

00233

SECRET

SUBJECT: Contacts With Other U.S. Government Agencies Which Could or Have Resulted In Use of CIA-Developed Technology in Addressing Domestic Problems

EPA (cont'd)

Technical discussions relating to using IR scanning equipment to detect underground fires in a sanitary land fill have been conducted.

(Mr. Gene James, EPA)

Federal Bureau of Investigation

At their request, we described Imagery Enhancement techniques germane to removing distortions from some photography they had on an alleged bank robber. Request for specific support in processing the imagery was turned down.

Secret Service
FBI
U.S. Customs

total contact with other agencies in terms of assistance with domestic operations has been in the field of audio surveillance countermeasures, anti-hijacking, or drugs.

(Mr. Robert Burnell, SS)
(Mr. Thomas Allen, FBI)
(Mr. Martin Pera, Customs)

NASA and USDA

We have an on-going program, to for earth resources assessments.

(Mr. William Ruble, USDA)
(Mr. Leonard Jaffe, NASA)
(General Smart)

00234

SECRET

SUBJECT: Contacts With Other U.S. Government Agencies Which Could or Have Resulted In Use of CIA-Developed Technology in Addressing Domestic Problems

Proposed Use of NASA ERTS Satellite (Agency association would be SECRET)

The Agency is preparing a proposal for an experimental program to aid in estimating the Soviet wheat crop. A part of the information would be obtained from a satellite launched for other announced programs. Ground-truth data will be collected on North American crops.

U.S. Department of Agriculture and Bureau of Narcotics and Dangerous Drugs

CIA has requested the establishment of a two-acre plot of opium poppies at a USDA research site in Washington state, to be used for tests of photo-recognition of opium poppies.

Army, Military Police Agency, Ft. Gordon
Air Force, Office of the Inspector General
Army, Office of Provost Marshall General

We have exchanged technical surveillance countermeasures and physical security information with them.

U.S. Army
Rocky Mountain Arsenal, Newport Army Ammunition Plant, Toelle Ordnance Depot

ORD tested environmental samples from testing, storage and production facilities in the U.S.

00235

SECRET

SUBJECT: Contacts With Other U.S. Government Agencies Which Could or Have Resulted In Use of CIA-Developed Technology in Addressing Domestic Problems

U.S. Army, Edgewood Arsenal

/ORD is sharing expenses with EA in field testing

U.S. Navy

U.S. Coast Guard

About six years ago, CIA infrared equipment was made available for USCG tests to evaluate IR as a means for night search of life boats.

(then-Lt. James McIntosh, USCG)

San Mateo County Sheriff's Office

ORD conducted polygraph tests on all applicants. Polygraph security findings were compared with the Sheriff's own security findings.

(Sheriff)

A study was made on con-men techniques and assessment methods in 1967-68.

(Sheriff)

00236

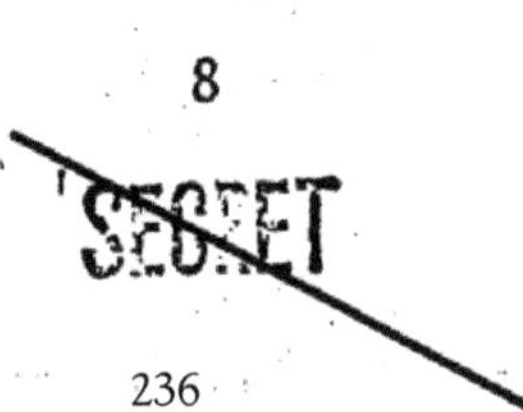

SUBJECT: Contacts With Other U.S. Government Agencies Which Could or Have Resulted In Use of CIA-Developed Technology in Addressing Domestic Problems

Chief, [redacted] Police

For security reasons, the Chief was made aware of a study to evaluate attempts [redacted] to penetrate [redacted] social groups. (1967)

(Police Chief)

9

SECRET

00237

DOMESTIC TESTS FOR
AGENCY RESEARCH AND DEVELOPMENT EFFORTS

1. As a normal part of ORD's efforts in the research and development of equipment and techniques for Agency applications in foreign intelligence, we conduct experiments and tests in the United States. Clearly, the design and development of our intelligence equipments can be done more economically and more securely in this country. Although most of the tests of our R&D equipments are performed in closed laboratories or in secure areas simulating the foreign environment, some of the tests and experiments, of necessity, reveal domestic information.

2. A review of the surveillance equipment or techniques which have at some time or other been exposed to domestic testing is as follows:

a. Laser Probe - About 1967, the laser probe developed by ORD was tested by TSD in San Francisco under very closely controlled conditions. The ORD Project Officer witnessed portions of the test. Recordings that were made of laser probe output were carefully controlled as classified material and it is believed that the tapes have long since been destroyed.

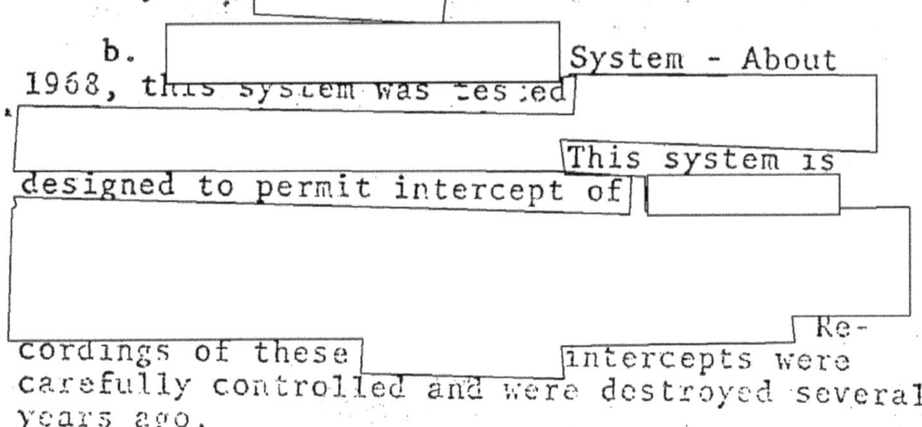

b. System - About 1968, this system was tested This system is designed to permit intercept of Recordings of these intercepts were carefully controlled and were destroyed several years ago.

ATTACHMENT 2

00238

SUBJECT: Domestic Tests for Agency Research and Development Efforts

c. Telephone Intrusion Study - [redacted] Many of these are patterned after the U.S. system and, for this reason, limited monitoring to test the operation of intercept equipment in the United States is planned. [redacted] Message content is of no interest and will not be recorded. Overseas testing is planned at a subsequent date. To date, some domestic testing of this concept has been carried out at the contractor's plant. No recordings have been made of such data. Extremely brief tests exercising U.S. and foreign telephone systems [redacted] have been carried out to verify initial concepts. The duration of testing was less than one-half hour.

d. Other Sensor Testing - Examples of engineering development tests of special sensors within the United States include [redacted] and [redacted] In all these cases, the data output of such testing has been used for engineering development and the content has been restricted to dissemination to those in Government involved with the engineering design.

SECRET

00239

e. Remote Physiological Measurements - An ORD-developed [redacted] is being tested at a contractor's site for use as a remote cardiograph [redacted] Some test subjects are witting, but most tests are on naive subjects (they do not know they are being tested). The [redacted] is completely harmless to the subject and the test results are closely held.

f. Personality Structure of Defectors Study - ORD undertook to determine the personality structure of defectors during the period 1966-69. The work primarily involved an analysis of the open literature on known defectors. An ancillary effort was concerned with a study of the phenomenon of defection itself, i.e., leaving one religion for another, or changing one set of political beliefs for another. The work was conducted at Stanford University. [redacted]

g. [redacted]

h. Communications Link Loading Study - [redacted] Under carefully controlled conditions, some U. S. microwave communications were recorded and passed through the intercept system under test to prove quality of performance. All intercept material connected with this was destroyed within a few weeks of the time of intercept and the material was never checked for substantive content. [redacted]

SECRET

00240

ORD-2274-73

7 May 1973

MEMORANDUM FOR: Deputy Director for Science and Technology

SUBJECT : Survey of ORD for Non-Foreign Intelligence Activities

At 11 a.m. today, each division and staff chief or his representative was instructed to query all of his people and report back by this afternoon whether or not they had provided any services or dealt with any other agencies on domestic, non-foreign matters. The attached list is an inventory of all items we were able to uncover. If additional information on any of these topics is desired, we can provide either a verbal or a written report on very short notice.

Scientific Advisor
to
Director of Research & Development

Attachment:
As stated

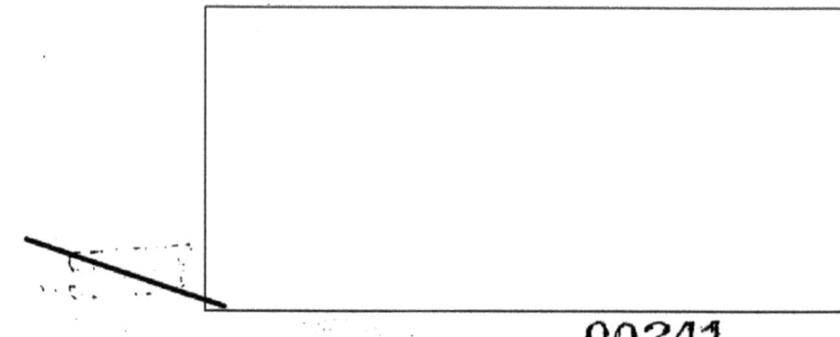

00241

Project [redacted] an on-going program which may be politically sensitive.

A proposed OER wheat estimate program which may be politically sensitive.

Narcotics--our foreign activities are well known in DDS&T.

A negative report from the Support Staff.

ORD's [redacted] work was reported to the FAA about three years ago. No action was taken, to our knowledge.

[redacted] Performed intelligibility enhancement of audio tapes for BNDD. Source of tapes unknown.

[redacted] - At the request of FBI, we described Imagery Enhancement Techniques germane to removing distortions from some photography they had on an alleged bank robber. Request for specific support in processing the imagery was turned down.

00242

7 May 1973

My total contact with other agencies in terms of assistance with domestic operations has been in the field of audio surveillance countermeasures, anti-hijacking, or drugs. Specifically, I participated in TSCC and R&D Subcommittee meetings which included technology exchanges and some equipment exchanges on a temporary basis ostensibly for testing or trial. I also assisted in x-raying the office walls of the Chairman of the AEC (then Mr. Schlesinger) at the request of Mr. Richard Cowan of AEC Security. The operation occurred one evening (date unknown) and was an attempt to resolve some anomalies created by the use of the

Other persons contacted over the years have been:

Mr. Robert Burnett, Secret Service

Mr. Martin Pera, U. S. Customs

Mr. Marvin Beasley, DASA

Mr. Thomas Allen, FBI

Major Jack Nelson, OSI/USAF

Major John Langager, ONI/USN

Mr. Richard Cowan, AEC

00243

5/7/73

1. Continuing contacts with intelligence community regarding technical surveillance countermeasures and physical security. This is an exchange of information and reports and has been conducted under the auspices of the USIB Technical Surveillance Countermeasures Community.

State
Air Force
Army
DIA
FBI
Navy
US Secret Service
NSA

2. Joint funding of two contracts with State Department (TRW/LLL). Two electret microphones were furnished to State Department for test purposes. Joint funding of one contract with NSA (Sandia). Participation in DNA/DOD contract (Bureau of Standards).

3. Other DOD and Government contacts for information collection or exchange only.

ARPA
LEAA/Dept. of Justice
DNA/DOD
Office Telecommunications Policy
Office of Army/Provost Marshal General
Army/Military Police Agency, Ft. Gordon
Air Force/Office of the Inspector General
Air Force/Electronic Systems Division

SECRET

00244

[redacted] has had communications with the Secret Service and the Bureau of Narcotics regarding navigation and tracking.

00245

OS&P—Contacts with Other U.S. Government Agencies which Could Have Resulted in Use of CIA-Developed Technology in Addressing Domestic Problems

EPA

- Exchange of technical information relating to detection of radio nuclides in the environment

- Technical discussions relating to using IR scanning equipment to detect underground fires in a sanitary land fill.

BNDD

- Exchange of technical information relating to the development of

USDA & BNDD

- CIA has requested the establishment of a two-acre plot of opium poppies at a USDA research site in Washington state, to be used for tests of photo-recognition of opium poppies.

US COAST GUARD

- About six years ago, CIA infrared equipment was made available for USCG tests to evaluate IR as a means for night search of life boats.

ALCOHOL & TOBACCO TAX DIV/IRS

- About five years ago assistance was requested in domestic search of "moonshine" stills using CIA infrared scanners. This was turned down.

SECRET

00246

[illegible]/TREASURY DEPT.

- Technical discussions relating to detecting illicit nighttime aircraft intrusions over the U.S.-Mexico border.

AEC

- Some of the AEC Laboratories, e.g. Savannah River Laboratory, are supported by CIA to develop radio nuclide sampling and detection techniques and devices. These Laboratories have used sampling techniques developed for CIA to measure CONUS nuclear plant releases.

2

00247

SECRET

7 May 1973

ORD CONTACTS WITH DOMESTIC CIVIL AGENCIES

1. BNDD(Charles Caskin) was given permission to receive proposals from Aerospace, Inc., concerning a Radar People Detector developed for ORD. Time: Fall of 1972. Action was approved by D/ORD.

2.

3. Developed Adhesive Restraint, Non-lethal Incapacitation System. Reports and information was made available to Department of Justice, LEAA in August 1972. If they developed the system, it would be used for civilian crowd and riot control.

00248

[illegible] -71

2 [illegible] 1971

MEMORANDUM FOR THE RECORD

SUBJECT: Processing Noisy Audio Tapes for Bureau of Narcotics Dangerous Drug Division

1. On 1 November 1971, Mr. Charles Gaskins of the Bureau of Narcotics Dangerous Drug Division called to request the assistance of ORD/[illegible]/SAW to improve the intelligibility of several tape recorded conversations. Mr. Gaskins had been employed by the Agency in the Technical Security Division and had become aware of the speech processing capability in the SAW laboratory through his Agency work. I suggested that he bring the tapes to the laboratory to determine the feasibility of enhancing the subject conversations.

2. On 2 November 1971, Mr. Gaskins appeared at the SAW laboratory with a tape containing a number of conversations recorded through legal wiretapping. The tape was to be used in the prosecution of one of the subject speakers on or about 4 November 1971. A cursory analysis indicated that most of the conversations could be made more intelligible through the processing available in the laboratory. In view of the time critical nature of the request, processing was begun immediatel However, Mr. Gaskins was informed that future processing might need to be handled more formally, i.e., with approval from higher levels within the Agency. If similar requests would be occuring on a frequent basis I suggested that BNDD personnel could be trained in the use of the processing system.

00249

1 MAY 1972

MEMORANDUM FOR THE RECORD

SUBJECT: Processing of Audio Tape for Bureau of Narcotics Dangerous Drug Division

1. On 13 April 1972 Mr. Charles Gaskins of the Bureau of Narcotics and Dangerous Drugs requested SAW/An/ORD assistance to improve the intelligibility of an audio tape that had been acquired by BNDD agents.

00250

SUBJECT: Processing of Audio Tape for Bureau of Narcotics Dangerous Drug Division

00251

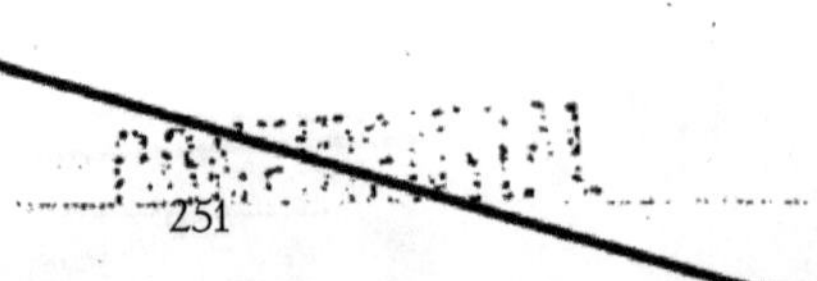

4 August 1972

MEMORANDUM FOR THE RECORD

SUBJECT: Assistance to Bureau of Narcotics: Enhancement of Noisy Audio Tape Recordings

1. On 7 June 1972, Mr. Marc R. Weiss of Federal Scientific Corp. (FSC) requested the cooperation of SAW in the processing of a noisy audio tape he had received from the Baltimore Regional Office of BNDD. Mr. John Bullard, Regional Director, had contacted Mr. Weiss to aid BNDD in the enhancement of the conversations on the tape recording which were masked by background music. The results of the processing will be used in a grand jury investigation and possible follow-on trial. Mr. Bullard did not indicate how he had become aware of Mr. Weiss's expertise in this area.

00252

SUBJECT: Assistance to Bureau of Narcotics: Enhancement of Noisy Audio Tape Recordings

ORD/DD/S&T

00253

WORKING PAPER ~~TOP SECRET~~

7 May 1973

MEMORANDUM FOR: Deputy Director for Science and Technology

SUBJECT: Telecon this morning concerning any OSA activities which could put the Agency into an embarrassing situation.

1. There are no missions which we have flown during the last four years with which I can associate the result directly to any activity potentially embarrassing to the Agency. There were a number of missions flown that indirectly have the potential for this embarrassment. Bear in mind that once we turn the film over to NPIC or any other agency, we have no control over subsequent distribution.

2. The missions listed on the attachment are in three categories:

a. Category A: These are missions flown in the U. S. that are very similar to the potential that you discussed with me using the example of the Santa Barbara oil disaster.

b. Category B: The (detection of illicit poppy grove) is a separate category because of the high sensitivity of this subject.

c. Category C: When we were developing LONG SHAFT, the In effect, we were Although to our knowledge nothing sensitive was picked up, in the broad sense this activity could be labeled illegal.

3. I have specifically looked to see where our U-2's were operating during the Watergate break-in discovery, Democratic National

~~TOP SECRET~~ 00254

Convention and Republican National Convention. All the above events occurred in the East and our aircraft on their missions during this time period was in the western part of the U. S.

WENDELL L. BEVAN, JR.
Brigadier General, USAF
Director of Special Activities

Attachment - 1
As noted above

TOP SECRET

00255

~~TOP SECRET~~

TASK	BY WHOM/WHEN	POSSIBLE IMPLICATION
CATEGORY A		
Santa Barbara Oil Disaster	Dept. of Interior. Feb 1969.	Potential for providing basis for criminal law suits. Pressure on oil company to change operation.
HILLTOP ( )	ORD/NASA Earth Resources Programs. Spring/Fall 1969	Possible use for industrial exploitation. Crop production control & estimates future market.
Snow Survey	Environmental Science Services Administration (ESSA), Dept. of Commerce thru COMIREX. Spring 1969.	Industrial exploitation. Water resource allocation.
Hurricane Base Line	Office of Economic Preparedness. Spring 1970.	Political leverage for disaster area funds.
Earthquake Damage	Self generated, NPIC processed. Feb 1971.	Political leverage. Criminal negligence suits. Reconstruction exploitation.
Minneapolis - Kansas City	OSI/AEC Division. Jan - Mar 1972.	Environmental applications, urban planning; exploitation.

~~TOP SECRET~~

00256

~~TOP SECRET~~

TASK	BY WHOM/WHEN	POSSIBLE IMPLICATION
CATEGORY A (continued)		
RIVER BOAT ([illegible])	NRO - ICRS. April 1973.	Political leverage. Industrial exploitation, civil damage suits.
West Virginia Dam Site Coverage	NRO - Army Corps of Engineers. Jan/Feb 1973.	Potential for real estate exploitation, water control.
CATEGORY B		
(Puerto Rico), Multi Spectral Sensor	BNDD, DDI/CIA, NPIC, ORD. Dept. of Agriculture. Fall 1972.	CIA extension of dope trafficking from SEA to CONUS. Better techniques to avoid detection of growth.
CATEGORY C		
LONG SHAFT	NSA/CIA COMINT collection.	

~~TOP SECRET~~

00257

Re Watergate question of this morning, the following called in:

[redacted] - contacted all in office with exception of four on TDY-- results negative

[redacted] - contacted all but two who were on leave--negative.

Parangosky -- negative on those he could contact. Following are people he could not reach:

[redacted]

[redacted] said FMSAC has negative results.

00258

OLC 73-0635

6 June 1973

MEMORANDUM FOR: Deputy Director for Science & Technology

SUBJECT: Correspondence Received by Chairman Hebert, House Armed Services Committee, Concerning [redacted]

The attached letter from Chairman Hebert, House Armed Services Committee, together with the enclosure from [redacted] [redacted] is forwarded for your information and such action as you deem appropriate. I have rechecked the Committee staff and have been advised that absolutely no response to Hebert's letter is expected.

[redacted]

Assistant Legislative Counsel

Atts

NOTE: This memo dtd 6 June 73 (OLC 73-0635) (pgs 259 thru 265) was sent to the IG for his information and was not considered a part of the DDS&T components' submissions to the IG in response to the Director's request on "Questionable Activities" and, therefore, it is believed that these documents should not be included in the Halperin request.

00259

U.S. House of Representatives
COMMITTEE ON ARMED SERVICES
Washington, D.C. 20515

NINETY-THIRD CONGRESS
F. EDWARD HÉBERT, CHAIRMAN

May 29, 1973

The Honorable James R. Schlesinger
Director
Central Intelligence Agency
Washington, D. C.

Dear Mr. Schlesinger:

Attached is correspondence from [redacted] [redacted] which is forwarded for information and whatever action might be appropriate.

With best regards.

Sincerely,

F. Edw. Hebert
Chairman

FEH:whb

Attachment

00260

OEL-010-73

MEMORANDUM FOR: Deputy Director for Science and Technology

SUBJECT: Policy Regarding Assistance to Agencies Outside the Intelligence Community on Speech Processing Problems

1. Recent public concern over Agency affiliations with law enforcement activities has made me wary of offering speech processing assistance to various other government agencies. My concern here is restricted to government activities outside the intelligence community. Because of a scientific community awareness of the expertise of members of OEL in speech processing problems, we are often asked by individuals in government for help on various speech problems. The requests are usually informal on a person-to-person basis. While most of these contacts involve only an exchange of unclassified information, several have involved the use of laboratory resources.

2. Contacts have come from the FBI, Attorney General's office, Bureau of Narcotics and Dangerous Drugs (BNDD), Post Office, and the Treasury Department. Of the above, assistance to BNDD had been specifically sanctioned by Mr. Helms. In one recent instance where a noisy tape was to be used in a court case, care was taken to insure that the processing of the tape was done entirely by a BNDD employee even though it was done in an Agency laboratory using the Agency's Coherent Spectrum Shaper equipment.

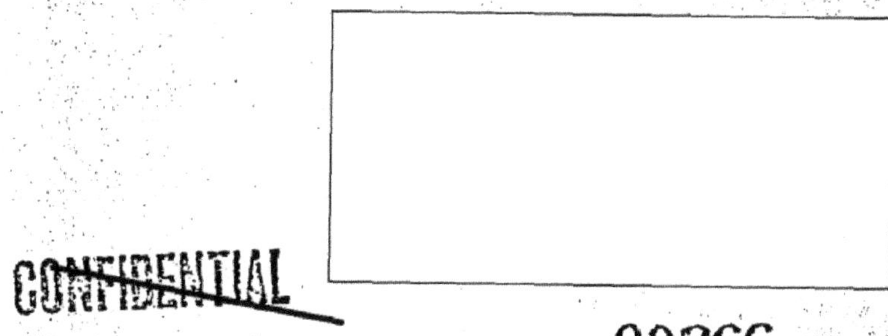

CONFIDENTIAL

00266

OEL-010-73
Page 2

3. Providing services of this kind to other agencies has not as yet imposed a significant workload on us and there is a benefit to us in that such contact enables the staff to test techniques and equipment on a variety of speech problems. Informal interactions at the technical level are fruitful in terms of helping us to accomplish Agency goals. Hence we would be willing to continue to support other departments on an ad hoc basis, but would appreciate your guidance re the wisdom of OEL's involvement in "domestic" activities.

JOHN N. MCMAHON
Director of ELINT
DD/S&T

CONFIDENTIAL

00267

Colby 13 05

Whistle if need people

News acct on burglary at Chilean Emb. Any ref to Hunt?
Send copy to [redacted]

00268

- Against whom do these agents work, on what do they report, and to whom?

1 Get copies of the reports on "Restless Youth" and black radicalism.

16x How is the cryogenic magnetometer used, on whom, and for what purpose?

2 Get copies of the reports on IOS.

7 Why does DCS collect information on What is done with it?

8 Why is DCS getting for whom, and for what purpose?

5 Get a rundown on

9 Give me a couple of paragraphs on Tofte.

3 Include the submission of FR Division.

10 Get the full story on providing alias documentation to the Secret Service.

14X Why did we pay the costs of the responses to letters received about the President's speech on Cambodia?

11 Supplying beacons to Ambassadors seems like a good idea. How many ~~MMMMMMM~~ are there in use and where?

12 Why is Logistics procuring police-type equipment for local police forces?

13 What is a telephone analyzer?

15X Why is it necessary ~~M~~ to continue

4 More on Vesco. How did it get started? What was done? Why was it stopped?

2 What were the multiple channels to CIA on the IOS matter?

DD –

1972 – 8 sets US alias Docs to Secret Service. (OS)

Beacons to Ambassadors.

OS –

OS – WOG's acquisition of police equip.

OS – What is a telephone analyzer

DDI –

Why continue [redacted]

~~OER~~ –

Vesco. How started? Why stopped.

?l –

What were multiple channels re IOS. USE CI Submission

File Coleman –

00270

Follow-ups

XEROX CI re IOS. Attach the six reports

XEROX FRD in its entirety.

00271

Tom Yale —

Will send copies re docs on postage for Cambodia speech letters.

00273

2 –

1 –

+ –

1 –

~~None issued + notes~~

All orig users still have.

Not surfaced to locals except in [redacted] recent highest levels.

~~thru~~ DCI

was off CIA rolls when WH consultant last summer.

CIA in touch with

00274

later moved to BNDD.

00275

Osborn —

April 71 - Wanted to use in convention. Wanted $ more. No follow up w/o letter.

00276

8 Sets of US alias docs to S/S.

Called [redacted] out.

Called Howard Osborn. Out.

[redacted] — 1315

13 Apr 72 memo from D/SS. Need for alias pocket litter. 8 sets as soon as poss. Will be stringently ~~security~~ controlled.

12 July 72 TSD passed docs to [redacted]. Non backstopped. 4 sets. Passed 14 July 72. by CSCI memo. Must be returned. No tell bearer CIA. Flash only. Not to rent or op motor vehicle.

S/S has undercover agents. ~~Protection of Pres. Use is both Nat-Cons.~~

00277

~~27 Dec~~ 29 Dec 72

Ltr AID/SS to Tom K.

Wanted 2 add sets. Will be used for intel coll ass by agents in Intel Div. Not aware of origin. No uso unless absol nec. Stringently controlled. Tom K. approved. Passed by asd memo.

00278

Bruce Clarke —

Bill Christeson, SAVA, in Bldg. Clarke called Bill. He knew subject + would take care of.

00279

Krueger.
11 including Helms. All overseas.
2 COS in past but not now.
Checked out mentally. All WRONG
with liaison for air support.
Izek + Find. Will confirm.

Mulholland —
Has report to DCI re
Vesco. Will → copy.

Walsh —
Will come up with
something on [redacted]

Joe O'Neill — 1577
Houston: content of memo
in Colby's folder

00280

00281

30 May 73

9 July 1970

The Director advised the DD/I that White House staffer Houston and Presidential Counsellor Pat Moynihan thought well of the memorandum on "Black Radicalism in the Caribbean."

10 July 1970

Maury briefed on his meeting yesterday with Congressman Richard Ichord, Chairman of the House Internal Security Committee, who had asked what we are doing to investigate "security leaks" connected with press accounts of Lon Nol's having sold rice to the Communists and having engaged in an attempted deal with Hanoi. Maury briefed on his explanation of why we are doing nothing, since such reports are not exclusively confined to our information.

1 September 1970

Maury noted that the Director sent a letter to Congressman Moss on telephone monitoring practices.

3 September 1970

The Director noted a 1 September memorandum from John Bross on Daniel Elsperg (sic). He asked the DDS to lift his clearances and to make this fact known in security channels.

15 October 1970

DDS reported that the Weathermen have declared this month for their fall offensive and have mentioned the Agency as a target for bombings and kidnapping. He briefed on precautionary measures adopted and asked senior officers to vary their route to and from work, and to report any peculiar telephone calls or unusual events around their residence.

28 October 1970

DDP reported that the FBI desires to check for fingerprints on all cryptogram messages mailed to high Government officials. The messages will then be passed to NSA for exploitation. DDP requested that Agency personnel who receive such messages pass them to him for transmittal to the FBI.

Copy given to
Bon Evans
5/30/73

00282

10 December 1970

DDI noted press accounts of FBI Director J. Edgar Hoover's 19 November statement that the Black Panthers are supported by terrorist organizations. He said that we have examined the FBI's related files and our own data and find no indication of any relationship between the fedayeen and the Black Panthers. He provided the Director with a memorandum on this topic.

23 December 1970

Executive Director called attention to the President's 21 December memorandum on "Disclosures of Classified Information and Coordination and Clearance of Official Statements," which is believed to be the result of representations by the Director and Admiral Anderson. Executive Director said that he will meet with selected Executive Committee Members next week to discuss the memorandum's implications and to develop recommendations for action by the Director in view of the special responsibilities placed on him by the President.

29 December 1970

Executive Director reminded Executive Committee participants about the meeting involving most of them this morning on the President's directive on disclosure of classified information.

30 December 1970

Executive Director briefed on the results of yesterday's meeting on what the Director now needs to do in pursuance of the Presidenc's directive on disclosure of classified information. He will outline in the Director's briefing book actions which are to be taken.

00283

14 January 1971

Bross said that he and Bronson Tweedy will have lunch today with General Bennett, Director of DIA. The Director said that he might ask Bross to take along a copy of his letter and guidance on the Disclosures of Classified Information and Coordination and Clearance of Official Statements but that he first wishes to clarify with the Executive Director some of the language in the guidance section.

18 January 1971

Maury said that he anticipates a number of questions from the Hill on the attached article by Jack Anderson in today's Washington Post, "6 Attempts to Kill Castro Laid to CIA."

Houston related that he will have lunch today with Assistant Attorney General Robert C. Mardian to discuss the Director's guidelines on the disclosure of classified information.

Bross related that Parrott met with General Bennett to review the Director's letter on disclosure of classified information and said that General Bennett will now discuss it with Deputy Secretary Packard, who may in turn review it with Secretary Laird. The Director asked to be advised of Secretary Packard's reactions and said that he wants to check the final guidance with Secretary Laird and with someone in the White House before it is issued.

23 February 1971

DD/P called attention to Jack Anderson's column in today's Washington Post, "Castro Stalker Worked For The CIA."

00284

1 July 1971

"Carver noted that Secretary Laird had requested that our printing plant assist in reproducing the forty-seven-volume secret Pentagon study on Vietnam for distribution to the press and others this morning. This request was aborted by the President." (DDCI in the chair)

2 July 1971

"DD/S said that in the absence of [redacted] attended a meeting at the White House yesterday of the interagency group which is reviewing classification and declassification policy. The President spent an hour with the group and said that he wants: ... and (6) the revocation of all clearances and the return of all classified material held at Harvard, Brookings, Rand, and Cal Tech, as well as the withdrawal of Q clearances held by the Regents of the University of California. A brief discussion followed, and the Executive Director noted that DOD has asked us to provide information on all our contracts with Rand, as well as all clearances held by Rand personnel for our purposes. Acting Director asked that we assemble data pertaining to the President's remarks but that we take no action until the President's guidance has been confirmed and the DD/S has provided a memorandum on it." (DDCI in the chair)

"Carver reported that they will probably complete their detailed review of the secret Pentagon papers by 6 July."

"Warner called attention to Secretary Rogers' request that the press permit the Government to review in advance potentially damaging documents from the Pentagon papers."

SECRET

6 July 1971

"Carver said that their review of the secret Pentagon study on Vietnam has almost been completed."

00285

7 July 1971

"Carver said that he will be attending a meeting today called by Assistant Secretary of Defense for Public Affairs Daniel Henkin. He added that he assumes it will concern the declassification of some of the secret Pentagon papers and that, if it does, he will seek the Director's advice." (DDCI in chai

"At the Executive Director's request, the DD/S agreed to get together with the DD/S&T and General Counsel to prepare a briefing paper for the Director on where we stand with respect to classified materials at Rand and efforts to safeguard them."

"Maury reported that Congressman Mahon would like to meet with the Director on 9 July to discuss the Pentagon papers and various world hot spots Carver said that he will prepare a briefing paper for the Director on the Pentagon study."

"Carver briefly noted [redacted] concern over the revelations in the Lansdale memorandum, which was surfaced as part of the Pentagon papers."

8 July 1971

"DD/S reported that a DOD security team is going to Santa Monica to repossess classified Defense materials held at Rand. He suggested that,

rather than take parallel action, we send a Security Officer to observe the operation and inventory Agency materials in the possession of Rand. In response to the Director's question he explained that we have seven contracts with Rand; only one is classified, and it is with Rand's Washington office, although some material could have been sent to Santa Monica. The Director concurred and requested a review to determine the essentiality of current proposed contracts with Rand. Houston commented that according to DOD General Counsel Buzhardt, DOD is technically under instructions to lift the security clearances of Rand contractors but has taken no action. DDCI reported that John Ehrlichman had telephoned to advise us that the White House is appointing former CIA employee Howard Hunt as a security consultant. Later in the meeting the Director asked all Executive Committee members to review their lists of consultants to determine whether each is really needed."

"Carver briefed on his meeting yesterday with Assistant Secretary of Defense for Public Affairs Daniel Henkin and noted that any further excisions from the text of the secret Pentagon papers must be provided by Monday. He added that no decision has yet been made on whether to release to the public the volumes or a version thereof. The Director noted that we should oppose any such course of action."

00286

<u>16 July 1971</u>

Carver said that [redacted] was most appreciative of the time which Houston spent with him yesterday.

00287

9 July 1971

"In response to the Director's question Carver reported that none of [redacted] contained in the secret Pentagon papers has yet appeared in the New York Times. He added, however, that the Soviet Embassy has a complete copy of the forty-seven volumes [redacted]

16 July 1971

"Carver reported that the book which General Lansdale has been writing for a year and a half is now in the hands of the publisher, with some minor changes being made in light of revelations resulting from the publication of the secret Pentagon papers. In response to the DD/P's question Carver said that he might be able to arrange for us to read the text."
(DDCI in the chair)

"Tweedy noted that at White House request a PFIAB committee composed of Franklin Lincoln, Dr. William Baker, ad Frank Pace will undertake a damage assessment of the publication of the secret Pentagon papers. He added that the committee will want to hear from us and spoke of plans for Houston and Carver to undertake this task."

20 July 1971

"Tweedy reported on a telephone call from Andy Marshall and said that Marshall and Rand President Henry Rowen are brooding about the security problem in Rand. Marshall expressed a desire to talk with one of our senior security officers when he next visits Washington in order to get a feel for security practices in general. Executive Director advised against our getting out front in terms of advising a major DOD contractor on security. The Director approved and requested that re respond to Mr. Marshall's request in low key and that the meeting be held in this building."

22 July 1971 (the day Howard Hunt came to see General Cushman)

"Carver highlighted his session yesterday with NSC staffer David Young, who is assisting John Ehrlichman in reviewing the secret Pentagon papers."

23 July 1971

"Carver highlighted his, Houston's, and [redacted] session with the PFIAB committee which is undertaking a damage assessment of the publication of the secret Pentagon papers. (See Morning Meeting Minutes of 16 July 1971.)

6 August 1971

The Director called attention to the article by Michael Getler in today's Washington Post, "CIA Patrols Into China Said Halted," and directed (1) that Maury write a letter for his signature to Senator Stennis making it clear that Senator Case was briefed on this topic and obviously leaked it; (2) that Maury brief Carl March on the background, including the fact that these operations were not terminated because of the President's projected trip to Communist China but because certain aspects of them were previously exposed in the press; (3) that the Director of Security (who was present at the Morning Meeting) get additional background from Maury and see White House staffer David Young; (4) that Goodwin reply to queries by saying that we know nothing about this matter; (5) that Houston and Maury utilize this incident in any material prepared for his use in opposing the Cooper bill; and (6) that the DDCI brief Dr. Kissinger or General Haig on this matter today.

** 13 August 1971

Knoche called attention to the article by Tad Szulc in today's New York Times, "Soviet Move to Avert War Is Seen in Pact with India," and said that the material contained therein on the reason for Foreign Minister Gromyko's visit to New Delhi is clearly from highly classified CS material. The A-DDP noted his concern over this breach of security.

16 August 1971

A-DDP noted that the article by Tad Szulc in Sunday's New York Times, "Attempted Pro-Soviet Coup in Yemen is Reported," contains information from a TDCS. The Director asked that he call this to the attention of White House staffer David Young.

00289

18 August 1971

A-DDP noted that he has reported to White House staffer David Young on the results of the Deputy Director of Security's survey of those who saw the classified assessment upon which Tad Szulc based his 13 August article (see Morning Meeting Minutes of 13 August 1971). **

19 August 1971

"Maury briefed on White House staffer John Lehman's request for our assistance in determining what four volumes of the secret Pentagon papers Senator Gravel reportedly provided to Beacon Press for publication. He noted that Paul Chretien of OTR is an acquaintance of the Senator and may be able to assist. Carver said that the four volumes probably pertain to efforts to negotiate a settlement and outlined the sensitive material contained therein. Houston recommended against our involvement in this matter and suggested that the Department of Justice query Beacon Press. Maury said that the Director instructed that we do nothing until Maury consults with Clark MacGregor, Counsel to the President for Legislative and Congressional Affairs, who is out of town and will not return until the first of next week. In the meantime, Maury noted that he will determine from John Lehman whether they have considered consulting the Department of Justice on this matter." (DDCI in the chair)

20 August 1971

"Maury said that he called White House staffer John Lehman yesterday and cited the Code which would permit the Justice Department to go after the four volumes of the secret Pentagon papers reportedly given to Beacon Press. Lehman's reaction was that, since there is an existing policy preventing the use of subpoenas on this matter, he still hopes we will assist in determining what Senator Gravel may have given Beacon Press. The DDCI asked Maury not to utilize Paul Chretien's entree to the Senator without prior consultation with the Director, and Carver commented that he is opposed to our involvement (see Morning Meeting Minutes of 19 August 1971." (DDCI in the chair)

---

23 August 1971

"The Director reviewed for Houston a conversation he had with a young lawyer who has reviewed the secret Pentagon papers in response to the Justice Department's efforts to prosecute. According to this attorney, Justice did not cite the appropriate provisions of the Code and has presented its case poorly."

10 November 1971

Lehman said that this is "leak day" in the Washington Post and called attention to the following articles: "Mao's Heir, Lin, Apparently Out in Power Shuffle" by Stanley Karnow, "North Vietnam's Next Move" by Evans/Novak, and "Lin Piao is 'Finished'" by Joseph Alsop (attached). He noted that, while the article by Stanley Karnow provides good coverage of the topic, it has a State Department flavor. He also recalled that on 25 October we disseminated information similar to that contained in the Evans/Novak article. He mentioned that the Alsop article is probably the most damaging, since it includes material [redacted] The Director noted plans to do something about this problem but advised the A-DDP to cope with any adverse reaction [redacted] by noting the large volume of reports on the political situation in Communist China.

11 November 1971

In response to the Director's question Carver said that some work requested by John Ehrlichman is pending. The Director asked to be filled in later on the details.

20 December 1971

Lehman said that Jack Anderson's column in today's Washington Post, "Hussein: 'Help or I'll Go on a Ghazou'," contains verbatim language from an ExDis message from King Hussein to the President and added that he is looking into the distribution of this message.

28 December 1971

A-DDI called attention to Jack Anderson's columns in yesterday's and today's Washington Post (attached). He noted that the 27 December piece contained material from three SALT ExDis memcons and added that today's column contains quotes from a State LimDis cable and two TDCSs. A brief discussion followed, the DDP observing that, if these security breaches continue, we will have to limit severely the distribution of sensitive intelligence information.

00291

7 January 1972

Maury said that according to Frank Slatinshek, Chairman Nedzi will rely on us rather heavily for support during his hearings on the problem of classification and handling of Government information (see Morning Meeting Minutes of 6 January 1972). The Director encouraged Maury to see Chairman Nedzi next week, and Houston suggested that the Chairman be provided with the Rehnquist study.

DDP briefed on work under way to limit distribution of reports [redacted] and noted that C/FI is completing a review of steps which might be taken to restrict dissemination of sensitive reports from all sources.

11 January 1972

Maury related that Frank Slatinshek is pressing for background materials pertaining to past efforts or studies related to the classification and control of information. He added that he and Houston will meet with the Director later today to discuss the availability of the Rehnquist study.

12 January 1972

Maury briefed on his and Houston's session with Frank Slatinshek and their provision of a large volume of material on past efforts to develop effective espionage laws.

Houston noted the President's nomination of Henry E. Petersen to become Assistant Attorney General in charge of the Criminal Division of the Justice Department. He observed that Mr. Petersen has been most helpful to the Agency in the past, particularly on the Itkin case.

13 January 1972

Maury noted that the draft revision of Executive Order 10501, "Security Classification Procedures," which is being circulated by the NSD staff for comment, is a follow on to the Rehnquist study.

18 January 1972

DDI called attention to the article in today's New York Times, "Nixon Acts to End Security Leaks." (Excerpt: "Last July, two members of the White House staff, David R. Young of the National Security Council and Egil Krogh Jr. of the Domestic Council, were asked to investigate earlier leaks and prevent recurrences.")

00292

3 February 1972

A/DDS reported the House Appropriations Committee request for a finance officer to assist them in work on the budget. He added that we have provided such assistance in the past, and the Director interposed no objection.

7 February 1972

Houston explained that no action will be taken in the near future with respect to the Hans Tofte case, since the judge has been stricken with hepatitis.

8 February 1972

DDI noted the article by Michael Getler in Today's Washington Post, "New Spy Satellites Planned for Clearer, Instant Pictures." Later in the meeting the Director asked the DDS to advise the Director of Security to undertake an investigation of this leak of EOI-related information and to convene the USIB Security Committee.

11 February 1972

Carver noted his handling of White House staffer Sven Kraemer's request to FBIS for material concerning U.S. POW's. The Director reminded Executive Committee members of Dr. Kissinger's request that any inquiries from elements of the White House staff be referred to his staff for conveyance to the Agency.

Houston highlighted the meeting with John Ehrlichman on the NSC draft Executive Order on security classification. He noted the related article by Sanford Ungar in today's Washington Post, "NSC Urges Stiffer Law On Secrets."

16 February 1972

Lehman noted plans to continue briefing Attorney General Mitchell, whose resignation is effective 1 March.

Houston related that White House staffer David Young has invited him to review another draft of the new Executive Order on security classification.

28 February 1972

Houston said that he and [redacted] Deputy Director of Security, recommend the Director concur in the new Executive Order on classification, in light of their understanding with NSC staffer David Young, that some of the features of the Executive Order may not materialize. A brief discussion followed and the Director asked Houston to review the matter with him.

2 March 1972

Houston reported that the draft Executive Order on classification has undergone a few minor changes. He noted Director's letter to John Ehrlichman, dated 7 December 1971, with respect to our position on problems related to declassification and suggested that a copy be provided David Young, NSC staffer. After a brief discussion, the Director interposed no objection.

6 March 1972

The Director noted his memorandum to the Deputies and Independent Office Heads, subject: "Allegations of Assassinations." He asked that it be mentioned at Staff Meetings.

21 March 1972

The Director said that the President has seen his 17 February memorandum on reducing disclosures of classified intelligence and directed the White House staff to prepare a memorandum urging that all agencies comply with proper disclosure procedures.

22 March 1972

Houston reported that he is scheduled to meet with John Ehrlichman this morning.

23 March 1972

Maury reported that, after checking with Egil Krogh of the White House staff, he has made arrangements to brief Congressman Lester Wolff of New York on the Agency's role in international narcotics control.

00294

1 May 1972

DDS related that the Director of Security has received a request from the Secret Service to provide two technicians in support of the Vice President's trip to Tokyo. The Director concurred.

2 May 1972

DDS reported that the Director of Security has received a request from the Secret Service for counteraudio technicians to support the President's trip to Moscow. The Director concurred.

11 May 1972

Houston noted his correspondence with White House staffer David Young pertaining to our problems with Executive Order 11652 and added that Mr. Young has accepted our position on about 90 percent of our problems with the implementing draft directive.

24 May 1972

Houston explained that he had obtained White House Staffer David Young's understanding that we will not meet the 1 June deadline for producing internal Agency regulations implementing the NSC directove on Executive Order 11652. A brief discussion followed on the cumbersome bookkeeping and declassification authorities which may be required. The Director observed that the topic was sufficiently important for us to be in no great rush to meet a 1 June deadline and Houston assured him that Mr. Young understands.

6 June 1972

Thuermer explained that he will continue working with the General Counsel in response to Charles Nesson's efforts to serve a subpoena on him in connection with the Ellsberg case. He noted the related article by Robert A. Wright in today's New York Times, "Hearing Is Asked In Ellsberg Case."

7 June 1972

Houston noted a letter from the Justice Department conveying a subpoena directed to Angus Thuermer in connection with the Ellsberg case. He highlighted the schedule of documents requested, most of which were mentioned in footnotes to the Pentagon papers. He noted plans to ask Justice to declare the material irrelevant to the case.

00295

8 June 1972

Houston said that he will be attending a meeting called by DOD General Counsel Buzhardt, who is recommending that Justice drop the case against Daniel Ellsberg.

19 June 1972

The Director noted the 17 June arrest of James W. McCord and four others who were apprehended at the Democratic National Committee headquarters at the Watergate. With the Director of Security present to provide biographic details, the Director made it perfectly clear that responses to any inquiry with respect to McCord or Howard Hunt, who may be implicated, are to be limited to a statement that they are former employees who retired in August and April 1970 respectively. The Director asked that this guidance be disseminated via staff meetings. The Director asked that any inquiry from other elements of the government be referred to the Director of Security who is to be the focal point. Inquiries from the press are to be referred to Mr. Unumb who may say that McCord worked in the Office of Security. The Director noted that we have no responsibility with respect to an investigation except to be responsive to the FBI's request for name traces. It was noted that Howard Hunt may have done some work since retirement in connection with the preparation of supporting material for some awards. The Executive Director was asked to review this topic and report to the Director.

20 June 1972

In response to the Director's request, the Director of Security highlighted developments over the past twenty-four hours with respect to the McCord/Hunt, et al., situation. He noted that the late edition of the New York Times carries a different story by Tad Szulc than that which appeared in the edition received here (attached). The Director of Security anticipates some inquiries on Bernard L. Barker's situation, and it was noted that Mr. Barker was hired by the Agency in 1960 and terminated in 1966. The Director complimented Unumb on his handling of inquiries and asked that future inquiries be met with a response confined to the fact that, now that we have acknowledged that both McCord and Hunt are former Agency employees, we know nothing more about the case and the caller should be referred to the FBI as appropriate.

00296

20 June 1972

DDS noted that in response to State's request its chauffeurs who drive the Secretary of State and other senior State officers will be given a one-day defensive driving orientation at [redacted]

20 June 1972

The Director noted receipt of a paper on a safehouse in Miami which is being made available to the Secret Service in support of its work in connection with the Republican and Democratic National Conventions. He asked the ADDP and the DDS to make it absolutely clear [redacted] that our cooperation in this undertaking is to be confined to provision of the safehouse and that it is not to be used as a site for investigations, interrogations, or "walk-ins", etc. The Director added that we will not loan people to the FBI or Secret Service in connection with their responsibilities at the Conventions nor will we provide equipment unique to the Agency.

21 June 1972

In view of the coverage in today's New York Times and Washington Post, Maury recommended that Chairman Nedzi be briefed on the McCord affair and that this briefing include all our information about the others involved. The Director asked Maury to touch base with the Director of Security and prepare a briefing paper on this topic for his review. Citing the number of distorted rumors about this matter, the Executive Director said that during the course of the day he hopes to provide a suggested Headquarters Bulletin for all employees for the Director's review.

Unumb noted a number of inquiries from the press with respect to the Cuban-Americans involved in the bugging attempt at the Democratic National Committee headquarters and their alleged involvement in the Bay of Pigs, etc. The Director asked that such inquiries be met with an explanation that we are not prepared to be helpful on this matter.

00297

22 June 1972

Unumb observed that inquiries on the McCord/Hunt situation seem to be slackening off.

23 June 1972

The Director called D/OCI's attention to coverage of the McCord affair in the Metro Section of today's Washington Post and asked that future issues of the "CIA Operations Center Morning Newspaper Highlights" include press items on this topic.

Maury noted that he briefed Chairman Nedzi on the McCord/ Hunt situation and on a security case.

26 June 1972

Houston noted the Fensterwald Freedom of Information case. The Director endorsed his plans to concur in the FBI's release of three photos, one being of Lee Harvey Oswald, which were acquired in Mexico and previously furnished to the Warren Commission.

00298

5 July 1972

Houston called attention to the judge's ruling in the Ellsberg/ Russo case denying the MMMMMM defense motion for an evidentiary hearing, as a result of which the subpoena directed at CIA is suspended.

11 July 1972

DDI noted press attention attached to Secretary of Commerce Peterson's planned trip to the Soviet Union and observed that [redacted]

It was also noted that [redacted] a secretary assigned to Peterson's office when he was Assistant to the President for International Economic Affairs, continues to work for him and may go to the Soviet Union. She will be in a LWOP status during the remainder of her tenure with the Secretary.

14 July 1972

Carver recalled that we have providdd some briefings to Senator Eagleton on Vietnam. The Director said that in time we will receive instructions from the White House on briefing Senators McGovern and Eagleton.

20 July 1972

Houston reported that the Justice Department is anxious that no comment be made on the Ellsberg/Russo trial and that any inquiries should be referred to the Justice Department's Public Relations Office.

24 July 1972

Houston noted that he had called David Young's attention to the fact that the White House (NSC Staff) is not utilizing the new classification procedures.

25 July 1972

Maury reported that according to White House Staffer John Lehman, David Young is of the opinion that Estimates are subject to declassification after ten years. Houston will see Mr. Young to straighten him out on this topic.

00299

26 July 1972

The Director . . . went on to ask the DDS for the background of a decision to have [redacted] of the Office of Security accompany Fred Flott on a White House survey of the drug scene in Southeast Asia. The Director said that in the future his or the DDCI's prior approval will be required in all cases where the Agency is asked by the White House or any other element of the Government to send an Agency officer on a narcotics-connected mission.

27 July 1972

DDP reported that Cord Meyer advised Bud Krogh of the White House staff of our unwillingness to have [redacted] accompany a new narcotics survey team to Southeast Asia and the possibility that Krogh may call the Director to reclama. The Director briefed on the background of this decision and noted his conversation with Al Haig on this topic.

1 August 1972

DDS related that Mr. [redacted] of the CI Staff received a call from the Secret Service requesting our training film on defensive driving. The Director interposed no objection to making this film available.

8 August 1972

Houston reported that Judge McArdle granted a motion for summary judgment in the Tofte case.

21 August 1972

Houston noted a telephone call from Howard Hunt who explained that his attorney was with him and had a question about a friend's past affiliation with the Agency. [redacted] DD/Sec, has reviewed the employment, and Houston reported that he replied directly to Hunt's friend, Mr. [redacted] that his old affiliation should create no problems in connection with his appearance before a grand jury.

00300

22 August 1972

Thuermer reported on a call from a Mr. Crewdson of the New York Times who said he was "formally requesting" a photograph of Howard Hunt. The DDP observed that we are under no obligation to provide a photograph, and Thuermer said he had declined.

23 August 1972

DDI noted a letter from the McGovern campaign headquarters requesting the FBIS daily white book and any recent studies on Southeast Asia. A brief discussion followed and the letter will be disregarded.

14 September 1972

Maury reported on his conversation with Messrs. Flug and Epstein of Senator Kennedy's staff in response to the Senator's 18 August letter to the Director alleging improper contact [redacted] (for details see OLC's Memorandum for the Record).

Thuermer noted that White House staffer David Young will hold a meeting today to brief the press on the implementation of Executive Order 11652.

21 September 1972

Warner reported that Marchetti's lawyers have been in touch with Justice in connection with ACLU's filing a secret brief with the Supreme Court and said that the Office of Security will pick it up as a convenience to Justice.

Warner noted that the Director is one of several defendants in a civil case filed by Ellsberg and Russo.

Unumb noted a request from the National Observer for biographic data on Howard Hunt and James McCord in connection with a story they are doing on the Watergate incident. The Director endorsed his having provided only the dates these individuals left the Agency.

25 September 1972

The Director noted a call from Assistant Secretary of State Sisco [redacted]

00301

18 October 1972

Maury noted his response to a request from CSC General Counsel Anthony Mondello, who was reacting to a request for the personnel files of those former Agency officers involved in the Watergate incident from Senator Kennedy's Subcommittee on Administrative Practices and Procedures. He added that we are exempted from related CSC regulations, and the Director endorsed his plan to provide only the dates of their departure from the Agency in the event the Senator's office calls us on this matter.

3 November 1972

Houston recalled that last August he reported on a call from Howard Hunt and his subsequent guidance to [redacted] on how to handle affiliation with the Agency, [redacted]

[redacted]

The Director highlighted his conversation with David Kraslow of the Washington Star News and his flat denial of a proposed story that the Agency was asked to report on the Democratic Party which led to the Watergate incident and others. The Director noted his plans to issue a statement of denial if such a story were to appear and suggested that Thuermer consider drafting one for contingency use.

15 November 1972

DDP noted a report from Chief, WH Division that on 9 October a Mr. Harper of the New York Times was working on a story which tries to link the Agency with Cuban emigres, the break-in at the Chilean Embassy, action against Daniel Ellsberg, and the Watergate case. Thuermer observed that this is the first he has heard about this topic, and the DDP concluded that such a story could have no basis in fact and it would be inadvisable to try to straighten out Mr. Harper.

20 November 1972

DD/I called attention to Jack Anderson's column in today's Washington Post and the quotes contained therein from an Agency report on a famous singer. The Director highlighted his brief conversation with Jack Anderson and explained that the Director of Security is looking into this matter.

00302

22 November 1972

Warner related that according to Assistant Attorney General Henry Petersen, U.S. Attorney Earl Silbert has several questions on the Watergate case. The Director indicated he will review this matter later.

12 December 1972

Thuermer noted an inquiry from Dave Burnham of the New York Times, who appears to be writing a story on the twelve New York Police officers who were briefed by the Agency on information processing. A brief discussion followed, and Thuermer will advise Burnham that we have occasionally provided briefings at the request of various police organizations, but these are exceptional cases.

13 December 1972

The Director noted the article by Thomas B. Ross in yesterday's Evening Star-News, "New Watergate Dimension?," and the impression left therein that the Agency was involved in the Watergate incident because a passport bearing the name Edward Hamilton was found on Frank Sturgis. Any inquiries from the press or elsewhere are to be met with a "this is nonsense" reply. The Executive Director noted work under way to identify the genesis of the passport story.

29 December 1972

Unumb reported that Seymour Hersh of the New York Times, who is preparing a story on the Watergate incident, had asked if Martinez had been employed by the Agency. Acting DCI recommended that the Agency not assist Mr. Hersh's efforts.

00303

10 January 1973

Maury related that we will be on firm ground in responding to Congressman Koch if we indicate that our assistance to the NY City Police Dept. was not training but a briefing on an essentially unclassified basis undertaken in response to the suggestion of a consultant to the N.Y.P.D. Thuermer reminded those concerned that [redacted] is a former Agency employee.

12 January 1973

[redacted]

15 January 1973

Maury noted press stories that Watergate defendant Martinez was on the Agency pay roll until 17 June and anticipated some inquiry on this topic. The DDP endorsed his view that Whereas Martinez was intermittently used as a source to report on Cuban exile matters, this relationship should cause no serious difficulty.

17 January 1973

The Director called attention to the article by James Reston "The Watergate Spies" contained in the New York Times, and wondered how Reston got the erroneous impression that Hunt was " . . . Operational head of the CIA's Cuban Bay of Pigs . . . "

18 January 1973

Maury reported that when he and Dave Blee, Chief/SB, saw Chairman Nedzi with respect to the Chairman's forthcoming trip to Finland, Leningrad, Sofia and Athens, Chairman Nedzi briefed on his November conversation with New York Times correspondent Seymour Hersh. Maury went on to highlight the several topics and allegations Hersh claims he has with respect to Agency activities, particularly allegations that we are engaged in extensive domestic operations. Maury will circulate a memorandum on the information Hersh claims he has. The Director explained that we should assemble a senior team to meet with Chairman Nedzi and clearly outline what we do and do not do in the United States. The Executive Director called attention to his 29 February 1972 memorandum to the deputies, Subject: Allegations of Agency involvement in the US, and suggested that it might serve as an outline for material to be covered with Chairman Nedzi.

00304

18 January 1973

Maury noted that in response to Tom Korologis' (Special Assistant tMM to the President for Legislative Affairs (Senate)) request for materials on instances where classified information had been leaked to the press, he assembled a paper on this topic and provided it with a note than an examination of most leaks reveals that MM the White House and Executive Branch are the guilty parties.

19 January 1973

Maury reported that Chairman Nedzi would like the full Subcommittee on Intelligence Operations to hear a presentation by us on Agency activitity in the United States sometime in mid-February. The Director noted that his decision of yesterday to turn out a senior team for this briefing stands.

22 January 1973

General Walters noted Howard Hunt's appearance on television last night. Thuermer will obtain a transcript of the program, and the Executive Director noted his concern over Hunt's suggestion that he is no longer bound by his secrecy agreement.

23 January 1973

Executive Director noted that the terminal secrecy agreement which Howard Hunt signed said that he will be acknowledged as an Agency employee. His assertion that he is not bound by the agreement because we did in fact acknowledge his employment here is therefore ill-advised.

The Director noted a call from Elliot Richardson asking about some information that Seymour Hersh has developed to the effect that HEW automatically provides the Agency with travel orders on its employees and that this agreement was made in Secretary Ribicoff's time. The DDI will determine what this is about and advise.

24 January 1973

Maury noted that he met with Congressman Koch on our minimal assistance in briefing the New York City police officers. The Congressman would like something in writing on this, which Maury will prepare and sign.

00305

24 January 1973

Thuermer noted advice from a former Agency employee that Seymour Hersh has been assigned full time to the Watergate story, but in the meantime, Mr. Hersh claims he has evidence of Agency interest in an arsenal in the Midwest, a map-making facility in Vermont, and in Camp Peary.

26 January 1973

The Director noted he has advised the Director of Training of Mrs. Lyndon Johnson's request for Marie Chiarodo to handle the large volume of mail she has received.

DDI reported that he has been unable to turn up any information which would lead Seymour Hersh to allege that we have a map-making facility in Vermont.

30 January 1973

Thuermer reported that the Virginia Gazette seems to be persisting in its efforts to embarrass Camp Peary and has been in touch with Victor Marchetti and Patrick McGarvey, who have tended to confirm allegations that the Phoenix program was supported by contract assassins.

7 February 1973

Maury noted that Mr. Helms is appearing before the Senate Foreign Relations Committee this morning on police training, ~~KMM~~ ITT, and the Watergate incident. He also noted that he has solicited the support of Senators Humphrey, McGee, and Scott to make appropriate public statements following Mr. Helms' appearance.

Mary advised that in response to Chairman Holifield's investigation of Agency training pf policemen, he will meet with Herbert Roback, Counsel of the House Government Operations Committee, to explain our briefing of various police departments.

8 February 1973

The Director noted his scheduled meeting tomorrow with Defense Secretary Richardson and asked Executive Committee members to give him a note on any item they wish him to raise with the Secretary. Candidates are . . . Secretary Richardsons' earlier concerns with respect to HEW providing the Agency with travel plans of officers going to Communist Bloc countries. On the latter item the DDI explained that since Secretary Richardson's inquiry to Mr. Helms (see minutes of 23 Jan 73), a survey had been undertaken and reviewed with HEW, which had no problems with these old arrangements but is shifting the point of pickup to its public affairs staff where such information is available to anyone.

00306

8 February 1973

Maury noted the statement by Senator Fulbight following Mr. Helms' appearance yesterday before the Senate Foregin Relations Committee in which the Sentator expressed his opposition to the whole concept of the Agency getting involved with the police even in an innocuous way. Maury added that he will see Chairman Holifield's staff assistant Herbert Roback today. Maury said that a stement had been transmitted to the White House yesterday for John Ehrlichman's possible use (attached). The Director asked that a contingency document be prepared along the lines that we will continue to comply with the Omnibus Crime Control and Safe Streets Act of 1968 which approves of our assistance to various police forces when MMMMMM authorized by the Justice Department. In response to the DDI's suggestions, the DDS will review what assistance to police forces had been given prior to 1968 and advise.

Maury concurred in the Director's judgment that it is impossible to keep all congressional elements happy and that we face a period of increased criticism from this quarter which must be met with firm assurances that what we are being criticized for is fully authorized and justified. Unless the facts justify such a statement, we would be well advised to terminate the activity in question.

Maury recalled that we are obligated to sit down with Chairman Nedzi and review what we do and don't do in the U.S. (see Momning Minutes of MMMM 18 and 19 January). The Director concurred. The DDI suggested that we undertake an in-house review of what it is we are doing within the U.S. and identify and eliminate the marginal.

9 February 1973

Maury said he spent an hour yesterday with Congressman Holifield and they decided to have their respective staffs work on a letter for Holifield to send to the Director suggesting restrictive, but not prohibitive, guidlines regarding such activities in the future. Maury noted Chairman Nedzi's current concerns about this topic and said the proposed MMMM letter may satisfy his worries.

14 February 1973

Thuermer noted advice from Hicholas Horrock of Newsweek that a "soft story" is floating around Newsweek on the general topic of political espionage and ex-CIA agents. Mr. Horrock asked what constraints we have on former employees. A lengthy discussion followed, noting in particular that the only legal constraint imposed is the terminal secrecy agreement as reinforced by the MMMMM courts in the Marchetti case. Other than this, there are no constraint except moral ones. Thuermer will advise Horrick that thousands of employees have gone through CIA, and it is a matter of considerable pride that only a handful have deported themselves improperly.

15 February 1973

. . . . . Maury added that he went over (with Nedzi) Seymour Hersh's charges with respect to the Agency and our position on each. DDI recalled our obligation to brief Chairman Nedzi on Agency activities in the US.

20 February 1973

Maury related that Herb Roback of Senator Holifield's staff is being asked by David Burnham of the New York Times for the names of those city police departments we have briefed in the past. The DDS called attention to our obligation to clear with these police departments any mention of their having been briefed. In response to the Director's suggestion that the Agency issue a press release on this topic, a lengthy discussion followed and the Director asked the DDS to report to him on what our understanding with various police departments has been prior to our agreement to brief same. He also asked that editorial comment on any past Agency briefing of the press or press releases be assembled and explained that in principle we should from time to time make it known that we are part of the U.S.Government.

23 February 1973

Maury noted that Herb Roback of Senator Holifield's staff and Chairman Nedzi have concurred in a letter for the Director's signature which will indicate that we will undertake training of U.S. police "only for the most compelling reasons." A brief discussion followed and the Director observed that it is important for us to decide what we do and then advise the Hill accordingly.

27 February 1973

The Director noted a call from Senator Jackson, who asked him to meet with Senator McClellan sometime next week with regard to Congressman Holifield's inquiry concerning Agency training of U.S. police departments.

1 March 1973

Maury related that former Director Richard Helms has been asked by Senator Fulbright to reappear before the Senate Foreign Relations Committee. Maury said that Mr. Helms would probably be queried on the Watergate incident, Agency training of police, and ITT and went on to describe Mr. Helms' anticipated reponse.

1 March 1973

Maury reported that Congressman Holifield's staff is anxiously awaiting a letter from the Director in response to the Congressman's written inquiry on police training. The Director noted plans to foward it.

2 March 1973

Maury highlighted yesterday's LIG meeting at the White House and his recommendation that we not provide examples of Congressional leaks of classified information for White House use in reacting to Congressional criticism of the Administration's "indiscretions." The DDS advised that the Office of Security is keeping a reasonably complete record of obvious leaks of intelligence information in the press and elsewhere.

5 March 1973

Maury highlighted the statement Congressman Holifield will introduce into the Congressional Record today on Agency briefing of U.S. police forces. He also noted a related news release that will be issued by the Congressman's office.

6 March 1973

Maury highlighted Congressman Koch's reaction to our response to Congressman Holifield's letter concerning police training, as reported in today's press. Maury noted that Congressman Koch plans to ask GAO for a ruling on this matter, and the Director suggested that Colby provide some guidance to Comptroller General Elmer Staats.

The Director noted advice that Hugh Sidey of Time magazine plans to write a story alleging that Howard Hunt was employed by a cover organization, i.e., Robert R. Mullen Company, when he left the Agency. Colby noted that this company is a completely private concern but has provided cover for one or two officers overseas. The Director asked Thuermer to be prepared to cope with any inquiries when the story appears.

00309

9 March 1973

DDI called attention to Joseph Alsop's article in today's Washington Post, "Analyzing the CIA's Analysts," which erroneously refers to Sam Adams as a former employee. Later in the meeting, Houston explained why the allegation that the Agency has tried to muzzle Adams is false. He went on to brief on [redacted] communications with Justice and the fact that the judge ruled Adams' material was not exculpatory. In response to the Director's question, the DDI reported that Mr. Adams has not been placed on probation. The Director found this unsatisfactory.

Houston explained the legal implications of the subpoena served on Thuermer for documents related to the Ellsberg case and advised that the Director may have to claim executive privilege.

15 March 1973

Houston said that the judge squashed the subpoena served on Thuermer (see Morning Minutes of 7 March).

Included in this folder are miscellaneous items, including the following:

Chuck Briggs' submission, including support of the Committee on narcotics

Review of Minutes of Morning Meetings

Agency funding of heroin study.

Tom Parrott's involvement with David Young

Cary's memo on briefing of Special Subcommittee on Intelligence Of House Armed Services Committee (this relates to the McCord letters to the Agency)

Broe's report of his and Colby's meeting with Nedzi

00311

☐ UNCLASSIFIED ☐ INTERNAL USE ONLY ☒ CONFIDENTIAL ☐ SECRET

ROUTING AND RECORD SHEET

SUBJECT: (Optional)

e of Disguise Materials and Alias Documentation Within the U.S.

FROM:	EXTENSION	NO.
Director of Training		

TO: (Officer designation, room number, and building)	DATE RECEIVED	DATE FORWARDED	OFFICER'S INITIALS	COMMENTS (Number each comment to show from whom to whom. Draw a line across column after each comment.)
1. Inspector General	5/19/73			copy is in disguise file.
2.	19 June			
3.				
4.				
5.				
6.				
7.				
8.				
9.				
10.				
11.				
12.				
13.				
14.				
15.				00312

FORM 3-62 610 USE PREVIOUS EDITIONS ☐ SECRET ☒ CONFIDENTIAL ☐ INTERNAL USE ONLY ☐ UNCLASSIFIED

~~CONFIDENTIAL~~

18 JUN 1973

MEMORANDUM FOR: Inspector General

SUBJECT : Use of Disguise Materials and Alias Documentation Within the U.S.

REFERENCE : Memo dtd 30 May 73 to DTR fm [redacted] Subj: Issuance of Disguise Materials for Probable Use Within U.S. or It's Territories

1. The Associate Deputy Director for Operations has asked that we give you a detailed report of the actual use that the Office of Training has made within the U.S. of all disguise materials and alias documentation we have obtained for our staff members and students.

2. Disguise Materials

OTR has obtained from OTS disguise materials - including glasses, wigs, mustaches, and special shoes to increase height - for 12 staff instructors at the Domestic Training Station. The purpose of these materials is to increase the difficulty that students in the Basic Operations Course and Advanced Operations Course will have in recognizing instructors during problems and exercises conducted [redacted] near DTS. Exercises include surveillance, countersurveillance, brush passes, and dead drop problems in which instructors monitor student activity. These exercises are run under carefully controlled conditions only in areas where adequate liaison exists with local authorities to avoid any flap should difficulty arise during an exercise.

00313

CONFIDENTIAL

The sole use of disguise materials by these instructors has been or will be in support of the training exercise noted above. At no time have the materials been used for other purposes.

3. Alias Documents

U.S. alias documents consisting primarily of business and social cards, but also including drivers' licenses and social security cards, have been used for more than a year by students [redacted] Such use is limited to establishing bona fides, if required, during the human assessment problem that is a part of the comprehensive exercise, [redacted] At the conclusion of the course, the alias documents are collected from the students and returned to OTS. Again, these documents are used only under carefully controlled conditions in an environment [redacted] where adequate liaison with local authorities exists to contain any flap; and the documents are used only for the purposes stated.

4. A thorough canvass of all elements of OTR discloses no other instance in recent years in which we have used disguise materials or alias documentation within the U.S. or obtained such materials for that purpose.

Director of Training

cc: ADDO

CONFIDENTIAL

00314

ꟽORANDUM FOR:

[redacted] HAS

JEWELS FILE

00315

(DATE)

FORM NO. 101 REPLACES FORM 10-101
1 AUG 54 WHICH MAY BE USED. (47)

☐ UNCLASSIFIED ☐ INTERNAL USE ONLY ☐ CONFIDENTIAL ☐ SECRET

ROUTING AND RECORD SHEET

SUBJECT: (Optional)

FROM:	EXTENSION	NO.
[redacted] Deputy Chief, WH Division		DATE 20 June 1973

TO: (Officer designation, room number, and building)	DATE RECEIVED	DATE FORWARDED	OFFICER'S INITIALS	COMMENTS (Number each comment to show from whom to whom. Draw a line across column after each comment.)
1. C/WHD	20 JUN 1973		[redacted]	
ADDO	21 JUN 1973			
2. DDO		6/22		
3. IG	6/22/73	6/25	[redacted]	
4. Executive Secretary, CIA Management Committee		6/28		
5. DDCI		6/29	W	
6. Return to O/IG	6/29/73	6/29		
7. JEWELS				
8.				
9.				
10.				
11.				
12.				
13.				
14.				
15.				

00316

FORM 3-62 610 USE PREVIOUS EDITIONS ☐ SECRET ☐ CONFIDENTIAL ☐ INTERNAL USE ONLY ☐ UNCLASSIFIED

DD/O 73-3355

Executive Registry
173-3501

20 June 1973

MEMORANDUM FOR THE RECORD

SUBJECT: John Dean Allegations to Newsweek Magazine

1. Mr. William Jorden, the Latin American referent on Dr. Kissinger's Staff, called today in reference to State cable No. 112189, dated 11 June (attached). He said that he had specific reference to paragraph 2 of that cable and would like to have "everything and anything we know" on that subject in the Agency.

2. The undersigned indicated to Mr. Jorden that he had checked out the allegation that some low level White House officials had considered assassinating Torrijos when the story first appeared in Newsweek and, despite checking outside WH Division also, could find no one in the Agency who could recollect or find anything relating to such a plan on the part of any portion of U.S. officialdom. I told him that I felt sure that nothing of this nature had come to WH Division's attention because for the period in question I had been Deputy Chief of WH Division and had heard nothing about any such plan. Mr. Jorden asked if the Agency knew anything about Howard Hunt having had a team in Mexico "before the mission was aborted" and I indicated that as far as I knew, the Agency had no information on Hunt being in Mexico on such a mission. I also indicated, however, they could have been and the Agency might well not know it simply because he could have used an alias and he is an American citizen, which is outside the Agency's province and really the FBI's business. I suggested that it might be best if he checked the FBI on that particular angle. Subsequently I checked with Mr. William V. Broe, the IG, and Mr. John Horton, recently returned

SECRET

00317

and both indicated that they had not run across any information concerning this latter allegation of Hunt and a team in Mexico on a mission related to Panama.

3. It was apparent that Mr. Jorden was under some pressure to refute these allegations and was casting about in all directions to make as certain of his ground as he possibly could before he tried to do so.

Deputy Chief
Western Hemisphere Division

Attachment:
As Stated Above

00318

OGC

BY 7 PER TOTAL COPIES 22 - 1 RUN BY

ADMIN INTERNAL USE ONLY

REPRODUCTION BY OTHER THAN ISSUING OFFICE IS PROHIBITED

UNIT NOTIFIED

STATE MESSAGE

COPY ISSUED/SLOTTED BY AT Z

UNIT

INFO RF. FILE VR. OCI/NAY, ONE, C/WH, OER3, SA3, WH3, OLC, DDO, C/SO 11, SEWR,

06383 PAGE 01-01 NC 02776

TOR:111326Z JUN 73

RUEAIIB
UUUUU ZOC STATE ZZH
RUESVA RULPALJ
RUEHC #2189 1621322
UUUUU ZZH
113122 JUN 73
SECSTATE WASHDC
RUESVA/AMEMBASSY PANAMA IMMEDIATE 2592
0 RULPALJ/PANCANAL IMMEDIATE
PA /USSOUTHCOM IMMEDIATE

LAS STATE 112189

. 11652: N/A
S: PFOR, PN
JECT: ALLEGATIONS MADE BY JOHN DEAN TO NEWSWEEK MAGAZINE

THE FOLLOWING IS EXCERPTED FROM A FRONT PAGE ARTICLE M TODAY'S NEW YORK TIMES WHICH REPORTS ON ALLEGATIONS E BY JOHN DEAN TO NEWSWEEK MAGAZINE.

"SOME "LOW-LEVEL" WHITE HOUSE OFFICIALS CONSIDERED AS-SINATING PANAMA'S RULER OMAR TORRIJOS, BECAUSE THEY PECTED THE INVOLVEMENT OF HIGH PANAMANIAN AUTHORITIES IN OIN TRAFFIC AND BECAUSE THEY FELT THE GOVERNMENT HAD N UNCOOPERATIVE ABOUT RENEGOTIATING THE PANAMA CANAL ATY. E. HOWARD HUNT JR., A LEADER OF THE WATERGATE GLARS, HAD A TEAM IN MEXICO "BEFORE THE MISSION WAS RTED," NEWSWEEK SAID." RUSH

DOCUMENT AS REFERRED TO Dept. of STATE Refer to State

00319

SENDER WILL CHECK CLASSIFICATION TOP AND BOTTOM

	UNCLASSIFIED		CONFIDENTIAL		SECRET

OFFICIAL ROUTING SLIP

TO	NAME AND ADDRESS	DATE	INITIALS
1	IG	6/8/73	
2			
3		8 June	
4	"Jewels" – where??		
5			
6	to file		

	ACTION		DIRECT REPLY		PREPARE REPLY
	APPROVAL		DISPATCH		RECOMMENDATION
	COMMENT		FILE		RETURN
	CONCURRENCE		INFORMATION		SIGNATURE

Remarks:

Cy to

00320

FOLD HERE TO RETURN TO SENDER

FROM: NAME, ADDRESS AND PHONE NO.	DATE
O/ES/MC	6/7/73

	UNCLASSIFIED		CONFIDENTIAL		SECRET

FORM NO. 1-67 237 Use previous editions (40)

MEMORANDUM FOR: IG

For the record —

[signature]
6/7/73

(DATE)

00321

FORM NO. 1 AUG 54 101 REPLACES FORM 10-101 WHICH MAY BE USED. (47)

NEW YORK TIMES

29 MAY 1973

Chilean Break-Ins Puzzle Watergate Investigators

By MICHAEL C. JENSEN

One unsolved puzzle that Watergate investigators are studying is the identity of intruders who broke into the offices and residences of Chilean diplomats in Washington and New York at least four times from April, 1971 to May, 1972.

Four break-ins against Chileans took place in the 14 months immediately preceding the break-in at the Democrats' Watergate headquarters last June. They also occurred at a time when the Chilean Government was negotiating with the International Telephone and Telegraph Corporation over compensation for Chile's take-over of the huge conglomerate's telephone subsidiary.

Because of far more sensational disclosures, Watergate investigators have not actively pursued the Chilean case in recent weeks, beyond asking a question or two about the break-ins during interrogations of the Watergate burglars.

However, Senate investigators have informed both the Senate Watergate committee and the Watergate prosecutors in Washington about the details of the four break-ins at the offices and residences of the Chileans.

3 Occurred in New York

Furthermore, a member of the special intelligence unit of the New York Police Department was said to have concluded that the three break-ins that occurred in Manhattan were no routine burglaries. And investigators in Washington said that the four break-ins had followed similar patterns.

They were apparently done by professionals, with a few items taken to make the break-ins appear to be burglaries, investigators said. Other valuable items were left behind, however, and sensitive papers were disturbed, possibly in the course of being photographed. Investigators reconstruct the break-ins as follows:

The first known break-in occurred on the afternoon of April 5, 1971 at the Manhattan residence on Lexington Avenue of Humberto Diaz-Casanueva, Chile's Ambassador to the United Nations. The Ambassador reportedly told the police that the intruders had stolen such items as a hair-dryer and a pair of boots and disturbed

The next break-in was said to have taken place six days later at the East 38th Street apartment in Manhattan of Javier Urrutia, president of the Chilean Development Corporation and a close economic adviser to Chile's president, Dr. Salvador Allende Gossens.

Pistol Stolen

Mr. Urrutia told the police that a .25-caliber Bernardelli pistol had been stolen. However, a fur coat in a closet was reportedly untouched. Government papers were said to have been disturbed, and chewing gum was edged into the apartment's lock, a familiar practice of professional intruders that gives them time to escape if they are surprised during the course of an entry.

The third reported break-in took place on Feb. 10, 1972, investigators said, at the New York residence on East 46th Street of Victor Rioseco, formerly a Chilean official at the United Nations. A radio and a television set were reportedly taken and papers disturbed.

The fourth and most publicized break-in took place over the weekend of May 13, 1972, at the Chilean Embassy in Washington. Files of the Ambassador and his first secretary, Fernando Bachelet, were reportedly rifled and two radios taken.

Chilean officials have been ordered by their Government not to discuss the matter, but sources close to the case said that the former Chilean Ambassador, Orlando Letelier, had confirmed that the Washington intruders apparently were seeking sensitive Government documents.

Speculation by Investigators

Capitol Hill investigators have speculated that the intruders might have been seeking evidence of links between Cuba and Chile, or looking for politically sensitive documents relating to the take-over by Chile of I.T.T. properties.

No evidence has turned up that members of the team that broke into the Watergate were involved in the entries, although hints that some of them may have participated have come from the authorities in Florida.

First reports about a break-in at the Chilean Embassy began to circulate in Miami a week or so after the Watergate break-in of June 17, 1972, and there was speculation that the two might have been related. That link never has been proved, and some investigators doubt that it exists.

One explanation offered for the Chilean break-in was that if any Cuban-Americans participated, as was the case in the Watergate, they might have been looking for documents that would indicate collusion between the Chilean and Castro governments.

Shortly after the speculation began in Miami, Chilean officials acknowledged the break-in and reported it to the city police, who started an investigation that has been inconclusive.

Earlier this month, a Cuban named Felipe de Diego was interrogated by State Attorney Richard E. Gerstein in Florida regarding participation in the break-in at the offices of Dr. Daniel Ellsberg's psychiatrist in Los Angeles.

He and his attorney indicated that, if granted immunity, Mr. de Diego might shed new light on other surreptitious operations in Washington. Investigators in Miami later indicated that these operations might include the Chilean break-in or break-ins.

SENDER WILL CHECK CLASSIFICATION TOP AND BOTTOM

UNCLASSIFIED | CONFIDENTIAL | SECRET

CENTRAL INTELLIGENCE AGENCY

OFFICIAL ROUTING SLIP

NO.	NAME AND ADDRESS	DATE	INITIALS
1	Mr. Colby	6/7	
2	WVB	6/8	
3		8/...	
4			
5			
6	OIG		

ACTION	DIRECT REPLY	PREPARE REPLY
APPROVAL	DISPATCH	RECOMMENDATION
COMMENT	FILE	RETURN
CONCURRENCE	INFORMATION	SIGNATURE

Remarks:

Nothing startling, but something you perhaps should be aware of.

00323

FOLD HERE TO RETURN TO SENDER

FROM: NAME, ADDRESS AND PHONE NO.	DATE
WVBroe, IG, 2E24	6/7/73

UNCLASSIFIED | CONFIDENTIAL | SECRET

FORM NO. 2-61 237 Use previous editions (40)

* U.S. GOVERNMENT PRINTING OFFICE : 1961 O—587282

25 May 1973

MEMORANDUM FOR THE RECORD

SUBJECT: Disposal of Classified Trash for the National Security Council (NSC)

1. A memorandum for the record by the Executive Officer of the Office of Logistics points out that this Agency is disposing of classified trash for the NSC. The material contains documents from the White House "Situation Room," codeword and other documents from the Intelligence community. This practice began in December 1971 and is still in effect. Pick-up of 30 bags of trash is made each Thursday.

2. Under normal times and circumstances such a routine matter would not be raised, but given the recent furor caused by the destruction of documents by the Acting FBI Director Patrick Gray it is felt that the matter should at least be highlighted for further consideration.

00324

TOP SECRET

UNCLASSIFIED when blank — TOP SECRET when attached to Top Secret Document — Automatically downgraded to SECRET when filled in form is detached from controlled document.

CONTROL AND COVER SHEET FOR TOP SECRET DOCUMENT

DOCUMENT DESCRIPTION		REGISTRY
SOURCE O/IG		CIA CONTROL NO. TS 185229/73
DOC. NO.	SENSITIVE	DATE DOCUMENT RECEIVED
DOC. DATE 30 May 1973	BY HAND	LOGGED BY
COPY NO. 1 ~~& 2~~		
NUMBER OF PAGES 1		
NUMBER OF ATTACHMENTS 2 (TS 185228/72/2 & TS 185228/72/3)		

ATTENTION: This form will be placed on top of and attached to each Top Secret document received by the Central Intelligence Agency or classified Top Secret within the CIA and will remain attached to the document until such time as it is downgraded, destroyed, or transmitted outside of CIA. Access to Top Secret matter is limited to Top Secret Control personnel and those individuals whose official duties relate to the matter. Top Secret Control Officers who receive and/or release the attached Top Secret material will sign this form and indicate period of custody in the left-hand columns provided. Each individual who sees the Top Secret document will sign and indicate the date of handling in the right-hand columns.

REFERRED TO	RECEIVED			RELEASED		SEEN BY		
OFFICE	SIGNATURE	DATE	TIME	DATE	TIME	SIGNATURE	OFFICE/DIV.	DATE
Mr. Colby						W E Colby	ES/DC	6/7
IG		6/5/73					O/IG	6/8
	Jewels? (copies of reports returned to EUR file) 8 June 73							8 June 73

NOTICE OF DETACHMENT: When this form is detached from Top Secret material it shall be completed in the appropriate spaces below and transmitted to Central Top Secret Control for record.

DOWNGRADED		DESTROYED		DISPATCHED (OUTSIDE CIA)	
TO		BY (Signature)		TO	
BY (Signature)		WITNESSED BY (Signature)		BY (Signature)	
OFFICE	DATE	OFFICE	DATE	OFFICE	DATE

TOP SECRET

SENSITIVE

30 May 1973

MEMORANDUM FOR: Mr. William E. Colby

SUBJECT MHCHAOS and

I call to your attention the attached sensitive annexes to our 1972 report of survey of EUR Division. You have seen them before, but a fresh look at them might be in order in the light of current developments. The recent revelations about the activities of the Intelligence Evaluation Committee are getting close to our MHCHAOS program. We are particularly concerned about MHCHAOS because of the high degree of resentment we found among many Agency employees at their being expected to participate in it.

William V. Broe
Inspector General

Attachments (SEE EUR GREEN FOLDER)
TS 185228/72/2, 9 Nov 72
TS 185228/72/3, 9 Nov 72

TOP SECRET

TS
Copy 1 of 4

00326

ROUTING AND RECORD SHEET

SUBJECT: (Optional)

DD/M&S Requiremtns - Watergate Incident

FROM: Howard J. Osborn Director of Security Room 4-E-60 Headquarters	EXTENSION 6777	NO. DATE

TO: (Officer designation, room number, and building)	DATE RECEIVED	DATE FORWARDED	OFFICER'S INITIALS	COMMENTS (Number each comment to show from whom to whom. Draw a line across column after each comment.)
1. Deputy Director for Mgmt. & Services Room 7-D-26	6/6	6/7	[illegible]	1. For Your Information Harold - This is supplemental. We may have more as our employee dredge their memories. Oz
2.				
3. JG	6/8		B	
4. KEG			[illegible]	
5. SDB				
6. (looks like "Jewel" too)				
7.				Chair - Let me have a Buray copy. [illegible]
8.				
9.				
10.				
11.				
12.				
13.				
14.				
15.				00327

FORM 3-62 610 USE PREVIOUS EDITIONS ☐ ~~SECRET~~ ☐ CONFIDENTIAL ☐ INTERNAL USE ONLY ☐ UNCLASSIFIED

SECRET

6 JUN 1973

MEMORANDUM FOR: Deputy Director for Management and Services

FROM : Director of Security

SUBJECT : DD/M&S Requirements - Watergate Incident

1. This memorandum is for information only.

2. In July 1971, the New York Times featured an article under the by-line of William Beecher which contained an exposition of the then current status of the Strategic Arms Limitation Talks (SALT). It was evident from this delineation of these talks that William Beecher had obtained the information from highly classified U.S. Government documents or from a person or persons having had access to such documents.

3. In this regard, Mr. Egil E. Krogh, Jr of the White House telephonically contacted the Director of Security of this Agency and requested that this Agency provide a polygraph examiner to conduct polygraph tests on four Department of State employees. In conjunction with Mr. G. Marvin Gentile, Deputy Assistant Secretary for Security, Department of State, this Office arranged for a polygraph examiner to conduct these examinations but with no CIA involvement to be acknowledged. In other words, this Office loaned the polygraph examiner to the Department of State and the polygraph examinations were conducted for Mr. G. Marvin Gentile.

4. This Office in 1970, requested approval to have disguise kits issued to approximately fourteen people. The disguise kits were never issued for operational

00328

SECRET

purposes, but they were issued for practice surveillance to train local field office personnel in their use, [redacted] Of these fourteen disguise kits, four were returned to the Office of Technical Services.

5. In regard to other activities that this Office has conducted domestically, the following two projects are submitted:

A. Project WESTPOINTER: In September 1969, February 1970, May 1970, and October 1971, a project, similar to Project SRPOINTER, was conducted by the Office of Security, East Asia Division, and the Office of Technical Services in the San Francisco, California, area. The target was mail to the United States from Mainland China.

[redacted]

6. [redacted] an Office of Security employee, who will retire effective 29 June 1973, had a chance meeting with Mr. James W. McCord, Jr. on 24 May 1973 near the Senate Office Building. According to Mr. [redacted] the substance of the chance meeting was an exchange of pleasantries.

Howard J. Osborn
Director of Security

00329

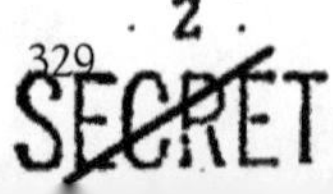

SECRET

Page 1 SDS and other student activist groups

OCI produced in December 1967 at Walt Rostow's request a 30-page typescript study of the SDS and its foreign ties.

In the summer of 1968 OCI produced--again at Rostow's request--a paper on Restless Youth. The first, and most sensitive section, was a philosophical treatment of student unrest, its motivation, history, and tactics. It drew heavily on overt literature and FBI reporting on SDS and affiliated groups. The second section comprised 19 chapters on foreign student dissidence.

Pages 11 & 12 Black radicalism

OCI began following Caribbean black radicalism in earnest in 1968. Two papers were produced on the subject, one in August 1969 and the other in June 1970.

OCI was asked in June 1970 to write a memo with special attention to links between black radicalism in the Caribbean and advocates of black power in the US. The memo was produced in typescript and given to the DCI.

OCI in 1968 wrote periodic typescript memos on Stokely Carmichael's travels abroad during a period when he had dropped from public view.

~~SECRET~~

Page 23 Prohibition against COMINT vs. US citizens

In September 1972 [redacted] Commo to conduct hearability tests of certain HF long-distance commercial telephone circuits between the US and South America. The circuits carried drug-related traffic. [redacted] The tests were successful. The activity was terminated on 30 Jan 73 following OGC determination that they were illegal.

We conduct an intercept operation in [redacted] targeted on radio telephone conversations [redacted] These intercepts contain a large number of unrelated conversations often involving US citizens.

Testing in the US of ORD-developed electronic collection systems occasionally result in the collection of domestic telephone conversations. When the tests are complete, the intercepted material is destroyed.

CIA [redacted] technicians conducted tests in the Miami area in August 1971 of DF gear intended for use against a Soviet agent in South Vietnam. While wholly innocuous, the tests preceded the holding of the conventions there and could be construed as being somehow related to them.

In February 1972 CIA asked an official of AT&T for copies of telephone call slips relating to US-China calls. The operation lasted for three or four months and then dried up. OGC stated its belief that the collection of these slips did not violate the Communications Act since eavesdropping was not involved.

Page 29 Mail coverage

Since 1953, CIA has operated a mail intercept program of incoming and outgoing Russian mail and, at various times, other selected mail at Kennedy Airport in New York City. This program is now dormant pending decision on whether to continue or to abolish it.

00331

SECRET

ATTACHMENT

FEDERAL BUREAU OF INVESTIGATION

TSD has had a close working relationship with the FBI over the past few years. The FBI is the only organization that has been fully briefed on TSD audio techniques and equipment. The following are situations where TSD equipment and guidance were involved in operations:

00332

SECRET

(G) TSD has furnished equipment items which constitute an on-the-shelf capability to engage in photo and audio surveillance operations which might not be known to the Agency. In one case it is known that a relatively unsophisticated device was used against a domestic target.

SECRET

00334

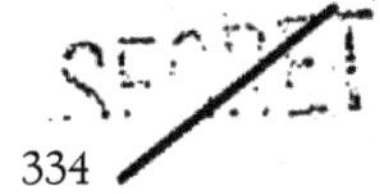

7

00335

Page 4 [illegible] other student radical groups

OCI produced in December 1967 at Walt Rostow's request a [illegible]-page typescript study of the SDS and its foreign ties.

In the summer of 1968 OCI produced--again at Rostow's request--a paper on Restless Youth. The first, and most sensitive section, was a philosophical treatment of student unrest, its motivation, history, and tactics. It drew heavily on overt literature and FBI reporting on SDS and affiliated groups. The second section comprised 19 chapters on foreign student dissidence.

Pages 11 & 12 Black radicalism

OCI began following Caribbean black radicalism in earnest in 1968. Two papers were produced on the subject, one in August 1969 and the other in June 1970.

OCI was asked in June 1970 to write a memo with special attention to links between black radicalism in the Caribbean and advocates of black power in the US. The memo was produced in typescript and given to the DCI.

OCI in 1968 wrote periodic typescript memos on Stokely Carmichael's travels abroad during a period when he had dropped from public view.

00336

Page [illegible] [illegible]

In September 1972 ██████ came to conduct feasibility tests of certain HF long-distance commercial telephone circuits between the US and South America. The circuits carried drug-related traffic. ██████ ██████ The tests were successful. The activity was terminated on 30 Jan 73 following OGC determination that they were illegal.

We conduct an intercept operation in ██████ targeted on radio telephone conversations by ██████ ██████ These intercepts contain a large number of unrelated conversations often involving US citizens.

Testing in the US of ORD-developed electronic collection systems occasionally result in the collection of domestic telephone conversations. When the tests are complete, the intercepted material is destroyed.

CIA ██████ technicians conducted tests in the Miami area in August 1971 of DF gear intended for use against a Soviet agent in South Vietnam. While wholly innocuous, the tests preceded the holding of the conventions there and could be construed as being somehow related to them.

In February 1972 CIA asked an official of AT&T for copies of telephone call slips relating to US-China calls. The operation lasted for three or four months and then dried up. OGC stated its belief that the collection of these slips did not violate the Communications Act since eavesdropping was not involved.

Page 29 Mail coverage

Since 1953, CIA has operated a mail intercept program of incoming and outgoing Russian mail and, at various times, other selected mail at Kennedy Airport in New York City. This program is now dormant pending decision on whether to continue or to abolish it.

00337

ATTACHMENT

FEDERAL BUREAU OF INVESTIGATION

TSD has had a close working relationship with the FBI over the past few years. The FBI is the only organization that has been fully briefed on TSD audio techniques and equipment. The following are situations where TSD equipment and guidance were involved in operations:

00338

SECRET

(G) TSD has furnished equipment items which constitute an on-the-shelf capability to engage in photo and audio surveillance operations which might not be known to the Agency. In one case it is known that a relatively unsophisticated device was used against a domestic target.

SECRET

10 July 1973

I talked with Ben Evans after the morning meeting today, about the skeletons assignment, mentioned yesterday morning by Mr. Colby. He and I both understood it to be a status report on where these items stand. I had spoken with Mr. Colby yesterday afternoon and gathered that it was based on the Nedzi briefing.

I proposed, and he agreed, that we prepare a status report on where the items covered in the Nedzi briefing stand now. A separate section would cover those things not included in the Nedzi briefing. He got the rough notes dictated by Mr. Colby on tape and transcribed. I had xerox copies made and returned the originals to [redacted]

When [redacted] reviewed the Colby notes, it became apparent that he was issuing instructions on what to do with the various items. This, in effect, pre-empted the status report we were preparing. I phoned Evans, saying that this was the case and that we proposed simply to edit the material for Colby (Colby had told me he planned to send it to us for editing after reviewing it himself). Evans said he would put a note on the papers telling Colby of this.

SDB

00341

MEMORANDUM FOR: DO

Pls find out what the two notes refer to — Maybe DDO files will show

WEC

23 MAY 1973

(DATE)

00342

(47)

FORM NO. 101 REPLACES FORM 10-101 WHICH MAY BE USED.
1 AUG 54

UNCLASSIFIED | CONFIDENTIAL | SECRET

OFFICIAL ROUTING SLIP

TO	NAME AND ADDRESS	DATE	INITIALS
1	W. E. Colby	5/23	
2			
3			
4			
5			
6			

ACTION		DIRECT REPLY		PREPARE REPLY
APPROVAL		DISPATCH		RECOMMENDATION
COMMENT		FILE		RETURN
CONCURRENCE		INFORMATION		SIGNATURE

Remarks:

See second sheet of notes on your copy only (at paragraph) Do not know if this was related in any way. We have no details in OPPB of this DCI-approved expenditure.

00343

FOLD HERE TO RETURN TO SENDER

FROM: NAME, ADDRESS AND PHONE NO.	DATE
Charles A. Briggs, D/PPB	5/23/73

UNCLASSIFIED | CONFIDENTIAL | SECRET

FORM NO. 1-67 237 Use previous editions (40)

23 May 1973

MEMORANDUM FOR: Deputy Director for Management and Services

SUBJECT: Watergate Principals - Direct or Indirect Involvement

1. This memorandum responds to the Director's request for a report of any involvement in any capacity since 1 January 1969 with Messrs. Hunt, McCord, Liddy, Young, or Krogh.

2. I have had none with Hunt, Liddy or Young.

3. My McCord contact was indirect and occurred sometime during the late 1960's when I was Director, Office of Computer Services. I opposed plans for Technical Division, Office of Security (under Mr. McCord) to acquire a separate computer for its In-Place Monitoring System. [redacted] of DD/S&T (then ORD) was the computer individual working with TD and, I think, would have details.

4. The Krogh contact also was indirect and involved his request, first through OMB, that CIA fund foreign travel on behalf of the Cabinet Committee on International Narcotics Control. Individual phone discussions are noted in the attached. The Agency focal points were [redacted] and [redacted] I understand [redacted] has forwarded relevant documentation. Copies of memoranda from Messrs. Krogh, [redacted] and Colby are attached also.

5. I held a staff meeting yesterday to pass the request to all OPPB employees. One officer who was attending a funeral will not be available until tomorrow.

/s/ Charles A. Briggs

Charles A. Briggs
Director of Planning,
Programming, and Budgeting

Distribution:
Orig & 1 - Addressee
1 - Mr. E. Colby
1 - D/PPB Chrono File
O/PPB/CABriggs/mm: 4420 (23May73)

Attachment
As stated

00344

SECRET

Attachment
23 May 1973

4 Feb 72 — Call from Jim Taylor, OMB re "Bud" Krogh and his deputy, Walter Minnick, of the Domestic Council who plan foreign travel in connection with their narcotics interests. Jim was alerting us to their intention to ask us for funds for the travel.

7 Feb 72 — Follow-up from Taylor: Plan 3-5 trips for 3 individuals--all in FY 72. Cost probably $10K. Minnick ready to make first trip. [redacted] is plugged in. ExDir said OK re Tehran visit.

7 Feb 72 — See attached memo from Egil Krogh, Jr. to Bill Colby and follow-on memos from [redacted] (21 Jul 72) and Colby (2 Aug 72).

12(?) May 72 — John Hurley, OMB called, mentioning possible Krogh/Minnick attendance at a Latin American (Station Chief?) conference on narcotics. He also said Jeff Shepherd, White House, was laying on a ~~trip~~ trip with [redacted] for himself, Shepherd and Mark Alger, OMB to Europe.

23 Jun 72 — [redacted] commented on Krogh/Minnick interest in getting CA activities, including large-scale PM, on narcotics front. [redacted]

6 Jul 72 — [redacted] called. Notes say only: "Minnick-Hurley film. We will send."

2 Aug 72 — [redacted] called re Colby letter (attached). Said travel orders ready; need money this PM (No record in my notes as to who was traveling when, but have faint recollection of its being to Mexico City). [redacted] and Ben Evans contacted by [redacted]

1 Nov 72 — Related? [redacted] call. Again notes are cryptic: [redacted] Survey BNDD problems/Mexico."

~~SECRET~~

00345

On Mr. Colby's copy only:

13 Jan 72 ExDir (Colby) said DCI had approved $30K for sensitive CS project - no details.

20 Jan 72 Reminded ExDir re $32K he said DCI OK'd.

SECRET

00346

THE WHITE HOUSE

WASHINGTON

February 7, 1972

MEMORANDUM FOR BILL COLBY

SUBJECT: BUDGETARY SUPPORT FOR THE CABINET COMMITTEE ON INTERNATIONAL NARCOTICS CONTROL

The Cabinet Committee on International Narcotics Control was created September 7, 1971, by the President to centralize his attack on the international drug traffic.

The Committee does not have a separate budget.

Salary and administrative support for its small, full-time staff has been provided by the Executive Office of the President. Other expenses are being charged to the constituent agencies and departments.

The Bureau of Customs, BNDD, and AID/Office of Public Safety have provided support to date.

The CIA should be prepared to defray not more than fifteen thousand dollars in overseas travel expenses for Cabinet Committee staff during the remainder of FY-1972.

Walter C. Minnick, the Committee's Staff Coordinator, can be contacted for further details.

Thank you for your assistance.

Egil Krogh Jr.

Egil Krogh, Jr.
Executive Director
Cabinet Committee on
International Narcotics Control

CC: John Ehrlichman
Assistant to the President for Domestic Affairs
Mark Alger
OMB, Chief, General Government Programs Division
[redacted]
CIA Representative, CCINC Working Group

00347

PPB 72-1063

2 AUG 1972

MEMORANDUM FOR: Deputy Director for Plans

SUBJECT: Fiscal Year 1973 Budgetary Support for the Cabinet Committee on International Narcotics Control (CCINC)

REFERENCE: Memo to ExDir from C/DDP/NARCOG dtd 21 July 1972; same subject

1. This is in response to the referenced memo regarding use of CIA funds to cover travel expenses for the White House Cabinet Committee Staff for Fiscal Year 1973.

2. You are authorized to obligated up to $15,000 for the use of the White House Cabinet Committee Staff for travel expenses during FY 1973. Obligation should be recorded against the O/DDP allotment and travel orders issued against your own appropriate fan number.

3. To the extent that you are unable to absorb this requirement within your present allotment, we will have to arrange some reprogramming later in the year to cover this unbudgeted item.

/s/

W. E. Colby
Executive Director-Comptroller

O/PPB/[redacted]hg 2 Aug 72
Distribution:
Orig & 1 - addressee
1 - ExDir
1 - ER
1 - PPB Subj (BMS
1 - O/F
1 - Reading
[redacted] Chrono

00348

21 July 1972

MEMORANDUM FOR: Executive Director - Comptroller

VIA : Deputy Director for Plans

SUBJECT : Fiscal Year 1973 Budgetary Support for the Cabinet Committee on International Narcotics Control (CCINC)

1. At our invitation, Mr. Walter C. Minnick, Staff Member of the CCINC, is scheduled to attend and participate in the Regional Narcotics Seminar sponsored by WH Division on 27-28 July 1972.

2. In accordance with procedures adopted for travel of White House Cabinet Committee Staff in FY 1972, it is requested that funds to cover the cost of Mr. Minnick's trip be released. Attached herewith is a copy of a formal request from Mr. Egil Krogh dated 7 February 1972 to Mr. William Colby requesting travel funds for the balance of FY 1972. Mr. Krogh is now preparing a formal request for $15,000.00 to cover travel expenses for White House Cabinet Committee staff for FY 1973. I will forward this request to your office as soon as it arrives.

C/DDP/NARCOG

Attachment: A/S

00349

RECORD COPY

SECRET

31 MAY 1973

6-1-73

MEMORANDUM FOR: Mr. Colby

SUBJECT : Review of Minutes of Morning Meetings

Per your request relayed through Ben Evans, we have read the minutes of the Director's morning meetings covering the period from 1 July 1970 through 31 March 1973 looking for items appearing to relate in any way to Watergate, the "plumbers," Agency involvement in the nominating conventions, or any other sensitive matters surfaced in the course of our present inquiries. We sifted rather finely and ended up with some 25-30 pages of material that we have in rough typescript. I doubt that it is worth while typing them in final, since you would be little enlightened by wading through them. We gave Ben Evans a copy at his request. The following are highlights:

There are about 25 entries during July and August 1971 relating to the Pentagon papers.

3 September 1970

The Director noted a 1 September memorandum from John Bross on Daniel Elsperg (sic). He asked the DDS to lift his clearances and to make this fact known in security channels.

23 December 1970 (DDCI in the chair)

Executive Director called attention to the President's 21 December memorandum on "Disclosures of Classified Information and Coordination and Clearance of Official Statements," which is believed to be the result of representations by the Director and Admiral Anderson. Executive Director said that he will meet with selected Executive Committee Members next week to discuss the memorandum's implications and to develop recommendations for action by the Director in view of the special responsibilities placed on him by the President.

00350

SECRET SENSITIVE

8 July 1971

DDCI reported that John Ehrlichman had telephoned to advise us that the White House is appointing former CIA employee Howard Hunt as a security consultant.

Another account of the Morning Meeting of this date reads:

It was also announced that Howard Hunt has been named security consultant to the White House. General Cushman told Ehrlichman that Mr. Hunt would have full cooperation from CIA.

16 July 1971

Carver said that [redacted] was most appreciative of the time which Houston spent with him yesterday.

22 July 1971 (the day Howard Hunt came to see General Cushman)

Carver highlighted his session yesterday with NSC staffer David Young, who is assisting John Ehrlichman in reviewing the secret Pentagon papers.

18 August 1971

A-DDP noted that he has reported to White House staffer David Young on the results of the Deputy Director of Security's survey of those who saw the classified assessment upon which Tad Szulc based his 13 August article.

11 November 1971

In response to the Director's question Carver said that some work requested by John Ehrlichman is pending. The Director asked to be filled in later on the details.

18 January 1972

DDI called attention to the article in today's New York Times, "Nixon Acts to End Security Leaks." (Excerpt from the article: "Last July, two members of the White House staff, David R. Young of the National Security Council and Egil Krogh, Jr., of the Domestic Council, were asked to investigate earlier leaks and prevent recurrences.")

SECRET SENSITIVE

8 February 1972

DDI noted the article by Michael Getler in today's Washington Post, "New Spy Satellites Planned for Clearer, Instant Pictures." Later in the meeting the Director asked the DDS to advise the Director of Security to undertake an investigation of this leak of EOI-related information and to convene the USIB Security Committee.

11 February 1972

The Director reminded Executive Committee members of Dr. Kissinger's request that any inquiries from elements of the White House staff be referred to his staff for conveyance to the Agency.

16 February 1972

Lehman noted plans to continue briefing Attorney General Mitchell, whose resignation is effective 1 March.

6 March 1972

The Director noted his memorandum to the Deputies and Independent Office Hea 's, subject: "Allegations of Assassinations." He asked that it be mentioned at Staff Meetings.

21 March 1972

The Director said that the President has seen his 17 February memorandum on reducing disclosures of classified intelligence and directed the White House staff to prepare a memorandum urging that all agencies comply with proper disclosure procedures.

8 June 1972

Houston said that he will be attending a meeting called by DOD General Counsel Buzhardt, who is recommending that Justice drop the case against Daniel Ellsberg.

00352

19 June 1972

The Director noted the 17 June arrest of James W. McCord and four others who were apprehended at the Democratic National Committee headquarters at the Watergate. With the Director of Security present to provide biographic details, the Director made it perfectly clear that responses to any inquiry with respect to McCord or Howard Hunt, who may be implicated, are to be limited to a statement that they are former employees who retired in August and April 1970 respectively. The Director asked that this guidance be disseminated via staff meetings. The Director asked that any inquiry from other elements of the government be referred to the Director of Security who is to be the focal point. Inquiries from the press are to be referred to Mr. Unumb who may say that McCord worked in the Office of Security. The Director noted that we have no responsibility with respect to an investigation except to be responsive to the FBI's request for name traces. It was noted that Howard Hunt may have done some work since retirement in connection with the preparation of supporting material for some awards. The Executive Director was asked to review this topic and report to the Director.

20 June 1972

In response to the Director's request, the Director of Security highlighted developments over the past twenty-four hours with respect to the McCord/Hunt, et al., situation. He noted that the late edition of the New York Times carries a different story by Tad Szulc than that which appeared in the edition received here. The Director of Security anticipates some inquiries on Bernard L. Barker's situation, and it was noted that Mr. Barker was hired by the Agency in 1960 and terminated in 1966. The Director complimented Unumb on his handling of inquiries and asked that future inquiries be met with a response confined to the fact that, now that we have acknowledged that both McCord and Hunt are former Agency employees, we know nothing more about the case and the caller should be referred to the FBI as appropriate.

20 June 1972

The Director noted receipt of a paper on a safehouse in Miami which is being made available to the Secret Service in support of its work in connection with the Republican and Democratic National Conventions. He asked the ADDP and the DDS to make it absolutely

00353

~~SECRET SENSITIVE~~

clear [redacted] that our cooperation in this undertaking is to be confined to provision of the safehouse and that it is not to be used as a site for investigations, interrogations, or "walk-ins", etc. The Director added that we will not loan people to the FBI or Secret Service in connection with their responsibilities at the Conventions nor will we provide equipment unique to the Agency.

21 June 1972

In view of the coverage in today's New York Times and Washington Post, Maury recommended that Chairman Nedzi be briefed on the McCord affair and that this briefing include all our information about the others involved. The Director asked Maury to touch base with the Director of Security and prepare a briefing paper on this topic for his review. Citing the number of distorted rumors about this matter, the Executive Director said that during the course of the day he hopes to provide a suggested Headquarters Bulletin for all employees for the Director's review.

Unumb noted a number of inquiries from the press with respect to the Cuban-Americans involved in the bugging attempt at the Democratic National Committee headquarters and their alleged involvement in the Bay of Pigs, etc. The Director asked that such inquiries be met with an explanation that we are not prepared to be helpful on this matter.

23 June 1972

Maury noted that he briefed Chairman Nedzi on the McCord/ Hunt situation.

21 August 1972

Houston noted a telephone call from Howard Hunt who explained that his attorney was with him and had a question about a friend's past affiliation with the Agency. [redacted] DD/Sec, has reviewed the employment, and Houston reported that he replied directly to Hunt's friend, Mr. [redacted] that this old affiliation should create no problems in connection with his appearance before a grand jury.

18 October 1972

Maury noted his response to a request from CSC General Counsel Anthony Mondello, who was reacting to a request for the personnel files of those former Agency officers involved in the

00354

SECRET SENSITIVE

Watergate incident from Senator Kennedy's Subcommittee on Administrative Practices and Procedures. He added that we are exempted from related CSC regulations, and the Director endorsed his plan to provide only the dates of their departure from the Agency in the event the Senator's office calls us on this matter.

3 November 1972

Houston recalled that last August he reported on a call from Howard Hunt and his subsequent guidance to [redacted] [redacted] on how to handle affiliation with the Agency, [redacted]

The Director highlighted his conversation with David Kraslow of the Washington Star News and his flat denial of a proposed story that the Agency was asked to report on the Democratic Party which led to the Watergate incident and others. The Director noted his plans to issue a statement of denial if such a story were to appear and suggested that Thuermer consider drafting one for contingency use.

15 November 1972

DDP noted a report from Chief, WH Division that on 9 October a Mr. Harper of the New York Times was working on a story which tries to link the Agency with Cuban emigres, the break-in at the Chilean Embassy, action against Daniel Ellsberg, and the Watergate case. Thuermer observed that this is the first he has heard about this topic, and the DDP concluded that such a story would have no basis in fact and it would be inadvisable to try to straighten out Mr. Harper.

22 November 1972

Warner related that according to Assistant Attorney General Henry Peterson, U. S. Attorney Earl Silbert has several questions on the Watergate case. The Director indicated he will review this matter later.

13 December 1972

The Director noted the article by Thomas B. Ross in yesterday's Evening Star-News, "New Watergate Dimension?" and the impression left therein that the Agency was involved in the Watergate incident because a passport bearing the name Edward Hamilton was found on Frank Sturgis. Any inquiries from the press or elsewhere are to be met with a "this is nonsense" reply. The Executive Director noted work under way to identify the genesis of the passport story.

15 January 1973

Maury noted press stories that Watergate defendant Martinez was on the Agency payroll until 17 June and anticipated some inquiry on this topic. The DDP endorsed his view that, whereas Martinez was intermittently used as a source to report on Cuban exile matters, this relationship should cause no serious difficulty.

18 January 1973

Maury reported that when he and Dave Blee, Chief/SB, saw Chairman Nedzi with respect to the Chairman's forthcoming trip to Finland, Leningrad, Sofia, and Athens, Chairman Nedzi briefed on his November conversation with New York Times correspondent Seymour Hersh. Maury went on to highlight the several topics and allegations Hersh claims he has with respect to Agency activities, particularly allegations that we are engaged in extensive domestic operations. Maury will circulate a memorandum on the information Hersh claims he has. The Director explained that we should assemble a senior team to meet with Chairman Nedzi and clearly outline what we do and do not do in the United States.

19 January 1973

Maury reported that Chairman Nedzi would like the full Subcommittee on Intelligence Operations to hear a presentation by us on Agency activity in the United States sometime in mid-February. The Director noted that his decision of yesterday to turn out a senior team for this briefing stands.

00356

22 January 1973

General Walters noted Howard Hunt's appearance on television last night. Thuermer will obtain a transcript of the program, and the Executive Director noted his concern over Hunt's suggestion that he is no longer bound by his secrecy agreement.

23 January 1973

Executive Director noted that the terminal secrecy agreement which Howard Hunt signed said that he will be acknowledged as an Agency employee. His assertion that he is not bound by the agreement because we did in fact acknowledge his employment here is therefore ill-advised.

7 February 1973

Maury noted that Mr. Helms is appearing before the Senate Foreign Relations Committee this morning on police training, ITT, and the Watergate incident. He also noted that he has solicited the support of Senators Humphrey, McGee, and Scott to make appropriate public statements following Mr. Helms appearance.

8 February 1973

Maury recalled that we are obligated to sit down with Chairman Nedzi and review what we do and don't do in the U.S. The Director concurred. The DDI suggested that we undertake an in-house review of what it is we are doing ~~in~~ within the U.S. and identify and eliminate the marginal.

14 February 1973

Thuermer noted advice from Nicholas Horrock of Newsweek that a "soft story" is floating around Newsweek on the general topic of political espionage and ex-CIA agents.

- 8 -

00357

1 March 1973

Maury related that former Director Richard Helms has been asked by Senator Fulbright to reappear before the Senate Foreign Relations Committee. Maury said that Mr. Helms would probably be queried on the Watergate incident, Agency training of police, and ITT and went on to describe Mr. Helms' anticipated response.

2 March 1973

Maury highlighted yesterday's LIG meeting at the White House and his recommendation that we not provide examples of Congressional leaks of classified information for White House use in reacting to Congressional criticism of the Administration's "indiscretions." The DDS advised that the Office of Security is keeping a reasonably complete record of obvious leaks of intelligence information in the press and elsewhere.

6 March 1973

The Director noted advice that Hugh Sidey of Time magazine plans to write a story alleging that Howard Hunt was employed by a cover organization, i.e., Robert R. Mullen Company, when he left the Agency. Colby noted that this company is a completely private concern but has provided cover for one or two officers overseas. The Director asked Thuermer to be prepared to cope with any inquiries when the story appears.

(Signed) William V. Broe
William V. Broe
Inspector General

Excerpt, WVB Daily Log of 30 May 1973.

1100: [redacted] called WVB, to bring to his attention the fact that Kissinger has asked for some papers he'd received in summer of 1970; now wants to see them again. One, Restless Youth (June 1970). OCI wrote a whole set of country chapters; and [redacted] of the CS (since left CIA) wrote a more sensitive piece drawing on US and other countries for examples to make its point. OCI balked--didn't want to do anything on the US side. The whole project eventually was turned over to CA. [redacted] worked under [redacted] supervision [redacted] also left--in Boston).

Thereafter XXXXXXXX, in August 1970, because we had done so much work we published a separate paper "Student Unrest Abroad"---compilation of the country studies.

WVB: There was a 3rd---on the Caribbean--black aspects.

WVB is familiar with the 3---but didn't know about the [redacted] aspects.

Per [redacted] Kissinger had told Latimer "You guys sent me a xxxxx paper; I sent it back with some nice words on it--would like to see again" (not a direct quote). WVB said he had the DDI's copy. Whitman says Latimer has copies of both reports. His records suggest that [redacted] paper was carried to San Clemente perhaps by Gen. XXXXX Cushman, but gathered Cushman had been unable to deliver it to Kissinger. Could be that Kissinger didn't see [redacted] only the others. Records do not confirm this in detail. Latimer is struggling with Kissinger's request.

WVB said he'd check with [redacted] who has all that stuff....

cm/30 May 73

00359

ROUTING AND RECORD SHEET

SUBJECT: (Optional)

FROM: Inspector General

EXTENSION | NO.

DATE 29 May 1973

TO: (Officer designation, room number, and building)	DATE RECEIVED	DATE FORWARDED	OFFICER'S INITIALS	COMMENTS (Number each comment to show from whom to whom. Draw a line across column after each comment.)
1. Executive Secretary, CIA Management Committee	5/29	5/31		
2.				
3. IG	5/30			
4. [redacted] Jewels				
5.				
6.				
7.				
8.				
9.				
10.				
11.				
12.				
13.				
14.				
15.				00360

FORM 3-62 610 USE PREVIOUS EDITIONS ☐ SECRET ☐ CONFIDENTIAL ☐ INTERNAL USE ONLY ☐ UNCLASSIFIED

~~SECRET SENSITIVE~~

00361

~~SECRET SENSITIVE~~

00362

- 2 -

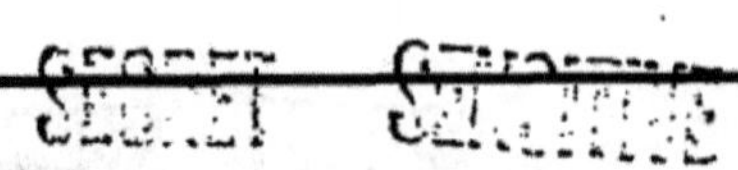

00363

00364

00366

SECRET SENSITIVE

- 2 -

00367

00368

CONFIDENTIAL

00371

[illegible] senators were kept under electronic surveillance, according to a source close to the defendants.

The operation at the Embassy of Chile, 1736 Massachusetts Ave. NW, involved three men, the source said. One pulled documents from the files, one photographed the documents, and one placed them back in the files. Embassy officials have said that last May their chancery was burglarized and the files of their ambassador and political chief were searched.

The source, a person well acquainted with the activities of the Watergate defendants, made the information available on the condition that his name not be used.

Among the senators whose activities were in some way allegedly monitored were Senate Majority Leader Mike Mansfield (D-Mont.), Senate Foreign Relations Committee Chairman J. William Fulbright (D-Ark.), and Sen. Frank Church (D-Idaho). This source also said that Sol Linowitz, former U.S. ambassador to the Organization of American States, was kept under similar surveillance.

While Newsday was able to confirm some of the source's statements through officials close to the investigation, allegations concerning the surveillance of senators neither could be confirmed nor denied.

The seven defendants in the Watergate case go on trial Monday in the U.S. District Court here.

It also has been learned that:

• Federal authorities have tracked down and questioned two men who had been involved in Washington with the Watergate group but who had not been caught at the Democratic headquarters scene June 17.

• Federal investigators have obtained a daily diary that was being written by one of the Watergate defendants, Eugenio Martinez.

[illegible] a CIA case officer—may have been monitoring the activities of the Watergate team. [illegible] work for the CIA in the years following his part in the Bay of Pigs affair, according to a well-informed defense source in the case. The source says that Martinez confessed to his fellow defendants that he had been keeping the diary, at the urging of his current CIA supervisor, after it was seized by federal officials.

Investigation sources acknowledge that FBI agents found the diary in the trunk of Martinez' car, which was parked at Miami International Airport.

Assistant U.S. Attorney Earl J. Silbert declined to say whether Martinez' diary would be introduced as evidence in the Watergate trial, which opens Monday.

De Diego, 43, is a real estate salesman who was employed in Miami real estate office of Bernard L. Barker, one of the Watergate defendants.

De Diego, who was granted immunity by the grand jury investigating the case, said he told the grand jury and the FBI that he had come to Washington last May with Pico and the four Watergate defendants from the Miami area (Barker, Martinez, Frank Sturgis and Virgilio R. Gonzales). He said that he believed he and his friends were waiting to see someone from the government [illegible] Miami.

[illegible] gate defendant [illegible] former security consultant for the President's re-election committee, was arrested in [illegible] the Watergate on June 17 with the four defendants from Miami.

While de Diego said he had no knowledge of any such [illegible] activities by the group while he was in Washington last May, other defense sources said the group was quite busy during that period.

During the weekend of May 13-14, the chancery of the [illegible] Embassy [illegible], first secretary of the embassy, said yesterday [illegible] reaction from police [illegible] government [illegible] committed the act.

00372

MEMORANDUM FOR: Deputy Director for Operations

SUBJECT: WH Comments on Jack Anderson Column

REFERENCE: Jack Anderson's Washington Merry-Go-Round Column of 8 March 1973: "Chilean Break-ins Reflect Watergate"

1. WH Division has reviewed the referenced column (copy attached) by Jack Anderson and finds that it contains no new information. To the best knowledge of the Division, there is no foundation to the allegation that E. Howard Hunt was engaged on behalf of ITT in breaking into Chilean diplomatic installations in Washington and New York.

2. Any connection between ITT and these break-ins is purely conjectural and the column takes care to point this out.

has told us that he had no relationship with Hunt on this or any ITT matter. He had anticipated that Anderson might imply such a relationship in his column and had assured us that this was not true.

Theodore G. Shackley

Theodore G. Shackley
Chief
Western Hemisphere Division

Attachment: As Stated

00373

SECRET/SENSITIVE

OFFICIAL ROUTING SLIP

TO	NAME AND ADDRESS	DATE	INITIALS
1	D/OS		
2	DD/PS		
3			
4			
5	A/EO	14 MAR 1973	
6	File		

ACTION		DIRECT REPLY		PREPARE REPLY
APPROVAL		DISPATCH		RECOMMENDATION
COMMENT		FILE		RETURN
CONCURRENCE		INFORMATION		SIGNATURE

Remarks:

This is of interest re Watergate & also Seymour Hersh.

00374

FOLD HERE TO RETURN TO SENDER

FROM: NAME, ADDRESS AND PHONE NO.	DATE
Executive Officer	12 MAR 1973

UNCLASSIFIED | CONFIDENTIAL | SECRET

FORM NO. 1-67 237 Use previous editions (40)

The Washington Merry-Go-Round — THE WASHINGTON POST [illegible]

Chilean Break-ins Reflect Watergate

By Jack Anderson

Senate investigators suspect that the "Mission Impossible" team arrested at the Watergate may also have broken into the Chilean Embassy several weeks earlier. And three Chilean diplomats in New York City, the investigators discovered, have been victims of similar, mysterious break-ins.

In a memo intended for the eyes only of senators investigating ITT's operations in Chile, staff director Jerry Levinson reported: "A source with excellent contacts in the Cuban community told the subcommittee staff that Frank Sturgis had told other people that he and Martinez and Gonzalez, two other Watergate defendants, had broken into the embassy to photograph documents."

Levinson was cautious, however, about implicating ITT in the alleged Chilean caper. "The staff of the subcommittee," he reported, "has developed a number of leads suggesting a relationship between ITT and the team which was arrested at the Watergate." But he stressed "that the case outlined in this memorandum is circumstantial and that there is no hard evidence of ITT involvement."

Suspicious Case

Here, however, is the circumstantial case, which the subcommittee staff has pieced together from jig-saw pieces of intelligence: "Government and non-government sources alike have told us that the Cuban exile community has a pool of talent which was trained by the CIA and is available for 'dirty tricks.' This talent has been used at one time or another by a number of federal agencies for missions of questionable legality inside and outside of the United States.

"Federal sources report the Cubans to be absolutely loyal, fanatically anti-Communist and willing to take any risk. It is also likely that when 'teams' were assembled for operations, only one or perhaps two members knew who had requested and was financing the operation.

"Washington business and political sources report that about eight months before the Watergate arrest, E. Howard Hunt let it be known around the city that he had a 'team' available for 'Mission Impossible' assignments and that the team would be willing to work for private clients.

"It is possible that E. Howard Hunt, acting as the contractor for the 'team,' had more than one client and that a second client was ITT, which was interested in obtaining information about its negotiations over the fate of its investment in the Chilean Telephone Company. The members of the team may have been recruited, thinking they were doing a patriotic thing to block a 'Communist' government.

"ITT is the only likely contractor for operations against the Chileans. It claims to have an investment worth $153 million in the Chilean Telephone Company; it knew that documents were leaking from its files; it asked the Chilean government to move negotiations from Santiago to Washington."

ITT and Watergate

We reported last week on other strange links between the ITT and Watergate scandals. We noted, for example, that acting FBI chief L. Patrick Gray and convicted Watergate felon E. Howard Hunt had been involved in an abortive effort to discredit the famous Dita Beard memo, which tied a $400,000 political pledge from ITT with a settlement of its antitrust troubles.

The Washington Post reported that Hunt, apparently disguised in an askew red wig, went to Denver to talk to Mrs. Beard about renouncing the memo. We reported that Gray, meanwhile, turned the original memo over to ITT for its experts to try to discredit.

Gray refused to comment when we called the FBI for his response. Questioned by senators under oath, however, he testified that he had not turned the memo over to ITT directly but had delivered it to White House aide John Dean. It was the White House, in other words, that not only dispatched the bewigged Hunt to Denver but also passed the document to ITT.

This makes the story even more sordid. It shows that the White House, while denying any involvement with ITT, was working closely with the giant conglomerate to discredit the Dita Beard memo.

The Chilean Embassy burglary was investigated by the FBI, which dismissed it as routine. But Senate investigators disagree. "Careful investigation of the circumstances leads us to the conclusion," Levinson wrote, "that it was not routine.

"Valuable office equipment and cash were left untouched. The Ambassador's office and the office of the First Secretary were both searched and files were inspected. The thieves walked past several more attractive offices to get to the First Secretary's office, suggesting they knew where they were going." The burglarizing of the New York apartments of Chilean diplomats were described in the memo as "similar clean break-ins."

Footnote: Jerry Levinson refused to comment on his memo, which he said wasn't intended for publication. An ITT spokesman called the allegations about Hunt "absolutely and totally untrue." He said ITT had never hired Hunt for any purpose.

00375

ROUTING AND RECORD SHEET

TO		DATE	INITIALS
1	DD/Security		
2			
3			
4			
5			
6			

	ACTION		DIRECT REPLY		PREPARE REPLY
	APPROVAL		DISPATCH		RECOMMENDATION
	COMMENT		FILE		RETURN
	CONCURRENCE		INFORMATION		SIGNATURE

Remarks:

FOLD HERE TO RETURN TO SENDER

FROM: NAME, ADDRESS AND PHONE NO.	DATE
DDO	

UNCLASSIFIED | CONFIDENTIAL | SECRET

FORM NO. 1-67 237 Use previous editions (40)

00375a

EXECUTIVE PROTECTIVE SERVICE
INCIDENT REPORT

1. CC/FMD CASE NUMBER: 72-328

3. LOCATION (NATION) (STREET ADDRESS)	5. NATURE OF INCIDENT
Chile 1736 Massachusetts Avenue, N.W.	Burglary II

6. REPORTED BY:	7. ADDRESS	8. HOME PHONE / 9. OFFICE PHONE
Hernan Navarro	1706 [illegible] Street, [illegible]	321-1021 / 785-1746

10. OFFICE ASSIGNED	11. DATE	12. HOUR	13. DAY OF WEEK
Sergeant Stevens E. Butler Sergeant Riley M. Richardson	05-15-72	1330 hrs.	(1) (2) 3 4 5 6 (7) (S) (M) T W T F (S)

14. WITNESS	15. ADDRESS	16. HOME PHONE / 17. OFFICE PHONE
N/A	N/A	N/A / N/A

18. WITNESS	19. ADDRESS	20. HOME PHONE / 21. OFFICE PHONE
N/A	N/A	N/A / N/A

22. DETAILS OF INCIDENT (BRIEFLY DESCRIBE INCIDENT. CONTINUE ABOVE ITEMS AS NECESSARY INDICATING ITEM)

At approximately 1330 hours, Monday, May 13, 1972, Foreign Missions Division-Control Center was advised by M.P.D.C., 3D, that a burglary had taken place at the Chancery of Chile, 1736 Massachusetts Avenue, N.W., sometime between 1600 hours on Friday, May 13, 1972, and on 0855 hours this date.

Sergeant Riley M. Richardson and the undersigned were dispatched at approximately 1335 hours in Cruiser # 23.

The undersigned was advised by Mr. Hernan (NMI) Navarro, Administrative Counselor of the Embassy of Chile, that the Chancery of Chile was entered and all the offices were ransacked. At this time the method of entry or items taken is unknown. Mr. Navarro advises that he will contact the Foreign Missions Division-Watch Command when determination of missing articles is made. (continued)

jam (USE EPS FORM 102 - SUPPLEMENT FOR ADDITIONAL DETAILS)

23. PHOTOS ☐ YES ☒ FS#

24. SUSPECT AND/OR ARRESTED PERSONS. IDENTIFY BY NAME, ADDRESS, SEX, RACE, SOCIAL SECURITY NUMBER, DOB, EYES, ETC. N/A

	LAST NAME	FIRST	MIDDLE	ADDRESS				
(1)	RACE	SEX	HEIGHT	WEIGHT	HAIR	EYES	DATE OF BIRTH	SOCIAL SECURITY NO. / NATIONALITY
	LAST NAME	FIRST	MIDDLE	ADDRESS				
(2)	RACE	SEX	HEIGHT	WEIGHT	HAIR	EYES	DATE OF BIRTH	SOCIAL SECURITY NO. / NATIONALITY

25. ARREST PD	26. ARREST NO.	27. ARREST OFFICER (NAME AND BADGE NO.)	28. DATE OF ARREST	29. HOUR

30. INCIDENT STATUS A. ☒ OPEN B. ☒ CLOSED C. ☐ UNFOUNDED D. ☐ CLEARED BY ARREST

31. REPORTING OFFICER (SIGNATURE) HOUR	DATE / HOUR	32. APPROVING OFFICIAL (SIGNATURE)	DATE / HOUR
Sgt. Stevens E. Butler [signature] Sergeant Stevens E. Butler	05-15-72 1500 hrs.	Pete N Manthos [signature] Captain Pete N. Manthos	05-15-7[2] 1505 h[rs.]

33. STATE DEPT. OFFICIAL NOTIFIED	DATE: / HOUR:	34. USSS-ID CASE NO.
N/A		N/A 0037

[illegible] 72-[illegible]3

3. TYPE OF INCIDENT

Burglary II

5. REPORTED BY: [illegible] (NMI) Navarro

4. ADDRESS: 7[illegible] [illegible] Street, Springfield, Va.

5. [illegible] 72[illegible]

6. [illegible] 6

7. ADDITIONAL DETAILS OF INCIDENT:

The following were previously on the scene: Sergeant Clifton O. Gill, Badge # [illegible], M.P.D.C., 3D, and Officer Michael S. [illegible], Badge # [illegible]0, M.P.D.C., 3D, also M.P. [illegible] Cruiser # 735.

S/A [redacted] USSS-PID (Foreign Branch), was notified.

jam

8. SUSPECT AND/OR ARRESTED PERSONS. IDENTIFY BY NAME, ADDRESS, SEX, RACE, SOCIAL SECURITY NUMBER, DOB, EYES, ETC.

N/A

	LAST NAME	FIRST	MIDDLE	ADDRESS
(1)				

RACE	SEX	HEIGHT	WEIGHT	HAIR	EYES	DATE OF BIRTH	SOCIAL SECURITY NO.	NATIONALI

	LAST NAME	FIRST	MIDDLE	ADDRESS
(2)				

RACE	SEX	HEIGHT	WEIGHT	HAIR	EYES	DATE OF BIRTH	SOCIAL SECURITY NO.	NATIONALI

9. ARREST PD	10. ARREST NO.	11. ARREST OFFICER (NAME & BADGE NO.)	12. DATE	13. HOUR

14. CURRENT CASE DISPOSTION

A. [X] OPEN B. [ ] CLOSED C. [ ] UNFOUNDED D. [ ] CLEARED BY ARREST

15. USSS-ID CASE NO.

N/A

16. FINAL CASE DISPOSITION

OPEN

00377

17. REPORTING OFFICER (SIGNATURE)	18. DATE	19. APPROVED (SIGNATURE & TITLE)	20. DATE
Sgt. Stevens E. Butler [signature] Sergeant Stevens E. Butler	05-15-72	Pete N Manthos [signature] Captain Pete N. Manthos	05-15

Burglary II

[illegible] (NMI) Navarro

[illegible] Springfield, Va.

[illegible]

ADDITIONAL DETAILS OF INCIDENT:

At approximately 1600 hours, Tuesday, May 16, 1972, Mr. Navarro contacted Officer Adrian Roman-Gonzalez at 1310 L Street, N.W. and stated the following items missing (4 Portable Radios), one (1) Sanyo AM/FM Portable Radio, two (2) Panasonic AM/FM Ra[illegible] and one (1) Westinghouse AM/FM/SW Radio. Also taken was one (1) Braun Electric Shave[illegible] one (1) Womens pullover sweater, and an unknown number of books.

jam

8. SUSPECT AND/OR ARRESTED PERSONS. IDENTIFY BY NAME, ADDRESS, SEX, RACE, SOCIAL SECURITY NUMBER, DOB, EYES, ETC. N/A

	LAST NAME	FIRST	MIDDLE	ADDRESS
(1)				

RACE	SEX	HEIGHT	WEIGHT	HAIR	EYES	DATE OF BIRTH	SOCIAL SECURITY NO.	NATIONALITY

	LAST NAME	FIRST	MIDDLE	ADDRESS
(2)				

RACE	SEX	HEIGHT	WEIGHT	HAIR	EYES	DATE OF BIRTH	SOCIAL SECURITY NO.	NATIONALITY

9. ARREST PD	10. ARREST NO.	11. ARREST OFFICER (NAME & BADGE NO.)	12. DATE	13. HOUR

14. CURRENT CASE DISPOSTION: A. [X] OPEN B. [X] CLOSED C. [ ] UNFOUNDED D. [ ] CLEARED BY ARREST

15. USSS-ID CASE NO.: N/A

16. FINAL CASE DISPOSITION: OPEN

00378

17. REPORTING OFFICER (SIGNATURE)	18. DATE	19. APPROVED (SIGNATURE & TITLE)	20. DATE
Sgt. Stevens E. Butler Sergeant Stevens E. Butler	05-15-72	Pete N. Manthos Captain Pete N. Manthos	05-15-

PERSON OR PREMISES				Embassy of Chile	338-42
14.	15. DIST. 3D	16.	17. P.A.	3. STREET ADDRESS 1736 MASS. Ave N.W.	4. HOME PHONE N/A
N/A				5. N/A	6. BUS. PHONE 785-177

DESCRIBE LOCATION OR TYPE OF PREMISES ▷ Chile Embassy	7. SEX	RACE	DOB	8. CRIME Burg. II	
VEHICLE USED N/A	9. LOCATION OF CRIME (Address) 1736 Mass Ave N.W.				10. DATE, TIME
YEAR MAKE MODEL COLOR(S)	11. WEAPON, TOOL, FORCE OR MEANS USED ▷ UNK				PHOTOS ☐ YES ☐ NO
CODE: O--OWNER R - REPORTING PERSON C--COMPLAINANT P - PARENT/GUAR	12. METHOD USED ▷ UNK				13. CLASSIFICATION ▷

22. NAME (Last, First, Middle)	CODE	RES. ADDRESS	HOME PHONE	BUS. PHONE
▷ NAVARRO, Hernan	R	7605 Hamlet St. Springfield VA	321-7121	785-17
23. Administrative Counselor ▷				
24. ▷				

25. IDENTIFY SUSPECTS BY NUMBER (Include Name, Address, Sex, Race, Age, Height, Weight, Eyes, Hair, Clothing etc.) IF ARRESTED GIVE ARREST NUMBER AND CHARGE (Omit description if arrested)

(1) ▷ N/A

(2) ▷

26. NATURE OF INJURIES AND LOCATION ON BODY ▷ N/A	27. HOSPITALIZED - WHERE? ▷ N/A ☐ ADM ☐ RELE
28. TRANSPORTED BY N/A	29. TREATED BY ▷ N/A

30. TYPE OF PROPERTY TAKEN ▷ UNK	31. LOSS VALUE ▷ UNK	32. TRADEMARKS, ACTIONS OR CONVERSATION OF SUSPECT N/A
33. EXACT LOCATION OF PROPERTY Inside Embassy	34. POINT OF ENTRY ▷ UNK	35. VEHICLE FROM WHICH THEFT OCCURRED TAG NO. STATE YEAR AND MAKE N/A

36. NARRATIVE: (1) CONTINUATIONS OF ABOVE ITEMS (INDICATE ITEM NUMBER) INCLUDE ADDITIONAL SUSPECTS AS OU LINED ABOVE. (2) BRIEFLY DESCRIBE INCIDENT AND ACTION TAKEN. (3) DESCRIBE EVIDENCE A PROPERTY INDICATE DISPOSITION AND DESCRIBE ALL PROPERTY INVOLVED. USE CONTINUATION R PORT IF MORE SPACE IS NEEDED. RECORD VALUE OF LOSS ESTIMATED BY VICTIM.

ITEM NO.

R-1 Reports Between The hours of 1600, 5-13-72 And 0855,
5-15-72 The Embassy of Chile was entered and ALL The
offices Ransaked. Unknown what was Taken AT This
Full Report To Follow Later.
CRU 244 SgT Gill on scene.
Print CRU 735 on Scene
OFF Leitz of E.P.S. Notified AT 1330 hrs.

OFFICE USE ONLY

9591	T.T. NUMBER	DATE & TIME THIS REPORT 5-15-72 1500	37. DATE/TIME TYPE NO.	38. REPRODUCE NO.

39. REPORTING OFFICER UNIT & BADGE NO. M.S. Kurdilla 3D 3770	40. STATUS (Check One) ☐ UNFOUNDED ☒ OPEN ☐ CLOSED ☐ SUSPENDED	41. UNIT REFERRED TO	42. UCR DISPOSITIC
43. SECOND OFFICER UNIT & BADGE NO. B.L. Dunning	44. SUPERVISOR APPROVING UNIT & BADGE NO. Sgt C.O. Gill 147	45. REVIEWER	NO 00379

PD 251 REVISED 3/71 METROPOLITAN POLICE DEPARTMENT WASHINGTON, D.C.

Department of State TELEGRAM

The "Family Jewels"

UNCLASSIFIED 154 OGC FILE

5-16-72

PAGE 01 SANTIA 02473 162301Z

72
ACTION ARA-16

INFO OCT-01 SS-14 CPR-02 SY-03 USSS-00 NSC-10 CIAE-00 DODE-00 INR-06 NSAE-00 P-03 RSC-01 USIA-12 PRS-01 RSR-01 /070 W

016973

R 162244Z MAY 72
FM AMEMBASSY SANTIAGO
TO SECSTATE WASHDC 1236

UNCLAS SANTIAGO 2473

SUBJ: UNAUTHORIZED ENTRY INTO CHILEAN EMBASSY: FONMIN STATEMENT

REF: SANTIAGO 2450 POL 17 Chile US

1. FOLLOWING IS OUR INFORMAL TRANSLATION OF STATEMENT (UNNECESSARY WORDS OMITTED) FONMIN UNDERSECRETARY PALMA GAVE PRESS EVENING MAY 15: QUOTE: CHILEAN AMBASSADOR IN US HAS INFORMED THIS MINISTRY THAT OVER WEEKEND CHANCERY OF EMBASSY IN WASHINGTON WAS ENTERED ILLEGALLY (VIOLADA) BY UNKNOWN INDIVIDUALS WHO PROCEEDED TO FORCE OPEN DESKS AND KARDEXES OF EMBASSY'S POLITICAL AFFAIRS OFFICE.

"OTHER CHANCERY OFFICES, IN ADDITION, WERE ENTERED ILLEGALLY ALBEIT ON LESSER SCALE. PRELIMINARY INVESTIGATION DISCLOSED REMOVAL OF DOCUMENTS, BOOKS, RADIOS, ETC. AS RESULT THESE SERIOUS ACTS, CHILEAN AMB TO US ADVISED STATE DEPT WHICH EXPRESSED 'ITS DEEP REGRET' AT WHAT HAD OCCURED.

"THIS AFTERNOON UNDERSECRETARY CALLED IN US AMBASSADOR TO EXPRESS GOC'S CONCERN ABOUT SECURITY OF ITS DIPLOMATIC MISSION IN US, REQUESTING RAPID AND RIGOROUS INVESTIGATION AS WELL AS ESTABLISHMENT OF POLICE GUARD TO PREVENT REALIZATION OF THESE LAMENTABLE ABUSES (DESMANES).

"FOR ITS PART OUR GOVT HAS ADOPTED MEASURES TO SAFEGUARD THE SECURITY OF OUR COMMUNICATIONS AND OBLIGATORY INVESTIGATION (SUMARIO) HAS BEEN ORDERED. UNQTE.

2. VIRTUALLY ALL SANTIAGO DAILIES THIS MORNING CARRY TEXT OR FAITHFUL SUMMARIES PALMA STATEMENT WITHOUT COMMENT OR FANCIFUL

(1)

UNCLASSIFIED

00380

Department of State TELEGRAM

UNCLASSIFIED

PAGE 02 SANTIA 02473 162301Z

HEADLINES. STORY BANNERED ACROSS FRONT PAGE, HOWEVER, BY COMMUNIST EL SIGLO AND INDEPENDENT LA TERCERA. GOVT TV NETWORK NEWS LAST EVENING RAN ANNOUNCEMENT AGAINST BACKDROP OF ITT EXPOSE POSTER.
DAVIS

00381

UNCLASSIFIED

POL 17 CHILE-US

Department of State TELEGRAM

CONFIDENTIAL 658 OGC FILE

5-15-72

PAGE 01 SANTIA 02450 152326Z

71
ACTION ARA-16

INFO OCT-01 CPR-02 SY-03 USSS-00 CIAE-00 DODE-00 INR-06
NSAE-00 P-03 RSC-01 USIA-12 PRS-01 SS-14 NSC-10 RSR-01

/070 W 008831

R 152306Z MAY 72
FM AMEMBASSY SANTIAGO
TO SECSTATE WASHDC 1218

C O N F I D E N T I A L SANTIAGO 2450

SUBJECT: UNAUTHORIZED ENTRY INTO CHILEAN EMBASSY

1. FOREIGN MINISTRY SUB-SECRETARY PALMA ASKED ME TO CALL ON HIM TODAY AT 5:30 P.M. I HAD JUST READ AP STORY FROM WASHINGTON ABOUT UNAUTHORIZED ENTRY INTO CHILEAN EMBASSY - AND KNEW WHAT TO EXPECT. PALMA EMPHASIZED THAT AMBASSADOR'S OFFICE SHOWED SIGNS OF HAVING BEEN CAREFULLY SEARCHED FOR PAPERS WHILE VALUABLES HAD NOT BEEN TOUCHED. HE SAID CHILEAN GOVERNMENT ASSUMED MOTIVE HAD BEEN POLITICAL. FROM HIS OWN RECENT EXPERIENCE IN WASHINGTON, PALMA SAID, HE KNEW PROTECTION GIVEN CHILEAN EMBASSY WAS LESS EFFECTIVE THAN IT MIGHT BE. HE SAID CHILEAN GOVERNMENT MADE SPECIAL EFFORTS TO PROTECT U.S. OFFICES AND RESIDENCES IN SANTIAGO IN PART BECAUSE OF DELICACY OF OUR RELATIONS - AND HE THOUGHT USG SHOULD ALSO STRIVE TO GIVE CHILEAN OFFICES AND HOMES BETTER THAN RUN-OF-THE-MILL PROTECTION. PALMA ASSURED ME THAT GOC HAS NO DESIRE THAT THIS INCIDENT BE MAGNIFIED. IN FACT, HE APPEARED SLIGHTLY TAKEN ABACK WHEN I MENTIONED THAT INCIDENT WAS ALREADY ON PRESS SERVICE WIRES.

2. I EXPRESSED REGRET THAT INCIDENT HAD OCCURRED AND THANKED PALMA FOR PROTECTION U.S. OFFICES ARE RECEIVING. (CARABINEROS BROKE UP DEMONSTRATION IN FRONT OF CONSULATE A FEW HOURS AGO.) I SAID I WOULD PASS ON GOC REQUEST FOR INCREASED PROTECTION.

3. STATE 84655 ARRIVED A FEW MOMENTS AGO. PALMA MADE NO MENTION OF PROPERTY DAMAGE OR THEFT OF RADIO.
DAVIS

00382

CONFIDENTIAL

XR SCC 11

FORM DS 322(OCR)

08465

| 084655 | 151903Z MAY 72 | ROGERS

OGC FILE

LIMITED OFFICIAL USE

ARA/BC/C:LGIRDLER
5/15/72 EXT 22575
ARA/BC:JWFISHER

S/CPR:HDAVIS

IMMEDIATE SANTIAGO

SUBJ: BREAK-IN AT CHILEAN CHANCERY

1. CHILEAN MINCOUNS VALDES PHONED DEPT (FISHER) MORNING MAY 15 TO REPORT THAT UPON ARRIVAL SAME MORNING THEY DISCOVERED PERSON OR PERSONS UNKNOWN HAD ENTERED CHANCERY (APPARENTLY SATURDAY NIGHT OR SUNDAY NIGHT) AND HAD SEARCHED SEVERAL OFFICES AND TAKEN SOME RADIOS AND BOOKS. DEPT IMMEDIATELY NOTIFIED APPROPRIATE AUTHORITIES THROUGH PROTOCOL AND SY CHANNELS, AND DEPTOFF (GIRDLER) VISITED CHANCERY TO EXPRESS CONCERN AND REGRET.

2. DURING VISIT, AMB LETELIER AND EMBOFFS DISMISSED ROBBERY AS POSSIBLE MOTIVE, STATING IT IMPOSSIBLE CONCEIVE THAT FOREIGN CHANCERY LOGICAL TARGET FOR STRAIGHT ROBBERY AND CONCLUDING THAT REAL PURPOSE WAS SEARCH FOR (UNSPECIFIED) DOCUMENTS. WHILE TERMING INCIDENT "DISAGREEABLE" THEY MADE NO HINT OF, OR REFERENCE TO, POSSIBLE PROTEST OR CLAIM FOR PROPERTY DAMAGE. YY

DOCUMENT AS REFERRED TO STATE DEPT.

00383

LIMITED OFFICIAL USE

OGC 73-0930
25 May 1973

MEMORANDUM FOR THE RECORD

SUBJECT: Chilean Embassy Break In on 15 May 1972

1. On 24 May 1973 I telephoned Mr. James Robinson, General Crime Section, Department of Justice and asked if he had any information as to criminal prosecution of persons involved in a break in at the Chilean Embassy in Washington, D.C. on 15 May 1972. Mr. Robinson stated he had no knowledge of this but suggested that it would be better to check with Mr. G. Marvin Gentile, Deputy Assistant Secretary for Security, Department of State, and the Secret Service since they had responsibilities for the Executive Protective Service (EPS). I telephoned Mr. Gentile and he identified two State Department cables relative to the incident; one from the embassy in Santiago to the Department, No. 2450, dated 15 May 1972, Subject: Unauthorized Entry Outlining the Protest of the Chilean Government presented to the American Embassy, and the State Department reply to Santiago, No. 084655, dated 15 May 1972. Mr. Gentile also identified the EPS report of investigation and suggested that I get a copy from the Secret Service. I then called [redacted] at Secret Service and he had his liaison man deliver me a copy of the EPS report of investigation.

2. On 25 May 1973 I received a call from FBI Agent [redacted] stating that he had received a telephone call from Mr. James Robinson relative to my inquiry about prosecution. [redacted] indicated that the FBI Washington Field Office had recontacted the Metropolitan Police Department (MPD) on 24 May and reviewed the report No. 248-424 filed with the 3rd District, MPD which states that a break in occurred at the Chilean Embassy between 5:00 and 8:00 a.m. on 15 May 1972.

00384

Reported loss at that time consisted of four am/fm radios and one electric razor. The police investigation identified some latent fingerprints but no identification of those prints was made. Since the reported loss was under $5,000 and there was no evidence of a crossing of state boundries, the FBI did not make an investigation of the incident. The MPD reported that there had been no prosecution and no suspect was identified.

Assistant General Counsel

cc: Legislative Counsel
Inspector General

25 May 1973

Note to : [illegible]

Names to be interviewed:

Mentioned at meeting of IG, DDO, and [illegible] -

Walt Elder

Left over from SDB's TSD (now OTS) interviews.

Names revealed in Office of Security report -

- Retiring June 1973, referred to McCord for job
- McCord offered part time work (still employed)
-
- Lectured for McCord at Mont. Jun Coll. Planed to work
- Wanted to raise bond for McCord

Where do we stand with:

Steve Kuhn)
Bruce Solie) Were to have been interviewed
Paul Gaynor)

I think WVB has interviewed following:

John Hart)
) Whose names appear in my notes to see
Ed Ryan)
Cord Meyer)

SDB 00386

~~SECRET~~

26 May 1973

MEMORANDUM FOR THE RECORD

SUBJECT: DDI "Trap" on Leaks of Narcotics Intelligence

1. In material provided by the DDI on contacts with certain persons on the White House Staff, there is a 9 September 1972 memorandum from Mr. Helms to Dr. Kissinger relating the identification of a leak to the press as having been in the BNDD. The memorandum states in part:

> "After noting that Jack Anderson had a continuing source for classified documents on narcotics, we arranged a trap so that recipient organizations of CIA Intelligence Memoranda (IM) on narcotics could be identified."

2.

3. This course of action was at the initiative of the Directorate of Intelligence, without consultation with persons elsewhere in the government, except in reporting the results to Dr. Kissinger. It represents a well-conceived attempt to target on a possible source of leaks. We doubt that it would be susceptible to misunderstanding if exposed to public view, but the fact is that it was something of an attempt to trap someone, and it was a part of the general attempt to seal off a leak similar to those leading to the "plumbing" operation. Because of the latter consideration it is noted for the record.

SIGNED

S. D. Breckinridge

cc:

00387

~~SECRET~~

25 MAY 1973

MEMORANDUM FOR: Mr. Colby

SUBJECT: Follow-ups on Potential Flap Activities

We have now completed the follow-ups requested by you and by Congressman Nedzi on our original submission summarizing potential flap activities. To the follow-ups given you on the afternoon of 24 May, we added the following on the afternoon of 25 May:

Tab 11: A second paragraph on the personnel locators (beacons) to make it more responsive to Congressman Nedzi's question.

Tab 16: An explanation of the magnetometer used for making cardiographs.

Tab 17: An IG-initiated follow-up on [redacted] which was merely noted on page 17 of the original sensitive summary.

Tab 18; Two IG-initiated follow-ups on items that were included in the initial Directorate submissions but were too fragmentary for inclusion in our ogiginal summary.

Tab 19: One completely new item that surfaced in the course of our inquiries.

The tabs are not arranged in any logical order, because we chose to place the bulkier items on the bottom of the file to make for easier handling of it. The following is a breakdown of the tabs by initiator of follow-up. (Both you and Nedzi asked for a follow-up on the item in Tab 2.)

Dolby-initiated	Nedzi-initiated	IG-initiated	New submission
1	2	17	19
2	4	18	
3	10		
5	11		
6	12		
7	13		
8	14		
9	15		
16			

William V. Broe
Inspector General

00388

25 May 1973

[illegible]

[illegible] files are being distributed as follows, to be [illegible] additional information is [illegible]. Please keep the files [illegible].

Q/DCI)
OGC)
OLC) Miss Gillard
OIG)

DDM&S

DDO

DDI

DDS&T Mr. Breckinridge

All material is to be read by COB Today.

It is requested that material be carded on 3 x 5 cards for future possible use. It should show (1) the name of the employee in upper lef hand corner, (2) name of person being reported on (e.g. Hunt, McCord, etc.)m (3) event reported, if significant,and the word "routine if not significant, (4) identifying reference to memo in which information is recorded.

If an event reported in this material is siginficant, please report it immediately for handling (either a "jewell" or something connected with Watergate and associated events)

Please raise any questions that occur as you get into the material. Especially, as you get ideas as work progresses, please put them forward.

SDB

PS. Add office symbol to employees name.

~~INTERNAL IG STAFF PAPER~~

00389

25 May 1973
Date

BROE

From: SDBreckinridge

Return to:

00390

25 May 1973

MEMORANDUM FOR: Mr. Broe

SUBJECT : Reported Agency Funding of Heroin Study

1. ORD, in reporting association of employees with Egil Krogh in connection with the government narcotics program, referred to an Agency funding action on 30 June 1972 whereby $37,500 was transferred to OST (the Office of Science and Technology under the Executive) from ORD's budget. The money was to fund a study proposed by IDA (I am told this is the Institute for Defense Analysis), and was approved by the DDI, ADD/S&T, [redacted] [redacted] acting for the DDS, and Mr. Colby as Executive Director-Comptroller.

2. I judge this to be a proper and normal expenditure within the government in connection with a high priority government program on narcotics. I recommend that this not be reported as an action subject to external criticism.

[redacted]

S. D. Breckinridge

00391

OPERATIONS CENTER

NEWS ANALYSIS SERVICE

DATE: 24 May

ITEM: NO. 24

REF : NO. ______

TRIBUTION:

DCI
DDCI
DCI/IC
DDI
DD/M&S
DDO (2
DDS/T
D/OCI
ONE
OSR
OSI (2
Ch/Ops
PDB
INDICO
DDO/DO
OSD

UPI155

(CIA)

WASHINGTON (UPI) -- CIA OFFICIALS TESTIFIED WEDNESDAY THEY FORGOT TO TELL CONGRESS OR THE AGENCY'S DIRECTOR, JAMES SCHLESINGER, ABOUT ANONYMOUS WARNINGS THEY RECEIVED THAT THE WHITE HOUSE WAS TRYING TO PIN BLAME ON THE AGENCY FOR THE WATERGATE SCANDAL.

REP. LUCIEN NEDZI, D-MICH., CALLED THREE OFFICIALS OF THE CIA TO EXPLAIN WHY THE LETTERS -- WHICH HAVE BEEN TRACED TO WATERGATE CONSPIRATOR JAMES MCCORD -- DID NOT SURFACE UNTIL TWO DAYS AGO.

"ONE OF THE REASONS THEY GAVE WAS THE FAMILIAR 'I FORGOT,'" NEDZI SAID. "THEY ALSO SAID IT WAS A MATTER OF TURNING IT OVER TO SOMEONE ELSE AND ASSUMING HE WOULD PASS IT ON."

THE SIX LETTERS -- ONE OF THEM SIGNED "JIM" AND THE OTHERS ANONYMOUS -- WERE SENT TO FORMER CIA DIRECTOR RICHARD HELMS BETWEEN JULY 1972 AND LAST JANUARY.

NEDZI SAID IT HAD BEEN "PRETTY DEFINITELY ESTABLISHED" THAT MCCORD, A FORMER CIA AGENT, WAS THE AUTHOR OF ALL THE LETTERS. NEDZI DECLINED TO SAY WHAT WAS IN THEM, BUT REP. WILLIAM BRAY, R-IND., SAID THEY WERE "CONFUSED" AND "DISJOINTED" WARNINGS THAT THE WHITE HOUSE WAS TRYING TO MAKE THE WATERGATE BREAK-IN AS A CIA PLOT.

BOTH NEDZI AND BRAY SAID THERE WAS NO EVIDENCE THAT CIA WAS IN ANY WAY RESPONSIBLE FOR THE WATERGATE BREAK-IN.

TESTIFYING AT THE SESSION WERE PAUL GAYNOR, HOWARD OSBORNE AND WILLIAM BRAUX, TOP CIA OFFICIALS WHO HAD CUSTODY OF THE MCCORD LETTERS AT VARIOUS STAGES AFTER THEY WERE SENT.

NEDZI INITIALLY SPELLED BRAUX'S NAME AS BROE AND SAID HE DID NOT KNOW IF IT WAS THE SAME MAN WHO TOLD THE SENATE COMMITTEE ABOUT MEETINGS HE HAD WITH ITT PRESIDENT HAROLD GENEEN TO DISCUSS THE CREATION OF INTERNAL ECONOMIC STRIFE IN CHILE.

UPI 05-24 05:12 PED

mea
fe
wh
eur
uermer
gco
uston
borne
oe
ynor

Comment:

00392

These comments represent the initial and tentative reaction of the Office of Current Intelligence to the attached item from the news services.

SECRET

SECRET

00395

2

00396

24 May 1973

MEMORANDUM FOR THE RECORD

SUBJECT: General: Watergate
Specific: Tom Parrott's Involvement with David Young

We met with Tom Latimer this morning to get from him the only existing copy of the sensitive attachment to our family jewels report in order that we might make a temporary stayback burn copy. At that time, Latimer said he had a call in to Broe to report that when Tom Parrott was DCI duty officer some time in September 1972 he received some calls from David Young.

I called Parrott's home (FE 7-3512) at 0925. The person answering, presumably Mrs. Parrott, gave me his telephone number at the Environmental Protection Agency (755-0533). I called Parrott there and told him that I would like to meet with him to debrief him on the substance of calls he received from the White House when he was DCI duty officer in September 1972. Tom said he would be happy to meet with me but that he saw no reason why he could not give me the information over the telephone.

Tom received a call from David Young at about midday on a Saturday. Young was calling about that morning's program by Dan Rather in which Rather included material from a classified report. Young wanted to come out to the headquarters building to see Parrott. Parrott started chasing it down. He spoke with Bruce Clarke who had the DDI duty. It turned out that Rather's comment was made on his program of the previous day and that it was based on a report that came out of George Carver's shop. The report was distributed in only seven or eight copies, and only two of them had gone outside the Agency--both to Kissinger.

Young got lost trying to find the building and did not arrive until about one. By then, Parrott had identified the Carver report and had a copy of the distribution list. Young was shaken upon discovering that the only external distribution was to Kissinger. He was extremely

00397

arrogant, wanting to know who each of the Agency recipients was and why he had received a copy. He wanted to know if any of the Agency recipients had talked with Rather. Parrott called Thuermer at home and found that no reports had been made of contacts with Rather. Young remarked to the effect "that's what they say" and asked if each of these people had been interrogated. Upon learning that the Agency had done nothing about the alleged leak, Young left in Huff saying that he would be back in touch.

Sometime later Parrott got the transcript of the Rather broadcast. Rather's comments bore only a remote connection to the content of the Carver report. Parrott cannot now recall specifically what the Carver report concerned. Rather did imply criticism of the President in his broadcast, and this may have been the basis of Young's concern. On Monday, Parrott got in touch with Carver, and the two of them met with Helms and briefed him on the episode. This is the last Parrott heard of it. Parrott commented that he had no other contacts with anyone remotely involved with Watergate or related matters. He thinks he may have written a memo for the record of the Young episode but is not sure. His duty secretary may remember. This would have been either [redacted] It is also possible that Carver made a M/R on the matter.

I called Carver. He said that he then had a memo in the mill, which will reach us during the course of the day.

[redacted] reports that she had traded the duty with [redacted] [redacted] that weekend. [redacted] thinks that Parrott wrote a memo on the episode, but he would have kept only a chrono copy, and his chrono files were destroyed when he left. She has no idea what might have happened to the original.

SIGNED

SECRET

00398

OLC 73-0611

24 May 1973

MEMORANDUM FOR THE RECORD

SUBJECT: Briefing of the Special Subcommittee on Intelligence of House Armed Services Committee

1. This morning Messrs. Lawrence Houston, General Counsel; William Broe, Inspector General; Howard Osborn, Director of Security; Paul Gaynor, Chief, Security Research Staff; and [redacted] Secretary to General Walters, appeared before the above Subcommittee about Agency action taken on letters received from James McCord. The meeting lasted from 1000 hours to 1245 hours. There was no technical sweep of the room, 2216 Rayburn House Office Building, and the room was not kept under technical monitoring. Discussions were on a Secret level. A transcript was taken and is on file in the Office of Legislative Counsel.

2. Present for the session were:

Lucien N. Nedzi (D., Mich.), Chairman
F. Edward Hebert (D., La.)
Melvin Price (D., Ill.)
William G. Bray (R., Ind.)
Leslie C. Arends (R., Ill.)
Bob Wilson (R., Calif.)

3. Present from the staff were:

Frank Slatinshek, Chief Counsel
William Hogan

00399

4. During the hearing, Chairman Nedzi and Mr. Slatinshek criticized Mr. Houston rather severely for the Agency's not reporting the existence of the McCord letters to the FBI at the time they were received. In this connection, Representative Wilson said he wondered if the Agency had actually gone along with "McCord's game plan." He said this would explain why these letters were just now being surfaced. Mr. Houston had a conversation with Nedzi and Slatinshek at the conclusion of the hearing and it seemed he was able to dispel some of their concern.

5. Followup action:

a. The Committee asked [redacted] to provide copies of her shorthand notes of the memorandum which she prepared for General Walters and copies of the Xerox copy which she made of each of these.

b. They asked for the exact date when Mr. Osborn was called [redacted]

[redacted]

GEORGE L. CARY, JR.
Acting Legislative Counsel

[redacted]

2

00400

SECRET

23 May 1973

MEMORANDUM FOR THE RECORD

On this date Mr. William E. Colby and the writer held a meeting with Congressman Lucien N. Nedzi. The reason for the meeting was to review with the Congressman material sent us by the Directorates describing the Agency activities that had flap potential.

At the outset, Mr. Colby advised that the Director had issued instructions to each directorate to come forward with descriptions of activities (especially involved in the domestic scene) that had flap potential. In addition, in a memorandum to all employees of the CIA, the Director had instructed all employees to report to him any activities the Agency was conducting that they construed as outside the Agency charter. Congressman Nedzi requested a copy of this Agency notice be furnished to him.

The full report, including the sensitive section, was discussed with the Congressman item-by-item and in most cases he actually read the text. This took two hours and the Congressman followed the material with great care.

With regard to the item concerning Mr. McCord's letters to the Agency in July and December 1972 and January 1973, he expressed astonishment that the material took so long to be surfaced and when surfaced took so long to get to the Director. He was very outspoken in his criticism of the people involved.

I will not try to set forth all his reactions to the material, which I believe he found sobering, but I will set out hereinafter the items in which he showed special interest:

a. Alien documentation furnished to the Secret Service. He desired more information concerning the reason why issued, the use, and how controlled.

SECRET

00401

b. Financial support to the White House in connection with the replies to letters and telegrams as a result of the President's speech on Cambodia in 1970. He requested more information on this subject.

c. Beacons furnished Ambassadors. He was interested in the number issued to Ambassadors and the position the State Department took on the use of these beacons. He was interested if the Department of State was pushing this program, as he believed they should be.

d. Logistics' acquisition of police equipment. He questioned whether LEAA, Department of Justice, should not be doing this rather than the Agency.

e. He noted Logistics furnished telephone analyzers, and desired to know what they were and how used.

f.

g. OER's crash project concerning Robert L. Vesco requested by the DCI. The Congressman was interested in who outside the Agency instigated the project and why was it stopped.

h. Several ORD projects indicated research done without knowledge of the host system or on unwitting subjects. He was of the opinion that this was risky and recommended it be terminated. He stated he would like to see a directive go out to the researchers concerning these practices.

i. John Dean's request re Investors Overseas Service. He reviewed the six reports that had been furnished. He noted, however, that the item stated "there were multiple channels to the Agency from the White House" and requested information concerning these channels.

j. Alien passports. Mr. Colby advised that he planned to review this whole subject and the Congressman agreed with the need to do so.

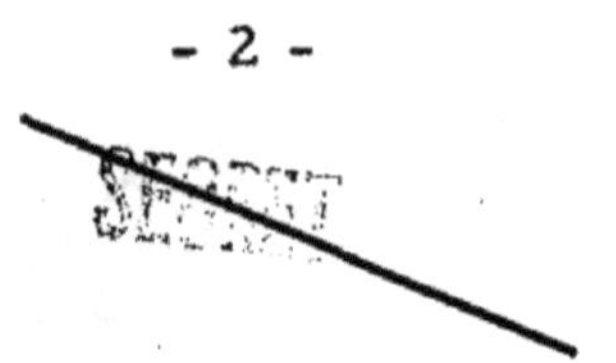

00402

The Congressman noted that in connection with John McCone's consultative role with the Agency the Director had stated some time in the past that he planned to take action regarding individuals in this category. The Congressman requested a report on what had been done.

Mr. Nedzi asked Mr. Colby if the Agency had considered how much of the information just reviewed with him could be made public. Mr. Colby stated this had not been done yet, and spoke to the question of sources, methods, and the impact on the institution. The Congressman stated that in the current climate he felt it was necessary to open up more information to help clear the air. Mr. Colby stated the Agency would give the matter deep consideration, and added he had been thinking of a general statement along these lines to be used at his confirmation hearing.

The meeting ended at 12 o'clock noon.

(Signed) William V. Broe

William V. Broe
Inspector General

Distribution:

Director of Central Intelligence
Mr. Colby
Office of Legislative Counsel

NOTE: The above listed items, except for item j, are being pursued by the Office of the Inspector General.

SECRET

00403

this date.

00404

Howard [redacted] orn
Director [redacted] urity

23 May 1973
(DATE)

FORM NO. 1 AUG 54 101 REPLACES FORM 10-101 WHICH MAY BE USED.

A F F I D A V I T

STATE OF VIRGINIA
COUNTY OF FAIRFAX, to-wit:

HOWARD J. OSBORN who, being first duly sworn, deposes and says as follows:

1. I am the Director of Security of the Central Intelligence Agency.

2. The purpose of this statement is to record, to the best of my knowledge and recollection, circumstances involved in the receipt of a series of unsigned correspondence received by the Agency during the period from 1 August 1972 to 7 January 1973. The significance of these letters is that by their content and by the handwriting on two of them, they are believed to have been written by James W. McCord, Jr., one of the defendants in the Watergate trial.

3. My first involvement in this matter occurred on the 2nd or 3rd of August 1972 when an envelope addressed to Mr. Helms, then Director of the Central Intelligence Agency, with no return address, and postmarked 30 July 1972 was routed to my desk from the Director's office as a routine piece of "crank mail". The envelope contained a carbon copy of a typewritten letter signed "Jim" with the name in the salutary address excised - "Dear _____". After dismissing the letter as a piece of crank mail, I had second thoughts and recognized the handwriting on the envelope and the signature "Jim" on the letter as being similar to that of Mr. McCord, who formerly worked for me as a security officer before his retirement from the Agency.

4. On that same day, I showed the letter to Mr. Helms and told him that although I was not positive, I was reasonably sure that the letter had been sent by Mr. McCord. Mr. Helms agreed that it was a strong probability that the envelope had been sent to him by Mr. McCord. I told him that I felt very strongly that the letter should be turned over to the Federal Bureau of Investigation. Mr. Helms, after some reflection, decided that he would like to have a legal opinion on the matter and summoned Mr. Lawrence Houston, General Counsel of the Agency, to his office and had him read the letter. After he had finished reading the letter the ensuing discussion, to the best of my recollection, centered about whether the Agency had any legal obligation to forward the letter to the Justice Department or the Federal Bureau of Investigation. Both Mr. Helms and Mr. Houston decided that there was no such obligation and I was told to hold the letter in a secure file in my office and take no further action on it. Mr. Helms instructed me to restrict knowledge of the existence of the letter to an absolute minimum number of people.

5. The next envelope received was addressed to Mr. Paul Gaynor, a staff chief in my office and a former close friend of Mr. McCord's, on or about the 23rd of December 1972. The next envelope received was addressed to Mr. Gaynor's residence and was undated but postmarked 27 December 1972. The two envelopes contained one or more unsigned typewritten pieces of correspondence which appeared to relate to Mr. McCord's involvement in the Watergate "affair". Both of these letters were handcarried by me to Mrs. Elizabeth

2

00406

[illegible] secretary to Mr. [illegible], and after he had reviewed them, they were returned to me personally by Mrs. Dunlevy. [illegible] file with the first one.

6. Subsequently, on 29 December 1972 and on 4 January 1973 and 6 January 1973, three additional envelopes containing unsigned typewritten correspondence were received by Mr. Gaynor at his residence and promptly delivered to me for review and subsequent inclusion in the secure file. I did not bring these to the immediate attention of Mr. Helms but a week or so later delivered to him a folder with all copies of the letters we had received. As I recall, my request to him was for guidance as to what action should be taken with regard to them in the light of his departure from the Agency incident to his nomination as United States Ambassador-designate to Iran. After reviewing them, he informed me that he did not see any reason to take any action at that time, but asked that I show them to Mr. Houston and if Mr. Houston had no objection, I was to retain them in a securo file and take no action with regard to them. As I recall, Mr. Houston was out of town at the time and it was several days before I had an opportunity to give him the folder with the copies of the letters in it for review. After reviewing them, he informed me that he had no objection to the instructions Mr. Helms had given me and I so informed Mrs. Elizabeth Dunlevy, secretary to Mr. Helms.

7. On 14 May 1973, Mr. William Broe, Inspector General of the Agency, and his Deputy, Mr. Kenneth Greer, met with me in my office in connection with an investigation they were undertaking at the direction of Mr. Schlesinger to determine if anyone in the Agency had any contact with

Mr. McCord since the Watergate incident or if Mr. McCord had contacted anyone in the Agency. I [illegible] them that, to the best of my knowledge, no one in the Agency had been in contact with Mr. McCord or [illegible] to the attention of my office. I told them that Mr. Paul Gaynor had been a close friend of Mr. McCord's but that I was satisfied, after interviewing him, that he had not seen or talked to Mr. McCord since the Watergate incident. (I subsequently determined from Mr. Gaynor that he has not seen or talked to Mr. McCord since his retirement from the Agency on 31 August 1970.) I also told them that a Mr. Leo Rosenbaum, an employee of the Agency, had requested an appointment with me to discuss the feasibility of contributing to Mr. McCord's defense fund and that I thought I had convinced him that this would be inimical to the best interests of himself, the Agency and Mr. McCord. I also stated that Mr. Rosenbaum had called me several weeks ago to say that he was well known as a close friend of Mr. McCord's and might be called to testify at the current Senate Hearings. I advised him to seek guidance in this regard from the Office of General Counsel. I do not know that he did so. I then remembered the envelopes and correspondence purportedly originated by Mr. McCord. I briefed Mr. Broe and Mr. Greer on the circumstances involved in the receipt and subsequent handling of them and made a copy of each of them and delivered them to Mr. Broe the next day. I also gave a copy, at the same time, to my immediate supervisor, Mr. Harold Browman.

8. A few days after this, I was contacted by Mr. John Greaney, Office of the General Counsel of the Agency, who asked me about any official or unofficial contacts anyone in the Agency had had with Mr. McCord. I mentioned

00408

[illegible] and suggested that he seek guidance from Mr. Lawrence Houston in this regard. Subsequently, [illegible] Mr. Houston's [illegible], Mr. Greaney [illegible] and [illegible] the original file containing the [illegible] letters. Mr. Greaney indicated that he would recommend to Mr. Houston that they be made [illegible] on 22 May 1973 Mr. Houston asked for a copy of the letters. On this same date, I was instructed by Mr. James R. Schlesinger, Director of the Central Intelligence Agency, to participate in certain Congressional briefings on this matter and to prepare this affidavit.

9. Up to the 14th of May 1973 when I informed Mr. Broe and Mr. Greer of the envelopes and their contents, the only persons knowledgeable of the existence of them, in addition to me, were: Mr. Helms, Mrs. Elizabeth Dunlevy, his secretary, Mr. Houston, Mr. Paul Gaynor of my staff, Miss Kathryn Aldridge, my secretary who prepared the file, Mr. Leo J. Dunn, my Executive Officer, knew of the first envelope and correspondence but not of subsequent envelopes.

10. The only other matter pertinent to this particular matter was the fact that an intermittent source of this Office, who was a close personal friend of Mr. McCord's has relayed to Mr. Gaynor and his staff certain information concerning the personal situation of Mr. and Mrs. McCord during and after the time he was in jail and since he has been released on bond. This source has been utilized by this office for many years and by my direction, no effort was made to solicit information from him about Mr. McCord and the information provided was done so purely gratuitously.

Howard J. Osborn [signature]

Howard J. Osborn

Subscribed and sworn to before me, a Notary Public, in and for the County of Fairfax, State of Virginia, this 23 day of May.
My commission expires September 29, 1976.

00409

/s/ Shirley [illegible]

23 May 1973

MEMORANDUM FOR THE RECORD

Bill Nelson called this date to advise that [redacted] had told him that [redacted] at the time he was in charge of narcotics matters for the DDP, knew Liddy and was probably involved with Hunt. At that same time Lou Conein was working at the White House and [redacted] wanted to meet Conein. It is [redacted] understanding that Hunt may have introduced [redacted] to Conein.

[redacted] queried as to what would be the best procedure. The writer advised that we should interview [redacted] concerning his relations with Liddy, Hunt, and Conein, and that this office would do so.

Will[redacted] Broe
Insp[redacted]eneral

00410

SECRET

23 May 1973

MEMORANDUM FOR: All Employees

SUBJECT : Agency Involvement in the Watergate Case

1. The leadership of the Agency continues to make a determined effort to investigate all aspects of Agency involvement with the "Watergate" case or any of those persons connected with it. The results of these investigations have been given to the appropriate legislative, executive, and judicial elements of the Government investigating these matters. Each employee has been asked and is directed to report to the Director any knowledge he or she has of the Watergate affair and related matters, any persons connected with it, or any other illegal activity in which they believe the Agency was involved in any way.

2. In consonance with the foregoing, anyone who has had any connection or contact with individuals on the attached list, or anyone in their offices or anyone purporting to act for them or acting pursuant to their authority, should report these contacts fully. Activities of these and other individuals include not only the Watergate affair, but any investigative work on the Pentagon Papers/ Ellsberg case and any contacts relating to the Executive Branch and White House efforts to locate and stem leaks of classified information to the press starting as early as July 1970.

3. Any work done by anyone in the Agency on any of these subjects, or any knowledge related thereto, should be reported to the IG through the appropriate Deputy Director, or directly and personally to the Director.

4. It is imperative that every piece of information bearing on these matters be reported immediately for evaluation by the senior management of the Agency. The public interest requires that all information be produced and reported to our oversight committees (on a classified basis if necessary) so that the Agency's actual role will be clarified with respect to various charges and speculation.

W. E. Colby
Executive Secretary
CIA Management Committee

Attachment

APPROVED

James R. Schlesinger
Director

Attachment

H. R. Haldeman
John D. Ehrlichman
John Dean
Egil Krogh
David Young
E. Howard Hunt
G. Gordon Liddy
James W. McCord
Charles W. Colson
John J. Caulfield
Eugenio Rolando <u>Martinez</u> Careaga
Juan Rigoberto <u>Ruiz</u> Villegas
Bernard L. Barker
Virgilio Gonzales
Frank Anthony Sturgis

SECRET

MEMORANDUM TO : Executive Secretary
CIA Management Committee

SUBJECT : Loan of Television System to Secret Service for Use at Democratic and Republican National Conventions in 1972

1. The attached ORD summary reports the loan of television equipment by the Agency to the Secret Service for use during the Democratic and Republican National Conventions last year. The equipment was for use in helicopter aerial surveillance, primarily for crowd control. The assumption is that it was used for that purpose. The equipment was recovered in November 1972.

2. The transaction seems a straightforward arrangement, related to the legal responsibility of the Secret Service. However, the fact that the Agency probided the equipment for use in a domestic political situation could be presented in a different light.

WVB

00412

MEMORANDUM TO : Executive Secretary
CIA Management Committee

SUBJECT : Drug Testing Program

1. The attached summary from ORD describes research into a behavioral drug. Conversations with Carl Duckett indicate that the reported drug was part of a larger program in which the Agency had relations with commercial drug manufacturers, whereby they passed on drugs rejected because of unfavorable side effects. The drugs were screened with the use of ADP equipment, and those selected for experimentation were tested at [redacted] [redacted] using monkeys and mice. Materials having further interest, as demonstrated by this testing, were then tested at Edgewood, using volunteer members of the Armed Forces.

2. The program was terminated last fall. The computer program remains in the machine, its final disposition not yet having been decided.

3. Carl Duckett emphasizes that the program was considered as defensive, in the sense that we would be able to recognize certain behavior if similar materials were used against Americans.

WVB

00413

SECRET

ORD-2550-73

23 May 1973

MEMORANDUM FOR: Deputy Director for Science and Technology

SUBJECT: ORD Involvement in Domestic Affairs

In surveying all of the people within the Office of Research and Development in search of specific contact or knowledge of Messrs. Hunt, Krogh, Young, and Liddy, an additional incident in which ORD supplied equipment for domestic use was uncovered. It is attached. I have also provided the additional information you requested on Project [redacted] and Project [redacted]

[redacted]

Sayre Stevens
Director of Research and Development

Attachments:
As stated

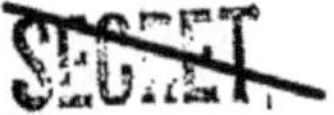

00414

KEG

22 May 1973

MEMORANDUM FOR THE RECORD

SUBJECT: General: The Family Jewels Exercise
Specific: Meeting with Colby This Date

Broe and [redacted] met with Mr. Colby at 1115 hours today. Colby asked that we provide him with fuller information on the following items:

DO [redacted] An EA Division project. What do these agents do in the States? What sort of reporting and to whom?

DDI ~~Get copies of OCI's reports on "Restless Youth" and Black Radicalism.~~

DDS&T ~~Get details on the cryogenic magnetometer that is used on unwitting subjects.~~ (S&T)

DDO ~~Get from CI Staff copies of the six reports sent to Fielding for John Dean on IOS.~~

DDI [redacted] For whom? For what purpose?

DDI [redacted]

~~Give Colby a rundown on~~ [redacted]

~~Give Colby a couple of paragraphs on the Tofte case.~~

~~Give Colby a copy of FR Division's contribution.~~

[redacted]

00415

EMPLOYEE BULLETIN

No. 359 21 May 1973

DDCI STATEMENT ABOUT THE WATERGATE CASE

The following statement was made by Lieutenant General Vernon A. Walters during a recent appearance before a Congressional Committee.

On 23 June 1972 I was ordered by a phone message from my office to be at the White House at about 1300 with Director Helms. I had lunch with Mr. Helms and we went to Mr. Ehrlichman's office at the White House. Present were Mr. Ehrlichman, Mr. Haldeman, Mr. Helms and myself. As I recall it, Mr. Haldeman said that the Watergate incident was causing trouble and was being exploited by the opposition. It had been decided at the White House that I would go to Acting FBI Director Gray and tell him that now that the five suspects were arrested, further enquiries into the Mexican aspects of this matter might jeopardize some of the CIA's covert activities in that area. An appointment was made for me to see Mr. Gray at 1430 that same day. I went over and told him that I had been directed by top White House officials to tell him that further investigation into the Mexican aspects of the Watergate episode might jeopardize some of the Agency's covert actions in that area. He said that he understood the agreement between the FBI and the Agency regarding their sources but that this was a complicated case. He would not violate the agreement with CIA regarding sources. On my return to the Agency I checked to see whether there was any danger in the Agency's covert sources if the Mexican part of the investigation continued and ascertained that no one believed that this was the case. No one had any knowledge of the plan to bug the Democratic National Committee.

On June 26 the Counsel to the President John Dean called me and asked me to come and see him about the matter I had discussed with Haldeman and Ehrlichman. He said I could check with Ehrlichman and I did. He said I could talk to Dean so I went to Dean's office at 1145 on June 26.

I informed Dean that I had checked carefully to see whether there was any jeopardy to the Agency's sources by a further investigation of the Mexican sources of this matter and had found there was none. Dean then asked whether the CIA might have taken part in the Watergate episode without my knowing it. I said that this was not

00416

possible. I knew that the Agency had had no part in the operation against the Democratic National Committee. I therefore could not say that further investigation would jeopardize Agency sources. I felt that someone had bungled badly and that the responsible parties should be fired. He asked whether there was not some way in which the Agency might have been involved. I said that I had checked with Director Helms and was convinced it was not. Any attempt to stifle this investigation would destroy the effectiveness of the Agency and the FBI and would be a grave disservice to the President. I would [illegible] issue. He asked whether I had any ideas [illegible] might be done and I replied that those responsible should be fired. He seemed [illegible] and I left.

The following day I saw Dean again in his office at his request. He again reviewed the Watergate Case saying that some witnesses were getting scared and were "wobbling". I said that no matter how scared they got, they could not involve CIA because it was not involved in the bugging of the Watergate. He then asked if the CIA could not furnish bail and pay the suspects' salaries while they were in jail, using covert action funds for this purpose.

I replied that this was out of the question. It would implicate the Agency in something in which it was not implicated. Any such action by the Agency would imply an order from the highest level and I would not be a party to any such action. It would be a grave disservice to the President and the country and would destroy the CIA's credibility with the Congress and the people. I would resign rather than do this and, if ordered to do it, I would ask to see the President to explain the reasons for my refusal. Furthermore, when the Agency expended funds in the U.S., we had to report this to the Oversight Committees of the Agency in Congress. He was much taken aback by this and agreed that risks of implicating the CIA and FBI in this matter would be enormous. I said that what was now a painful wound could become a mortal one. What was now a "conventional explosion could be turned into a multi-megaton explosion". I again advised him to fire the responsible parties.

Again Dean sent for me on the 28th of June and I saw him at his office at 1130 that day. He enquired whether I had learned anything more about CIA involvement. I replied that there was no involvement of the Agency in the bugging of the Watergate. He then asked whether I had any ideas and I said that I had none which could be helpful. Perhaps the Cubans who were anti-Castro might have had a hand in it but the CIA did not.

On July 5 I received a call from Acting Director of the FBI Gray saying that he could not stop further investigation of the Mexican aspects of this matter unless he had a formal letter from the Director of CIA [illegible] office and I saw him at [illegible] the following morning.

00416a

-3-

I told him that I could not tell him that further investigation would jeopardize the Agency's covert sources. I had checked on this and it was not so. I had ascertained that General Cushman had initially authorized the issuance of some equipment to Howard Hunt without knowing its purpose other than it was, as I understood it, to shut off "leaks". This was long before the Watergate bugging. Since then I had carefully checked and there was no other involvement of any sort by the CIA in the operation against the Watergate. I said that I felt that attempts to cover this up or to [illegible] the CIA or FBI would be [illegible] their integrity and a disservice to the President and the country. I would have no part in this and was quite prepared to resign on this issue. He said [illegible] integrity of our agencies and he too was prepared to resign on this issue. I gave Gray a list of the equipment the Agency had given Hunt and the account of our dealings with the former CIA employees up to the termination of their employment with the Agency long before the Watergate episode.

I saw Gray again on the 12th of July and gave him one additional memorandum regarding the contact furnished Hunt. We reviewed the matter reiterating the position we had taken previously. I said that I had told Dean that the best solution would be to fire those responsible. Gray said he had made the same recommendation. Once again we agreed that anything that might damage the integrity of the FBI and CIA would be a grave disservice to the President and the Government.

In February 1973 shortly after Dr. Schlesinger became Director I told him of my conversations with Haldeman, Ehrlichman and Dean. In February Dean called Dr. Schlesinger to see if the Agency could get back from the FBI the material it had sent to the Justice Department concerning our contact with Hunt. Dr. Schlesinger and I agreed that this could not be done. I attempted to contact Dean but he was in Florida. On his return I saw Dean at his office on February 21 and told him that we could not ask the FBI for the material back. That would only serve to implicate the CIA and I could not and would not do it. I had seen Acting FBI Director Gray that morning and told him of Dean's request and our refusal. He agreed saying that he could not do such a thing.

Since that date I have had no further contact with Dean. The above represents my recollection of what occurred and the dates are checked in my appointment book.

DISTRIBUTION: ALL EMPLOYEES

00417

~~ADMINISTRATIVE - INTERNAL USE~~

CENTRAL INTELLIGENCE AGENCY
WASHINGTON, D.C. 20505

OFFICE OF THE DIRECTOR

9 May 1973

MEMORANDUM FOR ALL CIA EMPLOYEES

1. Recent press reports outline in detail certain alleged CIA activities with respect to Mr. Howard Hunt and other parties. The presently known facts behind these stories are those stated in the attached draft of a statement I will be making to the Senate Committee on Appropriations on 9 May. As can be seen, the Agency provided limited assistance in response to a request by senior officials. The Agency has cooperated with and made available to the appropriate law enforcement bodies information about these activities and will continue to do so.

2. All CIA employees should understand my attitude on this type of issue. I shall do everything in my power to confine CIA activities to those which fall within a strict interpretation of its legislative charter. I take this position because I am determined that the law shall be respected and because this is the best way to foster the legitimate and necessary contributions we in CIA can make to the national security of the United States.

3. I am taking several actions to implement this objective:

- I have ordered all the senior operating officials of this Agency to report to me immediately on any activities now going on, or that have gone on in the past, which might be construed to be outside the legislative charter of this Agency.

- I hereby direct every person presently employed by CIA to report to me on any such activities of which he has knowledge. I invite all ex-employees to do the same. Anyone who has such information should call my secretary (extension 6363) and say that he wishes to talk to me about "activities outside CIA's charter."

~~ADMINISTRATIVE - INTERNAL USE ONLY~~

00418

ADMI RATIVE INTERNAL USE ONLY

4. To ensure that Agency activities are proper in the future, I hereby promulgate the following standing order for all CIA employees:

> Any CIA employee who believes that he has received instructions which in any way appear inconsistent with the CIA legislative charter shall inform the Director of Central Intelligence immediately.

James R. Schlesinger
Director

ADMINISTRATIVE - INTERNAL USE ONLY

00418a

DCI STATEMENT

BEFORE

SENATE APPROPRIATIONS SUBCOMMITTEE
ON INTELLIGENCE OPERATIONS

9 MAY 1973

OPENING STATEMENT

Mr. Chairman, I am here to discuss the questions which have arisen over CIA's real and alleged role in events that occurred in 1971 and 1972. I have opened a detailed investigation into the precise nature of that role. I can report to you on what Agency records, now being intensively reviewed, reveal at this juncture. However I do not yet know that I have all the facts in the matter. Nonetheless, I am pleased to present to you such facts as are now available, and I will certainly provide you with any further details as they come to my attention.

Let me start with the Agency's relationship with Mr. Howard Hunt, whose testimony has recently been made public. Mr. Hunt was a staff employee of the Agency from 8 November 1949 to 30 April 1970. At that time he retired from the Agency. He performed one editorial job of writing up a recommendation for an award for one of our officers in November 1970. He was not paid for these services, although the Agency placed the sums of $200.00 and $50.00 in two charitable organizations for the service performed.

In early July 1971, General Cushman, then the Deputy Director of Central Intelligence, received a telephone call from the White House. He was informed that Mr. Hunt had become a consultant on security affairs for the White House, and a request was made that Mr. Hunt receive assistance from the Agency. The minutes of the Agency Morning Meeting of 8 July 1971 indicate that the DDCI (General Cushman) reported a call by John Ehrlichman stating that Howard Hunt had been appointed a White House security consultant.

On 22 July 1971 Mr. Hunt visited General Cushman at the CIA building. According to the records, Mr. Hunt stated that he had been charged with a highly sensitive mission by the White House to visit and elicit information from an individual whose ideology he was not entirely sure of, and for that purpose he said he was asked to come to the Agency to see if he could get two things: identification documents in alias and some degree of physical disguise, for a one-time operation. He stressed that he wanted the matter to be held as closely as possible and that he would like to meet the Agency people in an Agency safehouse. Agency records indicate that, in the course of the conversation, Mr. Hunt referred to Mr. Ehrlichman by name and General Cushman acknowledged an earlier call from Mr. Ehrlichman to him. The Committee may desire to query General Cushman whose knowledge would not come from such secondary sources.

General Cushman directed the appropriate technical service of the Agency to be of assistance to Mr. Hunt, based on the above request. On 23 July 1971 Mr. Hunt was given alias documents, including a Social Security card, driver's license, and several association membership cards, in the name of "Edward Joseph Warren" similar to material he had been furnished for operational use while he had been an Agency employee, under the name of "Edward V. Hamilton." The same day Mr. Hunt was also given disguise materials (a wig, glasses, and a speech alteration device).

By calling an unlisted telephone number given him, Mr. Hunt arranged several additional meetings with Agency technical officers, the dates of which cannot be provided with precision. In these, he requested and was provided a commercial tape recorder (in a typewriter case) and a commercial Tessina camera disguised in a tobacco pouch. He also brought in a then-unidentified associate (later identified from press photos as Mr. G. Gordon Liddy) and secured for him a disguise (wig and glasses) and alias documents in the name of "George F. Leonard."

00420a

The Agency technical officers met these requests despite the absence of the procedural steps and approvals normally required by Agency regulations. However, they became increasingly concerned at the escalation of Mr. Hunt's requests for assistance. These finally included a request from Mr. Hunt to be met on the morning of 27 August 1971, upon his return from California, to have a film developed and returned to him. This was done the same day. He also asked for a New York mail address and telephone-answering service for operational use.

The technical officers raised their concern with senior officers, who noted the possibility that these activities could involve the Agency in operations outside its proper functions. As a result, again according to Agency records, General Cushman telephoned Mr. Ehrlichman at the White House on 27 August 1971 and explained that further such assistance could not be given. Mr. Ehrlichman agreed. The request for mail address and telephone answering service was not honored. On 31 August 1971, Mr. Hunt contacted the technical officers again, requesting a credit card, but this was refused. Mr. Hunt had also made a request on 18 August 1971 for the assignment of a secretary he had known during his Agency career. This was also refused. The earlier-furnished alias documents and other material were not recovered, however, except for the Tessina camera which was returned on 27 August as unsuitable. Since the end of August 1971, the Technical Services Division has had no further association with Mr. Hunt. As a point of reference, I would note that the break-in of the office of Mr. Ellsberg's psychiatrist took place on or about 3 September 1971.

00421

The Agency outlined the above events to Mr. Patrick Gray, Acting Director of the FBI, in letters dated 5 and 7 July 1972, and a meeting on 28 July 1972. A series of questions were asked the Agency on 11 October 1972 by Mr. Earl Silbert, Principal Assistant United States Attorney for the District of Columbia. On 24 October 1972, Attorney General Kleindienst and Assistant Attorney General Petersen reviewed the 5 and 7 July transmittals together with additional, more detailed but undated materials, that had been provided to Acting FBI Director Gray on 18 October 1972. The Agency is aware that this material was reviewed on 27 November 1972 by Mr. Silbert, who asked additional questions on that date as well as on 29 November 1972. Written responses to the foregoing questions were provided on 13 December 1972. An additional submission was made to the Assistant Attorney General Petersen on 21 December 1972. This material was discussed at a meeting held with Assistant Attorney General Petersen and Mr. Silbert on 22 December 1972. All of the foregoing materials can be made available to the Committee if it so desires.

As a separate matter, which was not known by those who prepared the material for the Department of Justice in the fall of last year, the Office of Medical Services of the Agency prepared and forwarded to the White House two indirect personality assessments of Mr. Daniel Ellsberg. The Agency has had a program of producing, on a selective basis, such assessments or studies on foreign leaders for many years. In July 1971 Mr. Helms, then Director, instructed Agency officers to work with Mr. David Young of the White House Staff relative to security leaks in the intelligence community.

-5-

Mr. Young requested a study on Mr. Ellsberg in the latter part of July 1971, which Agency activity was apparently approved by Mr. Helms. At that time, Mr. Young supplied raw material consisting principally of newspaper and magazine articles together with some State Department and Justice Department papers. The first assessment delivered to the White House dated 9 August 1971, was judged insufficient. As a result, there were several meetings between Dr. Malloy, Mr. Hunt, and Mr. Liddy, in which classified information of the Justice and State Departments was introduced. One such meeting occurred on 12 August 1971. Additional material was transmitted by Mr. Hunt on 12 October, and another meeting was held on 27 October. These meetings led to a second version of the assessment, dated 9 November 1971. This document was delivered to the Executive Office by Dr. Malloy on 12 November 1971. Agency records indicate that Mr. Helms had previously communicated with Mr. Young indicating he had read both reports.

In another contact "about October 1971," an Agency officer arranged to provide Mr. Hunt certain unclassified materials from CIA files relative to a 1954 French case of leakage of Government documents. These were delivered to his office at the White House.

In closing, I would like to stress several conclusions of my investigation so far:

a. CIA had no awareness of the details of Mr. Hunt's activities. The Agency's impression was that Mr. Hunt was engaged in an activity related to identifying and closing off the security leaks that were so much a preoccupation of the Government at the time.

b. The Agency clearly was insufficiently cautious in the initiation of its assistance to Mr. Hunt. Later, when the nature of Mr. Hunt's requests for assistance began to indicate a possible active involvement by the Agency in activities beyond its charter, the Agency terminated the relationship and refused further assistance.

c. The preparation of a profile on an American citizen under these circumstances lies beyond the normal activity of the Agency. It shall not be repeated -- and I have so instructed the staff. This shall be made a part of the regulations governing such activities.

d. As Director, I have called for a review of all Agency activities and the termination of any which might be considered outside its legitimate charter. In addition to requesting this review from my subordinates, I have directed each employee and invited each ex-employee to submit to me any cases which they may question. I am determined that the Agency will not engage in activities outside of its charter but will concentrate its energies on its important intelligence mission.

00422a

8 May 1973

DCI:

Sy Hersh's provocative teaser for the day:

"I have information that Cushman knew exactly what he was okaying when he gave approval to assist Hunt..."

I attentioned Sy H. again to the statement we had given to the Times already, and told him I "noted" what he had to say today.

He has calls in for you, Houston, and Colby.

attached:

AMT

cc: OGC
OLC
Mr. Colby

Prepared by OGC for press

RESPONSE TO PRESS INQUIRIES CONCERNING MR. HUNT'S GRAND JURY TESTIMONY

THE CENTRAL INTELLIGENCE AGENCY HAD NO ADVANCE NOTICE OF ANY SORT WHATSOEVER OF THE BREAK IN BY MR. HUNT OF THE OFFICE OF MR. ELLSBERG'S PSYCHIATRIST OR OF THE WATERGATE INCIDENT. THE NEWSPAPER REPORTS OF THESE TWO EVENTS WERE THE FIRST NOTICE TO ANYONE IN THE AGENCY. ALL AGENCY INFORMATION ON OUR CONTACTS WITH ANY PERSONS INVOLVED IN THESE INCIDENTS HAS BEEN REPORTED FULLY TO THE DEPARTMENT OF JUSTICE, AND AS INVESTIGATION OF THESE MATTERS IS IN THE HANDS OF THE COURTS AND THE GRAND JURY, ALL INQUIRIES SHOULD BE DIRECTED TO THE DEPARTMENT OF JUSTICE.

00424

~~SECRET EYES ONLY~~

8 May 1973

MEMORANDUM FOR: Executive Secretary, CIA Management Committee

SUBJECT: Potentially Embarrassing Agency Activities

The Office of the Inspector General has records on the following sensitive subjects that either have been or might in the future be the source of embarrassment to the Agency.

The report of the Board of Inquiry in the case of Hans Tofte. The Tofte affair was fully exposed in public, of course, but the report itself is closely held within the Agency. This office was designated as the custodian of the report, and we have the only surviving copy.

An annex to the Inspector General's report of survey of the Technical Services Division done in 1963. The annex deals with experiments in influencing human behavior through the administration of mind or personality altering drugs to unwitting subjects.

An Inspector General report of investigation of allegations that the Agency was instrumental in bringing about the assassination of President Diem. The allegations were determined to be without foundation.

An Inspector General report of investigation of allegations that the Agency was instrumental in bringing about the assassination of President Trujillo. The investigation disclosed quite extensive Agency involvement with the plotters.

An Inspector General report of investigation of allegations that the Agency conspired to assassinate Fidel Castro. The story first appeared in Drew Pearson's column and has since appeared in Jack Anderson's column. While the columns contained many factual errors, the allegations are basically true.

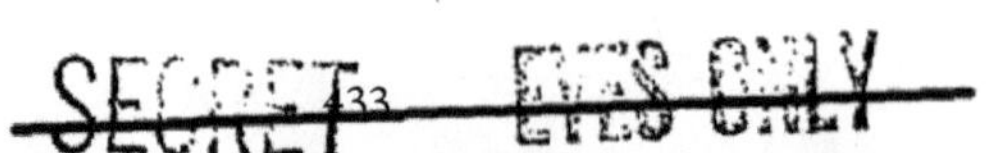

00425

Page 1 SDS and other student activist groups

OCI produced in December 1967 at Walt Rostow's request a 30-page typescript study of the SDS and its foreign ties.

In the summer of 1968 OCI produced--again at Rostow's request--a paper on Restless Youth. The first, and most sensitive section, was a philosophical treatment of student unrest, its motivation, history, and tactics. It drew heavily on overt literature and FBI reporting on SDS and affiliated groups. The second section comprised 19 chapters on foreign student dissidence.

Pages 11 & 12 Black radicalism

OCI began following Caribbean black radicalism in earnest in 1968. Two papers were produced on the subject, one in August 1969 and the other in June 1970.

OCI was asked in June 1970 to write a memo with special attention to links between black radicalism in the Caribbean and advocates of black power in the US. The memo was produced in typescript and given to the DCI.

OCI in 1968 wrote periodic typescript memos on Stokely Carmichael's travels abroad during a period when he had dropped from public view.

Page 23 Prohibition against COMINT vs. US citizens

In September 1972 [redacted] Commo to conduct hearability tests of certain HF long-distance commercial telephone circuits between the US and South America. The circuits carried drug-related traffic. [redacted] [redacted] The tests were successful. The activity was terminated on 30 Jan 73 following OGC determination that they were illegal.

We conduct an intercept operation in [redacted] targeted on radio telephone conversations [redacted] [redacted] These intercepts contain a large number of unrelated conversations often involving US citizens.

Testing in the US of ORD-developed electronic collection systems occasionally result in the collection of domestic telephone conversations. When the tests are complete, the intercepted material is destroyed.

CIA [redacted] technicians conducted tests in the Miami area in August 1971 of DF gear intended for use against a Soviet agent in South Vietnam. While wholly innocuous, the tests preceded the holding of the conventions there and could be construed as being somehow related to them.

In February 1972 CIA asked an official of AT&T for copies of telephone call slips relating to US-China calls. The operation lasted for three or four months and then dried up. OGC stated its belief that the collection of these slips did not violate the Communications Act since eavesdropping was not involved.

Page 29 Mail coverage

Since 1953, CIA has operated a mail intercept program of incoming and outgoing Russian mail and, at various times, other selected mail at Kennedy Airport in New York City. This program is now dormant pending decision on whether to continue or to abolish it.

n/R

00427

8 May 1973

MEMORANDUM FOR: Mr. W. E. Colby
Executive Secretary, CIA Management Committee

FROM : Director, National Estimates

SUBJECT : Comments on Proposed DCI Statement (Hunt Case)

Since you are aware that I have no facts bearing on the case, I take it that you asked for comment from the following point of view: will the proposed statement be well received by the committee?

The main questions in the committee's mind will be: Did CIA cooperate wittingly in activities which were both illegal and outside its charter? Or did it only respond supinely to higher authority even though it had some reason for suspecting illegal conduct?

Tactically, I think there would be advantage in coming to grips frankly with these questions in the statement itself. The text in its present form could be taken as a minimum factual response which doesn't quite get at the heart of the matter. I think it preferable, in the interest of the Agency's reputation on the Hill, to proceed to candor directly rather than to be drawn to it by subsequent questioning.

Key follow-up questions which can be anticipated would include the following:

Why is there no record of the initial Ehrlichman-Cushman contact?

If Cushman recorded the conversation with Hunt, was he not already suspicious of the latter's purpose and why didn't he ask? At a minimum, could he not have inquired whether "the individual whose ideology we aren't entirely sure of" was an American citizen?

00428

When Cushman told Ehrlichman on 27 August 1971 that CIA was suspending support to Hunt, was it only on the ground that the latter had become "too demanding"?

Why was the personality study on Ellsberg provided when it was obvious that this action transgressed the Agency's charter?

Obviously most questions which will be raised can only be answered by Helms and Cushman personally. Nevertheless, I think the DCI would be well advised to provide a candid evaluation of these proceedings in his initial statement. To do so voluntarily would make more persuasive the assurances the Committee will want that nothing of the sort will be done under his direction of the Agency.

John Huizenga

7 MAY 1973

MEMORANDUM FOR ALL CIA EMPLOYEES

1. Recent press reports implicate CIA in certain ~~illegal~~ activities allegedly committed in the United States. Without going into the details of these allegations, I can assure you that I intend to cooperate fully with the various law enforcement and Congressional investigations of these matters.

2. All CIA employees should understand my attitude toward matters of this sort. I shall do everything in my power to confine CIA activities to those which fall within the strictest interpretation of its legislative charter. I take this position because I am determined that the law shall be respected and because this is the best way to foster the legitimate and necessary contributions we in CIA can make to the national security of the United States.

3. I am taking several actions to implement this objective:

- I have ordered all the senior operating officials of this Agency to report to me immediately on any activities now going on, or that have gone on in the past, which might be construed by reasonable people to be outside the legislative charter of this Agency.

00430

~~CIA INTERNAL USE ONLY~~

- I hereby order every person presently employed by CIA to report to me directly on any such activities of which he has knowledge. I invite all ex-employees to do the same. Anyone who has such information shall call my secretary (extension 6363) and say that he wishes to talk to me about "questionable CIA activities".
- I intend to name a highly respected person from outside the Government to review, investigate, and prepare reports for me on any apparent violations of the CIA legislative charter which are brought to his attention or may be uncovered on his own initiative. I shall give this person complete and unrestricted access to all records and persons in the Agency.

4. To insure that Agency activities are proper in the future, I hereby promulgate the following standing order for all CIA employees:

> Any CIA employee who believes that he has received instructions which in any way appear inconsistent with the CIA legislative charter shall inform the Director of Central Intelligence immediately.

James R. Schlesinger
Director

00431

Retirement Information - E. Howard Hunt

1. Date of retirement: 30 April 1970

2. System: CIA Retirement and Disability System

3. Grade and salary at time of retirement: GS-15, Step 8 - $28,226

4. Creditable civilian service used in computing annuity:

   17 May 1948 to 8 June 1948 - Economic Cooperation Administration

   9 June 1948 to 19 February 1949 - State (ECA)

   8 November 1949 to 30 April 1970 - CIA

5. Annuity:

   At retirement - $1,020 per month

   At present - $1,181 per month (which includes cost-of-living increases since date of retirement)

6. At the time of retirement Mr. Hunt did not elect survivorship benefits. This meant that upon his death, his wife would not draw a survivorship annuity. By letter of 5 April 1971 he raised the question of changing his election but was informed by the General Counsel on 6 May 1971 that this could not be done. By letter dated 5 May 1972 Mr. Hunt asked Mr. Houston to raise with the Director the possibility of being recalled to duty for a short period of time, after which he could retire again and elect survivorship benefits. By letter of 16 May 1972 Mr. Houston advised Mr. Hunt that to call him back to duty solely for the purpose of permitting him to change survivorship benefits would be in violation of the spirit of the CIA Retirement Act.

00432

	SENDER WILL CHECK CLASSIFICATION TOP AND BOTTOM				
	UNCLASSIFIED		CONFIDENTIAL		SECRET

OFFICIAL ROUTING SLIP

TO	NAME AND ADDRESS	DATE	INITIALS
1	Inspector General	5/25	
2			
3			
4			
5			
6			

	ACTION		DIRECT REPLY		PREPARE REPLY
	APPROVAL		DISPATCH		RECOMMENDATION
	COMMENT		FILE		RETURN
	CONCURRENCE		INFORMATION		SIGNATURE

Remarks:

Attached in chronological order is that which MAG has produced and papers related to Management's reac.. on thereto on MAG's concern re domestic activities. It is provided for your review and comment to Mr. Colby. This is our file copy and I would hope it could be retrieved if required.

FOLD HERE TO RETURN TO SENDER

FROM: NAME, ADDRESS AND PHONE NO.	DATE
O/ES/CIA MC/Ben Evans	18May73

	UNCLASSIFIED		CONFIDENTIAL		SECRET

FORM NO. 1-67 237 Use previous editions (40)

00433

DIARY NOTES

Executive Director-Comptroller [signature] 4 January 1972

1. I met with the outgoing and incoming MAG Cochairmen. We discussed a number of topics but concentrated particularly on their two most recent memoranda concerning domestic activities. I expressed slight irritation with their second memorandum, which is a shotgun approach to the problem, and asked them to be specific if they have anything in mind. I said I understand they have heard that we sent a surveillance team to the Democratic National Convention. Mr. [redacted] said that he made this statement because an Office of Security employee reported in his presence that he personally was a member of a team which went to the Convention. (I subsequently raised this with Howard Osborn, who after investigating reported back that the Secret Service asked us for two technicians during the Democratic National Convention. These technicians were formally detailed to the Secret Service and went to Chicago, where they did RF monitoring under the supervision of the Secret Service. The Secret Service apparently calls RF monitoring "audio surveillance," and it seems that, during the discussion which took place at the Senior Seminar, those who heard this assumed that "surveillance" meant actual surveillance of the candidates, when actually the meeting rooms were being checked to ensure they had not been bugged. I have reported all this to the Director and shall discuss it with MAG when I have dinner with them on 11 January.)

00434

23 December 1971

MEMORANDUM FOR: The Executive Director-Comptroller

SUBJECT : CIA's Domestic Activities

REFERENCE : MAG Memoranda on same subject dated March 1971 and November 1971

As requested, MAG met with the DDP on 21 December and discussed with him the referenced memoranda on CIA's covert domestic activities. Our exchange consisted primarily of the DDP responding to the MAG memoranda as they related to activities of the Clandestine Service alone. The DDP made it clear that he spoke only for his Service. Since MAG's initial concern over covert domestic activities extended to, while not being restricted to, the Clandestine Service, it recommends that the referenced memoranda be also brought to the attention of appropriate senior officials in other Agency components.

The Management Advisory Group

UNCLASSIFIED ☐ USE ONLY ☐ CONFIDENTIAL ☐ SECRET

ROUTING AND RECORD SHEET

SUBJECT: (Optional)

FROM:	EXTENSION	NO.
DDP		DATE 22 Dec 71

TO: (Officer designation, room number, and building)	DATE RECEIVED	DATE FORWARDED	OFFICER'S INITIALS	COMMENTS (Number each comment to show from whom to whom. Draw a line across column after each comment.)
1. Executive Director				BY HAND
2.				
3.				
4.				
5.				
6.				
7.				
8.				
9.				
10.				
11.				
12.				
13.				
14.				
15.				00436

FORM 3-62 610 USE PREVIOUS EDITIONS ☐ ~~SECRET~~ ☐ ~~CONFIDENTIAL~~ ☐ INTERNAL USE ONLY ☐ UNCLASSIFIED

21 December 1971

MEMORANDUM FOR: Executive Director-Comptroller

SUBJECT: Meeting with MAG Group

1. I met with the MAG group this morning for little over an hour, and I set forth as candidly as possible those counter-intelligence and counterespionage responsibilities of ours overseas which make it mandatory for us occasionally to take an interest in American citizens overseas. I explained the requirements placed on us by the Department of Justice for overseas checks, and also the fact that our normal overseas operations against Soviets and others some times produce leads to Americans in conspiratorial contact with our Communist targets.

2. I was asked about our having sent Agency representatives to the Democratic National Convention in Chicago in 1968 and I explained that I never heard of such a thing and did not believe it. I pointed out that, as they knew, the press had reported fully on the Agency participation at the beginning of the sky marshalling program and I assumed they saw nothing wrong with this. They agreed. I also pointed out that, at President Kennedy's funeral, with scores of important foreign personalities here, the Agency lent some assistance to the Secret Service, and here again the group understood that this was a legitimate function.

3. The group made it clear that their concern was over the Agency image if the general public were aware that some of our activities, wherever they took place, were targeted against Blacks. I said that we did not target against Americans of any color in this country, and that the Clandestine Service was color blind when it came to carrying out its overseas CI responsibilities and it would continue to be so.

4. I agreed that the Director should be asked to speak a little more fully and clearly on whether we "target against American citizens" so that there is no ambiguity.

5. I told the group that we must expect all kinds of irresponsible accusations in the press, such as the one in the January 1972 issue of RAMPARTS magazine in which Bob Kiley and Drex Godfrey, it is suggested, are still in the employ of CIA working on a CIA plan to improve police organizations in this country. I said that this was palpably false as anyone who knows Kiley and Godfrey would understand. The group mentioned Dick Ober's unit and said that there was a lot of scuttlebutt that the purpose of this unit was to keep book on Black Power adherents. I denied this saying that our interest was as I had explained it previously.

6. I do not know whether this is a fair assumption, but Dick Ober's machine program is not handled in the Clandestine Service and it is possible that someone is misreading and misinterpreting the intent of Ober's program from fragmentary bits and pieces that may be discernible from the handling of the machine program. I do not state this as a fact because I have not examined it that closely.

7. I told the group that I had offered to enlighten it candidly on what we do so that they would at least have the facts and I said that I assume you would take it from here.

Thomas H. Karamessines
Deputy Director for Plans

00438

MEMORANDUM FOR: The Director

THROUGH: The Executive Director-Comptroller

SUBJECT: CIA's Domestic Activities

REFERENCE: MAG Memorandum, "CIA's Domestic Activities," March 1971

1. MAG is seriously concerned about possible repercussions which may arise as the result of CIA's covert domestic activities. Public revelation that CIA has become involved in collecting information on U.S. citizens would likely redound to the Agency's discredit and jeopardize overall Agency programs.

2. MAG first expressed its concern about CIA's covert domestic activities in a memo for the DCI, transmitted through the Executive Director-Comptroller in the Spring of 1971 (Attachment A). MAG's concern has increased recently because of such articles as Vic Marchetti's UPI interview (Attachment B) and the 10 October New York Times article concerning rupture of FBI-CIA relations (Attachment C). Both hint at extremely sensitive Agency involvement in domestic activities. Additionally, the DCI addresses to the American Society of Newspaper Editors (Attachment D) and to the CIA Annual Awards ceremony (Attachment E) make rather categorical denials of Agency covert targeting on U.S. citizens. Agency employees aware of the various sensitive operations in question know that there is qualifying language explaining CIA involvement. However, MAG believes that in the event of an expose, such esoteric qualifiers will be lost on the American public and that there is probably nothing the Agency could say to alleviate a negative reaction from Congress and the U.S. public. It is MAG's fear that such a negative reaction could seriously damage our Congressional relations, effect our work against priority foreign targets and have significant impact on the viability of CIA.

3. There are indications that the Agency, in responding to CE/CI requirements, is collecting information on selected

00439

U.S. citizen; both at home and abroad. In operational areas which are highly sensitive and potentially explosive (e.g., domestic radical or racial groups) this Agency must carefully weigh the needs and pressures for collecting and maintaining this information against the risk and impact of revelation should the operation become compromised or public knowledge. We therefore urge that all domestic collection and action programs be severely reviewed so that only those be continued which are of the highest priority and which absolutely cannot be undertaken by domestic agencies. CIA should not take on requirements of this type by default.

4. Not all of the members of MAG are privy to CIA's direct or indirect involvement in domestic activities. Those who are aware probably know only parts of the whole picture. But our increasing concern and our intense interest in maximizing the Agency's ability to do its proper job, impel us to bring our serious apprehensions to your attention.

THE MANAGEMENT ADVISORY GROUP

SECRET

EYES ONLY SENSITIVE

00440

Attachments B, C, D and E

Attachment B - Vic Marchetti's UPI Interview, from U.S. News and World Report, 11 October 1971:

"Fearing today that the CIA may already have begun 'going against the enemy within' the United States as they may conceive it--that is, dissident student groups and civil-rights organizations..."

"Because the men of the Agency are superpatriots, he said, it is only natural for them to view violent protest and dissidence as a major threat to the nation. The inbred CIA reaction, he said, would be to launch a clandestine operation to infiltrate dissident groups.

That, said Marchetti, may already have started to happen.

'I don't have very much to go on,' he said. 'Just bits and pieces that indicate the U.S. intelligence community is already targeting on groups in this country that they feel to be subversive.

'I know this was being discussed in the halls of the CIA, and that there were a lot of people who felt this should be done.' "

Attachment C - New York Times, 10 October, "FBI-CIA Relations:"

"Information generally exchanged between the FBI and the CIA might concern such subjects as officers of the Black Panther party traveling overseas...and American youngsters cutting sugar cane in Cuba."

Attachment D - DCI Address to the American Society of Newspaper Editors:

"And may I emphasize at this point that the statute specifically forbids the Central Intelligence Agency to have any police, subpoena, or law-enforcement powers, or any domestic security functions. I can assure you that except for the normal responsibilities for protecting the physical security or our own personnel, our facilities, and our classified information, we do not have any such powers and function; we have never sought any; we do not exercise any. In short, we do not target on American citizens."

00441

Attachment E - DCI Address to CIA Annual Awards Ceremony:

"I gave a talk to the American Society of Newspaper Editors last winter, as you know, and I did it for only one purpose. That was to try and put in the record a few of these denials that we've all wanted to see put in the public record for some time. And you can rely on those denials. They're true, and you can use that as any text that you may need to demonstrate that we're not in the drug traffic, and that we're not trying to do espionage on American citizens in the United States."

00442

EYES ONLY
SECRET/SENSITIVE

25 March 1971

CENTRAL INTELLIGENCE AGENCY

Management Advisory Group

MEMORANDUM FOR: The Director

THROUGH : The Executive Director

SUBJECT : CIA Domestic Activities

MAG is concerned that CIA avoid involvement in the current expose of the domestic intelligence activities of the Army and other federal agencies. We believe that there are CIA activities similar to those now under scrutiny which could cause great embarrassment to the Agency because they appear to exceed the scope of the CIA charter. Except for the Agency's statutory CE/CI responsibilities, MAG opposes any Agency activity which could be construed as targeted against any person who enjoys the protection of the US Constitution -- whether or not he resides in the United States. Except in those cases clearly related to national security, no US citizen should be the object of CIA operations. We realize that on occasion the Agency will develop information about some citizen who is engaged in activities inimical to the interests of the United States. Such information should quickly be turned over to the proper agencies of government for further action, even if it means that sometimes an essentially home-oriented agency may be asked to perform in a limited operational capacity overseas.

If we do not pursue such a course, one day the public and the Congress will come to have grave doubts about our role in government, and may severely restrict our ability to perform those tasks properly assigned to CIA.

SECRET/SENSITIVE
EYES ONLY

00443

72 2241

21 APR 1972

MEMORANDUM FOR: Deputy Director for Intelligence
Deputy Director for Plans
Deputy Director for Support
Deputy Director for Science and Technology
Heads of Independent Offices

(For Distribution to Office/Division Chief Level Only)

SUBJECT : CIA Activities in the United States

1. From time to time some of our employees express concern over various allegations or rumors of CIA activities in the United States. The attached memorandum is designed to clarify this subject so that supervisors can authoritatively reply to any employees indicating such concern. It is a statement of the facts of the situation. If incidents or activities are reported which appear to conflict with this statement, they should be reported to appropriate senior authority for resolution (or correction if unauthorized activities might have occurred).

2. Because of the possible sensitivity of this description of the Agency's methodology, this memorandum is not being given the usual broad circulation of the "FYI -- Allegations and Answers" series. Office and Division Chiefs are urged, however, to use it to inform Branch Chiefs so that its points can be readily available to supervisors to react to expressions of employee concern.

/s/ W. E. Colby

W. E. Colby
Executive Director-Comptroller

Attachment

WEC

Distribution:
O - DDI
1 - Each Other Addressee:

DDP	D/DCI/IC	A/DCI (Thuermer)
DDS	D/PPB	SAVA
DDS&T	ONE	USIB Secretary
OGC	OLC	IG

1 - ER 1 - ExDir

ExDir

00444

ALLEGATION:

In a variety of ways it has been alleged that CIA is working within the United States, with particular attention to extremist groups.

FACTS:

1. Section 102 of the National Security Act of 1947, subparagraph D3, states, "The Agency shall have no police, subpoena, law-enforcement powers, or internal security functions."

In his speech to the American Society of Newspaper Editors on 14 April 1971, the Director stated:

> "I can assure you that except for the normal responsibilities for protecting the physical security of our own personnel, our facilities, and our classified information, we do not have any such powers and functions; we have never sought any; we do not exercise any. In short, we do not target on American citizens."

In the Director's "State of the Agency" speech to employees on 17 September 1971, he said:

> "I gave a talk to the American Society of Newspaper Editors last winter, as you know, and I did it for only one purpose. That was to try and put in the record a few of these denials that we've all wanted to see put in the public record for some time. And you can rely on those denials. They're true, and you can use that as any text that you may need to demonstrate that we're not in the drug traffic, and that we're not trying to do espionage on American citizens in the United States, and we're not tapping telephone lines, and that we're not doing a lot of other things which we're accused of doing. One of the things that tends to perpetuate some of these silly ideas are jokes that are made about them, particularly about domestic espionage. Although the jokes have no basis in fact they nevertheless give us a name which we don't deserve. I don't say that that makes all that much difference, but it does make some difference, and this tends to spill over, so I would like to suggest that if you have it in your hearts to do so that you speak up when the occasion arises and try and set the facts straight."

00445

2. From time to time some employees have been concerned that Agency activities might conflict with these statements. They can be assured that Agency activities do not. For clarification, some activities which may have been subject to misunderstanding are listed as follows:

a. Domestic Contacts. The Domestic Contact Service establishes discreet but overt relationships with American private citizens, commercial, academic and other organizations and resident aliens for the purposes of collecting on a voluntary basis foreign intelligence information or soliciting their cooperation in assisting the Agency to perform its mission overseas. Records of the individuals and organizations cooperating with the Agency are maintained as a necessary practical element of this process.

b. Security Investigations. Security investigations are conducted on prospective employees, contractors, and consultants, and on security problems which arise. These investigations involve a wide range of investigative procedures, including neighborhood inquiries, checks with other Government agencies, review of credit reports, and interviews with former employers and business associates. This is essential to assure that our personnel possess a high degree of personal integrity, sense of responsibility, and competence and to protect classified information and sensitive intelligence sources and methods. The resulting files are held separately by the Office of Security and are not merged with other Agency files.

c. Foreign Resources. On some occasions, foreign citizens of interest to CIA are contacted and recruited in America for work abroad. The purpose of this activity is entirely restricted to the Agency's foreign operations.

d. Recruitment. CIA recruiters maintain a wide variety of contacts within the United States, assisting individuals interested in employment with CIA to learn more about it and to join its employee force.

e. Contracting. In the course of CIA business and operations, a number of contracts for procurement, research, or analysis are made with a variety of U.S. companies and individuals. This in no way constitutes operations in the U.S. but rather secures the assistance of these groups in carrying out the CIA mission against foreign targets.

00446

f. Operations. The 1967 Katzenbach Committee report was approved by the Director in March 1967 and is binding on any of our relations with American organizations today. It specifically prohibits covert financial assistance or support, direct or indirect, to any U.S. educational or private voluntary organization. Any relationship or operation the Agency has with an American organization must be and is within these guidelines.

g. Details or Loans. On rare occasions, details of technically qualified CIA personnel, technical advice, or loans of CIA equipment have been made available to other U.S. agencies at their request to assist them to carry out their responsibilities. An example is the skymarshal program, in which some CIA personnel were temporarily detailed to the FAA in order to assist in a rapid initiation of that program. Such personnel and equipment are under the operational control of the receiving agency. Assistance of this nature in no way constitutes an assumption of responsibility or authority by CIA for the program.

h. Counterintelligence and Drugs. To carry out its responsibilities for counterintelligence, CIA is interested in the activities of foreign nations or intelligence services aimed at the U.S. To the extent that these activities lie outside the U.S., including activities aimed at the U.S. utilizing U.S. citizens or others, they fall within CIA's responsibilities. Responsibility for coverage of the activities within the U.S. lies with the FBI, as an internal security function. CIA's responsibility and authority are limited to the foreign intelligence aspect of the problem, and any action of a law enforcement or internal security nature lies with the FBI or local police forces. (CIA's assistance to the U.S. Government program against narcotics and drugs is handled in the same fashion.)

i. Operational Support. To support CIA operations, arrangements are made with various U.S. business or other entities to provide cover or other support for CIA personnel or activities abroad. This can include proprietaries formed or controlled by CIA. While these may exist within the U.S., their purpose is to conduct or support operations abroad.

j. Defectors. As provided by law, CIA occasionally resettles in the U.S. defectors and other foreign individuals of operational interest. This resettlement may involve a new identity, relocation, employment, etc. Although this activity takes place in this country, its purpose is the support of operations abroad.

UNCLASSIFIED		CONFIDENTIAL		SECRET

OFFICIAL ROUTING SLIP

TO	NAME AND ADDRESS	DATE	INITIALS
1	MAG Co-Chairmen		
2			
3			
4			
5			
6			

	ACTION		DIRECT REPLY		PREPARE REPLY
	APPROVAL		DISPATCH		RECOMMENDATION
	COMMENT		FILE		RETURN
	CONCURRENCE		INFORMATION		SIGNATURE

Remarks:

For MAG review and return. Please do not reproduce.

FOLD HERE TO RETURN TO SENDER

FROM: NAME, ADDRESS AND PHONE NO.	DATE
O/Executive Director/[redacted]	15 May 72

UNCLASSIFIED		CONFIDENTIAL		SECRET

FORM NO. 1-67 237 Use previous editions (40)

00448

MEMORANDUM FOR : Deputy Director for Intelligence
Deputy Director for Plans
Deputy Director for Support
Deputy Director for Science and Technology
General Counsel
Inspector General
Assistant to the Director

SUBJECT : Allegation of Agency Involvement in the U. S.

1. The Management Advisory Group, among others, has reported on the concerns of some employees that the Agency is vulnerable to the charge of having an operational interest in U.S. citizens or organizations in violation of the National Security Act. Attached is my best understanding of the facts. If it is in error or incomplete, I ask that you let me know orally or in writing.

2. I have drafted the attached with two purposes in mind: First, as a basis for some type of issuance that would advise the command line and senior supervisors of policy and facts and, second, as a future issue of "FYI -- Allegations and Answers." I look forward to your comment in the not-too-distant future before it is formally distributed.

WEC

W. E. Colby
Executive Director-Comptroller

Attachment
O/ExDir/BEvans
Distribution:
O-DDI
1 - Each other addressee
1 - ExDir
1 - ER

Note. Attachment revised and issued in final form on 21 April 1973.

00449

FYI -- ALLEGATIONS AND ANSWERS

March 1972

ALLEGATION:

In a variety of ways it has been alleged that CIA is working within the United States, with particular attention to extremist groups. A recent example was in the Quicksilver Times of 20 January 1972 (attached)*.

FACTS:

1. Section 102 of the National Security Act of 1947, subparagraph D3, states, "The Agency shall have no police, subpoena, law-enforcement powers, or internal security functions."

In his speech to the American Society of Newspaper Editors on 14 April 1971, the Director stated:

> "I can assure you that except for the normal responsibilities for protecting the physical security of our own personnel, our facilities, and our classified information, we do not have any such powers and functions; we have never sought any; we do not exercise any. In short, we do not target on American citizens."

In the Director's "State of the Agency" Speech to employees on 17 September 1971, he said:

> "I gave a talk to the American Society of Newspaper Editors last winter, as you know, and I did it for only one purpose. That was to try and put in the record a few of these denials that we've all wanted to see put in the public record for some time. And you can rely on those denials. They're true, and you can use that as any text that you may need to demonstrate that we're not in the drug traffic, and that we're not trying to do espionage on American citizens in the United States, and we're not tapping telephone lines, and that we're not doing a lot of other things which we're accused of doing. One of the things that tends to perpetuate some of these

---

*COMMENT: The two gentlemen cited are former CIA employees. Neither they nor the organizations with which they are currently associated have any operational connection with the Agency.

00450

silly ideas are jokes that are made about them, particularly about domestic espionage. Although the jokes have no basis in fact they nevertheless give us a name which we don't deserve. I don't say that that makes all that much difference, but it does make some difference, and this tends to spill over, so I would like to suggest that if you have it in your hearts to do so that you speak up when the occasion arises and try and set the facts straight."

2. From time to time some employees have been concerned that Agency activities might conflict with the National Security Act and the Agency's statements. They can be assured that Agency activities do not. For clarification, some activities which may have been subject to misunderstanding are listed as follows:

a) Security Investigations. Security investigations are conducted on prospective employees, contractors, and consultants. They involve neighborhood checks on the background of these individuals. This is essential to meet the security requirements of the Agency. The resulting information is held in separate security office files and not merged in other Agency files.

b) Domestic Contacts. On an overt basis the Domestic Contact Service makes visits to American private citizens, firms, and other organizations, soliciting transmission to the Government of information they have learned abroad. The purpose and content of the information are restricted to foreign intelligence, i.e., intelligence on developments abroad. The records of the firms and individuals as sources are maintained as a purely practical element of this collection process.

c) Foreign Resources. A variety of foreign citizens of interest to CIA visit or on occasion reside in America. Occasionally they are contacted and recruited for work abroad in the course of travels to their homeland or for continuing collaboration with the Agency in their homeland after their return from the U.S. The purpose of this activity is entirely restricted to the collection of foreign intelligence.

d) Recruitment. CIA recruiters maintain a wide variety of contacts within the United States endeavoring to assist individuals interested in employment with CIA to learn more about it and to join its employee force.

e) Contracting. In the course of CIA business and operations, a number of contracts for procurement, research, or analysis are made with a variety of U.S. companies and individuals. This in no way constitutes operations in the U.S. but rather secures the assistance of these groups in carrying out the CIA mission of foreign intelligence.

f) Operations. The 1967 Katzenbach Committee report was approved by the Director in March 1967 and is binding on any of our relations with American organizations today. It specifically prohibits covert financial assistance or support, direct or indirect, to any U.S. educational or private voluntary organization. Any relationship or operation the Agency has with an American organization must be and is within these guidelines.

g) Details or Loans. On rare occasions, details of technically qualified CIA personnel or loans of CIA equipment have been made to other U.S. agencies to assist in the carrying out of their responsibilities. An example is the skymarshal program to which some CIA personnel were detailed in order to assist in a rapid initiation of that program. Assistance of this nature in no way constitutes an assumption of responsibility or authority by CIA for the program.

h) Counterintelligence. To carry out its responsibilities for counterintelligence, CIA is interested in the activities of foreign nations or intelligence services aimed at the U.S. To the extent that the activities lie outside the U.S., including activities aimed at the U.S. utilizing U.S. citizens or others, it falls within CIA's responsibilities. Responsibility for coverage of the activities within the U.S. lies with the FBI, as it involves an internal security function. CIA's responsibility and authority are limited to the foreign intelligence aspect of the problem and any action of a law enforcement or internal security nature lies with the FBI or local police forces.

i) Defectors. As provided by law, CIA occasionally resettles in the U.S. defectors and other foreign individuals of operational interest. This resettlement may involve their assumption of a new identity, location of employment, etc. Although this activity takes place in this country, its purpose is the support of operations abroad.

j) Cover. As a part of CIA operations abroad, arrangements are made with a number of U.S. entities to serve as the ostensible sponsor of individuals abroad. This can include business entities controlled by CIA, or proprietaries. While they may exist within the U.S., their purpose is to conduct or support operations abroad.

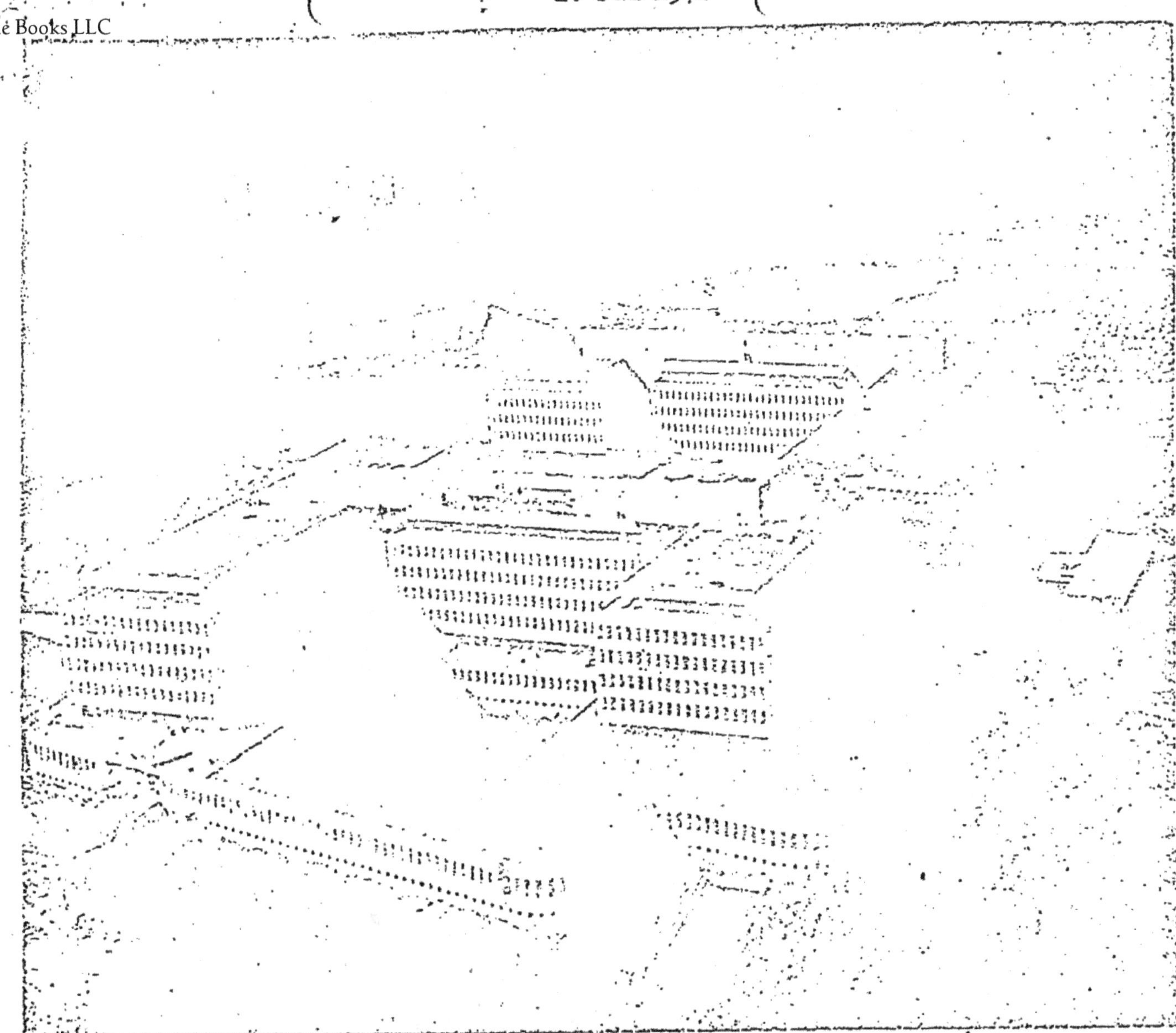

CIA Headquarters in Virginia

Back yard CIA

The Central Intelligence Agency always insists its men aren't involved in domestic police work. But in Chicago CIA agents have been working with the FBI and Tresury men in an effort to pin the bank bombings on radical groups.

Heretofore, clandestine CIA police work within the US was centered around counter espionage efforts aimed at the Soviet KGB. CIA maintains secret bases in all major US cities. The agency also has training camps in Virginia and the Carolinas. These are masked as regular military bases. Spooks are trained for duty at Williamsburg, Va.

Two years ago CIA employees were [illegible] when members of the Chicago

They met there with Helms, were shown around, and taken to the secret training camps. That was the beginning of rumors within the agency that the CIA had been given the go ahead to move into domestic police operations. While everyone denied it, the theory was that the CIA was told to get the radicals.

Two recent personnel changes increased speculation. One involved resignation of Helm's special assistant, Robert Kiley. Kiley handled the student operations through National Student Association facades. He recently turned up as associate director of the Police Foundation, a new group launched with a $30 million Ford Foundation grant. The money is meant to be used to improve local police. The second personnel shift involved Drexel Godfrey, who was head of the CIA's Office of Current Intelligence. He quit this high ranking job, turned up in the narcotics bureau of the Justice Commission at Harrisburg, Pa. The commission is another new [illegible]

police. Both personnel shifts a[re] cited by agency people to bols[ter] fronts in the US, thistime, mov[ed] into was given a new title rece[ntly] making him head of all intellig[ence] and presumably providing him wi[th] legitimate interest in internal operations. But such suggestio[ns] bitterly denied all around.

00454

TABLE OF CONTENTS

00455

SENDER WILL CHECK CLASSIFICATION TOP AND BOTTOM

	UNCLASSIFIED		CONFIDENTIAL		SECRET

EYES ONLY

OFFICIAL ROUTING SLIP

TO	NAME AND ADDRESS	DATE	INITIALS
1	Mr. William E. Colby		WEC
2	IG		
3			
4	B Y H A N D		
5			
6			

ACTION		DIRECT REPLY		PREPARE REPLY	
APPROVAL		DISPATCH		RECOMMENDATION	
COMMENT		FILE		RETURN	
CONCURRENCE		INFORMATION		SIGNATURE	

Remarks:

00456

FOLD HERE TO RETURN TO SENDER

FROM: NAME, ADDRESS AND PHONE NO.	DATE
Walter Elder EYES ONLY Ext.	1 Jun 1973

UNCLASSIFIED	CONFIDENTIAL	SECRET

SECRET/SENSITIVE

FORM NO. 1-67 237 Use previous editions (40)

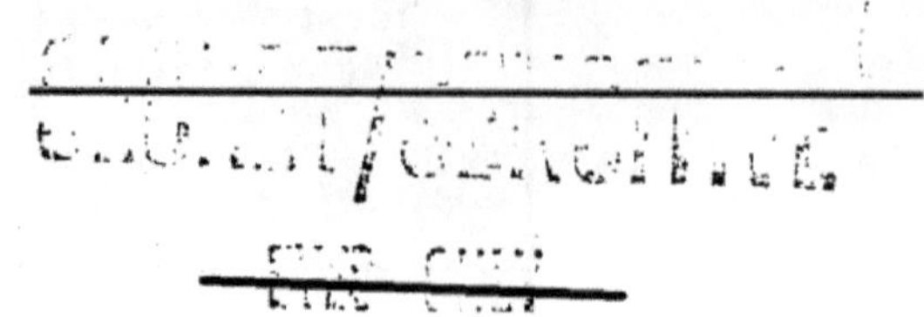

1 June 1973

MEMORANDUM FOR: Mr. William E. Colby

SUBJECT: Special Activities

1. Following our recent conversation, I have searched my memory and Mr. McCone's files for examples of activities which to hostile observers or to someone without complete knowledge and with a special kind of motivation could be interpreted as examples of activities exceeding CIA's charter.

2. First, as we discussed, on 7 March 1962, DCI McCone, under pressure from Attorney General Robert F. Kennedy, agreed to tap the telephones of columnists Robert S. Allen and Paul Scott in an effort to identify their sources for classified information which was appearing in their columns. Because the primary source appeared to be in the Department of Defense, McCone ordered me personally to brief General Joe Carroll, Director of DIA, orally, which I did. I understand more complete information on this operation is available from the Director of Security. I, personally, managed to avoid gaining any knowledge of what precise actions were taken, what information was gained, what was done with it, and when the operation was terminated.

3.

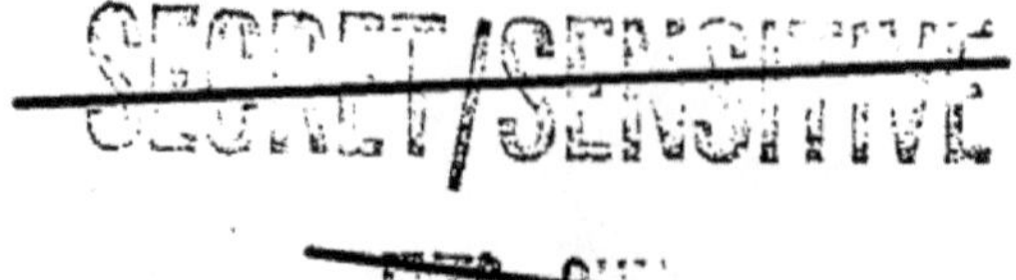

E 2, IMPDET CL BY 007789

00457

EYES ONLY

2

4. Although certain activities never got beyond the planning stage, there are, I believe, three examples of such planning which could be subject to misinterpretation. One involved chemical warfare operations against A second involved a paramilitary strike against Outside the United States Government, General Eisenhower was briefed on such planning. A third, which assumes a new significance today, involved a proposal by Angleton and Helms for a greatly increased intelligence collection effort against foreign installations in this country. This planning also involved a scheme for selected

EYES ONLY

00458

~~SECRET/SENSITIVE~~

~~EYES ONLY~~

3

exposure of KGB activities and counteractions against the Soviet intelligence service. The reasons are still unclear to me as to why the FBI chose to brief the PFIAB to the effect that CIA was planning to wiretap extensively and indiscriminately in this country, to greatly increase the Agency representation in the Moscow Embassy, and generally to use KGB-type tactics, also extensively and indiscriminately. This led to a heated exchange between DCI McCone and Mr. Belmont of the FBI, one such meeting taking place in the presence of the Attorney General. It is clear that the FBI was opposed to any such proposal then, as now, and the plan never went forward.

5. During the period when Des FitzGerald was in charge of the Cuban Task Force, DCI McCone's office learned, quite by accident, that FitzGerald had secured the cooperation of several prominent US business firms in denying economic items to Cuba. There was no question but that the businessmen were glad to cooperate, but knowledge of this operation had to be rather widespread.

6. [redacted] in connection with elections in Chile. On 12 May 1964 at a meeting of the 303 Committee, it was decided that the offers of American business could not be accepted, it being neither a secure way nor an honorable way of doing such business. This declaration of policy at this time bears on the recent ITT hearings, but I am not surprised that McCone has forgotten that he helped to set the precedent of refusing to accept such collaboration between the Agency's operations and private business.

7. At the direction of Attorney General Robert Kennedy and with the explicit approval of President Kennedy, McCone injected the Agency, and particularly Cord Meyer,

~~SECRET/SENSITIVE~~

~~EYES ONLY~~

00459

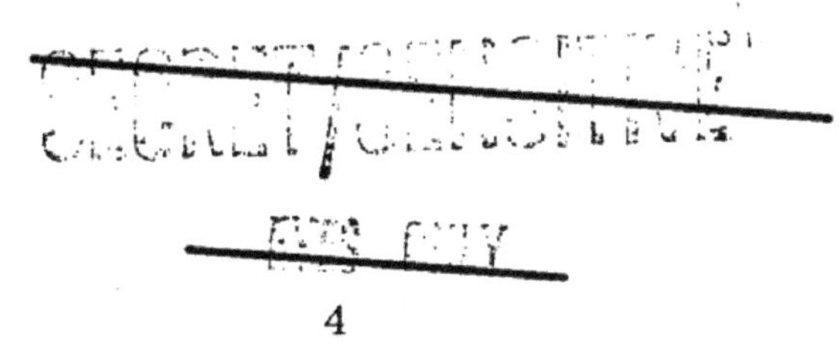

into the US labor situation, and particularly to try to ameliorate the quarrel between George Meany and Walter Reuther. Cord Meyer steered a very skillful course in this connection, but the Agency could be vulnerable to charges that we went behind Meany's back, or were somehow consorting with Reuther against Meany's wishes.

8. There are three examples of using Agency funds which I know to be controversial. One was the expenditure of money under Project MOSES in securing the release of Cuban Brigade prisoners. Details of this operation are best known to Larry Houston, Mike Miskovsky, George MacManus, and James Smith. Second, as you well know, when Lou Conein received his summons to report to the Joint General Staff Headquarters on 1 November 1963 a large amount of cash went with him. My impression is that the accounting for this and its use has never been very frank or complete. Third, at one of the early Special Group meetings attended by McCone he took strong exception to proposals to spend Agency funds to improve the economic viability of West Berlin, and for an investment program in Mali. His general position was that such expenditures were not within the Agency's charter, and that he would allow such spending only on the direct personal request of the Secretary of State or the Secretary of Defense, or the White House.

9. I raise these issues of funding because I remember the Agency's being severely criticized by the House Appropriations Subcommittee for having spent $3,000 for stamps in connection with a program to buy tractors to secure the release of prisoners from Cuba.

10. Under the heading of old business, I know that any one who has worked in the Director's office has worried about the fact that conversations within the offices and over the telephones were transcribed. During McCone's

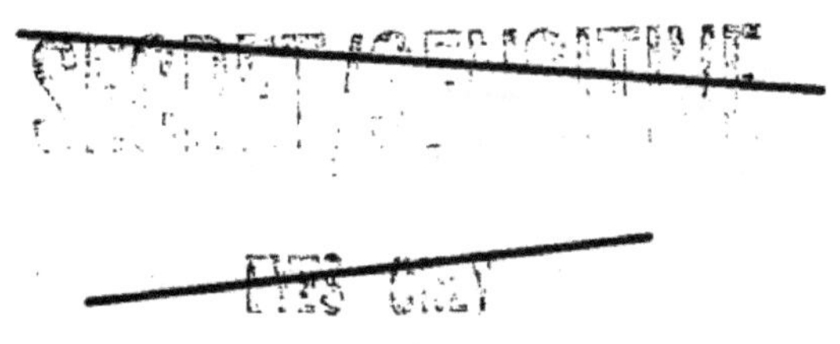

00460

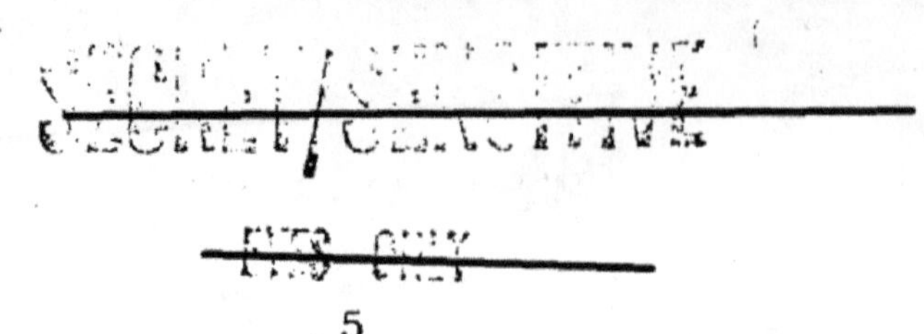

tenure, there were microphones in his regular office, his inner office, his dining room, his office in East Building, and his study at his residence on White Haven Street. I do not know who would be willing to raise such an issue, but knowledge of such operations tends to spread, and certainly the Agency is vulnerable on this score.

11. Also under the heading of old business, [redacted] Shortly after the Cuban missile crisis, there was a disposition in Washington to reexamine the Bay of Pigs, and the fact that several Alabama National Air Guard officers lost their lives in the Bay of Pigs was surfaced with surprisingly little excitement at the time.

12. During my stint on the 7th floor there was a special arrangement with the Office of Communications whereby the Director's office gained access to non-CIA traffic. This surfaced briefly at one point shortly after Admiral Rayborn became DCI. He had visited the Signal Center and removed a copy of a telegram from the Embassy in the Dominican Republic for Under Secretary George Ball, Eyes Only. He returned to his office and proceeded to discuss this telegram with George Ball who was naturally quite curious as to how Rayborn knew about it, and also as to how Rayborn had it in his possession before Ball did. Ben Read in the Secretary of State's office and I spent several weeks putting this one to rest.

13. Finally, DCI McCone, as you and I well know, operated on a very lofty plane, and I think certain of his activities could be misunderstood. One example was his decision in July of 1964 to have Aristotle Onassis and Maria Callas flown from Rome to Athens on Air Force KC 135. Their arrival in Athens in this airplane attracted the attention of the local press and in due course Mr. John

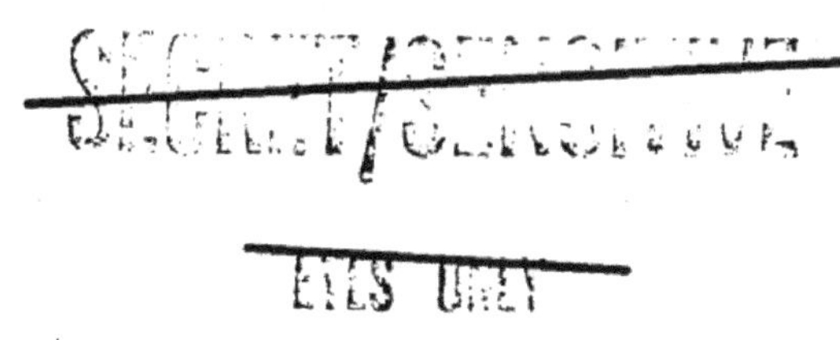

Hightower, Chief of the Associated Press Bureau for Washington, came to see me to ask about the propriety of this action.

14.

15. McCone dealt quite extensively with newsmen in Washington. In fact, they gave him a gift and a luncheon when he left Washington, which is perhaps indicative of the press's relations with him. However, in the case of the Ross and Wise book, The Invisible Government, he did try to bring pressure on the publisher and the authors to change things. They did not change a comma, and I doubt that this old saw will ever sing again.

16.

17. The above listing is uneven, but I have a sinking feeling that discipline has broken down, and that allegations from any quarter which cast these things in the wrong light would receive great publicity and attention, and no amount of denial would ever set the record straight. If I may be of any assistance in tracking down further details, I am of course at your disposal, but I would point

00462

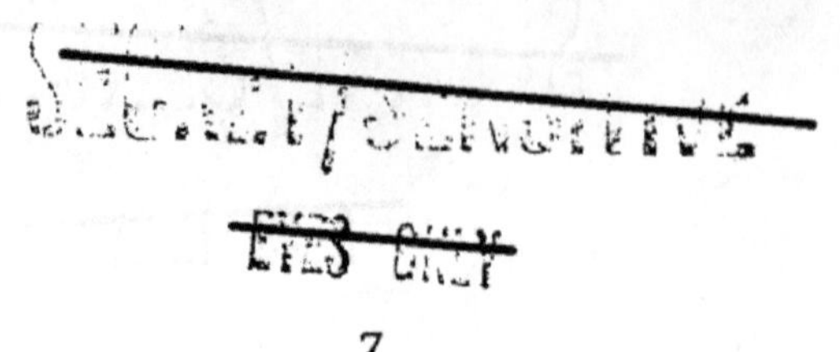

7

out that I was very much in the position of the enlisted man who knew that the commissioned officers were aware of these activities and better able to judge their propriety and possible impact or misinterpretation.

WALTER ELDER

SECRET/SENSITIVE

EYES ONLY

00463

14 February 1972

MEMORANDUM FOR THE RECORD:

In November 1962 Mr. [redacted] advised Mr. Lyman Kirkpatrick that he had, at one time, been directed by Mr. Richard Bissell to assume responsibility for a project involving the assassination of Patrice Lumumba, then Premier, Republic of Congo. According to [redacted] poison was to have been the vehicle as he made reference to having been instructed to see Dr. Sidney Gottlieb in order procure the appropriate vehicle.

00464

BALTIMORE NEWS AMERICAN
12 APR 1973

JOHN P. ROCHE

The CIA and Allende

The current imbroglio over the role that the Central Intelligence Agency and the International Telephone and Telegraph Co. played (or considered playing) in trying to block the election of Chilean President Allende has its tantalizing and perplexing aspects. Was the CIA's cash balance so low it needed a million dollars from IT&T? Did the CIA and IT&T really think they could pull off some of the stunts contemplated without the word getting out and working massively in favor of Allende? But underlying this brawl are a series of very difficult question of principle, to say nothing of definition.

First of all, what constitutes American (public or private) intervention in the internal affairs of another state? Obviously, sponsoring a revolution (as Teddy Roosevelt did to break Panama loose from Colombia) is at one pole. But between sponsoring revolutions and totally eliminating any American activity outside of the United States, there is a long line on the spectrum, a line that gets fuzzier and fuzzier the further you go.

Moreover, even doing nothing can be construed as intervention: Egypt's President Nasser throught that Secretary Dulles' refusal to help finance the Aswan Dam was a form of intervention, and some years ago six coffee-producing nations in Latin America protested to the Organization of American States that our refusal to rig coffee prices intervened in their internal affairs.

I would argue that the very existence of the United States as the most powerful nation in the world automatically intervenes in the affairs of every other state. Nasser and the coffee producers were right: Inaction on our part can have as great an impact as action. To take a vivid instance, if we had not shipped military equipment to Britain before Pearl Harbor, the war for Europe could have been lost.

If we accept that proposition, the futile argument over whether we should intervene automatically goes by the boards. Then we turn to the hard one: To what ends should we (publicly and privately) intervene? Should we protect democratic (or even undemocratic) nations from totalitarian invasion or subversion? Should we utilize our foreign aid to nourish democratic political development — as is provided in the Fraser Amendment to the foreign aid bill — or should we take a strictly hands-off approach?

It as at this point that the IT&T fracas comes back into focus, and as ideological shambles occurs. Let us suppose for a moment that the Chase Manhattan Bank, influenced by the World Council of Churches and black militants, decided to provide a condult to black-liberation movements in South Africa, using its business connections to provide arms and other aid to the revolutionaries. Would this be a "bad" thing? Was it a "bad" thing when the CIA, using a business cover, shipped into Santo Domingo the weapons used to kill the brutal dictator Trujillo? (I don't know how he feels about it today, but in 1961 the Dominican statesman Juan Bosch thought that intervention was the greatest thing since the discovery of America.)

Colby! true?

What this comes down to is that intervention is a "good" thing when you happen to favor the cause involved, but is wicked and immoral if you disapprove of the goals. A perfectly human response; but hardly one on which sound public policy can be formulated. The though of IT&T losing its Chilean assets does not bring tears to my eyes or lead me to wish we still had a supply of gunboats in stock. Capitalism. I'm told, involves taking risks, and the corporation may in the end be reimbursed by a federal agency set up to provide insurance for such contingencies.

No, what bothers me is the wholly ad hoc reaction of the Senate committee investigating the matter. We would be far better served by Sen. Church and his colleagues if they spent less time being outraged and a little more trying to formulate general guidelines, guidelines which would apply to South America and South Africa, to the just and the unjust alike, however defined.

00465

UNCLASSIFIED ☐ INTERNAL USE ONLY ☐ CONFIDENTIAL ☐ SECRET

ROUTING AND RECORD SHEET

SUBJECT: (Optional)

~~EYES ONLY~~

FROM:	EXTENSION	NO.
DC/WHD		DATE 2 April 1974

TO: (Officer designation, room number, and building)	DATE RECEIVED	DATE FORWARDED	OFFICER'S INITIALS	COMMENTS (Number each comment to show from whom to whom. Draw a line across column after each comment.)
1. IG. Attn: [redacted]			[redacted]	Per our conversation. [redacted]
2. [redacted]				
3. [redacted]	2 April '74			
4. Jewel File				~~BY HAND & EYES ONLY~~
5.				
6.				This material was forwarded by DC/WH as a late discovery re the Jewels exercise last summer. He did not know if they had been submitted at the time. Comments as follows:
7.				
8.				
9.				
10.				
11.				
12.				1. Re Vesco. We don't have this piece, but other material related.
13.				
14.				2. Chilean question re deaths and reported re Watergate
15.				3. Health matter covered by Watergate

00466

FORM 3-62 610 USE PREVIOUS EDITIONS ☐ SECRET ☐ CONFIDENTIAL ☐ INTERNAL USE ONLY ☐ UNCLASSIFIED

~~SECRET~~

MEMORANDUM FOR THE RECORD

SUBJECT: Robert L. Vesco

1. On 31 July 1972 C/WHD was contacted by Mr. Jorden, Latin American referent at the NSC, by telephone in order to determine if BKHERALD had any information on Vesco. Mr. Jorden was advised that a check would be made. A file review uncovered [redacted] C/WH[illegible] called Mr. Jorden (31 July 1972) and informed him of the following:

a) Vesco was known to us as head of IOS, had recently visited Costa Rica and expressed a desire to settle there. In addition, it was known that Vesco [redacted]

b) C/WHD also advised Mr. Jorden that Vesco had come to the attention of [redacted] and they were aware that he was President of the International Control Corporation of Fairfield, N.J. Subsequently, [redacted] was advised that the NSC was making inquiries about Vesco.

2. [redacted]

3. [redacted]

~~SECRET~~

00467

00468

SECRET

SENSITIVE
SECRET

00469

~~SECRET~~

~~SENSITIVE~~

-3-

~~SENSITIVE~~

~~SECRET~~

00470

~~SECRET~~

~~SECRET~~

00471

7 September 1973
DATE

~~CHAMBERLAIN~~

BRECKINRIDGE

~~GILLARD~~

A sample of a short, to-the-point special study, approved by WEC and now the subject of activity by DDO, DDM&S and DDS&T to do new regulation.

RETURN TO: SDB.

Scott:
Is there any control, or need for such, overseas?

00472

21 AUG 1973

MEMORANDUM FOR: Director of Central Intelligence

FROM : Inspector General

SUBJECT : Use and Control of Disguise and Alias Documents

Action Requested:

1. The attached report resulted from our general inquiries into Watergate-related issues and contains recommendations in paragraph 9 for your approval.

Background:

2. In the course of collecting information on various activities of the Agency with flap potential, we received a number of reports on issuance and use of disguise and alias documentation. The Executive Secretary, CIA Management Committee noted on the face of the summary submitted by the Office of Technical Services (OTS) on materials issued by it that it would be interesting to check the reports of other components to see if they matched with OTS issuances. In fact, OTS is not the only component to issue alias documentation, and the review was broadened to include the other issuing components and their procedures for controlling the materials. The attached report summarizes the findings.

Donald F. Chamberlain
Inspector General

Attachment
As Stated Above

APPROVED: [signature] DATE: 24 AUG 1973

DISAPPROVED: ______ DATE: ______

00473

USE AND CONTROL OF DISGUISE AND ALIAS DOCUMENTS

General

1. The policy, responsibilities, and procedures concerning U.S. documentation issued to authenticate a false identity used in the Directorate of Operations are set forth in CSI (now DOI) 240-4 dated 23 August 1972. This instruction, a revision of CSI 220-7 dated 12 May 1959, represents an extensive upgrading in the definition of responsibilities and in establishing procedures ensuring that each request has the approval of a designated senior official in the component. The current instruction, furthermore, requires that each request be routed through Cover and Commercial Staff, Official Cover Branch (CCS/OCB) for concurrence, which, in effect, makes CCS/OCB the one component retaining complete records and details of every request. There are no other regulations applying to this subject, but it currently is observed by all components.

Issuing Responsibilities and Procedures

2. Three major components are responsible for issuing alias documentation and/or disguise. The specific responsibilities are:

this office issues non-backstopped documents in alias which are used exclusively for flash identification purposes. Birth certificates in alias are considered to be a special document and require a uniquely prescribed approval procedure and control. This Branch also responds to requests for disguises.

b. issues driver's licenses which are fully backstopped as well as fully backstopped investigative credentials

c.

00474

3. All requests to any of the above three components for alias documentation or disguise must be by memorandum and must be signed by one of two authorized officers designated by the requesting component. The instruction requires that this approval authority be confined to the chief of the division or staff, or to a senior operations officer specifically designated by the division or staff chief to exercise this function. The request is routed through CCS/OCB for concurrence at which time the requesting signature is verified as being on the approved list and all of the documents requested are recorded in the OCB file. All requests for documents to be used in CONUS are then routed to Office of Security, Operational Support Division, Special Activities Branch for approval and then are forwarded to the component which is to issue the documents. Issuing components are required to maintain controls on accountability and establish conditions for use of documents that they issue. OTS is developing a new computerized system which is scheduled to become operational in November 1973. Every six months each component will be given a complete listing of all documentation and disguises issued to them and they will be required to either justify the continued retention of the documents or return them.

Component Controls

4. There is no established procedure prescribing how each component is to control the documents issued to it. The instructions do require, however, that the documents will be handled as controlled documents from the time of issue until their ultimate disposition. The general practice is to maintain a record of all documents received within the component, but to issue the documents to the appropriate officers who assume responsibility for handling them properly. There is no evidence of periodic spot checking. At least one area division of the Directorate of Operations follows a procedure which requires that the documents be retained in the front office until needed for an operation, being returned after the operation is completed. On the surface this may appear to be a strict control, but in actuality the documents are retained in individual packages for each senior officer, and are never inspected before they are issued nor after they are returned; in effect, no record accountability by the officer is required.

Ultimate Document Retrieval

5. Every employee using alias documents is now required to process through CCS as part of his exit-out process for either resignation or retirement. It is at this time that he is given a list of all alias documentation issued to him and is requested to return all such documents. If there are any of these documents

00475

which he is unable to produce, the employee must submit a signed written statement describing, to the best of his ability, the conditions under which the document or documents were either lost or destroyed. The controls that now exist were not in operation when Howard Hunt was an employee, which may explain how he was able to retain documents issued in the 1960s. Nor do these controls apply effectively to non-employees over whom the Agency has no control. Most disguise material -- other than documents -- is regarded as perishable and non-sensitive and OTS is not too concerned if disguise material is not returned.

6. A new computerized system is being readied called CENBAD (Central Badge and Credential System). Initially this system will include all of the issuances of the badge office, CCS, Central Processing and the motor pool. The system will provide a monthly listing to these four components of all credentials issued and could be used to request outstanding credentials at the time of checkout. As a follow-up the system will provide a weekly credential status of all employees who have separated but for whom CENBAD still shows outstanding credentials.

Conclusions

7. Since the issuance of DOI 240-4 there has been a very definite improvement in the controls exercised over alias documentation. By requiring that every request be routed through CCS/OCB for concurrence, a very complete file of all alias documents issued has been compiled. The probability is slight that an Agency employee could resign or retire without having been queried about all the alias documents which had been issued to him. This procedure, while currently observed in the Agency, has no standing as a general requirement and exists only as an administrative instruction in one of the Agency's directorates.

8. The OTS computerized system, when operational, should tend to reduce the number of outstanding documents since a justification every six months will be required for their retention. The CENBAD system will not only make the CCS/OCB control even more effective by mechanizing the up-to-date listing but in the rare instances when an officer might depart without turning in his documents, CENBAD will provide this data weekly to allow for a follow-up.

00476

SECRET

9. Recommendations:

a. That an Agency Headquarters Regulation be issued formalizing the requirement for a central Agency control over issuance, accountability and recovery of alias documentation.

b. That each component designate an alias documentation control officer who would retain all documents, issuing them only for specific operations and institute a policy of signed receipts and return of documents upon the completion of the operation.

UNCLASSIFIED [ ] INTERNAL USE ONLY [ ] CONFIDENTIAL [X] SECRET

~~SECRET~~

ROUTING AND RECORD SHEET

SUBJECT: (Optional)

ACTVITIES OF POSSIBLE INTEREST TO THE DIRECTOR

FROM:	EXTENSION	NO.
[redacted]	[redacted]	DATE 25 May 1973

TO: (Officer designation, room number, and building)	DATE RECEIVED	DATE FORWARDED	OFFICER'S INITIALS	COMMENTS (Number each comment to show from whom to whom. Draw a line across column after each comment.)
1. [redacted]		5/29	[redacted]	1-2: Pls bring to attn of whomever is handling this mtl & getting for DDO. [redacted]
2.				
3.				
4. ADDO	30 MAY 1973	31 MAY 1973	[initials]	[redacted] sent this to you as a skeleton in the closet that you should know of for background purposes. [redacted] does not foresee any real problems with support by [redacted]
5.				
6.				
7. IG	5/31		B	
8. [redacted]		31 May	[initials]	
9. [redacted] "Jewels" (chrono).			[initials]	
10.				
11.				
12.				This was also reported by ORD/DDS&T and called to attention of WEC. [redacted]
13.				
14.				
15.				00478

~~SENSITIVE~~

~~SECRET~~

610 USE PREVIOUS EDITIONS [ ] SECRET [ ] CONFIDENTIAL [ ] INTERNAL USE ONLY [ ] UNCLASSIFIED

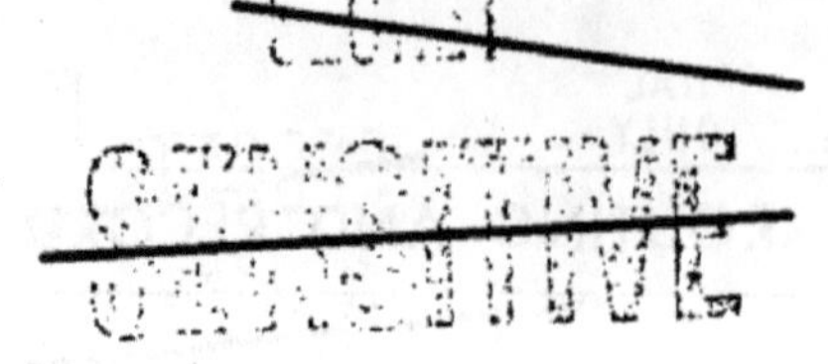

24 May 1973

MEMORANDUM FOR: Acting Chief, [redacted]

SUBJECT: Activities of Possible Interest to the Director

1. A few years ago the [redacted] Branch was asked to support a test program and feasibility study being conducted by DD/S&T/ORD. [redacted] When this project concluded, the [redacted] Branch was given permission by DD/S&T/ORD to retain the camera and TV image transmission system for further experimentation. [redacted]

2. In early June 1972 [redacted] DD/S&T/ORD, who had been the Project Officer in evaluating this TV data link system, phoned the [redacted] Branch. He stated that the U.S. Secret Service had a requirement for this TV camera and data link system. It was our understanding that the camera would be carried in a helicopter and would be used for crowd surveillance during the Democratic and Republican Conventions at Miami Beach, Florida. Mr. [redacted] asked that we make the equipment available for the period desired by the Secret Service and indicated that the equipment would be returned to us when no longer needed. On 19 June 1972, Mr. Michael T. Casey, accompanied by Mr. [redacted] visited [redacted] to pick up the equipment. Mr. Casey of the Secret Service was not made witting of the fact that [redacted] is an Agency facility. [redacted]

3. On 13 November 1972, the equipment, as a result of a phone call from [redacted] was picked up at Secret Service Headquarters by [redacted] A few of the system's

~~SENSITIVE~~

~~SECRET~~

00479

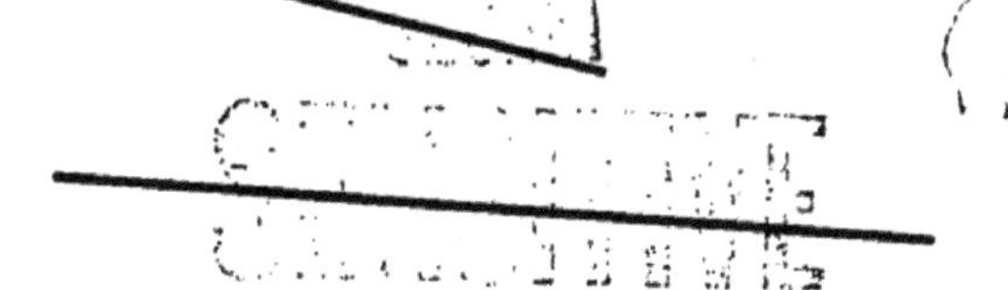

components were missing when it was returned. These components were the handle, tripod and electrical adapter. Later the missing components were returned to us by the Secret Service.

4. A few months ago, Mr. [redacted] called me about this equipment and said that S&T would like to get the equipment off its books since none of it would be needed in the future by S&T. He offered to transfer the equipment at no cost to [redacted] Branch. A short time later the necessary paper work was performed to reflect the receipt of this equipment into the [redacted] Branch inventory.

[redacted]

Chief, [redacted] Branch
Special Operations Division

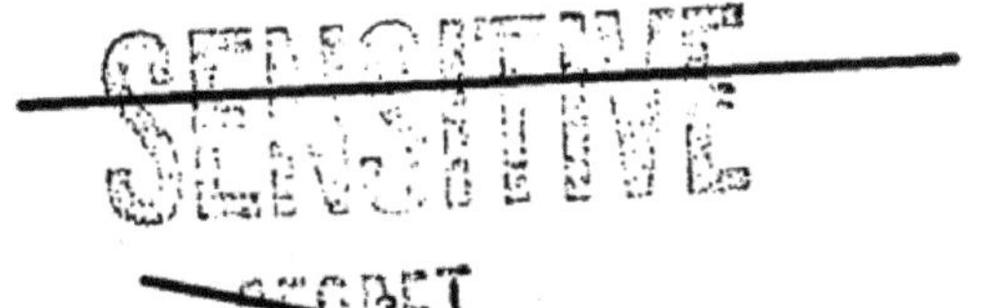

00480

~~SECRET~~ SENSITIVE

SUBJECT: [redacted]

Project [redacted] is a Headquarters initiated program which has as its fundamental objective the long term manipulations of selected agent assets operating against EA Division difficult targets in the leftist and communist milieu in various parts of the world. Although targetted overseas these agents are often exposed to and directed against American radical, leftist, and communist targets to gain a practical knowledge of the leftwing, radical, communist world. There is a possibility that an asset might become suspect and be accused of being an employee of the Agency or the Bureau; or it might happen some asset would, for some reason, become disenchanted with his role and expose his Agency relationship and his activities, with resultant embarrassment. To minimize potential problems, therefore, each case is cleared with the FBI and through CI/SO the Bureau is kept informed on a regular basis.

~~SECRET~~ SENSITIVE [redacted]

00482

Central Cover Staff

00483

SECRET
EYES ALONE

Subject: Cover Support

Bill:

1. In addition to the matters listed in the CCS memorandum on CCS Cover Support Within the United States the following bigoted cases should be noted:

2. We have no indications that either of these cases might create problems. As I told you on 5 March 1973, I don't feel the same way in regard to the cover situation of the personnel in projects

7 May 1973

00484

[ ] UNCLASSIFIED [ ] INTERNAL USE ONLY [ ] CONFIDENTIAL [X] SECRET

ROUTING AND RECORD SHEET

SUBJECT: (Optional)

Alias Passports

FROM:	EXTENSION	NO.
CHIEF, CCS		DATE 8 MAY 1973

TO: (Officer designation, room number, and building)	DATE RECEIVED	DATE FORWARDED	OFFICER'S INITIALS	COMMENTS (Number each comment to show from whom to whom. Draw a line across column after each comment.)
1. Mr. Colby,				BY HAND
2.				
3.				
4.				
5.				
6.				
7.				
8.				
9.				
10.				
11.				
12.				
13.				
14.				
15.				00485

FORM 3-62 610 USE PREVIOUS EDITIONS ~~[ ] SECRET~~ ~~[ ] CONFIDENTIAL~~ [ ] INTERNAL USE ONLY [ ] UNCLASSIFIED

8 May 1973

MEMORANDUM FOR: Deputy Director for Operations

SUBJECT: Alias Passports

Chief, Central Cover Staff

~~FULL TEXT COPY - DO NOT RELEASE~~

00486

~~SECRET~~

COUNT 1
DO-10

8 May 1973

MEMORANDUM FOR: Deputy Director for Operations

SUBJECT: Alias Passports

Chief, Central Cover Staff

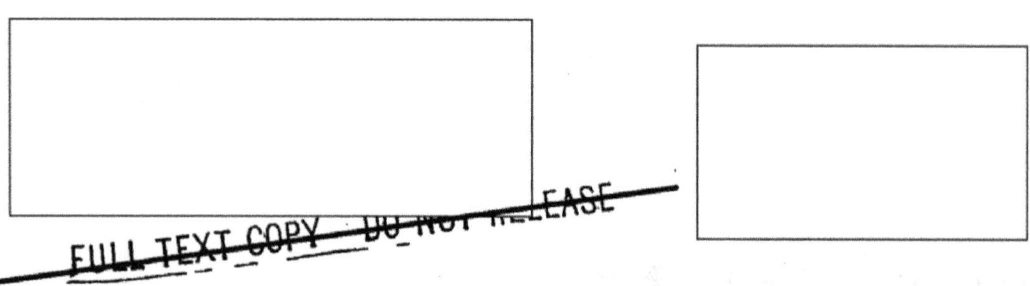

00487

SECRET

ROUTING AND RECORD SHEET

SUBJECT (Optional)

Count 1

FROM: C/CCS

EXTENSION

NO. DO-11

DATE 7 MAY 1973

TO: (Officer designation, room number, and building)	DATE RECEIVED	DATE FORWARDED	OFFICER'S INITIALS	COMMENTS (Number each comment to show from to whom. Draw a line across column after each comment.)
1. DDO				
2.				
3.				
4.				
5.				
6.				
7.				
8.				
9.				
10.				
11.				
12.				~~488 Not a record~~
13.				Deny 488–516 (b)(1) (b)(3)
14.				00488
15.				

FORM 3-62 610 USE PREVIOUS EDITIONS ☑ ~~SECRET~~ ☐ ~~CONFIDENTIAL~~ ☐ INTERNAL USE ONLY ☐ UNCLASSIFIED

7 May 1973 (Revised)

MEMORANDUM FOR: Deputy Director for Operations

SUBJECT : CCS Cover Support Provided Within the United States

1. The following specific information regarding domestic cover support provided by Central Cover Staff is submitted in response to your request:

a. Aliases Used in Conjunction with Documentation.

NOTE: The above figures are based on the CCS record-keeping system initiated in April 1972.

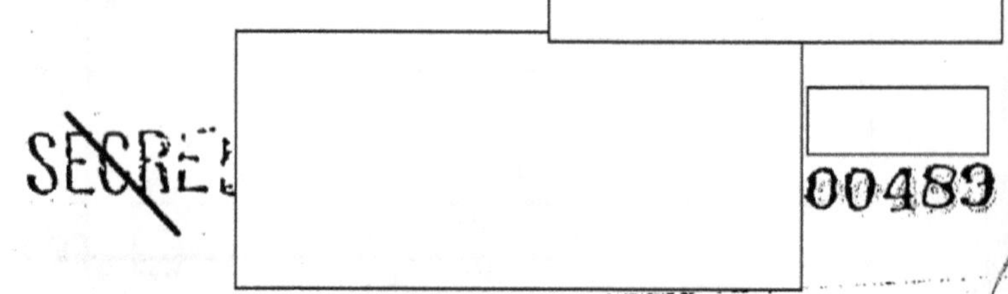
SECRET
00489

c. Alias U.S. Birth Certificates.

d. Alias Credit Cards.

-2-

~~SECRET~~

e. Alias Social Security Cards.

-3-

00491

~~SECRET~~

-4-

~~SECRET~~

00492

1. Support to BNDD Activities.

2. The following general information pertains to domestic cover support activities outside the purview of CCS:

a. Alias U.S. drivers licenses

b. Alias CIA credentials

Chief, Central Cover Staff

~~SECRET~~

7 May 1973 (Revised)

MEMORANDUM FOR: Deputy Director for Operations

SUBJECT : CCS Cover Support Provided Within the United States

1. The following specific information regarding domestic cover support provided by Central Cover Staff is submitted in response to your request:

a. Aliases Used in Conjunction with Documentation.

NOTE: The above figures are based on the CCS record-keeping system initiated in April 1972.

~~SECRET~~

00494

c. <u>Alias U.S. Birth Certificates.</u>

d. <u>Alias Credit Cards.</u>

-2-

SECRET

00495

e. Alias Social Security Cards.

-3-

00496

SECRET

-4-

SECRET

00497

SECRET

1. Support to BNDD Activities.

2. The following general information pertains to domestic cover support activities outside the purview of CCS:

a. Alias U.S. drivers licenses

b. Alias CIA credentials

Chief, Central Cover Staff

-5-

00498

C:/HB

SECRET

CSI 240-4

CLANDESTINE SERVICE
INSTRUCTION 240-4

COVER
23 August 1972

ALIAS U.S. DOCUMENTATION

SECRET

00499

CLANDESTINE SERVICE
INSTRUCTION 240-4

COVER
23 August 1972

SECRET

CSI 240-4

CLANDESTINE SERVICE
INSTRUCTION 240-4

COVER
23 August 1972

3

SECRET

00501

~~SECRET~~

CSI 240-4

CLANDESTINE SERVICE INSTRUCTION 240-4

COVER
23 August 1972

Thomas H. Karamessines
Deputy Director for Plans

4

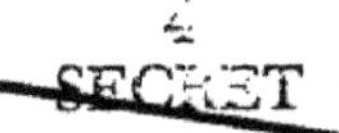

00502

SECRET

CSI 240-4

Attachment 1
23 August 1972

5

SECRET

00503

SECRET

CSI 240-4

Attachment 1
23 August 1972

6

SECRET

00504

CLANDESTINE SERVICES
INSTRUCTION NO. 220-7

TECHNICAL SUPPORT
12 May 1959

U. S. DOCUMENTATION IN CLANDESTINE SERVICES OPERATIONS

SECRET

CSI NO. 220-7

CLANDESTINE SERVICES
INSTRUCTION NO. 220-7

TECHNICAL SUPPORT
12 May 1959

00506

CSI NO. 220-7

CLANDESTINE SERVICES
INSTRUCTION NO. 220-7

TECHNICAL SUPPORT
12 May 1959

RICHARD M. BISSELL, JR.
Deputy Director
(Plans)

Released by:
Richard Helms
Chief of Operations

7 May 1973

MEMORANDUM FOR: Deputy Director for Operations

SUBJECT : CCS Cover Support Provided Within the United States

1. The following specific information regarding domestic cover support provided by Central Cover Staff is submitted in response to your request:

a. Aliases Used in Conjunction with Documentation.

SECRET

00508

b.

c. Alias U.S. Birth Certificates.

d. Alias Credit Cards.

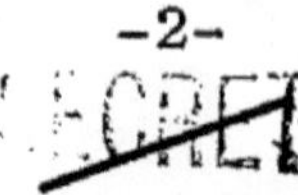

00509

e. Alias Social Security Cards.

f.

g.

h.

-3-

SECRET

00510

-4-

00511

k.

l. Other Special Arrangements.

(1) Alias U.S. drivers licenses

~~SECRET~~

(5) Alias CIA credentials

Chief, Central Cover Staff

00513

CORPORATE COVER

00514

DEVISED FACILITIES COVER

00515

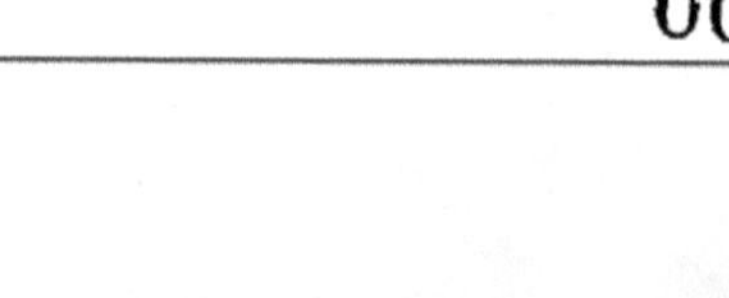

SECRET

PROPRIETARY ENTITY COVER

00516

SECRET

00517

7 May 1973

MEMORANDUM FOR: Deputy Director for Operations

SUBJECT : Research Project on Robert L. Vesco

1. In mid-October 1972, [redacted] of the Office of Economic Research asked [redacted] to participate in a meeting with a number of OER officers. During the meeting, [redacted] explained that the Director of Central Intelligence had levied a crash project on Dr. Edward Proctor, the Deputy Director for Intelligence, to produce a paper on international financier Robert L. Vesco. Since the Director had specifically requested contributions from the field [redacted] asked our Division to help in procuring them.

2. We thereupon cabled various questions suggested by OER to [redacted] and asked for replies by 19 October. Relevant answers were turned over to OER in memorandum form. In the case of a brief reference in one of the field messages to an earlier high-level American intercession on behalf of Mr. Vesco, we asked Mr. Helms through his secretary whether this was relevant information. The response, again received through the secretary, was that it was not relevant.

3. Soon after our memoranda had been submitted, [redacted] advised [redacted] that the Director wanted everyone to forget the Vesco project. This was communicated to all DDP Headquarters personnel who had had a hand in the project or had been made aware of it.

[redacted]

00518

4. We never had any indication as to the reason for or the purpose of the project.

5. We understand that OER has recently written a memorandum on this matter for the DCI.

Archibald B. Roosevelt
Chief, European Division

00519

Soviet Bloc Division

DO 48

7 May 1973

MEMORANDUM FOR: Deputy Director for Operations

SUBJECT: Items for Possible Use in Briefing the DCI

1. This Memorandum is submitted in order to identify to you for possible briefing of the Director activities which in certain contexts could be construed as delicate or inappropriate.

2. At the request of the Director of Security, from approximately mid-October 1972 to mid-January 1973 safesite [redacted] was made available to the U.S. Marshal's Service for use as a secure residence by an Assistant U.S. Attorney who reportedly was under threat of assassination by organized criminal elements.

3.

4.

5. Since late 1972 CIA has taken part in seven FBI training courses at Quantico, Virginia in response to requests from the FBI. We have shared with them through lectures and discussions lessons we have learned which are relevant to their counter-espionage responsibilities.

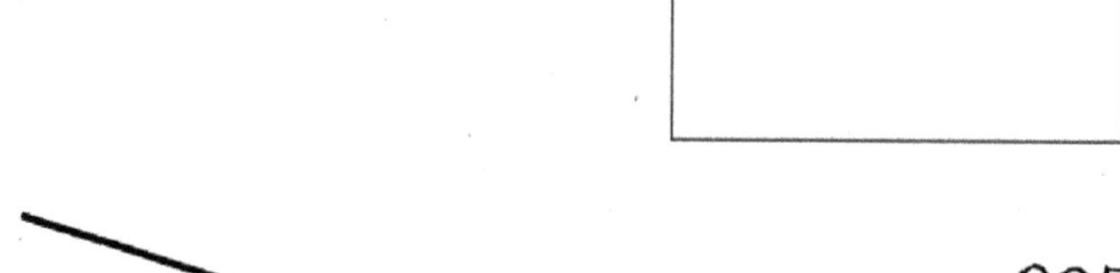

00521

SECRET

6. As a means of sharing more fully our operational experience we have invited three FBI officers to be students in our [redacted] Course from 14 to 25 May 1973.

7. The Soviet defector Yuriy NOSENKO was confined at a CIA facility from April 1964 to September 1967 while efforts were being made to establish whether he was a bona fide defector. Although his present attitude toward the Agency is quite satisfactory, the possibility exists that the press could cause undesirable publicity if it were to uncover the story.

[redacted]

David H. Blee
Chief
Soviet Bloc Division

SECRET

00522

NARCOG

00523

00524

7 MAY 1973

MEMORANDUM FOR: Deputy Director for Operations

SUBJECT: CIA Narcotics Activities Having Domestic Implications

1. This memorandum is in response to your request for a review of activities and relationships that might have domestic implications.

2. We occasionally report on the activities of American citizens involved in narcotics trafficking abroad. This information is normally disseminated to U.S. law enforcement agencies and other recipients of our reports. We also occasionally request U.S. law enforcement agencies for name traces on U.S. citizens who are known or suspected to be involved in narcotics trafficking abroad.

00525

00524

SECRET

7 MAY 1973

MEMORANDUM FOR: Deputy Director for Operations

SUBJECT: CIA Narcotics Activities Having Domestic Implications

1. This memorandum is in response to your request for a review of activities and relationships that might have domestic implications.

2. We occasionally report on the activities of American citizens involved in narcotics trafficking abroad. This information is normally disseminated to U.S. law enforcement agencies and other recipients of our reports. We also occasionally request U.S. law enforcement agencies for name traces on U.S. citizens who are known or suspected to be involved in narcotics trafficking abroad.

5. We have occasionally received requests for alias documentation for U.S. narcotics law enforcement

00525a

SECRET

officials working abroad on foreign narcotics investigations. The present method of handling such requests is for us to request the approval of the Deputy Director for Operations prior to asking the Technical Services Division to comply. We insist on knowing the true identity of the persons to use such documentation and limit them to staff officers of the U.S. law enforcement agencies. We also require that we know the purpose and intended use of the documents. Finally, we require receipts from the headquarters of the agency involved and the individual, and also require these documents to be returned to us for destruction after they have fulfilled their use. We have turned down requests from BNDD for alias documentation for domestic use. There are some indications in the files that there have been requests from BNDD for domestic documentation in connection with their domestic investigations. These predate NARCOG, and we are unable to determine how these requests were handled.

6. We periodically receive requests for technical assistance in the form of photographic and audio devices or guidance for use of such items by U.S. law enforcement agencies in connection with their foreign investigations of illicit narcotics activities. We require these agencies to adhere to the same procedures we require in our own operations. From time-to-time we have honored these requests and have provided sterile equipment when the requests have been properly presented and approved. Our records show evidence that several such requests were made prior to the existence of NARCOG in connection with narcotics law enforcement investigations in the United States. We are unable to determine whether the requests were fulfilled.

Chief, DDO/NARCOG

2

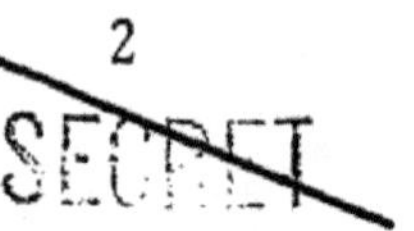

00526

Division D

00527

~~TOP SECRET~~
~~SECRET~~
~~CONFIDENTIAL~~

~~EYES ONLY~~

DOCUMENT DESCRIPTION	REGISTRY
SOURCE: C/Div. D.	CONTROL NUMBER:
DATE OF DOCUMENT: 29 May 1973.	DATE DOCUMENT RECEIVED: 5/29/73
COPY NUMBER (S): 1 & 2	LOGGED BY:
NUMBER OF PAGES: 2 DOCUMENT N	
NUMBER OF ATTACHMENTS: none	

FROM: Division D/CIB
Headquarters

DATE: 29 May 1973

	TO OFFICE	NAME	SIGNATURE	DATE
1	Inspector General	W V Broe Room	Seen -	5/29
2				
3				
4				
5				

- [ ] Approval
- [ ] Action
- [ ] Comment
- [ ] Concurrences
- [ ] Information
- [ ] Direct Reply
- [ ] Preparation of Reply
- [ ] Recommendation
- [ ] Signature
- [ ] Return
- [ ] Dispatch
- [ ] File

REMARKS

~~EYES ONLY~~
~~BY HAND~~

~~CONFIDENTIAL~~
~~SECRET~~
~~TOP SECRET~~

~~EYES ONLY~~

00528

~~TOP SECRET~~

~~EYES ONLY~~

29 May 1973

~~TOP SECRET~~

~~EYES ONLY~~

~~FULL TEXT COPY - DO NOT RELEASE~~

00529

~~TOP SECRET~~

~~TOP SECRET~~

~~EYES ONLY~~

~~FULL TEXT COPY - DO NOT RELEASE~~

00530

~~TOP SECRET~~

~~EYES ONLY~~

29 May 1973

~~TOP SECRET~~

~~EYES ONLY~~

00531

~~TOP SECRET~~

~~EYES ONLY~~

29 May 1973

~~TOP SECRET~~

~~EYES ONLY~~

(Orig)

DOCUMENT DESCRIPTION	REGISTRY
SOURCE:	CONTROL NUMBER:
DATE OF DOCUMENT:	DATE DOCUMENT RECEIVED:
COPY NUMBER (S):	LOGGED BY:
NUMBER OF PAGES: DOCUMENT NO:	
NUMBER OF ATTACHMENTS:	

FROM: Chief, Division D - 7B44 Hqs - Red

DATE: 7 May 1973

	TO OFFICE	NAME	SIGNATURE	DATE
1				
2				
3				
4				
5				

- [ ] Approval
- [ ] Action
- [ ] Comment
- [ ] Concurrences
- [ ] Information
- [ ] Direct Reply
- [ ] Preparation of Reply
- [ ] Recommendation
- [ ] Signature
- [ ] Return
- [ ] Dispatch
- [ ] File

REMARKS

00533

CONFIDENTIAL
SECRET
TOP SECRET

SECRET

D0 71

7 May 1973

MEMORANDUM FOR: Deputy Director for Operations

FROM : Chief, Division D

SUBJECT : Potentially Embarrassing Activities Conducted by Division D

REFERENCE : Your staff meeting, 7 May 1973

1. There is one instance of an activity by Division D, with which you are already familiar, which the Agency General Counsel has ruled to be barred to this Agency by statute: the collection [redacted] of international commercial radio telephone conversations between several Latin American cities and New York, aimed at the interception of drug-related communications. The background on this is briefly as follows:

[redacted] Therefore on 29 September 1972 NSA asked if Division D would take over the coverage, and on 12 October 1972 we agreed to do so. On 14 October a team of intercept operators from the [redacted] began the coverage experimentally. On 13 January 1973, NSA wrote to say that the test results were good, and that it was hoped this coverage could continue.

Because a question had arisen within Division D as to the legality of this activity, a query was addressed to the General Counsel on this score (Attachment A hereto). With the receipt of his reply (Attachment B), the intercept activity was immediately terminated. There has been a subsequent series of exchanges between Division D and the General Counsel as to the legality of radio intercepts made <u>outside</u> the U.S., but with one terminal being in the U.S., and the General Counsel

SECRET

00534

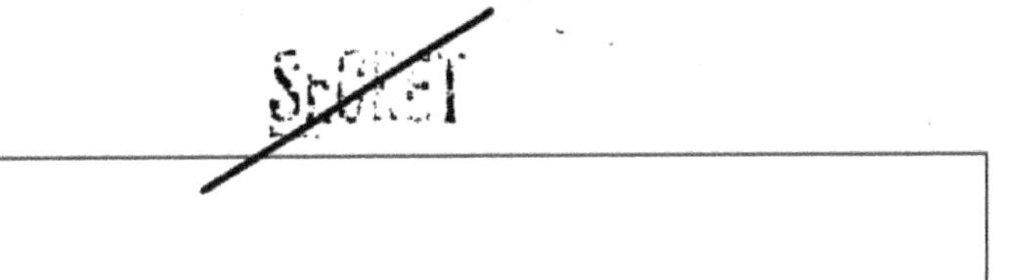

has ruled that such intercept is also in violation of CIA's statutory responsibilities.

2. We are carrying out at present one intercept activity which falls within this technical limitation--i.e., of having one terminal in the U.S.

Since the link being monitored carries a large number of totally unrelated conversations, the operators do intercept other traffic, frequently involving U.S. citizens--for example, BNDD staffers talking to their agents. I have described this situation to the General Counsel, and his informal judgment was that, as long as the primary purpose of the coverage is a foreign target, this is acceptable. He suggests, however, that it might be desirable to inform the Attorney General of the occasional incidental intercept of the conversations of U.S. citizens, and thus legalize this activity. We will pursue this with Mr. Houston.

4. An incident which was entirely innocent but is certainly subject to misinterpretation has to do with an equipment test run by CIA technicians in Miami in August 1971. At that time we were working jointly to develop short-range agent DF equipment for use against a Soviet agent in South Vietnam. and a field test was agreed upon. The Miami area was chosen, and a team consisting of Division D, Commo, personnel went to Miami during the second week of August. Contact was made with a Detective Sergeant of the Miami Beach Police Department, and tests were made from four different hotels, one a block away from the Miami Beach Auditorium and Convention Hall. A desk clerk in this hotel volunteered the comment that the team was part of the official security checking process of all hotels prior to the convention. (The Secret Service had already been checking for possible sniper sites.) As the team's report notes, "The cover for the use of the hotel is a natural."

2

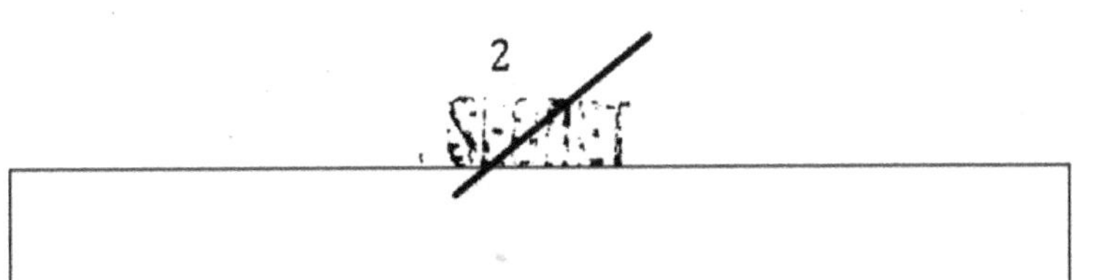

00535

SECRET

5. Another subject worthy of mention is the following:

In February 1972, contacts in U.S. telecommunications companies for copies of the telephone call slips pertaining to U.S.-China calls. These were then obtained regularly by Domestic Contact Service in New York, pouched to DCS Washington, and turned over to Division D for passage to FE/China Operations. The DDP was apprised of this activity by Division D in March 1972, and on 28 April 1972 Division D told DCS to forward the call slips to CI Staff, Mr. Richard Ober. Soon thereafter, the source of these slips dried up, and they have ceased to come to Mr. Ober. In an advisory opinion, the Office of General Counsel stated its belief that the collection of these slips did not violate the Communications Act, inasmuch as they are a part of a normal record-keeping function of the telephone company, which does not in any way involve eavesdropping.

Atts:

A. DivD memo to OGC 26 Jan 73

B. OGC memo to DivD 29 Jan 73

SECRET

3

00536

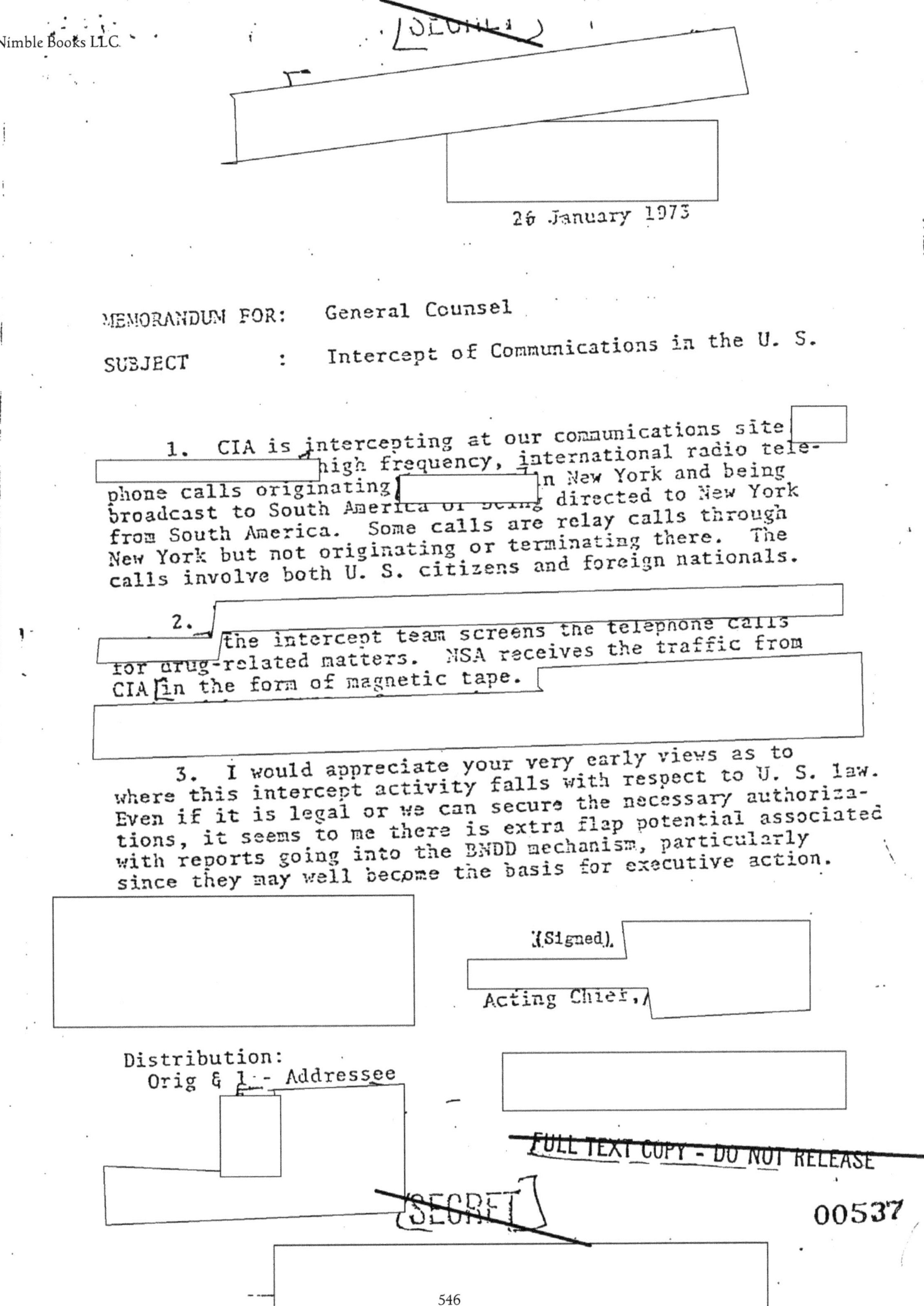

SECRET

26 January 1973

MEMORANDUM FOR: General Counsel

SUBJECT : Intercept of Communications in the U. S.

1. CIA is intercepting at our communications site high frequency, international radio telephone calls originating in New York and being broadcast to South America or being directed to New York from South America. Some calls are relay calls through New York but not originating or terminating there. The calls involve both U. S. citizens and foreign nationals.

2. the intercept team screens the telephone calls for drug-related matters. NSA receives the traffic from CIA in the form of magnetic tape.

3. I would appreciate your very early views as to where this intercept activity falls with respect to U. S. law. Even if it is legal or we can secure the necessary authorizations, it seems to me there is extra flap potential associated with reports going into the BNDD mechanism, particularly since they may well become the basis for executive action.

(Signed)

Acting Chief,

Distribution:
Orig & 1 - Addressee

FULL TEXT COPY - DO NOT RELEASE

SECRET

00537

Copy 1 of 2

29 January 1973

MEMORANDUM FOR: Acting Chief, Division D

SUBJECT: Intercept of Communications in the U. S.

REFERENCE: 26 Jan 73 Memo for GC fr AC/Division D, Same Subject

1. In referent you request our views as to the legal aspects of a radio telephone intercept activity carried on at our communications site

2. The basic law is contained in section 605 of the Communications Act of 1934, 47 U. S. C. 605, which prohibits interception of any radio communication without the authorization of the sender and also prohibits divulging the substance thereof to any person. Chapter 119 of Title 18, U. S. C., makes the interception of any wire or oral communication a crime punishable by $10,000 or five years' imprisonment, or both. There are two exceptions to these prohibitions:

a. The first provides for application through the Department of Justice to a Federal court for a court order authorizing such interception for specific purposes in connection with law-enforcement duties. Since this Agency is prohibited by statute from any police or law-enforcement activities, obviously we cannot operate under this exception.

b. The other exception is contained in section 2511 of Title 18, U. S. C., at subsection (3). This provides that the prohibition cited above on interception shall not

00538

limit the constitutional power of the President to take such measures as he deems necessary to protect against attack, to obtain foreign intelligence information deemed essential to the security of the United States or to protect such information, and to protect the United States against overthrow by force or other unlawful means or against any other clear and present danger to the structure or existence of the Government.

3. The type of information you describe in your memorandum does not appear to fall within any of these categories and since its ultimate destination is BNDD, it appears to be collection for law-enforcement purposes, which as noted above is barred to this Agency by statute.

4. For your information, in most cases where there is a criminal prosecution for violation of the narcotics laws, the Department of Justice queries us as to whether we have engaged in any interception in connection with the defendants. If a case should involve the interception being made [redacted] it would be deemed to be unauthorized and in all probability the prosecution would have to be dropped by the Government. It is our view, therefore, that such interception should be carried on by appropriate law-enforcement agencies in accordance with the authority of chapter 119 of Title 18, U.S.C.

LAWRENCE R. HOUSTON
General Counsel

Distribution:
Copy 1-Addressee
Copy 2-General Counsel

00539

Foreign Intelligence Staff

00540

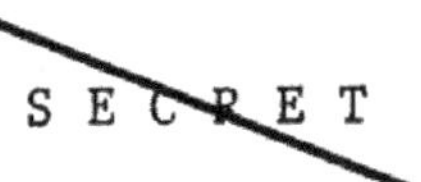

7 May 1973

MEMORANDUM FOR: Deputy Director for Operations

SUBJECT: Item for the List of Delicate Matters

The Securities and Exchange Commission has asked CIA to provide information on any foreign connections with organized crime in the United States. The record indicates that Mr. David Young, of the White House Staff, asked Mr. Colby to set up a contact for Mr. T. C. Barreaux, of SEC. Mr. Barreaux discussed the matter with Mr. Paul V. Walsh, of DDI, and on 4 April 1973, Mr. Barreaux and Mr. Timmeny came to a meeting at CIA with Mr. Lawrence Houston (General Counsel) [redacted] (Chief, FI Staff, DDO).

Since that meeting, we have received no specific requirements from Mr. Barreaux, but have provided him with one piece of information involving a banking transaction of a [redacted] associate of Robert Vesco.

[redacted]
Chief
Foreign Intelligence Staff

S E C R E T

00541

Counterintelligence Staff

00542

SE[ ]R WILL CHECK CLASSIFICATION TOP AN[ ]OTTOM

	UNCLASSIFIED		CONFIDENTIAL		SECRET

OFFICIAL ROUTING SLIP

TO	NAME AND ADDRESS	DATE	INITIALS
1	Inspector General		
2	"Jewels"		
3			
4			
5			
6			

	ACTION		DIRECT REPLY		PREPARE REPLY
	APPROVAL		DISPATCH		RECOMMENDATION
	COMMENT		FILE		RETURN
	CONCURRENCE		INFORMATION		SIGNATURE

Remarks:

Mr Colby has not seen

00543

FOLD [ ]URN TO SENDER

FROM: NAME, ADDRESS AND PHONE NO.	DATE
O/ES/CIA MC/Ben Evans	6June73

	UNCLASSIFIED		CONFIDENTIAL		SECRET

FORM NO. 1-67 237 Use previous editions (40)

~~EYES ONLY~~

15 May 1973

Dear Bill,

Prior to my assignment to Nha Trang I was assigned to the CI Staff for approximately 20 months. While I was with the Staff I was led to believe that one of their "Groups" on the ground floor, [redacted] was involved in domestic operations. I believe their target (s) were minority group (s). The Chief and Deputy Chief of the Group at that time were Dick Ober and [redacted] respectively. One of their Case Officers, [redacted] spent over 50% of his time TDY within the United States. It was my understanding they reported only to the White House and to Dick Helms. Other members of the Staff, including myself, had limited access to the [redacted] area, only when necessary and escorted at all times. Perhaps you were or are now aware of what the operations are. However, I believe I would be remiss in not responding to the book cable (407190). And perhaps their operations might have been outside the legislative charter.

Also, during my tour with the CI Staff I accidently learned they launched someone into Vietnam while you and [redacted] were there. I believe this was without the knowledge or approval of Chief, [redacted] (If I recall, the Case Officer was [redacted] I mention the latter only because of the following: When they learned that [redacted] was being reassigned from Saigon to Chief, Operations, FE, they also learned that I was a friend of [redacted] and from the same area [redacted] As a result they cautioned me not to discuss any of their operations with [redacted] This I did not do.

[redacted]

00544

Sincerely,

[redacted]

~~EYES ONLY~~

TRANSMITTAL MANIFEST

No. 446603

TO	FROM
Chief, BKHERALD	

ITEM NO.	DESCRIPTION	USE
1.	~~EYES ONLY~~ envelope under separate cover for Chief, BKHERALD	From [ ] in response to DIRECTOR 407190 (BOOK CABLE)

00545

FORM 2-64 1236 USE PREVIOUS EDITION

~~SECRET~~

(13-47)

MEMOR...DUM FOR: Mr. Colby

Attached is the material we requested of D
Ober:

A. Ten Reports, Subj: Foreign Support for
Activities Planned to Disrupt or Harass the
Republican National Convention

B. Five Reports, Subj: Foreign Support fo
Activities Planned to Disrupt or Harass the
Democratic National Convention

C. Two Memoranda re Agency support to
Secret Service for Democratic and Republican
Conventions

Ober advises that the only American we repor
on to the IEC is Rennie Davis

(14 May 73)
DATE)

00540

FORM NO. 101 REPLACES FORM 10-101
1 AUG 54 WHICH MAY BE USED.

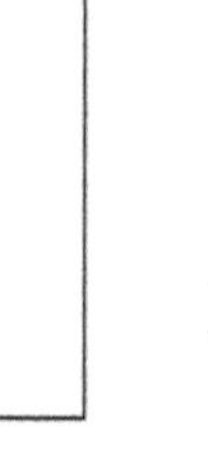

Not a record

SENDER WILL CHECK CLASSIFICATION TOP AND BOTTOM

	UNCLASSIFIED		CONFIDENTIAL		SECRET

OFFICIAL ROUTING SLIP

TO	NAME AND ADDRESS	DATE	INITIALS
1	Inspector General		
2			
3			
4			
5			
6			

	ACTION		DIRECT REPLY		PREPARE REPLY
	APPROVAL		DISPATCH		RECOMMENDATION
	COMMENT		FILE		RETURN
	CONCURRENCE		INFORMATION		SIGNATURE

Remarks:

Mr. Broe:

Dick Ober has been advised that this package is being sent to you. Since knowledge of the existence of this Committee has been strictly limited, I've asked that it be delivered to you unopened. Although it has an ER number on it, it has not been sent through that office -- I gave them only the day, subject, and originator.

00547

FOLD HERE TO RETURN TO SENDER

FROM: NAME, ADDRESS AND PHONE NO.	DATE
O/ES/MC/	15 May 73

	UNCLASSIFIED		CONFIDENTIAL		SECRET

FORM NO. 1-67 237 Use previous editions (40)

UNCLASSIFIED | INTERNAL USE ONLY | ~~CONFIDENTIAL~~ | ~~SECRET~~

ROUTING AND RECORD SHEET

SUBJECT: (Optional)

FROM: Richard Ober

EXTENSION

NO.

DATE 14 May 1973

TO: (Officer designation, room number, and building)	DATE RECEIVED	DATE FORWARDED	OFFICER'S INITIALS	COMMENTS (Number each comment to show from whom to whom. Draw a line across column after each comment.)
1. Mr. Evans O/DCI	14 May	14 May		Attached are:
2. Mr Colby	5/14	5/15		1. Background note on the Committee per your request of this morning.
3.				2. Copies of memoranda concerning Agency support to Secret Service (7 April and 23 June 1972).
4. IG				
5.				
6.				EYES ONLY
7.				Not to go through any registries
8.				
9.				
10.				
11.				
12.				
13.				
14.				00548
15.				~~Not to record~~

610 USE PREVIOUS EDITIONS ~~SECRET~~ ~~CONFIDENTIAL~~ INTERNAL USE ONLY UNCLASSIFIED

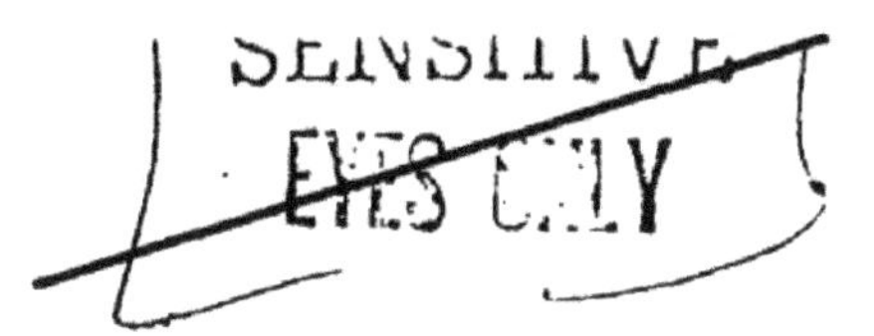

Count 1

14 MAY 1973

DO-25

SUBJECT: Intelligence Evaluation Committee and Staff

1. Background: Formed December 1970 to produce fully-evaluated national domestic intelligence studies, including studies on demonstrations, subversion, extremism and terrorism. Membership: Department of Justice (Chairman); Federal Bureau of Investigation; Department of Defense; Secret Service; National Security Agency; Central Intelligence Agency; and as necessary representatives of other Departments or Agencies (following have participated: Treasury and State). Staff: IES, Executive Director John Dougherty and later Bernard Wells supplied by Department of Justice with title of Special Assistant to the Attorney General reporting to the Assistant Attorney General for Internal Security Robert Mardian and later William Olson. IES has received requirements directly from and delivered reports directly to John Dean of the White House. The White House has insisted that the existence of this Committee be kept secret. Awareness of its existence within this Agency has been limited to DCI, DDO (DDP), C/CI and four officers of this office.

2. CIA Participation: Contributions on foreign aspects (by memorandum with no Agency letterhead or attribution). Contributions occasionally include foreign intelligence provided by FBI and NSA. The Chief of the Special Operations Group serves as the Agency representative on the Intelligence Evaluation Committee Staff and as the alternate to the Agency representative on the Committee (who is the Chief, Counter Intelligence Staff).

3. Special Report: The Unauthorized Disclosure of Classified Information, November 1971. This study was initiated in July 1971 by the White House as a consequence of the President's concern about the release of the Pentagon Papers by Daniel Ellsberg. Both Robert Mardian and G. Gordon Liddy initially involved in tasking the IES to produce this evaluation. Drafting done by IES Staff members from Justice and FBI. Only Agency participation was editorial review.

FULL TEXT COPY - DO NOT RELEASE

00549

EYES ONLY
SENSITIVE
SECRET

EYES ONLY

4. Republican National Convention (21-24 August 1972): At the request of the White House, a series of estimates was prepared by the IES on "Potential Disruptions at the 1972 Republican National Convention, Miami Beach, Florida." The Agency provided from February through August 1972 periodic contributions for these estimates concerning foreign support for activities planned to disrupt or harass the Republican National Convention (copies attached).

5. Democratic National Convention (10-13 July 1972): At the request of the White House, a series of estimates was prepared by the IES on "Potential Disruptions at the 1972 Democratic National Convention, Miami Beach, Florida." The Agency provided between March and July 1972 contributions on foreign support for activities planned to disrupt or harass the Democratic National Convention (copies attached).

Attachments: a/s

FULL TEXT COPY - DO NOT RELEASE

EYES ONLY
SENSITIVE
SECRET

00550

~~EYES ONLY~~

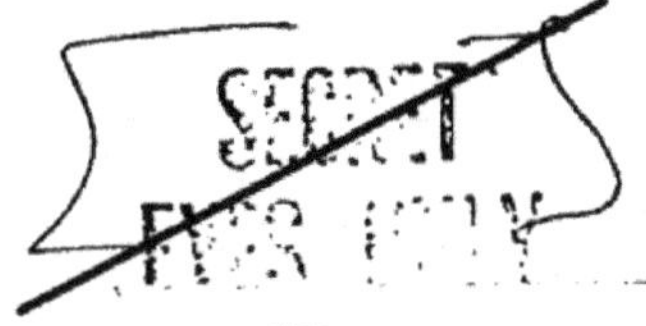

00551

Conf 1
Do 26

23 FEB 1972

SUBJECT: Foreign Support For Activities Planned to Disrupt or Harass the Republican National Convention

1. There are only limited indications thus far of foreign efforts to inspire, support or take advantage of activities designed to disrupt or harass the National Convention of the Republican Party in San Diego, 21-23 August 1972.

2. Some American participants at the Soviet-controlled World Assembly for Peace and Independence of the Peoples of Indochina, held 11-13 February 1972 in Paris/Versailles, attempted unsuccessfully to include a call for international demonstrations to take place at the time of the Republican National Convention. A representative of the San Diego Convention Coalition (SDCC), one of the domestic action groups targetting on the Republican Convention, requested the American Delegations' Steering Committee at the World Assembly to include a specific call for international support of activities against the Republican convention in their proposal to the Action Commission of the World Assembly. This request, however, was dropped as too divisive by the Steering Committee, despite initial indications that the proposal would be taken to the floor of the Assembly.

3. John LENNON, a British subject, has provided financial support to Project "YES", which in turn paid the travel expenses to the World Assembly of a representative of leading antiwar activist Rennie DAVIS. (DAVIS' representative is tentatively planning to assist in preparations for disruptive actions at the San Diego Convention.) Project "YES" is an adjunct to another LENNON-supported project, the Election Year Strategy Information Center (EYSIC), of which Rennie DAVIS is a key leader, which was set up to direct New Left protest activities at the Republican National Convention. In Paris Rennie DAVIS' representative to the World Assembly met at least once with officials of the Provisional Revolutionary Government of South Vietnam; it is not known if the Republican National Convention was discussed.

00552

SECRET

4. The SDCC is planning for foreign support for its harassment of the Republican convention. A working draft plan of the SDCC includes proposals for (a) the use of a special television network to broadcast video-taped messages from other countries, including coverage of sympathetic demonstrations elsewhere; and (b) broadcasts over public address systems of live telephone calls from the Vietnamese in Paris and from the Communist Chinese and others at the United Nations.

00553

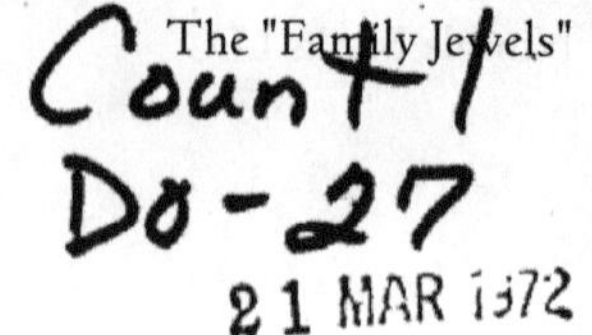

21 MAR 1972

Foreign Support for Activities Planned to Disrupt or Harass the Republican National Convention

SUMMARY AND CONCLUSION:

Indications remain limited, thus far, of foreign efforts to inspire, support or take advantage of activities designed to disrupt or harass the National Convention of the Republican Party in San Diego, 21-23 August 1972. The concept of coordinated international support for domestic activities in the United States was generally endorsed at the recent World Assembly for Peace and Independence of the Peoples of Indochina; however, the Conference issued no specific call for international support of disruptive actions at the American national political conventions.

BACKGROUND:

At the Soviet-controlled World Assembly for Peace and Independence of the Peoples of Indochina, held in Versailles from 10-13 February 1972, there was mention of American plans for demonstrations at both the Republican and Democratic National Conventions. The final draft resolution from the Conference's "Action Commission" contains an appendix submitted by American delegates whose goal was to secure global coordination for domestic actions in the United States. It calls for international support to six weeks of domestic antiwar actions and demonstrations, from 1 April to 15 May 1972, and concludes with the statement: "This campaign will lead up to the Democratic Party Convention at Miami on July 9, 1972, and the Republican Party Convention in San Diego on August 21, 1972."

The final "Resolution of the Paris World Assembly for the Peace and Independence of the Indochinese People" of 13 February 1972, drafted by the "Political Commission" states:

> "In the United States particularly, the protest against the war is voiced more and more strongly, under various forms, such as draft evasions, desertions, resistance, demonstrations which now affect even the soldiers. The Assembly calls for support to these progressive and antiwar forces in the United States, and asks the governments to grant asylum to deserters and to support their right to repatriation. All together, the peoples of the world will efficiently help to impose on the U.S. Government the restoration of peace, and independence and freedom in Vietnam, Laos, and Cambodia."

~~FULL TEXT COPY - DO NOT REL~~

00554

DEVELOPMENTS:

The San Diego Convention Coalition (SDCC), one of the domestic action groups targetting on the Republican Convention, is planning, in addition to demonstrations, for a "large exposition in the campsights (sic) called Expose 72, which with movies, exhibits, displays will portray the struggles of people all over the world." Plans for activities at Expose 72 are believed to include (a) the use of a special television network to broadcast video-taped messages from other countries, including coverage of sympathetic demonstrations elsewhere; and (b) broadcasts over public address systems of live telephone calls from the Vietnamese in Paris and from the Communist Chinese and others at the United Nations. In addition, the SDCC has suggested that, in order to "outflank NIXON domestically and internationally," international opposition can be expressed "by obtaining the authority of other countries and liberation movements to carry their flags in SDCC demonstrations."

Count 1
DO-2

Foreign Support for Activities Planned to Disrupt or Harass the Republican National Convention

SUMMARY:

There is little new evidence of foreign plans or efforts to inspire, support, or take advantage of actions designed to disrupt or harass the Republican National Convention in San Diego, 21 to 23 August 1972. The Students for a Democratic Society, in joining the ranks of domestic groups planning actions at the Republican Convention, has adopted a proposal to cooperate with Mexican workers and students in a demonstration in Tijuana, Mexico, during the Convention. The San Diego Convention Coalition (SDCC), another domestic group targetting on the Convention, has received a letter of solidarity from the North Vietnamese. The letter is of interest as an indication of North Vietnamese contact with the SDCC; such contact will be required for the SDCC to implement its earlier-reported plans for broadcasts over public address systems during the Convention of live telephone calls from the Vietnamese in Paris.

DEVELOPMENTS:

At its recent convention in Cambridge, Massachusetts, held 30 March to 2 April 1972, the Students for a Democratic Society (SDS) adopted a proposal to hold demonstrations at the San Diego-Tijuana border during the Republican National Convention. The proposal included a call for SDS to cooperate with Mexican workers and students in an action to occur during a fiesta in Tijuana, where Convention delegates will be entertained.

The North Vietnamese have given their endorsement to the San Diego Convention Coalition (SDCC) in the form of a letter from the Vietnam Committee for Solidarity with the American People (VCSWAP), a quasi-official organ of the North Vietnamese Government. The letter, which has been circulated by the SDCC and is dated 27 January 1972, expresses "great delight" with the formation of the SDCC, and conveys the Committee's "best wishes of militant solidarity and friendship." The VCSWAP requests that the SDCC write often and "send us materials you have."

00556

Count/
DO-29
23 MAY 197

Foreign Support for Activities Planned to Disrupt or Harass the Republican National Convention

SUMMARY:

Indications remain limited of foreign plans or attempts to inspire, support, influence, or exploit actions designed to disrupt or harass the Republican National Convention in Miami, Florida, 21-23 August 1972.

The British-based International Confederation for Disarmament and Peace (ICDP) has distributed a "Spring Offensive Calendar" of activities in the United States against the war based on a submission by the Peoples' Coalition for Peace and Justice (PCPJ). The calendar includes actions planned in connection with the Republican Convention.

DEVELOPMENTS:

The International Confederation for Disarmament and Peace, a British-based antiwar organization and one of the more prominent member organizations of the Stockholm Conference, has attached a "Spring Offensive Calendar" to the April-May 1972 issue of its regular international publication Vietnam International. The calendar had been furnished by the People's Coalition for Peace and Justice (PCPJ) and included the following entry:

August 21-23 Republican Convention, San Diego. Demonstrations organized by the San Diego Convention Coalition, Box 8267, San Diego, Ca. 92103.

The ICDP commentary on the PCPJ calendar urges demonstrations in support of some of the dates listed but does not specificall call for actions in connection with the Republican Convention.

14 JUN 1972

Count 1

DO-3(

Foreign Support for Activities Planned to Disrupt or Harass the Republican National Convention

SUMMARY:

The only new indication of foreign plans or efforts to inspire, support, influence, or exploit actions designed to disrupt or harass the Republican National Convention in Miami, Florida, 21-23 August 1972, is an expression of interest by a member of the North Vietnamese Delegation to the Paris Peace Talks in the plans of the major antiwar organizations in the United States for demonstrations in connection with the political conventions of both major parties.

DEVELOPMENTS:

In mid-May 1972, a member of the North Vietnamese Delegation to the Paris Peace Talks invited a visitor to contact him again when the visitor returned from an imminent trip to the United States. The North Vietnamese official gave the visitor the New York City addresses of the People's Coalition for Peace and Justice (PCPJ) and the National Peace Action Coalition (NPAC), and asked the visitor to inquire at their offices regarding their plans for demonstrations during the coming summer. The North Vietnamese official stated that he was especially interested in plans for actions in connection with the Democratic and Republican National Conventions.

00559

28 JUN 1972

Foreign Support for Activities Planned to Disrupt or Harass the Republican National Convention

There are no additional indications of any substantial foreign plans or efforts to inspire, support, or take advantage of activities designed to disrupt or harass the National Convention of the Republican Party in Miami, Florida, 21-24 August 1972.

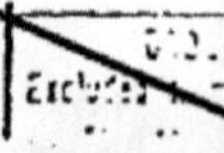

-Count/

26 JUL 1972

DO-31

Foreign Support for Activities Planned to Disrupt or Harass the Republican National Convention

SUMMARY:

New indications of foreign plans or efforts to inspire, support, influence, or exploit activities designed to disrupt or harass the Republican National Convention in Miami, Florida, 21-24 August 1972, consist of the following: A leader of the People's Coalition for Peace and Justice (PCPJ) has stated that demonstrations will be organized to take place at United States and allied military installations abroad during the period immediately before and during the Republican Convention. The PCPJ leader also stated that representatives of the Stockholm Conference on Vietnam will participate in activities in connection with the Convention. The Anti-War Union (AWU), a domestic organization which has been active in planning demonstrations in connection with the Republican National Convention, has sent a delegation to Paris, France, to meet with officials of the Democratic Republic of Vietnam (DRV) and the Provisional Revolutionary Government of South Vietnam (PRG). No information is presently available, however, indicating that actions at the Republican Convention have been discussed at these meetings.

DEVELOPMENTS:

In an early July 1972 meeting with prominent members of foreign antiwar organizations, a representative of the People's Coalition for Peace and Justice (PCPJ), who occupies an important position within that organization, discussed the plans of the PCPJ in connection with the upcoming election campaign in the United States. The PCPJ representative stated that during the period 14-23 August, a "Peoples Campaign Against Bombing" would be waged in U.S. cities involved in the manufacture and shipping of materials for use in Vietnam, and that similar actions will be organized at United States and allied military installations abroad. The PCPJ representative further stated that "dramatic demonstrations" in protest

00561

of the bombing in Vietnam are being organized by the "Republican Party National Convention Coalition" to occur on 21 August 1972. In an apparent reference to the 21 August actions, the PCPJ leader added that representatives of the Stockholm Conference on Vietnam will speak on the subject of the alleged American bombing of dikes in North Vietnam. (Comment: We have no present information concerning plans of Stockholm Conference representatives to travel to the United States during the Republican National Convention; nor do we have any additional information concerning plans of Stockholm Conference representatives to participate in activities connected with the Republican Convention.)

The Anti-War Union (AWU), a domestic group engaged in organizing counter-activities at the Republican National Convention, has sponsored the travel of a delegation of activists to Paris, France, to meet with officials of the Democratic Republic of North Vietnam (DRV) and the Provisional Revolutionary Government of South Vietnam (PRG). An advance party has already met with DRV and PRG representatives to discuss the agenda for meetings with the full AWU delegation. Although no information is presently available indicating that actions at the Republican Convention have been discussed or are scheduled to be discussed at meetings between the AWU delegation and the DRV/PRG officials, it is known that members of the AWU advance party have asked for advice from the PRG officials regarding the stance the AWU should take on certain questions relating to the presidential elections. It is also known that the DRV officials have questioned the AWU advance party about the political mood in the United States. One of the AWU delegation members has stated that upon their return to the United States about 26 July 1972, some of the members will speak at rallies, over the radio, and on television, to "educate the American people about the consequences of voting for Nixon, and the need to end the war and defeat Nixon." The delegation member added that the demonstrations at the Republican Convention will be "unique."

00562

2 AUG 1972

Count I
DO-32

Foreign Support for Activities Planned to Disrupt
or Harass the Republican National Convention

SUMMARY:

There are no new indications of specific foreign plans or efforts to inspire, support, influence, or exploit activities designed to disrupt or harass the Republican National Convention in Miami, Florida, 21-24 August 1972. Although meetings have been held recently in Paris, France, between American antiwar activists and representatives of the Democratic Republic of North Vietnam (DRV) and the Provisional Revolutionary Government of South Vietnam (PRG), currently available information indicates that the DRV/PRG officials made no efforts to encourage or give guidance to the American participants with respect to the upcoming Republican National Convention. Private discussions, separate from the meetings with the entire American delegation, were conducted by both the DRV and the PRG officials; at present, we have no information regarding the substance of these private exchanges. A second group of activists, considered more important than the first delegation, is scheduled to travel to Paris on or about 1 August 1972 for further consultations with the PRG and DRV representatives.

DEVELOPMENTS:

In recent meetings in Paris, France, with members of an American delegation sponsored by the Anti-War Union (AWU), representatives of the Democratic Republic of Vietnam (DRV) and the Provisional Revolutionary Government of South Vietnam (PRG) were very guarded with respect to discussing activities at the Republican National Convention. Although the Vietnamese repeatedly questioned the Americans concerning the mood of the antiwar movement in the United States, they made no direct reference to the Republican Convention, except for one instance when PRG Deputy Chief Nguyen Van TIEN accused President Nixon of using the private and public sessions of the Paris peace talks as "propaganda for the Republican Convention." TIEN then urged the Americans to promote and propagandize the Seven Point Plan offered by the PRG. The Americans, too, for the most part, refrained from discussing the Convention, other than to estimate that demonstrators will number about 10,000 at the Convention.

00563

Following their meeting on 22 July 1972 with the AWU delegation, the PRG officials held additional talks with sub-groups of the delegation. Additionally, at least one of the American participants was invited by the DRV officials to return for further discussions. At present, there is no information available concerning the substance of these private exchanges.

A second, more important delegation of Americans connected with the Anti-War Union is scheduled to travel to Paris circa 1 August 1972 for further consultation with DRV and PRG representatives. This second group is scheduled to be led by Rennie DAVIS, founder and leader of the AWU. This will be DAVIS' second trip to Paris within recent months for discussions with DRV and PRG representatives. Upon his return from his first trip, DAVIS publicly stated that the AWU would demonstrate at both the Democratic and the Republican Convention, but that the AWU's chief target would be the Republican Convention.

Countl
DO-33

9 AUG 1972

Foreign Support for Activities Planned to Disrupt
or Harass the Republican National Convention

There are no new indications, as of this date, of foreign plans or efforts to inspire, support, or take advantage of activities designed to disrupt or harass the National Convention of the Republican Party in Miami, Florida, 21-24 August 1972.

~~FULL TEXT COPY - DO NOT RELEASE~~

00565

Count/
DO - 34

16 AUG 1972

Foreign Support for Activities Planned to Disrupt or Harass the Republican National Convention

There are no new indications, as of this date, of foreign plans or efforts to inspire, support, or take advantage of activities designed to disrupt or harass the National Convention of the Republican Party in Miami, Florida, 21-24 August 1972.

00566

~~FULL TEXT COPY - DO NOT RELEASE~~

~~SECRET~~

Count 1
DO-35

FULL TEXT COPY - DO NOT RELEASE

SECRET

00567

06 MAR 1972

Foreign Support for Activities Planned to Disrupt Or Harass the Democratic National Convention

SUMMARY AND CONCLUSION:

There are no direct indications thus far of foreign efforts to inspire, support or take advantage of activities designed to disrupt or harass the National Convention of the Democratic Party in Miami, 10-13 July 1972. The concept of coordinated international support for domestic activities in the United States was generally endorsed at the recent World Assembly for Peace and Independence of the Peoples of Indochina; however, the Conference issued no specific call for international support of disruptive actions at the American national political conventions.

BACKGROUND:

At the Soviet-controlled World Assembly for Peace and Independence of the Peoples' of Indochina, held in Versailles from 10-13 February 1972, there was mention of American plans for demonstrations at both the Republican and Democratic National Conventions. The final draft resolution from the conference's "Action Commission" contains an appendix submitted by American delegates whose goal was to secure global coordination for domestic actions in the United States. It calls for international support to six weeks of domestic antiwar actions and demonstrations, from 1 April to 15 May 1972, and concludes with the statement: "This campaign will lead up to the Democratic Party Convention at Miami on July 9, 1972, and the Republican Party Convention in San Diego on August 21, 1972."

The final "Resolution of the Paris World Assembly for the Peace and Independence of the Indochinese People" of 13 February 1972, drafted by the "Political Commission" states:

"In the United States particularly, the protest against the war is voiced more and more strongly,

00568

under various forms, such as draft evasions, desertions, resistance, demonstrations which now affect even the soldiers. The Assembly calls for support to these progressive and antiwar forces in the United States, and asks the governments to grant asylum to deserters and to support their right to repatriation. All together, the peoples of the world will efficiently help to impose on the U.S. Government the restoration of peace, independence and freedom in Vietnam, Laos and Cambodia."

Count 1
DO-36

Foreign Support for Activities Planned to Disrupt or Harass the Democratic National Convention

SUMMARY:

New indications of foreign efforts or plans to inspire, support, influence, or exploit actions designed to disrupt or harass the Democratic National Convention in Miami, 10-13 July 1972, are limited to a reiteration by a member of the Secretariat of the Stockholm Conference on Vietnam of a statement previously issued by the World Assembly for Peace and Independence of the Peoples of Indochina. The Assembly's pronouncement generally endorsed the concept of international support to a campaign of anti-Vietnam War activities in the United States leading up to the Democratic and Republican Conventions, but made no specific call for support of disruptive actions at the conventions themselves.

DEVELOPMENTS:

The World Assembly for Peace and Independence of the Peoples of Indochina, of which the Stockholm Conference was a major organizer, had earlier enunciated a similar statement in an appendix to the final draft resolution of the Assembly's "Action Commission." The appendix called for international support to six weeks of domestic antiwar actions and demonstrations, from 1 April to 15 May 1972, and concluded with the statement: "This campaign will lead up to the Democratic Party Convention at Miami on July 9, 1972, and the Republican Party Convention in San Diego on August 21, 1972."

FULL TEXT COPY - DO NOT RELEASE

00570

23 MAY 1972

Count 1
DO-37

Foreign Support for Activities Planned to Disrupt or Harass the Democratic National Convention

SUMMARY:

Indications remain limited of foreign plans or attempts to inspire, support, influence, or exploit actions designed to disrupt or harass the Democratic National Convention in Miami, Florida, 10-13 July 1972. The British-based International Confederation for Disarmament and Peace (ICDP) has distributed a "Spring Offensive Calendar" of activities in the United States against the war based on a submission by the Peoples' Coalition for Peace and Justice (PCPJ). The calendar includes actions planned in connection with the Democratic Convention.

DEVELOPMENTS:

The International Confederation for Disarmament and Peace, a British-based antiwar organization and one of the more prominent member organizations of the Stockholm Conference, has attached a "Spring Offensive Calendar" to the April-May 1972 issue of its regular international publication Vietnam International. The calendar had been furnished by the People's Coalition for Peace and Justice (PCPJ) and included the following entry:

July 9 - 12 Democratic Convention, Miami Beach. Demonstrations organised by Florida People's Coalition, Box 17521, Tampa, Florida 33612.

FULL TEXT COPY - DO NOT RELEASE

00571

The ICDP commentary on the PCPJ calendar urges demonstrations in support of some of the dates listed but does not specifical call for actions in connection with the Democratic Convention.

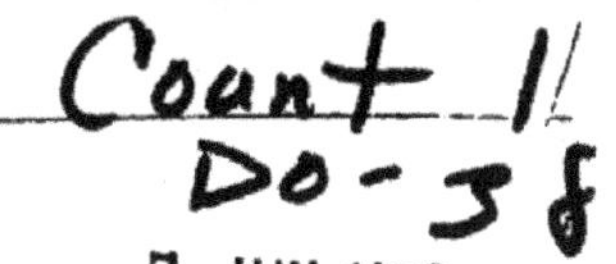

7 JUN 1972

Foreign Support for Activities Planned to Disrupt or Harass the Democratic National Convention

SUMMARY:

The only new indication of foreign plans or efforts to inspire, support, influence, or exploit actions designed to disrupt or harass the Democratic National Convention in Miami, Florida, 10-13 July 1972, is an expression of interest by a member of the North Vietnamese Delegation to the Paris Peace Talks in the plans of the major antiwar organizations in the United States for demonstrations in connection with the political conventions of both major parties.

DEVELOPMENTS:

In mid-May 1972, a member of the North Vietnamese Delegation to the Paris Peace Talks invited a visitor to contact him again when the visitor returned from an imminent trip to the United States. The North Vietnamese official gave the visitor the New York City addresses of the People's Coalition for Peace and Justice (PCPJ) and the National Peace Action Coalition (NPAC), and asked the visitor to inquire at their offices regarding their plans for demonstrations during the coming summer. The North Vietnamese official stated that he was especially interested in plans for actions in connection with the Democratic and National Conventions.

00573

Count 1
DO-3

21 JUN 1972

Foreign Support for Activities Planned to Disrupt
or Harass the Democratic National Convention

There are no additional indications, as of this date, of foreign plans or efforts to inspire, support, or take advantage of activities designed to disrupt or harass the National Convention of the Democratic Party in Miami, Florida, 10-13 July 1972.

00574

C

23 JUN 1972

MEMORANDUM FOR: Executive Director/Comptroller

VIA : Acting Deputy Director for Plans

SUBJECT : Agency Support to the U.S. Secret Service (USSS) for National Democratic (10-14 July 1972) and National Republican (21-24 August 1972) Conventions

1. This memorandum is for the information of the Executive Director/Comptroller.

2. Authorization for CIA support to the U.S. Secret Service for the Democratic and Republican National Conventions is contained in a memorandum of 7 April 1972 from Chief, CI Staff to the DCI which was concurred in by the ADDP and approved by the DCI on 10 April 1972 (copy attached).

3. On 13 April 1972 the [redacted] met with the Miami USSS representative and Mr. [redacted] of USSS Headquarters to discuss preliminary planning for [redacted] support to the USSS prior to and during subject conventions. On 17 April 1972 the [redacted] and [redacted] met with Mr. [redacted] at Headquarters to implement the preliminary planning agreed upon in Miami and to determine the extent of Headquarters support required by the USSS.

4. The basic agreement mutually concurred in by the USSS and Headquarters representatives provided that:

a. [redacted] would conduct name traces on all Cubans of interest to the USSS.

b. CIA Headquarters would conduct name traces on all other foreign born persons of interest to the USSS.

c. CIA would keep the USSS informed of any events in the Caribbean and Latin American areas that would have any bearing on the USSS protective mission during the convention periods. This would include briefings on Cuba and Cuban policies toward the United States and on activities of Cuban intelligence operations which could affect the security of the conventions.

00576

d. Coverage of Latin American exile groups in the United States would be the responsibility of the FBI since CIA had ceased the extensive coverage formerly targeted against these groups since it was now considered an internal security function.

5. [redacted]

6. [redacted] has arranged the rental of a safehouse about five minutes from convention center which will provide a secure and nearby meeting site for USSS and Agency personnel. This safehouse will be available just prior to and during both conventions. A Headquarters officer will TDY to Miami prior to the conventions and remain until the conventions adjourn to assist [redacted] in providing the support described in paragraph four above.

7. Station WH/Miami is in daily contact with the USSS in Miami, utilizing JMFALCON as a meeting site when necessary. The location of Station WH/Miami (JMCOBRA) has not been revealed to the USSS. (JMCOBRA is located some distance from JMFALCON.) Additionally, the Miami Security Field Office maintains normal liaison with the local USSS Miami unit.

8. The [redacted] understands that no personnel will be present at the convention hall, that they will not provide any equipment unique to the Agency, nor will it provide the use of any other facilities other than the safehouse described in paragraph six.

9. A copy of this memorandum is being sent to [redacted] [redacted] to insure that the [redacted] is fully conversant with the guidelines and basic agreements with the Secret Service, and has all of the information agreed upon in Headquarters.

signed

Theodore G. Shackley
Chief
Western Hemisphere Division

Attachment

Distribution:

Orig & 1 - Exec. Dir/Comptroller
2 - Acting DDP
1 - [redacted]
2 - [redacted]
2 - [redacted]
2 - [redacted]

[redacted] (Typed 23 June 1972)

00578

7 APR 1972

MEMORANDUM FOR: Director of Central Intelligence

VIA: Deputy Director for Plans

SUBJECT: CIA Support to the Secret Service for the Democratic National Convention in Miami, Florida July 9 - 15, 1972

1. This memorandum describes the support which the Secret Service has requested from CIA with regard to the Democratic National Convention. It is recommended that the Agency furnish the support outlined in paragraph 3 of this memorandum and your approval is requested.

2. By memorandum 1-30-610.53 of 30 March (attached as reference), the Secret Service has requested a meeting with appropriate Agency officers to discuss the Agency's support to the Secret Service prior to and during the Democratic National Convention. The Secret Service plans to send an agent to Miami on 11 April to commence preparations for the convention and wishes to have the meeting with Agency Headquarters officers prior to the agent's departure for Miami.

3. While details regarding the type of support which the Secret Service will request of the Agency will not be known until there has been a meeting with the Secret Service on this matter, it is evident from the Secret Service memorandum and from our experience in supporting the Secret Service at the Republican Convention in Miami in 1968 that the Secret Service desires:

A) Briefings on Cuba and Cuban policy towards the United States. Counterintelligence information on Cuban operations against the United States which could affect the security of the convention.

B) Briefings on Cuban exile activities in the United States.

C) Name checks on hotel and convention employees; name checks on those persons in the Miami area whom the Secret Service considers a threat to its protective mission.

D) A watchlist of persons whom the Agency considers a potential threat to the security of the convention.

E) Liaison with a designated officer [redacted] for the purpose of conducting name checks against [redacted] files and other files available [redacted]

4. Agency support to the Secret Service for the convention will be centralized at Headquarters and will be controlled by Headquarters. Chief, [redacted] under the general supervision of the CI Staff, will serve as the coordinator of this support.

[redacted]

James Angleton
Chief, CI Staff

1 Attachment

cc: DDCI

CONCUR:

[redacted]

Deputy Director for Plans

The recommendation contained in paragraph 1 is approved:

[signature]

Director of Central Intelligence

Date 5 APR 1972

~~FULL TEXT COPY - DO NOT RELEASE~~

00580

THE DEPARTMENT OF THE TREASURY

UNITED STATES SECRET SERVICE

WASHINGTON, D.C. 20226

OFFICE OF THE DIRECTOR

1-30-610.53

Date: March 30, 1972

BY LIAISON: [redacted]

TO : Central Intelligence Agency
ATTN: Mr [redacted]

FROM : JAMES J. ROWLEY - DIRECTOR

SUBJECT: Democratic National Convention - Miami, Florida - July 9-15, 1972

In view of our responsibilities regarding the protection of Presidential candidates, we have initiated security preparations for the Democratic National Convention, which will be held in Miami, Florida, between July 9-15, 1972.

We request a meeting as soon as possible between representatives of our Intelligence Division and your agency to discuss intelligence support prior to and during the Democratic National Convention. We are specifically interested in discussing the appropriate channels for routing name checks of hotel and convention employees, as well as other individuals of protective interest to this Service. We anticipate there will be several thousand names to be checked. We would also like to discuss the current Cuban situation, particularly any existing relationships between pro-Cuban groups in the Miami area and mainland Cuba, since we consider these groups to be a potential threat to our protective mission.

Attachments

00581

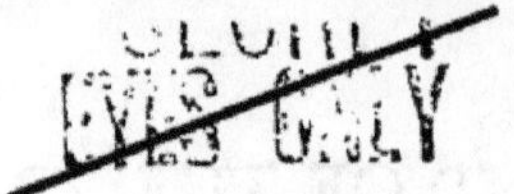

7 May 1973

SUBJECT: Request for Information on Sensitive Activities

You will recall that in Fiscal Years 1971 and 1972, I believe, Agency funds were made available to the FBI. These funds may still be possibly held in a special account for that use. This is one of the areas where TSD has been very much involved. Chuck Briggs would have the details as this was handled through the Executive Director's office and of course Angleton would have additional information.

Edward L. Sherman
Chief
Missions and Programs Staff

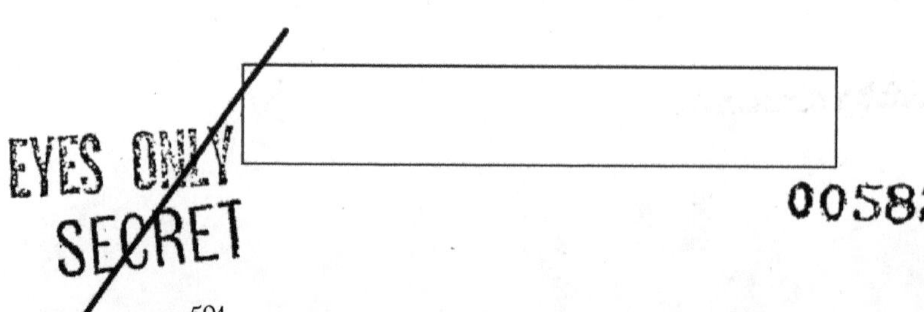

00582

8 May 1973

MEMORANDUM FOR : Deputy Director for Operations

SUBJECT : Areas of Possible Embarrassment to the Agency

1. Sometime in the spring or early summer of 1971, Mr. John Dean levied the requirement on the Agency for information relating to the Investors Overseas Service (IOS). The original request was non-specific but it gradually emerged that Dean was concerned with the possible adverse publicity that might develop regarding the President's nephew, who was employed by IOS.

2. There were multiple channels from the White House to the Agency on this subject:

a. Presumably Haldeman and/or Ehrlichman to Director Helms.

b. Someone (unnamed) in the White House to the DDCI, General Cushman (see attached telephone conversation). Note that Ehrlichman is mentioned, and

c. John Dean to the CI Staff. These various channels were sorted out in time and six reports were passed by the CI Staff to Mr. Fred Fielding for Mr. John Dean.

3. The telephone call of General Cushman's is of interest since it gives the flavor of White House concern. It took several days to uncover the fact that the White House interest centered on the involvement of the President's nephew with IOS and possible adverse publicity. The reports submitted to Dean's office were routine in nature and were coordinated with the DCI. After a few months, interest in this subject died down and we did not pursue it further.

4. Please return the attachments when they have served your purpose.

00583

5. I also include a short note on the Intelligence Evaluation Committee and Staff prepared by Richard Ober. The original meetings were held in the office of John Dean at the White House and the principal sparkplug for this group activity was the then Assistant Attorney General for Internal Security, Robert Mardian and then later his assistant, William Olsen. It is noted that Mr. Mardian is now appearing before the Grand Jury and it is always possible that he might draw in the Agency.

6. Before appointing Ober to the IES Staff as the Agency representative, I had attended various inter-agency meetings presided over by Mardian. I expressed the view to Director Helms that Mardian would require very careful handling due to his inexperience. Furthermore, Mardian was deeply involved in the split between Bill Sullivan and Mr. Hoover. On a confidential basis one or two senior FBI officials stated that Sullivan was secretly passing files to Mardian without Mr. Hoover's permission. This was one of the important reasons why Sullivan was dismissed from the Bureau.

James Angleton
Chief, Counter Intelligence Staff

Attachments (5)

00584

Telephone conversation of General Cushman and someone in White House, 23/7/71

Bob, how are you.

DDCI: Just fine; I just talked to Jack Sherwood and he suggested I give you a buzz.

I deeply appreciate it. I asked Jack to call you. I spoke to Rose yesterday, and told her "I had a little project here for John Ehrlichman and I need very discreet assistance from the Company, and I should like to touch base with Bob. I met him at Jack Sherwood's."

DDCI: That's right.

That's right and beyond that I would like to just establish a relationship because from time to time we have a few needs in your area. Let me tell you what we need to know here. Your Agency would be the only one to help. I have checked with the Bureau, Bob, and they have nothing on this fellow. Just a mere name check but it apparently has some significance, of course. Ray Finkelstein; born in Belgium about 1940; moved to Brazil about age 12 with his family. This might be helpful. He now is working with one Gilbert Straub, apparently Straub is hooked up with that Kornfeld outfit: IOS. We have a need to know what Finkelstein is all about.

DDCI: We will do our best, of course; we have some counterintelligence files which sometimes turn up people but ordinarily, of course, we don't surveil any Americans but this fellow might have come to our notice.

He may not be an American, just a European Jew; that is the problem, the Bureau has come up with zero.

DDCI: Do you know where he is physically located?

He may be in Geneva; Straub is apparently in Geneva.

DDCI: Well, let me get on this and I will get back to you.

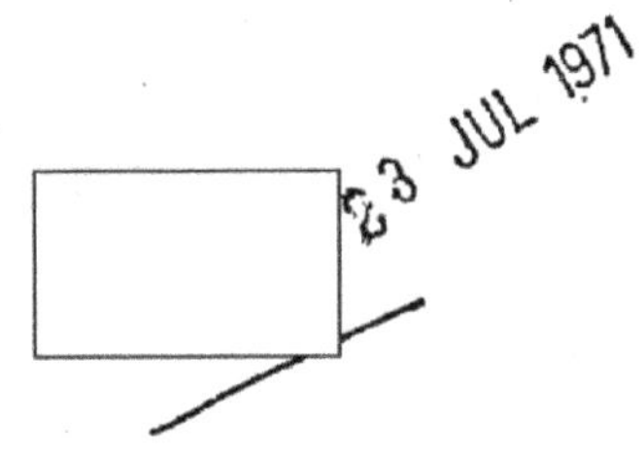

00585

The Washington Merry-Go-Round THE WASHINGTON POST Wednesday, Feb. 16, 1972 D7

Nixon Puts an Eye on His Brother

By Jack Anderson

President Nixon has given aide John Ehrlichman a delicate personal assignment to keep the President's irrepressible brother, Donald, out of hot water.

Donald Nixon has a weakness for fattening foods and easy money. He tried to satisfy both appetites in the 1950s by borrowing $205,000 from billionaire Howard Hughes to operate a restaurant chain, the Home of the Nixonburger, in Southern California.

Two months after the loan was made, some of Hughes' top assistants sat down with Donald to survey the chaos of his accounts. Noah Dietrich, who then directed the day-to-day operations of Hughes' empire, complained that Donald had gone through the money without paying off important creditors.

But it was too late. Donald's restaurants went bankrupt, and the Nixonburger was lost to mankind.

The story of the $205,000 loan leaked out during Richard Nixon's 1960 campaign for the presidency, causing him political pain.

At one time, Donald incorporated himself and began selling shares to citizens who might have an interest in his blood line. Ehrlichman explained gently to Donald that such ventures could embarrass his brother and that, for his brother's sake, he should avoid deals that might reflect unfavorably on the President.

Not long afterward, Donald began dickering with John Hill, a Boston manufacturer of playground equipment, who wanted the government to consider installing his products in urban riot areas. Hill told us Donald merely wanted to be the company's West Coast representative, and did not want to put in the fix for federal money. But Ehrlichman quietly vetoed the project, and the President's brother wrote to Hill saying he was no longer interested in the company.

No Longer Adviser

Donald also made contact with Elmer Stone a lawyer for the Ryan Aeronautical Company. But in deference to his brother, Donald took Stone through the guarded White House gates to see Ehrlichman. Afterward, a spokesman for Ryan Aeronautical explained that the pair had just dropped by to let it be known that Stone was no longer acting as Donald's legal adviser.

When Donald finally joined the Marriott Corporation in January, 1970, Ehrlichman summoned J. Willard Marriott and his son, Bill, to the White House for an audience with the President. Marriott had been chairman of the Nixon Inaugural and is trusted by the President.

Delicately, the President asked the Marriotts to keep his brother out of trouble. "I want to be sure that Don has no dealings with the federal government," said the President. "I want to be sure that Don is never asked to do anything that would embarrass this office."

Then the President added as an afterthought: "Don is the best salesman in the Nixon family."

The Marriotts agreed to watch over Donald, and they have scrupulously kept him away from Washington. There has been only one awkward incident. Donald flew to Greece as one of the three-man team that offered Marriott's airline-catering service to Aristotle Onassis' Olympic Airlines.

Greeks Bearing Gifts

The Greeks, whose military government is unpopular in the U.S., rolled out the red carpet for the President's brother. Tom Pappas, a big Republican money raiser with oil interests in Greece, threw a lavish dinner for Donald in Athens and invited members of the Greek military junta. And Onassis, the husband of the widow of the man who defeated Richard Nixon for President in 1960, sent long-stemmed roses to Donald's hotel room.

Washington whispers that Donald used his White House influence to get catering contracts for Marriott with American Airlines and TWA, we have established, are strictly untrue.

Ehrlichman also gave Donald's son, Donald, Jr., a lecture before the boy went to Switzerland last summer to work for International Controls. The company has now transferred young Nixon to the Bahamas.

His father, talking to a few visitors, including my associate George Clifford, considered that Donald, Jr., was something of a disappointment to the family. He had been off in the mountains associating with hippies before the overseas job was arranged.

The boy had said he was going to work for Investors Overseas Service, which has been in financial difficulty.

"I told him not to say that," said Donald, a note of exasperation in his voice. "If that gets around, he's going to be in a lot of trouble. I told him he was to say he was going to work for International Controls. IOS and International Controls are allied companies, but he's not supposed to say he's working for IOS. You know what would happen if that got around.

"That dumb so-and-so," Donald said of his son. "John Ehrlichman talked to him for a couple of hours and told him to behave himself over there. You know, he told him he was the President's nephew and couldn't do anything to embarrass the President."

MS. Comp

Nixon Kin Is Mum On Vesco Cash Gift

By JAMES R. POLK
Star-News Staff Writer

Edward C. Nixon, brother of the President, is keeping his silence in the face of court testimony that he played a role in arranging a $200,000 campaign contribution in cash from a financier accused of fraud.

"No comment that is newsworthy. Thank you. Goodbye," Nixon said when finally reached yesterday at his unlisted telephone number in Edmonds, Wash., after a week of calls. Then he hung up.

A New Jersey campaign official, Harry L. Sears, has testified he was told the Nixon brother made a call to Washington to confirm that the donation by financier Robert L. Vesco was wanted in cash.

Sears said under oath he was present when the 42-year-old Nixon arrived at Vesco's business headquarters in Fairfield, N.J., after a helicopter flight from New York City. However, Sears said he didn't stay for the meeting among Nixon, Vesco and business associates.

The Securities and Exchange Commission has filed a civil suit against Vesco accusing him of a $224 million fraud in looting the assets of his Swiss-based IOS, Ltd., mutual fund network.

Edward Nixon, who Sears said is a former director of a Vesco company, is the second member of the President's family to be linked to the financier. Donald A. Nixon, a son of the President's other brother, is Vesco's personal administrative assistant, usually based in Nassau, the Bahamas.

The SEC probe has indicated the $200,000 cash donation came from funds at Vesco's Bahamas Commonwealth

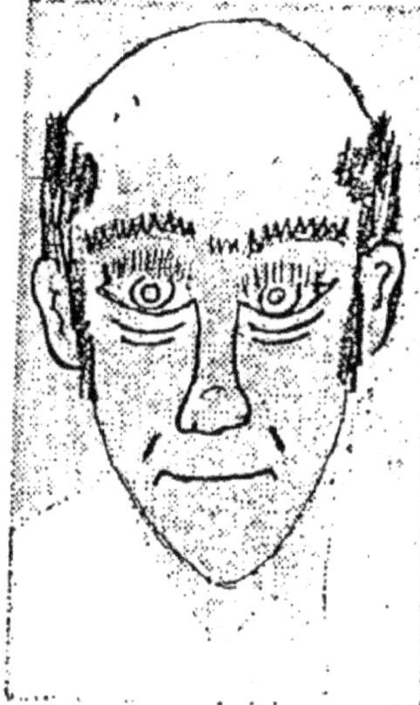

EDWARD C. NIXON

Bank in Nassau. The money was flown to Washington April 10, although the Nixon campaign failed to report the donation under the new disclosure law.

A federal court hearing is scheduled Monday in New York City on the SEC's bid for an injunction against violation of securities laws. Sears' testimony came in a pretrial deposition in the SEC case.

STAR 3.3.73

Pre… his t… the … searc… probl… ing fo… value …

A W… said th… sion o… Treasu… Shultz, … man A… agemen… Roy As… bert St… Economi… tended t… range of…

High c… closed do… buffeting… week in i… markets… to new … currenci… Frankfu… and To… day to… ferver.

Nixon…

Papers Called Embarrassing …

00587

THE WALL STREET JOURNAL, Friday, May 4, 1973 5

Vesco Arrest Warrant Issued by Federal Judge For Grand Jury Inquiry

Financier Hasn't Been in the U.S. For Months; His Lawyer Fears Panel Will Produce Indictment

By a WALL STREET JOURNAL *Staff Reporter*

NEW YORK — Federal Judge Edmund L. Palmieri issued a warrant for the arrest of embattled New Jersey financier Robert L. Vesco, in order to bring him as witness before a grand jury here investigating his activities. Mr. Vesco has been out of the U.S. for several months.

No criminal charges have been brought against Mr. Vesco. But the U.S. Attorney's office, which requested the bench warrant, previously had asked the judge to find Mr. Vesco in contempt of court for failing to heed a subpoena ordering him to appear before the grand jury. The government tried to serve the subpoena on April 15 in Nassau, Bahama Islands.

The grand jury is understood to be investigating the circumstances of Mr. Vesco's $250,000 in contributions to President Nixon's 1972 reelection campaign. At the time, the Securities and Exchange Commission was conducting a well publicized inquiry into Mr. Vesco's business affairs. The SEC file dahuge civil suit against him and 41 other men and concerns on Nov. 27. The Nixon finance committee returned Mr. Vesco's contributions to him on Jan. 31.

Mr. Vesco's attorney, Edward Bennett Williams, told the judge yesterday he had reason to believe that Mr. Vesco would be indicted by the grand jury. Mr. Wiliams said that if forced to appear, Mr. Vesco would invoke his constitutional privilege against self-incrimination, unless he were granted immunity against prosecution. Mr. Williams added that the U.S. Attorney's office had already replied to him that it wouldn't offer immunity.

Mr. Williams, who earlier had asked the judge to dismiss the contempt application on technical grounds, said the circumstances didn't call for Mr. Vesco's arrest.

After the court was adjourned, Mr. Williams declined to discuss reports that the 37-year-old Mr. Vesco intended to renounce his U.S. citizenship, even though the attorney at an earlier hearing had said he would raise the question of citizenship.

James W. Rayhill, an assistant U.S. attorney, brought the matter up in court, saying the government had information that Mr. Vesco was "currently attempting to renounce his U.S. citizenship in Costa Rica," where he last year took up legal residence. It's understood that Mr. Rayhill wasn't referring to a disclosure made late Wednesday by Costa Rica's president, Jose Figueres.

President Figueres, on a two-day visit to this country, said that Mr. Vesco in an audience two or three weeks ago formally announced his intention to renounce U.S. citizenship.

In Washington, the State Department said Mr. Vesco has told Costa Rican authorities that he already has renounced American citizenship before two notaries, with his lawyer's help. However, the U.S. Embassy in Costa Rica contended that didn't count, because it wasn't done before a consular officer. The State Department's legal experts are checking to determine whether that view is correct.

The U.S. has a 1922 extradition treaty with Costa Rica, covering 21 crimes, including robbery, forgery, embezzlement, and fraud. The U.S. considers its 1931 extradition treaty with Britain to apply to the Bahamas, but it isn't clear whether the Bahamas agrees. The British treaty covers such crimes as fraud and misrepresentation, but the warrant issued yesterday for a grand-jury appearance isn't a matter for which extradition is possible.

Mr. Vesco has a home and family in Boonton, N.J., but has bases of operations in Nassau and in San Jose, Costa Rica. Government prosecutors declined to comment when asked what steps they would take to have Mr. Vesco arrested if he were located in either of those countries.

The SEC's civil suit accuses Mr. Vesco of directing the "looting" of $224 million in assets of four foreign mutual funds managed by I.O.S. Ltd. Mr. Vesco formerly headed both I.O.S. and International Controls Corp., of Fairfield, N.J.

00588

~~SENSITIVE~~

7 MAY 1973

SUBJECT: Intelligence Evaluation Committee and Staff

1. Background: Formed December 1970. Membership: Department of Justice (Chairman); FBI (active staff participation agreed to only in May 1971); Department of Defense; Secret Service; National Security Agency; CIA and any necessary representatives of other Departments or Agencies. (Following have participated: Treasury, State.) Staff: IES Executive Director John Dougherty and later Bernard Wells supplied by Department of Justice with title of Special Assistant to the Attorney General in reporting through the Assistant Attorney General for Internal Security Robert Mardian and later William Olsen. IES has received requirements directly from and delivered reports directly to John Dean of the White House.

2. CIA Participation: Contributions on foreign aspects (by memorandum with no agency letterhead or attribution). Contributions occasionally include foreign intelligence provided by FBI and NSA.

3. Special Report: <u>The Unauthorized Disclosure of Classified Information</u>, November 1971. Initiated July 1971 by the White House as a consequence of the President's concern about the release of the Pentagon Papers by Daniel Ellsberg. Both Robert Mardian and G. Gordon Liddy initially involved in tasking the IES to produce this evaluation. Drafting done by IES Staff members from Justice and FBI. Only Agency participation was editorial review.

(Table of contents attached).

~~FULL TEXT COPY - DO NOT RELEASE~~

00589

~~SENSITIVE~~
~~SECRET~~

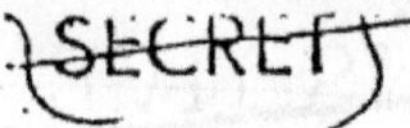

TABLE OF CONTENTS

00590

SECRET

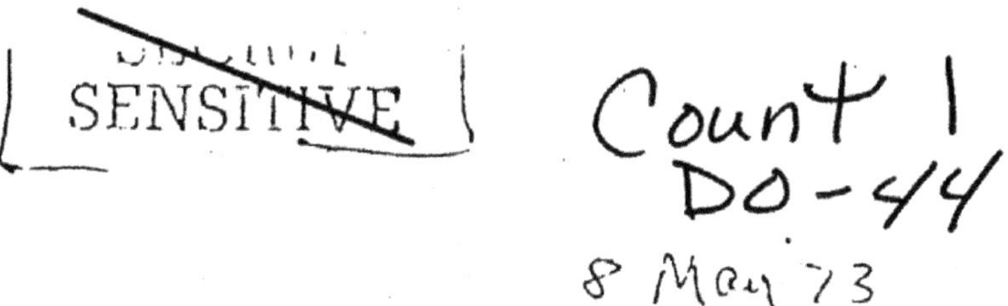

SUBJECT: The MHCHAOS Program

1. The MHCHAOS program is a worldwide program for clandestine collection abroad of information on foreign efforts to support/encourage/exploit/manipulate domestic U.S. extremism, especially by Cuba, Communist China, North Vietnam, the Soviet Union, North Korea and the Arab fedayeen.

2. The MHCHAOS program has not and is not conducting efforts domestically for internal domestic collection purposes. Agency efforts are foreign. Foreign-oriented activity in the United States has been of two types:

a. Selected FBI domestic sources who travel abroad in connection with their extremist activity and/or affiliations to make contact with hostile foreign powers or with foreign extremist groups have been briefed and debriefed by Headquarters officers. The briefing has included appropriate operational guidance, including defensive advice.

b. Americans with existing extremist credentials have been assessed, recruited, tested and dispatched abroad for PCS assignments as contract agents, primarily sources offered for such use by the FBI. When abroad they collect information responsive to MHCHAOS program requirements, as well as other Agency requirements. They are thus used primarily for targeting against Cubans, Chinese Communists, the North Vietnamese, etc., as their background and their particular access permits. It should be noted that the [redacted] aspect of the [redacted] project of the East Asia Division is similar to the MHCHAOS PROGRAM.

U.S. citizens recruited to go abroad

3. As indicated earlier, MHCHAOS is a foreign program, conducted overseas, except for the limited activity described above. The program is and has been managed so as to achieve the maximum feasible utilization of existing resources of the Operations Directorate. No assets

FULL TEXT COPY - DO NOT RELEASE

00591

SENSITIVE
SECRET

have been recruited and run exclusively for the MHCHAOS program. Instead, emphasis has been placed on the exploitation of new and old Agency assets who have a by-product capability or a concurrent capability for provision of information responsive to the program's requirements. This has involved the provision of custom-tailored collection requirements and operational guidance. This collection program is viewed as an integral part of the recruitment and collection programs of China Operations, Vietnam Operations, Cuban Operations, Soviet Bloc Division operations and Korean Branch operations. Agents who have an American "Movement" background or who have known connections with the American "Movement" are useful as access agents to obtain biographic and personality data, to discern possible vulnerabilities and susceptibilities, and to develop operationally exploitable relationships with recruitment targets of the above programs. These assets are of interest to our targets because of their connections with and/or knowledge of the American "Movement." Over the course of the MHCHAOS program, there have been approximately 20 important areas of operational interest, which at the present time have been reduced to about ten: Paris, Stockholm, Brussels, Dar Es Salaam, Conakry, Algiers, Mexico City, Santiago, Ottawa and Hong Kong.

4. The MHCHAOS program also utilizes audio operations, two of which have been implemented to cover targets of special interest.

a.

b.

00592

SENSITIVE

5. [MH]CHAOS reporting from abroad relating to the program originates in two ways: Individuals who are noted in contact with Cubans, the Chinese Communists, etc., and who appear to have extremist connections, interests or background are reported upon. Other individuals are reported upon in response to specific Headquarters requirements received from the FBI because such individuals are of active investigatory security interest to the FBI.

6. All cable and dispatch traffic related to the [MH]CHAOS program is sent via restricted channels. [It is not processed by either the Cable Secretariat or the Information Services Division.] The control and retrievability of information obtained, including information received from the FBI, is the responsibility of the Special Operations Group.

7. Information responsive to specific FBI requirements is disseminated to the FBI via special controlled dissemination channels, i.e., by restricted handling cable traffic or via special pouch and specially numbered blind memoranda.

8. Information of particular significance, when collected, has been disseminated by special memorandum over the signature of the Director of Central Intelligence to the White House (Dr. Kissinger and John Dean), as well as to the Attorney General, the Secretary of State and the Director of the FBI.

00593

CI/Police Group

00594

SENDER WILL CHECK CLASSIFICATION TOP AND BOTTOM

	UNCLASSIFIED		CONFIDENTIAL		SECRET

OFFICIAL ROUTING SLIP

TO	NAME AND ADDRESS	DATE	INITIALS
1	Mr. Halpern		✓
2			
3			
4			
5			
6			

	ACTION		DIRECT REPLY		PREPARE REPLY
	APPROVAL		DISPATCH		RECOMMENDATION
	COMMENT		FILE		RETURN
	CONCURRENCE		INFORMATION		SIGNATURE

Remarks:

Sam:

Attached are the following:

1-background paper on TIC #7
2-comments on facts and statistics
3-comments on AID by Mr. Schlesinger 1963 (which Mr. Colby might find of interest)

00595

FOLD HERE TO RETURN TO SENDER

FROM: NAME. ADDRESS AND PHONE NO.	DATE
	25/4/73

	UNCLASSIFIED	✓	CONFIDENTIAL		SECRET

FORM NO. 237 1-67 Use previous editions (40)

~~CONFIDENTIAL~~
~~SECRET~~

00596

~~SECRET~~
~~CONFIDENTIAL~~

MEMORANDUM FOR: Deputy Director for Operations

SUBJECT : Counter Intelligence Staff, Police Group Activities

1. Counter Intelligence Staff, Police Group (CI/PG) is responsible for Staff coordination within the Office of the Deputy Director for Operations for activities and programs involving assistance to foreign police/security forces for the purpose of exploiting such activities and programs for intelligence purposes.

2. CI/PG maintains liaison with the Office of Public Safety, Agency for International Development (OPS/AID) and its training facility, the International Police Academy (IPA). CI/PG also administers and supervises Project [redacted] In addition, CI/PG coordinates a joint [redacted] [redacted] Central Intelligence Agency [redacted] Technical Investigations Course. CI/PG provides guidance and counsel to the Area Divisions in matters pertaining to police/security functions and activities. Specific details of these functions are as follows:

LIAISON WITH OPS/AID

CI/PG liaison with OPS/AID and IPA is conducted on a daily basis and consists principally of:

A. exchange of information on IPA participants, some of whom later attend [redacted] courses [redacted] [redacted]

B. arranging for inclusion of Agency sponsored participants in IPA/OPS/AID training programs,

C. arranging for IPA/OPS/AID briefings and tours for foreign police/security representatives sponsored by CIA Area Divisions,

00597

SECRET

D.

E. providing general information pertaining to police/security organizations, activities, equipment, and personalities requested by Agency operating components,

F. coordinating the Agency's participation in the Technical Investigations Course designed to familiarize the trainees with the technique required to properly investigate terrorist activities wherein explosives have been utilized,

G.

H.

PROJECT

It is engaged principally in training foreign police/security personnel under and selling police/security equipment to foreign police/security personnel and organizations. also provides special training programs and briefings to foreign police/security personnel of interest to Agency operating divisions.

Recently has acquired the capability of providing training to foreign police/security personnel in VIP protective security for Chiefs of State.

*

00598

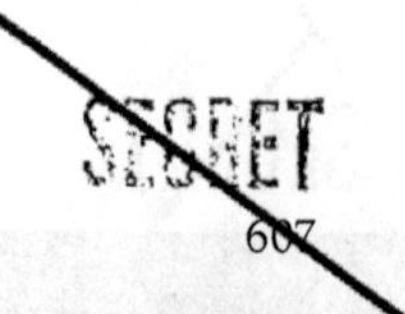

COMMENT

[redacted] does not maintain direct contact or liaison with any law enforcement organization, local or federal, at home or abroad. When the need arises, such contact is sometimes made on our behalf by [redacted] has such contacts at home and abroad because of the nature of its activities (training of foreign police/security personnel at home and abroad), and its Public Safety programs around the world. [redacted] has such contacts at home - local and federal level - because its personnel are personally acquainted with law enforcement officers throughout the United States. Members of the [redacted] have appeared as guest lecturers at such federal institutions as the U.S. Park Police, IPA, the U.S. Secret Service, and the U.S. Treasury Enforcement Division.

3. In addition to the liaison mentioned in the previous paragraph, the Agency maintains liaison in varying degrees with foreign police/security organizations through its field stations. The existence and extent thereof, however, is a decision to be made by the Area Division, and is not the responsibility of [redacted]

4. [redacted] with Dan Mitrione, who was murdered by the Tupamaros. Dan Mitrione, an experienced and respected law enforcement officer, was a bona fide OPS/AID officer assigned to the AID mission in Uruguay, and was never a CIA employee or agent.

for [redacted]
James Angleton
Chief, Counter Intelligence Staff

00599

SECRET

27 MAR 1973

29 March
J.A. sign

MEMORANDUM FOR: Deputy Director for Operations

SUBJECT : Joint CIA/USAID Terrorist (Technical) Investigations Course #7 (English language) CI Staff's Project [redacted]

1. This effort is a joint CIA/USAID training program for foreign police/security personnel. The initial phase of the training will be conducted at the International Police Academy (IPA), Washington, D.C. during the period 2-27 April 1973. The following subject matter is covered in this phase of the training: investigative techniques, collection and preservation of evidence, records, files, and reporting, gathering of information on terrorist groups and their activities, a student seminar devoted to discussions on terrorist and other hostile activities currently existing in their respective countries, etc. This phase of the training is concluded by a two day orientation by the Bomb Squad of the Dade County Police Department in Florida.

2. The second phase of this training will be conducted by Agency [redacted] during 30 April - 25 May 1973. The [redacted] technicians utilize [redacted] cover. The objective of this phase of the training is to develop individual student technical capability to realistically conduct investigations into known or suspected incidents of sabotage/terrorist bombings by:

a. Providing trainees with basic knowledge in the uses of commercial and military demolitions and incendiaries as they may be applied in terrorism and industrial sabotage operations.

b. Introducing the trainees to commercially available materials and home laboratory techniques likely to be used in the manufacture of explosives and incendiaries by terrorists or saboteurs.

00600

SECRET

c. Familiarizing the trainees with the concept of target analysis and operational planning that a saboteur or terrorist must employ.

d. Introducing the trainees to booby trapping devices and techniques giving practical experience with both manufactured and improvised devices through actual fabrication. Emphasize the necessity of alertness for detecting and countering booby traps placed by saboteurs or terrorists.

e. Conducting several field exercises to give each trainee the opportunity for detecting and neutralizing various explosive and incendiary devices likely to be used by terrorists or saboteurs, including letter bombs, packages, attache cases, etc.

f. Conducting several investigative field exercises of explosive incidents to alert the trainee to the need for and manner in which to collect, identify, and preserve legally admisable evidence for prosecutive action.

3. The program provides the trainees with ample opportunity to develop basic familiarity and use proficiently through handling, preparing and applying the various explosive charges, incendiary agents, terrorist devices and sabotage techniques. USAID, International Police Academy (IPA) has received reports from former foreign police/security personnel who participated in the program indicating that they were called upon to utilize the skills they acquired through this training in the handling of explosive devices in their respective country. Attached is a letter from a participant in TIC #6 [redacted] stating that he deactivated a letter bomb device which was sent to the [redacted] Embassy in [redacted]

4. Subject course will have 26 participants from ten (10) foreign countries. Nine (9) are financed by AID, eight (8) by CIA and nine (9) by their own governments.

00601

5. Separate end of course reports will be prepared by USAID and CIA, TSD personnel/

James Angleton
Chief, Counter Intelligence Staff

00602

FACTS AND STATISTICS

AID/OPS TRAINING

AID/OPS, International Police Academy sponsors some seven hundred (700) foreign police officers for training in the United States each year. These officers are selected from underdeveloped countries. [redacted]

[redacted] TRAINING

[redacted] trains some 350-400 of these officers in specialized areas of law enforcement. [redacted]

During FY 1973 [redacted] supported two of our field stations by providing training in VIP protective security for [redacted] personnel.

AID/OPS-CIA TRAINING

During FY 1973 two joint USAID/OPS/CIA Technical Investigations training programs were conducted for [redacted] foreign police/security personnel representing [redacted] countries. The purpose of the training is to develop individual student technical capability to realistically conduct investigations into known or suspected incidents of sabotage/terrorist bombing or other activities.

NATIONAL SECURITY

Political, Military, and Economic Strategies in the Decade Ahead

Edited by

David M. Abshire *and* Richard V. Allen

Introduction by

Admiral Arleigh Burke, *Director*

THE CENTER FOR STRATEGIC STUDIES
GEORGETOWN UNIVERSITY

Published for the
HOOVER INSTITUTION ON WAR, REVOLUTION
AND PEACE
by
FREDERICK A. PRAEGER, *Publisher*
New York · London

1963

00604

Strategic Leverage from Aid and Trade

—JAMES R. SCHLESINGER

Summary

The analysis of this paper rests on the assumption that American policy-makers should not be so concerned with the pursuit of hard-to-obtain ideological objectives that they exhaust the power potential implicit in trade and aid relationships. Rather the trade and aid programs should be managed so as to preserve an environment in which pressures can be brought to bear to serve the national interest at a later, and perhaps more critical, date. This emphasis on power considerations implies both (a) that the assistance program cannot be based primarily on humanitarian or idealistic goals, and (b) that economic ties with other nations should not be severed simply because of our disapproval of other social systems, including those based on communism. Though typically public opinion vastly overstates the strategic leverage that can be gained through economic weapons, this leverage is still not negligible. One can argue that in the past the United States has failed to take advantage of the power potential implicit in aid and trade through its failure to develop concepts and mechanisms of deterrence in ways akin to what has been done in the military field. Much of the difficulty may be ascribed to a failure to develop sanctions, which discourage actions unfavorable to our interests, as well as incentives, which encourage cooperation. No system of deterrence can exclusively stress the carrot and ignore the stick.

More is being demanded of the aid program than it can reasonably achieve. Assuming that the primary emphasis of the aid program is to encourage social and economic development rather than to elicit direct support for American foreign policy objectives, it is argued that we should attempt to develop stable social and political conditions by strengthening the "legitimacy" of the developing social order in the eyes of the respective publics—rather than attempting to export the trappings of American democracy.

Technological change, the easy availability of substitutes, and the lengthy period for adjustment in a prolonged struggle have all reduced the impact of the "supply effect" which was at one time the main weapon of economic warfare. If the economic weapons of strategy are to be at all effective under today's conditions, the "influence effect" must rise correspondingly in importance. This implies that we should be in a position to threaten to do damage to other economies through the curtailment of access to Western markets. In order to keep this threat an ever-present one, we must, however, continue to trade in volume with other countries, including Communist ones. Particularly in dealing with the underdeveloped nations the potential effectiveness of such threats may prove to be considerable.

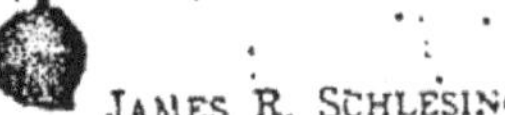

One final consideration—it would be unwise to use potential weapons of this sort for niggling purposes. The balance of payments has been troublesome and is properly an object of concern in Washington, but surely it is not a first-order consideration in our relations with the underdeveloped nations. Suggestions have been bruited about that we should make use of the aid program to force recipients to buy from us in ways that go beyond tied aid. Under the best of circumstances, our bargaining power is limited, and shooting away strategic ammunition for so paltry an economic goal would seem to reflect a poor sense of proportion.

Aid

Within an over-all framework designed to discourage hostile or predatory attitudes toward the West, the aid program may seek to foster the maximum rate of economic and social progress. In the basic policy of AID, the Kennedy Administration has explicitly adopted this goal. As has been indicated there are costs to this decision. Outsiders are not likely to be much liked even under the best of circumstances, which hardly apply to the underdeveloped countries, and their intervention in whatever direction will in the long run excite antagonism based on real or fancied wrongs. Nevertheless, the basic decision has been made. Let us examine in what way we may proceed so that the good effects clearly outweigh the ill effects.

There are two initial postulates: (1) our bargaining power will be limited, and (2) American notions of social reform and of equity are neither necessarily applicable in the underdeveloped lands, nor need we assume that those whose cooperation we must win will find them appealing. These postulates are interrelated. Jointly they imply that we cannot press forward on all fronts to create a society in which a good American democrat will feel at home, but must instead concentrate our energies on those social changes which will spur economic growth even if the immediate results are more consistent with the cultural genius of the peoples involved rather than our own tastes. We ought not expect them to make the same choices as we would, or, if they make the same choices, to achieve in a ten-year period what it took us eighty years to achieve. Finally, in reaching judgments on social processes in other lands, we cannot apply what are our own—or, in reality, higher—standards of purity.

As outsiders, we will be unable to perceive the social function of behavior which is superficially corrupt, and will tend to lump it together with that which is purely parasitical. With respect to our own history, retrospectively we have come to find merit in what once were regarded as the disreputable procedures of an organization like Tammany Hall in that it provided a kind of social security and a welcome for the newly arrived immigrant. We are accustomed to the daily dangling of new post offices, good committee assignments, and bridges over creeks in the outback before wavering Congressmen, and warm approval is given, for its fine sense of political realism, to whatever administration is doing the dangling by those who agree with its goals. Toward similar procedures abroad we are inclined to take a simple muckraking attitude. We look askance at the higgling of the political market—with a naiveté that would do credit both to missionaries and old-style political reformers. If we hope to achieve a fair measure of success, we shall have to sharpen our critical faculties and learn to distinguish between unappetizing social devices which are functional and those which are simple barriers to progress.

The statement of objectives by AID is a very ambitious one. The purposes of the assistance program include stimulation of self-help, encouragement of progressive forces, and achievement of governments based on consent, which recognize the dignity and worth of individuals who are expected to participate in determining the nation's goals. No doubt, a statement of aspirations is in large part window dressing, but the criteria by which self-help is moving toward social and political progress are more specific: a more equitable distribution of income, a more equitable tax system with increased yields, expanded welfare programs, increased political participation and civil liberties, and so on. Several points may be made regarding the objectives: first, there are too many; second, they are to some extent inconsistent; and third, they ignore the real resources available.

There is, in the first place, the long-perceived clash between economic progress, on the one hand, and the combined goals of equitable distribution of income, immediate improvement in living standards, and security on the other. This underlying conflict spills over into a tension between rapid economic progress and the introduction of democratic processes. On this issue there appears to have been a revolution in informed opinion in the United States during the past five years. During the late fifties, it had become almost an axiom that authoritarian, if not totalitarian, governments had innate advantages in guiding economies toward rapid growth. The prevailing view was based, no doubt, on an assessment of the record of the Soviet regime, and an exaggerated notion of how much the Chinese "Great Leap Forward" would accomplish. Perhaps the earlier "pessimism" regarding the relative performance potential of "free" and "controlled" economies was overdone, but have we not gone too far in the now prevailing "optimism" that any clash between economic progress and the democratic institutions which insure the dominance of the *vox populi* is minimal?

The average citizen—particularly when he is ill-housed, ill-clothed, ill-fed, and ill-educated—seems most likely to be interested in the here and now. A government which is responsive to the desires of the public will continually be tempted to mortgage the future for the present. The "abstinence" or "waiting" which classical and neoclassical economics state to be necessary ingredients in economic progress will be hard to require, as will be the incentive schemes (and the accompanying conspicuous consumption) which are likely to strike the average voter as inequitable. We may recall that the Perón regime was (and still may be?) the most popular regime in recent Latin American history. Or we may observe the economic consequences of Brazilian democracy, and have our doubts. The inflow of American resources may be able to make showpieces out of several small, recently-democratized nations like the Dominican Republic, but we ought not assume either that democracy assists in economic development, or that the Dominican example is widely applicable. This is not to say that some judicious prodding in the direction of democracy may not be a wise policy, but it must be *judicious*, and cannot be based on the assumption that democracy necessarily fosters the political stability essential to growth.

One of the criteria by which self-help can be judged as justifying additional aid is an improvement in the savings ratio. Some students of the aid program would put major emphasis on changes in the savings ratio in that it provides a relatively objective standard by which an improvement in economic performance can be judged.* If we apply an objective standard, complaints about the distribution of aid and subjectivity in the

* Charles Wolf, Jr. of RAND has been attempting to develop an econometric model which will provide an objective measure of the performance of aid recipients in terms of self-help. The criterion is the savings ratio. In the model the attempt is made to eliminate the influence of other variables, such as per capita income, income distribution, and degree of urbanization, which account for a good deal of the observed variation in the savings ratio as between nations and between different periods of time.

SECRET/SENSITIVE

8 May 1973

MEMORANDUM FOR: Deputy Director for Operations

SUBJECT: Foreign Resources Division Operational Activities with Possible Flap Potential

REFERENCE: FR Memorandum, [redacted] dated 7 May 1973, same subject

1. The answers to your questions are as follows:

a. Question: Do we recruit Americans?

Answer: Yes, we recruit Americans to be used as [redacted] support assets and access agents. These Americans are used for spotting and assessment purposes only and do not perform any recruitments.

b. Question: Do we use alias documents on Americans in course of operations?

Answer: Yes, we do use alias documents when recruiting American support assets. The great majority of these recruitments are done in alias. All recruitments of foreign targets are done in alias.

c. Question: What disciplinary controls do we have over alias documents?

Answer: We maintain a current list in FR Division Headquarters of the alias documents issued to each Base.

SECRET/SENSITIVE

00611

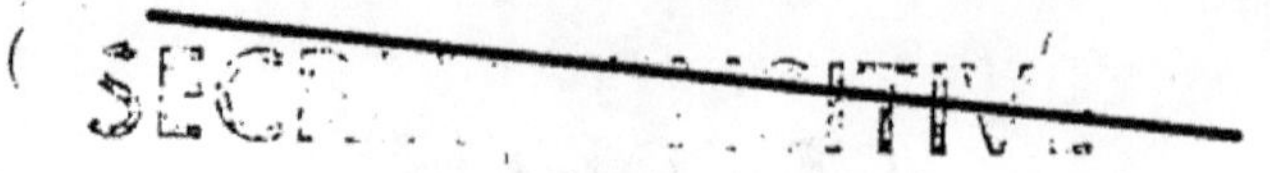

/2/

More importantly, each Base Chief is responsible for supervising and maintaining control over the alias documents used by the case officers on his Base.

d. Question: Any clearances or prohibitions?

Answer:

2. If you have further questions, please let me know.

Acting Chief
Foreign Resources Division

00612

SECRET/SENSITIVE

UNCLASSIFIED ☐ INTERNAL USE ONLY ☐ CONFIDENTIAL ☐ SECRET

ROUTING AND RECORD SHEET

SUBJECT: (Optional)

COUNT 1
DO-55

FROM: Acting Chief, FR Division

EXTENSION

NO.

DATE 7 May 1973

TO: (Officer designation, room number, and building)	DATE RECEIVED	DATE FORWARDED	OFFICER'S INITIALS	COMMENTS (Number each comment to show from whom to whom. Draw a line across column after each comment.)
1. EA/DDO				~~SECRET/SENSITIVE~~
2.				~~BY HAND~~
3. DDO				
4.				
5.				
6.				
7.				
8.				
9.				
10.				
11.				
12.				
13.				
14. ~~FULL TEXT COPY — DO NOT RELEASE~~				
15. Exempt (b)(1) (b)(3)				

Conversation with FR Div (R-

He indicated that the introductory and closing paragraphs

~~of this memo could be released in the sanitized form shown.~~

OGC January 13, 1981

(1) Do we recruit Americans?

(2) Do we use a[illegible] docs on Ameri[illegible] in course of [illegible]

(3) What discipline controls do [illegible] have over a[illegible] docs?

(4) [illegible] -Am[illegible] or prohibit[illegible]

00613

FORM 3-62 610 USE PREVIOUS EDITIONS ☐ SECRET ☐ CONFIDENTIAL ☐ INTERNAL USE ONLY ☐ UNCLASSIFIED

7 May 1973 DO 55

MEMORANDUM FOR: Deputy Director for Operations

SUBJECT: Foreign Resources Division Operational Activities with Possible Flap Potential

1. At thr risk of stating the obvious, almost all of the operational activities carried on by FR Division [redacted] run the risk that unauthorized disclosure could create embarrassment to the Agency. We have accepted this as a condition precedent and have proceeded with our operational activities in the most professional manner possible under the circumstances. There are certain rather unusual activities in which FR Division has participated and/or is participating that contain somewhat greater possibility for embarrassment if discovered. I have listed these below, not necessarily in order of embarrassment potential:

a. [redacted] provides a fairly considerable amount of support to Dr. Kissinger in his contacts with the Chinese. This support was authorized by Mr. Karamessines and Mr. Helms. Thus far there has been no problem other than the inordinate amount of time spent by [redacted] personnel, not to mention the fairly sizeable amount of money that has been expended in support of these efforts.

b. [redacted]

FULL TEXT COPY - DO NOT RELEASE

00614

SECRET/SENSITIVE Exempt (b)(1) (b)(3)

c. Alias Documentation: Clearly, FR Division does the great majority of its operational work by having its case officers utilize alias documents. All recruitments are done in alias. Thus, the alias documentation is a prerequisite for effective operations [redacted] Furthermore, our case officers have utilized fully backstopped alias credit cards for renting automobiles, motel rooms, hotel rooms for operational meetings, etc. These credit cards are backstopped by accounts in alias which are promptly paid at the appropriate time. I see no problem in the continued use of alias documentation and moreover, I feel it is absolutely essential to continue using alias documentation wherever and whenever possible.

d. [redacted]

e. [redacted]

00615
Exempt (b)(1)
(b)(3)

/3/

2. Summarizing the above, I believe that all of the activities outlined are clearly within the acceptable risk frame. [redacted] The other activities, although clearly involving some degree of risk are necessary and valuable and in my opinion should be continued.

[redacted]

Acting Chief
Foreign Resources Division

00616

Exempt (b)(1)
(b)(3)

DRAFT OUTLINE FOR DDO BRIEFING

I. Statement of Organization and Functions

II. Official T/O

III. Location of Field Units

IV. Cover

V. Targets

VI. Methodology

VII. Budget

VIII. Coordination

A. Internal

B. External

X. Statistics:

A. Recruitments

B. General Support Assets

C. Positive Intelligence Reporting

FOREIGN RESOURCES DIVISION

I. Statement of Organization and Functions

SECRET

SECRET

00621

SECRET

SECRET

00626

~~SECRET~~

~~SECRET~~

00627

SECRET

SECRET

00628

~~SECRET~~

~~SECRET~~

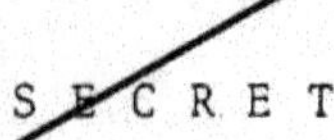

SECRET

SECRET

00632

6 JUN 1973

MEMORANDUM FOR: Director of Central Intelligence

THROUGH : Executive Secretary, CIA Management Committee

SUBJECT : Alleged CIA Involvement in the Ballou Case

1. By memorandum dated 25 May 1973, I informed you of the results of an interview of Mr. [redacted] who reported that Mr. [redacted] an employee of the Office of Security, had stated during a discussion period at Advanced Intelligence Seminar No. 6 in September 1971 that the Office of Security had been involved in the "Ballou case." (The residence of Mr. Ballou, an antique gun collector in Silver Spring, Maryland, was raided on 7 June 1971 by Montgomery County Police and Federal law enforcement officers. When the officers, dressed in civilian clothes, forced their way into the house, Ballou picked up an antique pistol. The officers opened fire and seriously wounded Ballou. He was hospitalized for several months and was left partially paralyzed. I believe he is now suing over the incident.)

2. We interviewed Mr. [redacted] certain other employees who attended the Seminar, and the Director of Security to determine just what was said at the Seminar and the extent of any Agency involvement in the Ballou case. We find that participants in the Seminar were encouraged to discuss the details of their work and associated problems. Mr. [redacted] mentioned an assignment he had been on with the U. S. Secret Service at the 1968 National Conventions and his liaison activities with the Montgomery County Police.

3. [redacted] reports that in discussing the latter subject he related a conversation he had with Inspector [redacted] of the Montgomery County Police, sometime in June 1971 after the Ballou incident had been reported in the newspapers. According to [redacted] the police inspector had thanked him for some amplifying equipment the Agency had given to the Montgomery County Police and remarked that

00634

SECRET

this equipment had probably saved a policeman's life. The inspector commented that the account of the Ballou incident appearing in the press was not the whole story. With the aid of the equipment the Agency had provided, the police had intercepted a telephone call from Ballou to a friend in which Ballou outlined plans to "kill a cop." The police then staged a raid to forestall Ballou's plan, and it was during this raid that Ballou was shot.

4. [redacted] said that he has no other knowledge of the Ballou case, except for what he has read in the newspapers, and that he has not had any other conversations about the case with any members of the Montgomery County Police. We learned nothing from our inquiries that would indicate any other Agency involvement in the Ballou case.

5. The following are related excerpts from the "Family Jewels" submission of the Director of Security on 16 May 1973:

> During the period from 1968 to 1973, several items of positive audio equipment consisting primarily of clandestine transmitters and touch-tone dial recorders were loaned to the Metropolitan Police Department; Fairfax County, Virginia, Police Department; Montgomery County, Maryland, Police Department; New York City Police Department; and the San Francisco, California, Police Department.
>
> On 25 July 1968, and at the specific request of the United States Secret Service, this Office provided two audio countermeasures technicians to the United States Secret Service in connection with the Democratic National Convention held in Chicago, Illinois. This was not an official detail although both men were provided with temporary credentials identifying them as being affiliated with the United States Secret Service.
>
> On 15 August 1968, we detailed the same two men to the United States Secret Service to cover the Republican National Convention in Miami, Florida. On both occasions, the team members were debriefed upon their return and it is clear that their activities were confined exclusively to sweeping the candidates' and potential candidates' quarters.

(Signed) William V Broe

William V. Broe
Inspector General

OIG: [redacted] (6 June 1973)
Distribution:
Orig & 1 - Addressee
1 - ExecSec/CIA MC

00635

MEMORA JM FOR: The Record

Mr. F. P. Bishop is following up per para 7 of IG memo to DCI dtd 25 May -

cm/31 May

00636

(DATE)

FORM NO. 1 AUG 54 101 REPLACES FORM 10-101 WHICH MAY BE USED. (47)

☐ UNCLASSIFIED ☐ INTERNAL USE ONLY ~~☐ CONFIDENTIAL~~ ☐ SECRET

ROUTING AND RECORD SHEET

SUBJECT: (Optional)

FROM:	EXTENSION	NO.
Inspector General		DATE 25 May 1973

TO: (Officer designation, room number, and building)	DATE RECEIVED	DATE FORWARDED	OFFICER'S INITIALS	COMMENTS (Number each comment to show from whom to whom. Draw a line across column after each comment.)
1. Mr. Wm. E. Colby	5/22	5/25	C	
2. The Director				BY HAND, NOT THROUGH REGISTRY.
3.				
4. IG	5/29			
5.				
6.				
7.				
8.				
9.				
10.				
11.				
12.				
13.				
14.				
15.				00637

FORM 610 USE PREVIOUS EDITIONS ~~☐ SECRET~~ ~~☐ CONFIDENTIAL~~ ☐ INTERNAL USE ONLY ☐ UNCLASSIFIED

CIA INTERNAL USE ONLY

25 May 1973

MEMORANDUM FOR: Director of Central Intelligence

THROUGH : Mr. William E. Colby

1. On 17 May the name of [redacted] was referred to this office as having attempted to contact the Director concerning "activities outside the Agency." I attempted to contact [redacted] on 21 and 22 May, but he was on leave. On 23 May he stated he wanted to check a portion of his information and asked if he could come to my office on 24 May.

2. [redacted] came into the Agency as a JOT in October 1957 and is currently a [redacted] assigned to the Soviet/EE Section. He has a very strong personnel file.

3. [redacted] advised that in August 1971 he attended the Advanced Intelligence Seminar. On the first evening of the seminar the students had a "getting acquainted" session where each one gave a brief description of his duties. One of the students, [redacted] of the Office of Security, however, carried on after the session was over and expanded on the briefing he had given. He claimed that CIA was cooperating with the Montgomery County Police, stating that the Office of Security gave electronic and other support to that organization.

4. He further indicated that the Office of Security had been involved in the "Ballou case". [redacted] described the Ballou case as follows: The residence of Mr. Ballou, an antique gun collector in Silver Spring, Maryland, was raided on 7 June 1971 by the Montgomery County Police and some Federal law enforcement officers. After the officers, dressed in civilian clothes, had forced their way into the house Ballou picked up an antique pistol. The officers immediately opened fire and wounded Ballou seriously. He spent a long time in the hospital and is partly paralyzed at the present time.

CIA INTERNAL USE ONLY

00638

His case was given much publicity in the Washington Post at the time. There was additional publicity in the last several months when Ballou instigated a lawsuit against the raiding officers.

5. [redacted] identified another student, [redacted] who was assigned to IAS, as a friend of [redacted] He stated that [redacted] also seemed to know the specifics of the Ballou case.

6. I thanked [redacted] and told him this was just the type of information we wanted to receive so that it can be investigated and appropriate action taken if the information is borne out.

7. This office will follow up on this allegation and advise the Director concerning our findings.

[redacted]
William V. Broe
Inspector General

Noted
WVB

Mr. [redacted] called the Director on 16 May at 3:05 re "activities outside the Agency". I told him Director was out of the office, but we would return his call. Mr. [redacted] called back that day and said he was going to Fubini lecture and would call us back. He never did call back. Mr. Colby said to turn over to Mr. Broe. [redacted]

00640

~~SECRET~~
~~EYES ONLY~~

~~EYES ONLY~~

00641

~~SECRET~~

SECRET

EYES ONLY

EYES ONLY

2

SECRET

00642

☐ UNCLASSIFIED ☐ INTERNAL USE ONLY ~~☐ CONFIDENTIAL~~ ~~☐ SECRET~~

ROUTING AND RECORD SHEET

SUBJECT: (Optional)

FROM:	EXTENSION	NO.
Inspector General 3		DATE 22 May 1973

TO: (Officer designation, room number, and building)	DATE RECEIVED	DATE FORWARDED	OFFICER'S INITIALS	COMMENTS (Number each comment to show from whom to whom. Draw a line across column after each comment.)
1. Mr. Wm. E. Colby	5/23	5/23	[initials]	
2. The Director			[initials]	Recommend the IG express your appreciation to [redacted] & assure we will follow this up (which, of course, we already have done by terminating the activity) WEC
3.				
4. IG	5/24		B	
5.				
6.				
7.				
8.				
9.				
10.				
11.				
12.				
13.				DONE - 29 May 73 [redacted]
14.				
15.				00643

FORM 3-62 610 USE PREVIOUS EDITIONS ~~☐ SECRET~~ ~~☐ CONFIDENTIAL~~ ☐ INTERNAL USE ONLY ☐ UNCLASSIFIED

22 May 1973

MEMORANDUM FOR: Director of Central Intelligence

THROUGH : Mr. William E. Colby WEC

Mr. Colby advised me that [redacted] extension [redacted] had called the Office of the Director in line with the Director's memorandum to all employees dated 9 May 1973, requesting all employees to report activities which might be construed to be outside the legislative charter of the Agency.

[redacted] is employed as a GS-5 clerk in the Cable Secretariat. He joined the Agency in September 1967 and worked in the Office of Security for 3-1/2 years before transferring to the Cable Secretariat in 1970.

While in the Office of Security he was assigned to a support desk, SD3. The primary function of this desk was to [redacted] During his assignment to this desk, [redacted] supported a project entitled SRPOINTER-HTLINGUAL [redacted] described the project as follows. The Office of Security [redacted] had a unit at the JFK International Airport that photographed mail going to Soviet Bloc countries. This work was done by Agency staff employees. The mail was placed in bags by the regular Post Office employees and stacked. After their departure for the night, the Agency employees would open the mail and photograph it. Both incoming and outgoing mail, including postcards, were photographed. A watch list was maintained and priority was given to the names listed, but generally all mail was processed.

The results of the operation were sent to Washington Headquarters where they were handled by [redacted] He would receive a teletype advising him of the registry number and the number of items. He would check to see if the number of items received was correct and route the material to the appropriate offices. Generally about 1/4 of

00644

SECRET [redacted]

the material was separated into bundles bound with rubber bands. This portion was sent to TSD for technical processing. The remaining material was sent to the CI Staff, [redacted]

About twice a month the CI Staff would add names to or delete names from the list. [redacted] would send the changes in the list to the field office. The watch list was made up primarily of [redacted] [redacted] who were in the United States. When [redacted] left the Office of Security in 1970, the project was still active.

[redacted] was in no way emotional or belligerent. He presented the facts quickly and clearly and said he had no other information. He stated he would have come forward with the information sooner but he had only recently had time to read the Director's memorandum. The writer thanked him for his interest.

William V. Broe
Inspector General

6 JUN 1973

MEMORANDUM FOR: Director of Central Intelligence

THROUGH : Executive Secretary, CIA Management Committee

SUBJECT : Alleged CIA Involvement in the Ballou Case

1. By memorandum dated 25 May 1973, I informed you of the results of an interview of Mr. [redacted] who reported that Mr. [redacted] an employee of the Office of Security, had stated during a discussion period at Advanced Intelligence Seminar No. 6 in September 1971 that the Office of Security had been involved in the "Ballou case." (The residence of Mr. Ballou, an antique gun collector in Silver Spring, Maryland, was raided on 7 June 1971 by Montgomery County Police and Federal law enforcement officers. When the officers, dressed in civilian clothes, forced their way into the house, Ballou picked up an antique pistol. The officers opened fire and seriously wounded Ballou. He was hospitalized for several months and was left partially paralyzed. I believe he is now suing over the incident.)

2. We interviewed Mr. [redacted] certain other employees who attended the Seminar, and the Director of Security to determine just what was said at the Seminar and the extent of any Agency involvement in the Ballou case. We find that participants in the Seminar were encouraged to discuss the details of their work and associated problems. Mr. [redacted] mentioned an assignment he had been on with the U. S. Secret Service at the 1968 National Conventions and his liaison activities with the Montgomery County Police.

3. [redacted] reports that in discussing the latter subject he related a conversation he had with Inspector [redacted] of the Montgomery County Police, sometime in June 1971 after the Ballou incident had been reported in the newspapers. According to [redacted] the [redacted] had thanked him for some amplifying equipment the Agency had given to the Montgomery County Police and remarked that

00646

SECRET SENSITIVE

this equipment had probably saved a policeman's life. The inspector commented that the account of the Ballou incident appearing in the press was not the whole story. With the aid of the equipment the Agency had provided, the police had intercepted a telephone call from Ballou to a friend in which Ballou outlined plans to "kill a cop." The police then staged a raid to forestall Ballou's plan, and it was during this raid that Ballou was shot.

4. [redacted] said that he has no other knowledge of the Ballou case, except for what he has read in the newspapers, and that he has not had any other conversations about the case with any members of the Montgomery County Police. We learned nothing from our inquiries that would indicate any other Agency involvement in the Ballou case.

5. The following are related excerpts from the "Family Jewels" submission of the Director of Security on 16 May 1973:

> During the period from 1968 to 1973, several items of positive audio equipment consisting primarily of clandestine transmitters and touch-tone dial recorders were loaned to the Metropolitan Police Department; Fairfax County, Virginia, Police Department; Montgomery County, Maryland, Police Department; New York City Police Department; and the San Francisco, California, Police Department.
>
> On 25 July 1968, and at the specific request of the United States Secret Service, this Office provided two audio countermeasures technicians to the United States Secret Service in connection with the Democratic National Convention held in Chicago, Illinois. This was not an official detail although both men were provided with temporary credentials identifying them as being affiliated with the United States Secret Service.
>
> On 15 August 1968, we detailed the same two men to the United States Secret Service to cover the Republican National Convention in Miami, Florida. On both occasions, the team members were debriefed upon their return and it is clear that their activities were confined exclusively to sweeping the candidates' and potential candidates' quarters.

(Signed) William V. Broe

William V. Broe
Inspector General

OIG: [redacted] (6 June 1973)
Distribution:
Orig & 1 - Addressee
1 - ExecSec/CIA MC

4 June 1973

Date

BROE

Follow-up interview re Mr. [redacted] request ~~xxx~~ to see DCI.

FROM: FPBishop

RETURN TO: 1. FPB. 2. File on Interviews held on behalf of DCI re Watergate/Jewels

00648

31 May 1973

MEMORANDUM FOR THE RECORD

SUBJECT: Interview with [redacted] Office of Security

1. On 31 May 1973 I questioned [redacted] about what he had said at the Advanced Intelligence Seminar No. 6 and the extent and nature of the relations he had had with the Montgomery County Police. He said that he and others had been encouraged to discuss their work and the problems related thereto with other Seminar members and told that what they said would be "non-attributable." In this context he had discussed the Office of Security's relations with local Police Forces including the Police Force in Montgomery County. He said he mentioned the "Ballou Case" as an example of how the Montgomery County Police had used equipment provided by the Agency in their work, but denied that he had said or implied that the Agency was "involved" in the Ballou case. He said that he had also related to the other Seminar members the fact that the Agency had provided assistance to the Secret Service in connection with the protection of the President and Vice President and that he and others had been detailed to work with the Secret Service on counter-audio activities at the 1968 Democratic National Convention in Chicago and the Republican National Convention in Miami. I asked [redacted] who was on the Chicago detail, if he was detailed to protect the Vice President. He said that he was detailed to Tom Kelly, Deputy Chief of the Secret Service and worked in effect as a member of the Secret Service under Mr. Kelly.

2. I questioned [redacted] as to whether his relations with the Montgomery County Police was training oriented, equipment oriented, or if he had engaged in any operations or activities with the police. He said his relations with the Police had been entirely equipment oriented and had been limited to the Chief of Police and one or two senior Inspectors. The extent of assistance given consisted of the Agency providing the Police with surplus technical

SECRET

00649

equipment which was of no further use to the Agency, and briefing them as to its use. He said he would not define these briefings as training, but admitted that it might be so construed.

3. [redacted] said that his only knowledge of the "Ballou Case", except what he had read in the papers, came from one telephone conversation he had with Inspector [redacted] of the Montgomery County Police sometime after accounts of the Ballou shooting had appeared in the press. He said the Inspector called to thank him for some amplifying equipment the Agency had given the Police and mentioned that it had probably saved the life of a policeman. He said that the Inspector explained to him that the account of the incident appearing in the press was not the whole story, that with the aid of the equipment the Agency had provided the Police had been able to intercept a telephone call from Ballou to a friend in which Ballou had outlined plans to "kill a cop ." The Police had then staged a raid to forestall Ballou's plan and it was during this raid that Ballou was shot. [redacted] said that he had had no other conversations with the Montgomery County Police on that subject. He said he had mentioned it at the Seminar as an example of the sensitivity involved in the Agency's dealings with domestic Police Forces. He said he recalled that there was quite a bit of discussion and argument by the Seminar members about the propriety of the Agency assisting local police forces and working with the Secret Service in the U.S., but that he did not recall any extensive discussion about the Ballou Case and that at no time had he said that the Agency was directly involved. [redacted] said he remembered that [redacted] seemed particularly concerned about the Agency's involvement in domestic activities and that sometime later, around January or February 1972, [redacted] talked to Colonel White about his concern and Colonel White in turn talked to the Director of Security. Since that date, he said, he has not had any further direct contact with the Montgomery County Police, based upon orders of the Director of Security.

[redacted]
F. P. Bishop
Inspector

2

SECRET

00650

SECRET

31 May 1973

MEMORANDUM FOR THE RECORD

SUBJECT: Interview with [redacted] Office of Security

1. On 31 May 1973 I questioned [redacted] about what he had said at the Advanced Intelligence Seminar No. 6 and the extent and nature of the relations he had had with the Montgomery County Police. He said that he and others had been encouraged to discuss their work and the problems related thereto with other Seminar members and told that what they said would be "non-attributable." In this context he had discussed the Office of Security's relations with local Police Forces including the Police Force in Montgomery County. He said he mentioned the "Ballou Case" as an example of how the Montgomery County Police had used equipment provided by the Agency in their work, but denied that he had said or implied that the Agency was "involved" in the Ballou case. He said that he had also related to the other Seminar members the fact that the Agency had provided assistance to the Secret Service in connection with the protection of the President and Vice President and that he and others had been detailed to work with the Secret Service on counter-audio activities at the 1968 Democratic National Convention in Chicago and the Republican National Convention in Miami. I asked [redacted] who was on the Chicago detail, if he was detailed to protect the Vice President. He said that he was detailed to Tom Kelly, Deputy Chief of the Secret Service and worked in effect as a member of the Secret Service under Mr. Kelly.

2. I questioned [redacted] as to whether his relations with the Montgomery County Police was training oriented, equipment oriented, or if he had engaged in any operations or activities with the police. He said his relations with the Police had been entirely equipment oriented and had been limited to the Chief of Police and one or two senior Inspectors. The extent of assistance given consisted of the Agency providing the Police with surplus technical

00651

SECRET

equipment which was of no further use to the Agency, and briefing them as to its use. He said he would not define these briefings as training, but admitted that it might be so construed.

3. [redacted] said that his only knowledge of the "Ballou Case", except what he had read in the papers, came from one telephone conversation he had with Inspector [redacted] of the Montgomery County Police sometime after accounts of the Ballou shooting had appeared in the press. He said the Inspector called to thank him for some amplifying equipment the Agency had given the Police and mentioned that it had probably saved the life of a policeman. He said that the Inspector explained to him that the account of the incident appearing in the press was not the whole story, that with the aid of the equipment the Agency had provided the Police had been able to intercept a telephone call from Ballou to a friend in which Ballou had outlined plans to "kill a cop." The Police had then staged a raid to forestall Ballou's plan and it was during this raid that Ballou was shot. [redacted] said that he had had no other conversations with the Montgomery County Police on that subject. He said he had mentioned it at the Seminar as an example of the sensitivity involved in the Agency's dealings with domestic Police Forces. He said he recalled that there was quite a bit of discussion and argument by the Seminar members about the propriety of the Agency assisting local police forces and working with the Secret Service in the U.S., but that he did not recall any extensive discussion about the Ballou Case and that at no time had he said that the Agency was directly involved. [redacted] said he remembered that [redacted] seemed particularly concerned about the Agency's involvement in domestic activities and that sometime later, around January or February 1972, [redacted] talked to Colonel White about his concern and Colonel White in turn talked to the Director of Security. Since that date, he said, he has not had any further direct contact with the Montgomery County Police, based upon orders of the Director of Security.

F. P. Bishop
Inspector

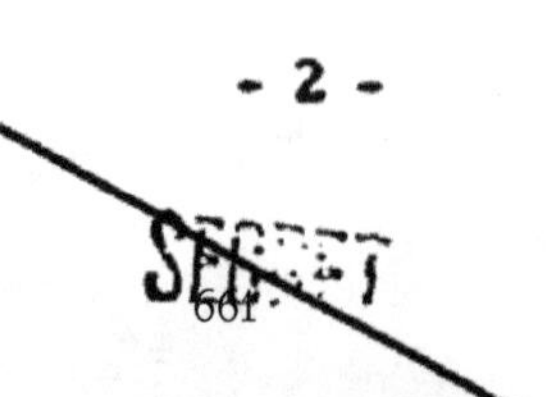

31 May 1973

MEMORANDUM FOR THE RECORD

SUBJECT: Interview with [redacted] FMSAC

1. [redacted] said he recalled [redacted] talking about the Office of Security's liaison with the Police Forces in the Metropolitan Area and that the Ballou case was mentioned. He also recalled that [redacted] had mentioned that the Agency had provided assistance to the Secret Service in connection with surveillance work against radical groups at the 1968 Democratic National Convention in Chicago. He said that he could not remember exactly what [redacted] said, but he did recall that there was considerable discussion and debate among the class members about the propriety of the Agency engaging in such activities.

2. Later in January or February 1972, at a time when [redacted] was Chairman of the Management Advisory Group (MAG), he said he discussed these matters, and questioned the extent to which the Agency should become involved in domestic intelligence activities, with Colonel White and later with Mr. Colby. The MAG also raised the general problem in a couple of their papers, but without citing specific detailed examples. He said he understood that Colonel White had taken the matter up with the Director of Security and that some changes had been made as a result.

[redacted]
F. P. Bishop

Orig - File w/ [redacted] Interview

00653

29 May 1973

MEMORANDUM FOR THE RECORD

SUBJECT: Possible Agency Involvement in Outside Activities on Basis of Information Provided by

On 29 May 1973 I talked to Mr. who was a classmate of and at the Advanced Intelligence Seminar No. 6 held on 8-24 September 1971. Mr. said that each student was asked to describe and talk about his work in the Agency and he recalled that Mr. had talked about the Office of Security's liaison with, and assistance given to and received from, the Police Departments in the Washington Metropolitan area. He said he could not recall specifically what was said, but to the best of his memory Mr. described training given to either the Prince George's or Montgomery County Police concerning surveillance methods and electronic techniques. He said that he did not recall any discussion of the "Ballou case" and that he had no knowledge of that case other than what he had read in the newspapers.

F. P. Bishop

00654

SECRET

30 May 1973

MEMO OF RECORD:

SUBJECT: Talk with Howard Osborne, Dir. Security Re: Report of Statements made by

I talked with Mr. Osborne on 30 May about Mr. statements concerning remarks made by Mr. at the Advanced Intelligence Seminar No. 6 during the period 8=24 Sept. 1971. Mr. Osborne said that fact that the Office of Security had relations with the local police forces in the Metropolitan Washington Area had been reported to the DCI in the Family Jewel(s Memo dated 16 May 1973, but that he had no knowledge of the Ballou Case and had not previously heard of any Agency involvement in or connection with the case.

He suggested that I go ahead and talk to Mr. and get what facts I could from him, but that he also intended to talk to Mr. later himself. He remarked that Mr. was a very good briefer, but inclined to be over-expansive at times and talk to much.

... Bishop

4 June 1973

Talked again with Osborne. He had checked on story and to see if there was any further involvement by the Agency in the Ballou case. The facts he had obtained corresponded with the stories I had got from and — Mr Osborne said that the OS relations with the local police and the detail of two OS officers to the Secret Service for work with a counter sniper team at the 1968 Democrat Nat'l Convention had been reported to the DCI as items No. 5 and 7 respectively in the "Family Jewels" memo of 16 May 1973.

00655

25 May 1973

MEMORANDUM FOR: Director of Central Intelligence

THROUGH : Mr. William E. Colby

1. On 17 May the name of [redacted] was referred to this office as having attempted to contact the Director concerning "activities outside the Agency." I attempted to contact [redacted] on 21 and 22 May, but he was on leave. On 23 May he stated he wanted to check a portion of his information and asked if he could come to my office on 24 May.

2. [redacted] came into the Agency as a JOT in October 1957 and is currently [redacted] assigned to the Soviet/EE Section. He has a very strong personnel file.

3. [redacted] advised that in August 1971 he attended the Advanced Intelligence Seminar. On the first evening of the seminar the students had a "getting acquainted" session where each one gave a brief description of his duties. One of the students, [redacted] [redacted] of the Office of Security, however, carried on after the session was over and expanded on the briefing he had given. He claimed that CIA was cooperating with the Montgomery County Police, stating that the Office of Security gave electronic and other support to that organization.

4. He further indicated that the Office of Security had been involved in the "Ballou case". [redacted] described the Ballou case as follows: The residence of Mr. Ballou, an antique gun collector in Silver Spring, Maryland, was raided on 7 June 1971 by the Montgomery County Police and some Federal law enforcement officers. After the officers, dressed in civilian clothes, had forced their way into the house Ballou picked up an antique pistol. The officers immediately opened fire and wounded Ballou seriously. He spent a long time in the hospital and is partly paralyzed at the present time.

00656

His case was given much publicity in the Washington Post at the time. There was additional publicity in the last several months when Ballou instigated a lawsuit against the raiding officers.

5. [redacted] identified another student, [redacted] who was assigned to [redacted] as a friend of [redacted] He stated that [redacted] also seemed to know the specifics of the Ballou case.

6. I thanked [redacted] and told him this was just the type of information we wanted to receive so that it can be investigated and appropriate action taken if the information is borne out.

7. This office will follow up on this allegation and advise the Director concerning our findings.

William V. Broe
Inspector General

00657

ADVAN(INTELLIGENCE SEMINAR N(;

8-24 Sept 71

List of Students

Name	Office	Room No.	Extension

Ballon case, Silver Spring, 7 June 71

C

S E C R E T

00658

MEMORANDUM FOR: File

Original of this file handed Dr. Chamberlain by Mr. Colby. We made the copies and returned the original to [redacted] who wanted a copy.

[redacted]

13 AUG '73
(DATE)

00659

FORM NO. 101 REPLACES FORM 10-101 WHICH MAY BE USED.
1 AUG 54 (47)

5317 Briley Place, N. W.
Washington, D. C. 20016
29 February 1972

Mr. Lloyd Shearer
Editor-at-Large
Parade Magazine
140 N. Hamilton Drive
Beverly Hills, California 90211

Dear Mr. Shearer:

Thank you for your letter of February 7, 1972, and its kind words about me. As you can imagine, your challenge set me to work to meet it. As a result I can say, under oath if need be, that CIA has never carried out a political assassination, nor has it induced, employed or suggested one which occurred. Whether this fully meets your challenge, I cannot say (it takes two to tango), but it is a long way from the original statement in Mr. Scott's column that CIA "uses political assassination as a weapon." Perhaps I am too sensitive, but I would hope you could set the record straight for your readers.

Sincerely,

W. E. Colby

W. E. Colby

NB - Mr. Helms approved the dispatch of this letter —

WEC

00660

PARADE

LLOYD SHEARER
Editor-at-Large

Parade Publications, Inc. • *OL 3-2073*
140 N. Hamilton Drive
Beverly Hills, Calif. 90211

February 7, 1972

Mr. W.E. Colby
5317 Briley Pl.
Washington, D.C. 20016

Dear Mr. Colby:

Thank you for your kind and informative letter of January 11 concerning Operation Phoenix.

I don't want to get into a running word-battle with you on the subject of political assassination in Indo-China or the role of CIA and other of our agencies in Operation Phoenix.

I am just wondering if you would care to say flatly that the CIA has never used political assassination in Indo-China or elsewhere and has never induced, employed, or suggested to others that such tactics or devices be employed.

If you will make that flat statement under oath, I will not only apologize, I will tango with Dick Helms in Garfinckel's largest show window at 14th and F--providing, of course, Mrs. Helms gives her permission.

Again, I thank you for your interest and commend you for the really outstanding service you have rendered the country. You are indeed one of Helms' finest.

Respectfully,

Lloyd Shearer

LLOYD SHEARER

00661

SENDER WILL CHECK CLAS[SIFI]CATION TOP AND BOTTOM

	UNCLASSIFIED		CONFIDENTIAL		SECRET

OFFICIAL ROUTING SLIP

TO	NAME AND ADDRESS	DATE	INITIALS
1	DCI		
2	DDCI – FYI		
3	Mr Thuermer		
4			
5			
6			

	ACTION		DIRECT REPLY		PREPARE REPLY
	APPROVAL		DISPATCH		RECOMMENDATION
	COMMENT		FILE		RETURN
	CONCURRENCE		INFORMATION		SIGNATURE

Remarks:

I suggest we let the whole thing drop

F[OLD HERE TO RETURN TO SENDER]

FROM: N[AME, ADDRESS AND PHONE NO.]	DATE
Executive Director	4 MAY 1972

	UNCLASSIFIED		CONFIDENTIAL		SECRET

FORM NO. 1-67 237 Use previous editions (40)

00662

00663

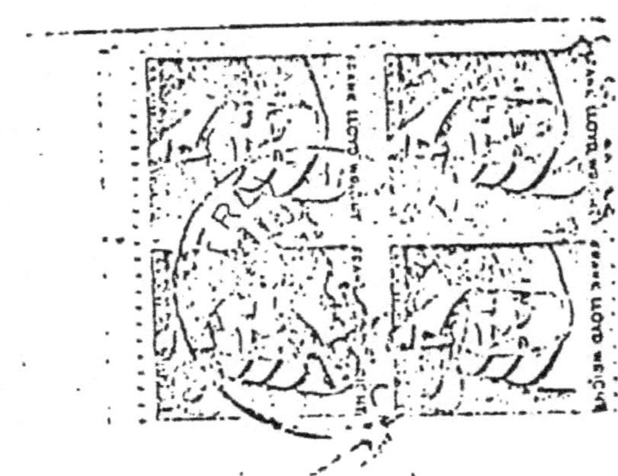

PARADE
140 North Hamilton Drive
Beverly Hills, Calif.

Mr. W. E. Colby
COLBY, KOMER & HELMS
5317 Briley Place, N.W.
Washinxton D.C. 20016

PARADE

LLOYD SHEARER
Editor-at-Large

Parade Publications, Inc. • *OL 3-2073*
140 N. Hamilton Drive
Beverly Hills, Calif. 90211

April 30, 1972

Dear General Colby:

(1) Thank you for your article, "Should Lesbians Be Allowed To Play Professional Football?" I found it intriguing, and we plan to run it in a future issue under your by-line, of course.

(2) Thank you for arranging a tango with me and Dick Helms of Her Majesty's Tel Aviv Rifles. Even At Williams, Dick was one of the great tango-artists of our time. Carfinkels, Woodrop-Lathrop, even Hechts---in fact, any place and time of your choosing is O.K. with me.

(3) One sad note! Will you tell Angus we cannot use his new car bumper sticker: LICK DICK in "72, because it is open to misinterpretation. In addition, we try to remain politically neutral.

(4) As to your willingness to say under oath that the CIA has never been party to political assassination, I, of late, have been travelling a good deal. In the course of my travels I happened to encounter Oleg Penkovsky--not your Oleg---but Penkovsky, a bartender, in Cleveland, Ohio. Penkovsky told me that you signed a secrecy agreement, Form 270, witnessed by Victor L. Marchetti. Under the terms of this agreement you are pledged to eternal silence concerning CIA activities. Unless you have a special Papal dispensation--- the kind given Allen Dulles and Lyman Kirkpatrick, Jr., it seems to me you are lip-sealed.

Perhaps this does not apply to hearings before the Senate Foreign Relations Committee or the prestigious Council on Foreign Relations. If this is so, please let me know; and we will take it from there.

(5) I will be in Washington shortly staying at the home of Jack Anderson out in Silver Spring. Perhaps we can meet there for a small summit. I will have with me several former Green Beret members who want to discuss with you the subject of CIA imposters in South Vietnam, who lied to them and me, too.

Let me hear from you. All the best,

00664

72-2785/2

5317 Briley Place, N. W.
Washington, D. C. 20016
29 February 1972

Mr. Lloyd Shearer
Editor-at-Large
Parade Magazine
140 N. Hamilton Drive
Beverly Hills, California 90211

Dear Mr. Shearer:

Thank you for your letter of February 7, 1972, and its kind words about me. As you can imagine, your challenge set me to work to meet it. As a result I can say, under oath if need be, that CIA has never carried out a political assassination, nor has it induced, employed or suggested one which occurred. Whether this fully meets your challenge, I cannot say (it takes two to tango), but it is a long way from the original statement in Mr. Scott's column that CIA "uses political assassination as a weapon." Perhaps I am too sensitive, but I would hope you could set the record straight for your readers.

Sincerely,

/s/ W. E. Colby

W. E. Colby

VII.35

00665

22-27/1

PARADE

LLOYD SHEARER
Editor-at-Large

Parade Publications, Inc. • *OL 3-2073*
140 N. Hamilton Drive
Beverly Hills, Calif. 90211

February 7, 1972

Mr. W.E. Colby
5317 Briley Pl.
Washington, D.C. 20016

Dear Mr. Colby:

Thank you for your kind and informative letter of January 11 concerning Operation Phoenix.

I don't want to get into a running word-battle with you on the subject of political assassination in Indo-China or the role of CIA and other of our agencies in Operation Phoenix.

I am just wondering if you would care to say flatly that the CIA has never used political assassination in Indo-China or elsewhere and has never induced, employed, or suggested to others that such tactics or devices be employed.

If you will make that flat statement under oath, I will not only apologize, I will tango with Dick Helms in Garfinckel's largest show window at 14th and F--providing, of course, Mrs. Helms gives her permission.

Again, I thank you for your interest and commend you for the really outstanding service you have rendered the country. You are indeed one of Helms' finest.

Respectfully,

Lloyd Shearer

LLOYD SHEARER

00666

5317 Briley Place
Washington, D. C. 20016
January 11, 1972

Mr. Lloyd Shearer
Editor at Large
Parade Magazine
733 Third Avenue
New York, New York 10017

Dear Mr. Shearer:

In your issue of January 9th, one of Walter Scott's Personality Parade responses stated that CIA "uses political assassination as a weapon" and that Operation Phoenix "run by the CIA established a new high for U. S. political assassinations in Vietnam." Since I have held responsible positions in CIA for many years and was also (during detached service from CIA) responsible for U. S. support to Operation Phoenix, I believe I am uniquely qualified to testify (as I have in public session under oath to Senate and House Committees) that:

a. CIA does not and has not used political assassination as a weapon.

b. Operation Phoenix was run not by the CIA but by the Government of Vietnam, with the support of the CORDS element of the U. S. Military Assistance Command in coordination with several U. S. agencies including CIA.

c. Operation Phoenix is not and was not a program of assassination. It countered the Viet Cong apparatus attempting to overthrow the Government of Vietnam by targetting its leaders. Wherever possible, these were apprehended or invited to defect, but a substantial number were killed in firefights during military operations or resisting capture. There is a vast difference in kind, not merely in degree, between these combat casualties (even including the few abuses which occurred) and the victims of the Viet Cong's systematic campaign of terrorism to which Mr. Scott quite accurately referred.

In order to clarify this important question to the millions of concerned Americans who read Parade, I should appreciate your publishing this letter.

Sincerely,

/s/ W. E. Colby

W. E. Colby

WEC:blp

00667

Distribution:
Orig - Addressee 1 - ER 1 - ExDir 1 - Mr. Thuermer
1 - William Sullivan of State (via SAVA - 12 Jan) 1 - Colonel Farnham (OSD/ISA

5317 Briley Place
Washington, D. C. 20016
January 11, 1972

Mr. Lloyd Shearer
Editor at Large
Parade Magazine
733 Third Avenue
New York, New York 10017

Dear Mr. Shearer:

In your issue of January 9th, one of Walter Scott's Personality Parade responses stated that CIA "uses political assassination as a weapon" and that Operation Phoenix "run by the CIA established a new high for U. S. political assassinations in Vietnam." Since I have held responsible positions in CIA for many years and was also (during detached service from CIA) responsible for U. S. support to Operation Phoenix, I believe I am uniquely qualified to testify (as I have in public session under oath to Senate and House Committees) that:

a. CIA does not and has not used political assassination as a weapon.

b. Operation Phoenix was run not by the CIA but by the Government of Vietnam, with the support of the CORDS element of the U. S. Military Assistance Command in coordination with several U. S. agencies including CIA.

c. Operation Phoenix is not and was not a program of assassination. It countered the Viet Cong apparatus attempting to overthrow the Government of Vietnam by targetting its leaders. Wherever possible, these were apprehended or invited to defect, but a substantial number were killed in firefights during military operations or resisting capture. There is a vast difference in kind, not merely in degree, between these combat casualties (even including the few abuses which occurred) and the victims of the Viet Cong's systematic campaign of terrorism to which Mr. Scott quite accurately referred.

In order to clarify this important question to the millions of concerned Americans who read Parade, I should appreciate your publishing this letter.

Sincerely,

W. E. Colby

00668

quested. Volume of ... received makes personal replies ... impossible.

11 Jan 71

Nimble Books LLC

Q. *Four years ago actress Hedy Lamarr had a man named Donald Blyth jailed for attempted rape. He claimed at the time that Hedy had invited him to share her bed. What ever happened to that case?—D.L., Lubbock, Tex.*

...pairman for the Los Angeles ... the charge and sued Hedy ...g that she had willingly ac... ...veral weeks ago Miss Lamarr ...urt to answer Blyth's charges, ...dered her to pay him $15,000 ...lenouncing him as a rapist.

...aid of girls and marriage?— ...C.

...ly too engrossed in his work.

...Hope and does he still fool ... Chicago, Ill.

...n in Eltham, England, on July ...t his zest for living it up.

...nan is one with whom you can ...ke." Who said that?—Louise ...il.

...alery.

...AND RICHARD BURTON.

...n wear lifts in his shoes? And ...eth Taylor, rule the roost?— ...ale, Ariz.

... lifts to make him taller. Yes, ...hots in the family. Of the two ...ger and more responsible. It is ... scripts they do, which may ...s of recent flops.

ACTOR ERNEST BORGNINE WITH HIS FOURTH WIFE.

Q. *How many times has actor Ernest Borgnine been married, and is he a wife-beater?—E.T.R., Springfield, Mass.*

A. Borgnine has been married four times. His last wife, Donna, has charged him with beating her, is seeking a divorce.

Q. *Is there any agency of the U.S. Government which has been authorized to include political assassination in its practices?—M. Wilson, Austin, Tex.*

A. The one U.S. agency which uses political assassination as a weapon is the Central Intelligence Agency. Many of its men in Vietnam have assassinated civilian Communists in an effort to destroy the Vietcong infrastructure. Operation Phoenix run by the CIA established a new high for U.S. political assassinations in Vietnam, largely in response to enemy terrorist tactics which also include assassination, kidnapping, terrorism of all sorts.

Q. *Does Richard Nixon have his own private golf course at Key Biscayne?—Emma Reynolds, Orlando, Fla.*

A. Not at Key Biscayne. He owns a six-hole pitch-and-putt course on his San Clemente, Calif., estate.

Q. *How long does it take radioactive fallout from Chinese nuclear tests to reach the U.S.?—Mark Cheseboro, Barstow, Calif.*

A. Approximately three days depending on the wind.

...resident, DANIEL D. KINLEY editor, JESS GORKIN publisher, WARREN J. REYNOLDS
...or, CAMPBELL GEESLIN senior editor, DAVID PALEY

associate editors, LINDA GUTSTEIN, HERBERT KUPFERBERG, MARTIN MARGULIES, JOHN G. ROGERS
...F. MILKUHN art associate, AL TROIANI
...assistants, MARY HODOROWSKI, SUZANNE CURLEY, DORIS SCHORTMAN
...s, DEMETRIA TAYLOR fashion, VIRGINIA POPE cartoon editor, LAWRENCE LARIAR
...BLUMENTHAL, OPAL GINN

00669

5317 Briley Place
Washington, D. C. 20016
January 11, 1972

Mr. Lloyd Shearer
Editor at Large
Parade Magazine
733 Third Avenue
New York, New York 10017

Dear Mr. Shearer:

In your issue of January 9th, one of Walter Scott's Personality Parade responses stated that CIA "uses political assassination as a weapon" and that Operation Phoenix "run by the CIA established a new high for U. S. political assassinations in Vietnam." Since I have held responsible positions in CIA for many years and was also (during detached service from CIA) responsible for U. S. support to Operation Phoenix, I believe I am uniquely qualified to testify (as I have in public session under oath to Senate and House Committees) that:

a. CIA does not and has not used political assassination as a weapon.

b. Operation Phoenix was run not by the CIA but by the Government of Vietnam with the support of the CORDS element of the U. S. Military Assistance Command in coordination with several U. S. agencies including CIA.

c. Operation Phoenix is not and was not a program of assassination. It countered the Viet Cong apparatus attempting to overthrow the Government of Vietnam by ~~apprehending or defecting~~ its leaders. ~~Some of these~~ were killed in firefights during military operations or resisting capture. There is a vast difference in kind, not merely in degree, between these combat casualties (even including the few abuses which occurred) and the victims of the Viet Cong's systematic campaign of terrorism to which Mr. Scott quite accurately referred.

In order to clarify this important question to the millions of concerned Americans who read Parade, I should appreciate your publishing this letter.

Sincerely,

W. E. Colby

00670

5317 Briley Place
Washington, D. C. 20016
January 10, 1972

Mr. Lloyd Shearer
Editor at Large
Parade Magazine
733 Third Avenue
New York, New York 10017

Dear Mr. Shearer:

In your issue of January 9th, one of Walter Scott's Personality Parade responses stated that CIA "uses political assassination as a weapon" and that Operation Phoenix "run by the CIA established a new high for U. S. political assassinations in Vietnam." Since I have held responsible positions in CIA for many years and was also (during detached service from CIA) responsible for U. S. support to Operation Phoenix, I believe I am uniquely qualified to testify (as I have in public session under oath to Senate and House Committees) that:

a. CIA does not and has not used political assassination as a weapon.

b. Operation Phoenix was run not by the CIA but by the Government of Vietnam with the support of the CORDS element of the U. S. Military Assistance Command in coordination with several U. S. agencies including CIA.

c. Operation Phoenix is not and was not a program of assassination ~~but rather endeavored to~~ counter the Viet Cong apparatus ~~leading the~~ attempt to overthrow the Government of Vietnam by apprehending or defecting its ~~members~~. Some of these were killed in firefights during military operations or resisting capture. There is a vast difference in kind, not merely in degree, between these combat casualties (even including which occurred occasional -- and few -- abuses) and the victims of the Viet Cong's systematic campaign of terrorism ~~referred to by Mr. Scott~~.

In order to clarify this important question to the millions of concerned Americans who ~~might be misled by Mr. Scott's column~~, I should appreciate your publishing this letter.

Sincerely,

W. E. Colby

00671

	SENDER WILL CHECK CLASSIFICATION TOP AND BOTTOM				
	UNCLASSIFIED		CONFIDENTIAL		SECRET

OFFICIAL ROUTING SLIP

TO	NAME AND ADDRESS	DATE	INITIALS
1	Colonel White		
2			
3			
4			
5			
6			

	ACTION		DIRECT REPLY		PREPARE REPLY
	APPROVAL		DISPATCH		RECOMMENDATION
	COMMENT		FILE		RETURN
	CONCURRENCE		INFORMATION		SIGNATURE

Remarks:

Mr. Colby asked that the attached be sent to you for comments.

Right on target, I think. If you have not already done so I suggest you ask Houston to have a look at it.

FOLD HERE TO RETURN TO SENDER

FROM: NAME, ADDRESS AND PHONE NO.	DATE
O/ExDir	10 Jan 72

	UNCLASSIFIED		CONFIDENTIAL		SECRET

FORM NO. 1-67 237 Use previous editions (40)

00672

5317 Briley Place
Washington, D. C. 20016
10 January 1972

Mr. Lloyd Shearer
Editor at Large
Parade Magazine
733 Third Avenue
New York, New York 10017

Dear Mr. Shearer:

In your issue of January 9th, one of Walter Scott's Personality Parade responses stated that CIA "uses political assassination as a weapon" and that Operation Phoenix "run by the CIA established a new high for U. S. political assassinations in Vietnam." Since I have held responsible positions in CIA for many years and was also (during detached service from CIA) responsible for U. S. support to Operation Phoenix, I believe I am uniquely qualified to testify (as I have in public session under oath to Senate and House Committees) that:

a. CIA does not and has not used political assassination as a weapon.

b. Operation Phoenix was run not by the CIA but by the Government of Vietnam with the support of the CORDS element of the U. S. Military Assistance Command.

c. Operation Phoenix is not a program of assassination. Members of the Viet Cong apparatus were killed in the course of military operations or resisting police arrest. There is a vast difference in kind, not merely degree, between these (even including occasional -- and few -- abuses) and the Viet Cong's conscious campaign of terrorism referred to by Mr. Scott.

In order to clarify this important question to the millions of concerned Americans who might be misled by Mr. Scott's column, I should appreciate your publishing this letter.

Sincerely,

W. E. Colby

00673

SENDER WILL CHECK CLASSIFICATION TOP AND BOTTOM		
UNCLASSIFIED	CONFIDENTIAL	SECRET

OFFICIAL ROUTING SLIP

TO	NAME AND ADDRESS	DATE	INITIALS
1	Mr. George Carver		
2			
3			
4			
5			
6			

	ACTION		DIRECT REPLY		PREPARE REPLY
	APPROVAL		DISPATCH		RECOMMENDATION
	COMMENT		FILE		RETURN
	CONCURRENCE		INFORMATION		SIGNATURE

Remarks:

Mr. Colby asked that the attached be sent to you for comments. If possible, we should appreciate receiving your response this afternoon.

FOLD HERE TO RETURN TO SENDER

FROM: NAME, ADDRESS AND PHONE NO.	DATE
O/Executive Director/	10 Jan 72

UNCLASSIFIED	CONFIDENTIAL	SECRET

FORM NO. 1-67 237 Use previous editions (40)

00674

5317 Briley Place
Washington, D. C. 20016
10 January 1972

Mr. Lloyd Shearer
Editor at Large
Parade Magazine
733 Third Avenue
New York, New York 10017

Dear Mr. Shearer:

In your issue of January 9th, one of Walter Scott's Personality Parade responses stated that CIA "uses political assassination as a weapon" and that Operation Phoenix "run by the CIA established a new high for U. S. political assassinations in Vietnam." Since I have held responsible positions in CIA for many years and was also (during detached service from CIA) responsible for U. S. support to Operation Phoenix, I believe I am uniquely qualified to testify (as I have in public session under oath to Senate and House Committees) that:

a. CIA does not and has not used political assassination as a weapon.

b. Operation Phoenix was run not by the CIA but by the Government of Vietnam with the support of the CORDS element of the U. S. Military Assistance Command in coordination with several US agencies ~~including CIA and was not~~

c. Operation Phoenix is not a program of assassination, but rather endeavored to counter the Viet Cong apparatus. Some of these were ~~Members of the Viet Cong apparatus~~ were killed ~~in the course of~~ during firefights military operations or resisting ~~police arrest~~ capture. There is a vast difference in kind, not merely degree, between these (even including occasional -- and few -- abuses) and the victims of the Viet Cong's systematic ~~conscious~~ campaign of terrorism referred to by Mr. Scott.

In order to clarify this important question to the millions of concerned Americans who might be misled by Mr. Scott's column, I should appreciate your publishing this letter.

Sincerely,

W. E. Colby

leading the attempt to overthrow the Government of Vietnam by apprehension or defection its members

combat casualties

00675

a. The CIA does not and has never ~~used assassination as a weapon~~ engaged in assassination operations. The often repeated charge that it does, reflected in Mr. Scott's 9 January "Personality Parade", is a calumny without any foundation whatsoever in fact.

c. Operation Phoenix is not and never has been a program of assassination. "Phoenix" is a label for the structure and process through which the ~~GVN~~ Government of Vietnam has endeavored to coordinate the activities of all of its components -- military, police and civilian ministries -- who have some measure of responsibility for coping with various facets of the Vietnamese Communist Party's continuing effort to overthrow the Government by force of arms. The members of the Communist Party hierarchy and apparatus -- the Viet Cong -- against which the Government is endeavoring to protect itself almost invariably carry arms and 0067
the more senior members ~~[illegible]~~ are usually

guarded by an armed military escort or bodyguard unit. Since any attempt to arrest Party members or, particularly, Party officials ~~always invariably~~ frequently entails some kind of fire fight, members of the Viet Cong apparatus have, obviously, been killed in the course of military operations or while resisting police arrest. There is, ~~a vast di~~ however, a vast difference in kind, not merely degree, between those casualties deriving from armed combat (even including occasional -- and few -- Government abuses) and the Viet Cong's conscious, systematic campaign of terrorism against unarmed non-combatants referred to by Mr. Scott.

00677

SENDER WILL CHECK CLASSIFICATION TOP AND BOTTOM

	UNCLASSIFIED		CONFIDENTIAL		SECRET

OFFICIAL ROUTING SLIP

TO	NAME AND ADDRESS	DATE	INITIALS
1	DD/P 10 JAN 1972	10 Jan	
2			
3	Mr. Colby		
4			
5			
6			

	ACTION		DIRECT REPLY		PREPARE REPLY
	APPROVAL		DISPATCH		RECOMMENDATION
	COMMENT		FILE		RETURN
	CONCURRENCE		INFORMATION		SIGNATURE

Remarks:

Mr. Colby asked that the attached be sent to you for comments. If possible, we should appreciate your response this afternoon.

FOLD HERE TO RETURN TO SENDER

FROM: NAME, ADDRESS AND PHONE NO.	DATE
O/Executive Director	10 Jan 72

	UNCLASSIFIED		CONFIDENTIAL		SECRET

FORM NO. 1-67 237 Use previous editions (40)

00678

5317 Briley Place
Washington, D. C. 20016
10 January 1972

Mr. Lloyd Shearer
Editor at Large
Parade Magazine
733 Third Avenue
New York, New York 10017

Dear Mr. Shearer:

In your issue of January 9th, one of Walter Scott's Personality Parade responses stated that CIA "uses political assassination as a weapon" and that Operation Phoenix "run by the CIA established a new high for U. S. political assassinations in Vietnam." Since I have held responsible positions in CIA for many years and was also (during detached service from CIA) responsible for U. S. support to Operation Phoenix, I believe I am uniquely qualified to testify (as I have in public session under oath to Senate and House Committees) that:

a. CIA does not and has not used political assassination as a weapon.

b. Operation Phoenix was run not by the CIA but by the Government of Vietnam with the support of the CORDS element of the U. S. Military Assistance Command.

c. Operation Phoenix is not a program of assassination. Members of the Viet Cong apparatus were killed in the course of military operations or resisting police arrest. There is a vast difference in kind, not merely degree, between these (even including occasional -- and few -- abuses) and the Viet Cong's conscious campaign of terrorism referred to by Mr. Scott.

In order to clarify this important question to the millions of concerned Americans who might be misled by Mr. Scott's column, I should appreciate your publishing this letter.

Sincerely,

W. E. Colby

00679

Mr. Houston
Mr. Warner

I have asked [redacted] to look this over and give you his comments. J. 1/10/72

00680

SENDER WILL CHECK CLASSIFICATION TOP AND BOTTOM

	UNCLASSIFIED		CONFIDENTIAL		SECRET

OFFICIAL ROUTING SLIP

TO	NAME AND ADDRESS	DATE	INITIALS
1	General Counsel		
2			
3			
4			
5			
6			

	ACTION		DIRECT REPLY		PREPARE REPLY
	APPROVAL		DISPATCH		RECOMMENDATION
	COMMENT		FILE		RETURN
	CONCURRENCE		INFORMATION		SIGNATURE

Remarks:

Mr. Colby asked that the attached be sent to you for comments. If possible, we should appreciate your response this afternoon.

FOLD HERE TO RETURN TO SENDER

FROM: NAME, ADDRESS AND PHONE NO.	DATE
O/ExDir/	10 Jan 72

	UNCLASSIFIED		CONFIDENTIAL		SECRET

FORM NO. 1-67 237 Use previous editions (40)

00681

5317 Briley Place
Washington, D. C. 20016
10 January 1972

Mr. Lloyd Shearer
Editor at Large
Parade Magazine
733 Third Avenue
New York, New York 10017

Dear Mr. Shearer:

In your issue of January 9th, one of Walter Scott's Personality Parade responses stated that CIA "uses political assassination as a weapon" and that Operation Phoenix "run by the CIA established a new high for U. S. political assassinations in Vietnam." Since I have held responsible positions in CIA for many years and was also (during detached service from CIA) responsible for U. S. support to Operation Phoenix, I believe I am uniquely qualified to testify (as I have in public session under oath to Senate and House Committees) that:

a. CIA does not and has not used political assassination as a weapon.

b. Operation Phoe ix was run not by the CIA but by the Government of Vietnam with the support of the CORDS element of the U. S. Military Assistance Command, in coordination with CIA and other US agencies.

c. Operation Phoenix is not a program of assassination. Members of the Viet Cong apparatus were killed in the course of military operations or resisting police arrest. There is a vast difference in kind, not merely degree, between these (even including occasional -- and few -- abuses) and the Viet Cong's conscious campaign of terrorism referred to by Mr. Scott.

In order to clarify this important question to the millions of concerned Americans who might be misled by Mr. Scott's column, I should appreciate your publishing this letter.

Sincerely,

W. E. Colby

00682

SENDER WILL CHECK CL[ASSI]FICATION TOP AND BOTTOM

	UNCLASSIFIED		CONFIDENTIAL		SECRET

OFFICIAL ROUTING SLIP

TO	NAME AND ADDRESS	DATE	INITIALS
1	Mr. Angus Thuermer	10 JAN 1972	
2			
3	MR Colby		
4			
5			
6			

	ACTION		DIRECT REPLY		PREPARE REPLY
	APPROVAL		DISPATCH		RECOMMENDATION
	COMMENT		FILE		RETURN
	CONCURRENCE		INFORMATION		SIGNATURE

Remarks:

Mr. Colby asked that the attached be sent to you for comm[e]nts. If possible, we should appreciate receiving your response this afternoon.

FOLD HERE TO RETURN TO SENDER

FROM: NAME, ADDRESS AND PHONE NO.	DATE
O/Executive Director [redacted]	10 Jan 72

	UNCLASSIFIED		CONFIDENTIAL		SECRET

FORM NO. 1-67 237 Use previous editions (40)

00683

The noted phrases should, in my opinion,

be cut out. They are the kind that lead to the italticized "Editor's Note" at the end of the letter which rebuts the whole point being made by the letter writer.

"Resisting police arrest" will get you, with the press, nothing but snide snicking cracks... and as we're really not going to win too much in such a short letter anyway, why not skip the occassional abuses bit.

Them's my thots.

AMT

00684

5317 Briley Place
Washington, D. C. 20016
10 January 1972

Mr. Lloyd Shearer
Editor at Large
Parade Magazine
733 Third Avenue
New York, New York 10017

Dear Mr. Shearer:

In your issue of January 9th, one of Walter Scott's Personality Parade responses stated that CIA "uses political assassination as a weapon" and that Operation Phoenix "run by the CIA established a new high for U. S. political assassinations in Vietnam." Since I have held responsible positions in CIA for many years and was also (during detached service from CIA) responsible for U. S. support to Operation Phoenix, I believe I am uniquely qualified to testify (as I have in public session under oath to Senate and House Committees) that:

a. CIA does not and has not used political assassination as a weapon.

b. Operation Phoenix was run not by the CIA but by the Government of Vietnam with the support of the CORDS element of the U. S. Military Assistance Command.

c. Operation Phoenix is not a program of assassination. Members of the Viet Cong apparatus were killed in the course of military operations ~~or resisting police arrest.~~ There is a vast difference in kind, not merely degree, between these ~~[even including occasional and few abuses]~~ and the Viet Cong's conscious campaign of terrorism referred to by Mr. Scott.

In order to clarify this important question to the millions of concerned Americans who might be misled by Mr. Scott's column, I should appreciate your publishing this letter.

Sincerely,

W. E. Colby

00685

Dear Mr Shearer

Thank you for your letter of Feb 7, 1972 and its too kind words about me. As you can imagine, your quite appropriate challenge set me to work to see if I could meet it. ~~I share the results of my inquiries with you~~ as a result, I can say ~~that~~ CIA has never carried out a political assassination, nor has it induced, employed or suggested one which occurred. I cannot say that it never suggested one but ~~for the two~~ ~~[illegible]~~ occasions I find this was done.

00686

So I can't ask you to tango (although it takes two to do so).

~~but the three persons~~

~~I think~~ we called off the idea before the action took place. ~~We~~ We make our policy crystal clear ~~to~~ instructions have been issued to our employees ~~have carefully~~ that no such action be suggested, ~~or~~ undertaken or assisted.

In summary, I cannot ~~tell you to~~ meet your challenge, I still think, however, that the facts are a long way from ~~the~~ original statement in Walter Scott's column ~~that~~ CIA "uses political assassination as a weapon." Perhaps we in CIA are ~~too~~ sensitive, but we would hope you could set the record straighter than that to your readers.

00687

was induced employ by suggested (

CIA has never carried out a political assassination, Such proposals were discussed among staff members on a few occasions, but rejected by senior CIA officials. Implementation was on two occasions but called off before the action was accomplished. Other than these two instances (both some time ago), CIA has never induced, employed or suggested to others that ~~such~~ political assassination be employed. A clear instruction has been ~~circulated~~ issued that this not be done and that ~~any indications of this nature~~ any indications of such activity which might in any way be ascribed to CIA be reported ~~through~~ to the Director at once.

00689

Notes:

Diem: CIA had no forewarning of Diem's assassination. CIA attempted to arrange a safe-conduct out of Vietnam for Diem and Nhu

Lumumba: CIA had nothing to with Lumumba's death. Earlier however, an action was initiated but abandoned. ~~as infeasible~~

Castro: Part of the Bay of Pigs plan involved a commando unit ~~targetted on Castro~~ the leader of the defending forces. This was a part of a large paramilitary operation not a political assassination. On a separate occasion, an action was initiated but abandoned, ~~as [illegible]~~

Counter-Terror: In Vietnam in 1964, teams were organized and paid by CIA to conduct operations against the Viet Cong. These teams later became the Provincial Reconnaissance Units (PRU). These were a part of

00690

the war effort, not political assassination squads. When questions arose as to their tactics CIA tightened its and the GVN controls over them.

Laos: In the war in La[os] commando and guerrilla squads played an important role against the North Vietnamese. These were a part of paramilitary and military operations not political assassinat[ion]

00691

Phoenix This has been described in detail to Congressional committees. It was not a program of assassination!

00692

for over 30 years, will receive an annuity at full pay for life.

00693

www.ingramcontent.com/pod-product-compliance
Lightning Source LLC
Chambersburg PA
CBHW061833260326
41914CB00005B/976
9781608880973